The Chapel of St John the Baptist in the Church of São Roque

THE COMMISSION, THE BUILDING, THE COLLECTIONS

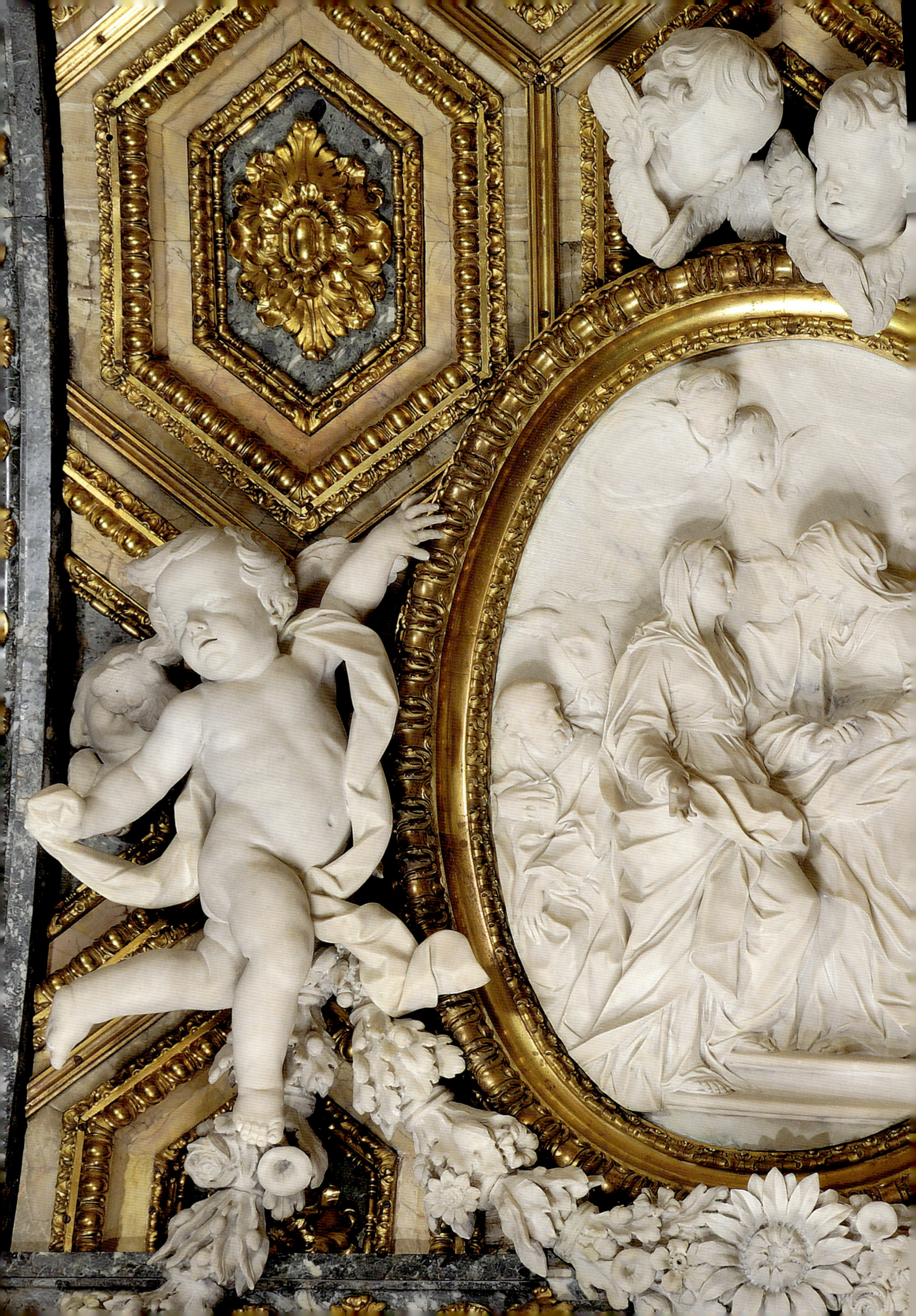

The Chapel of St John the Baptist in the Church of São Roque

THE COMMISSION, THE BUILDING, THE COLLECTIONS

Edited by TERESA LEONOR M. VALE

SCALA

SANTA CASA
Misericórdia de Lisboa. Por boas causas.

edições
SANTA CASA

MUSEU
SÃO ROQUE
Santa Casa da Misericórdia de Lisboa

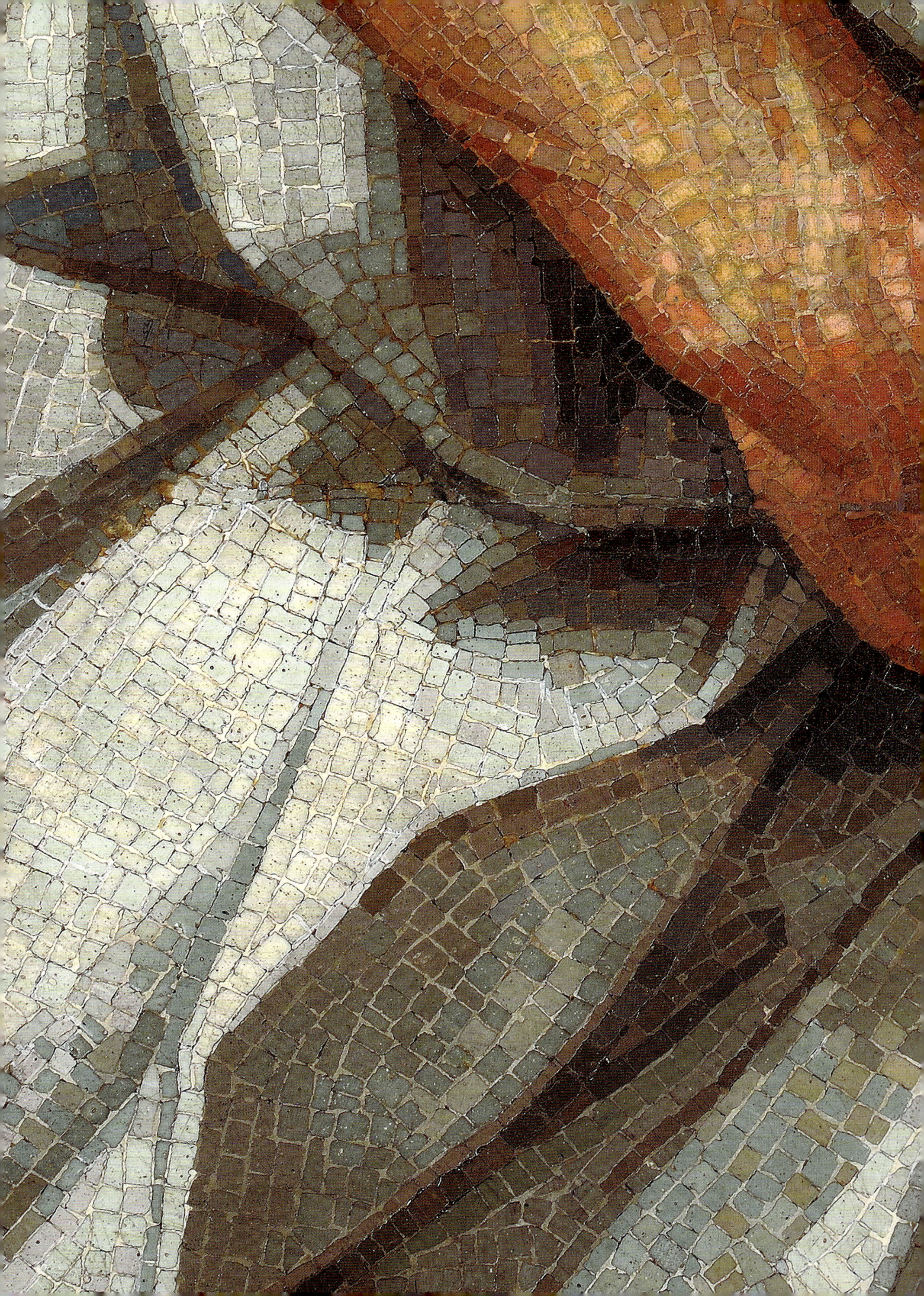

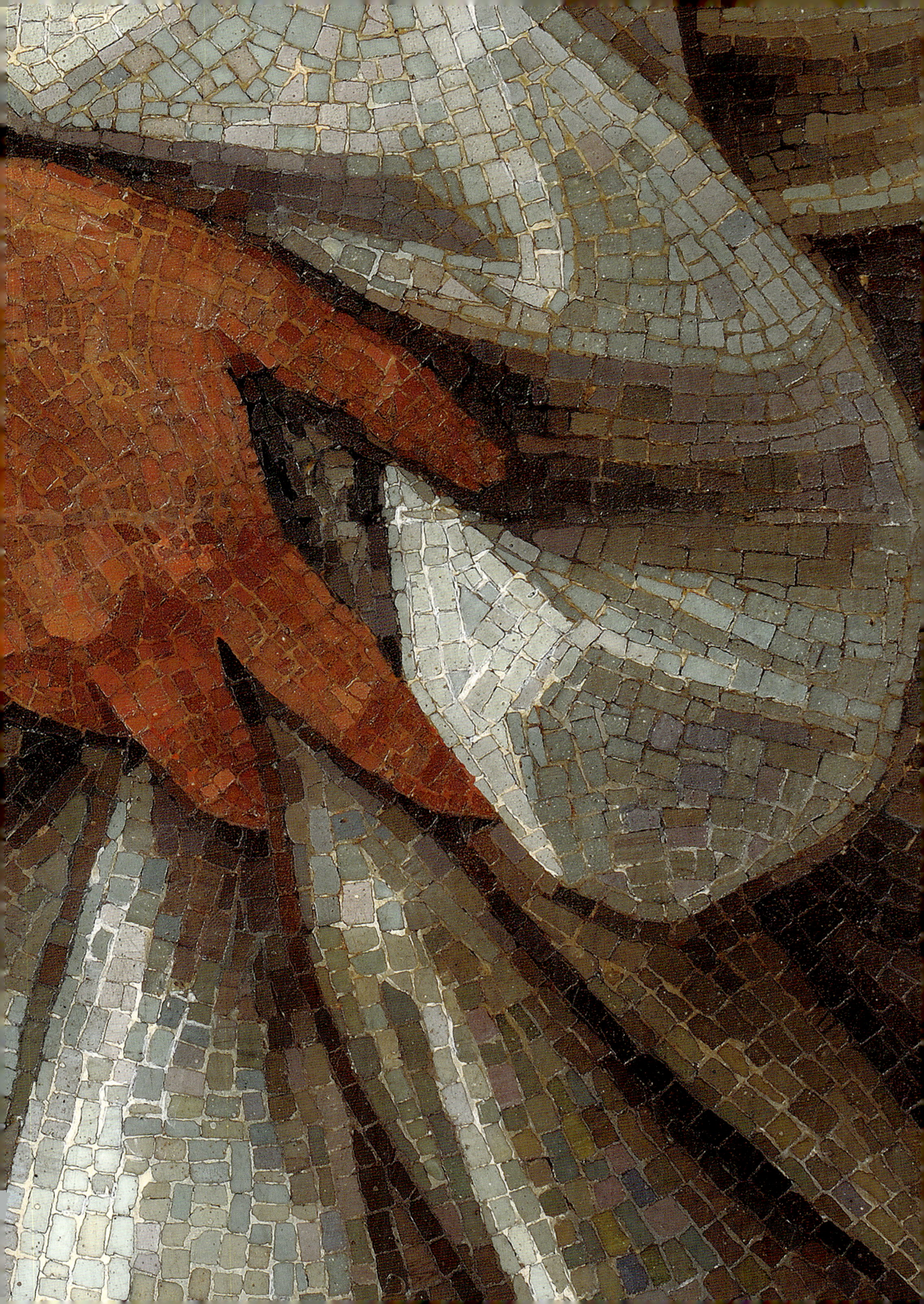

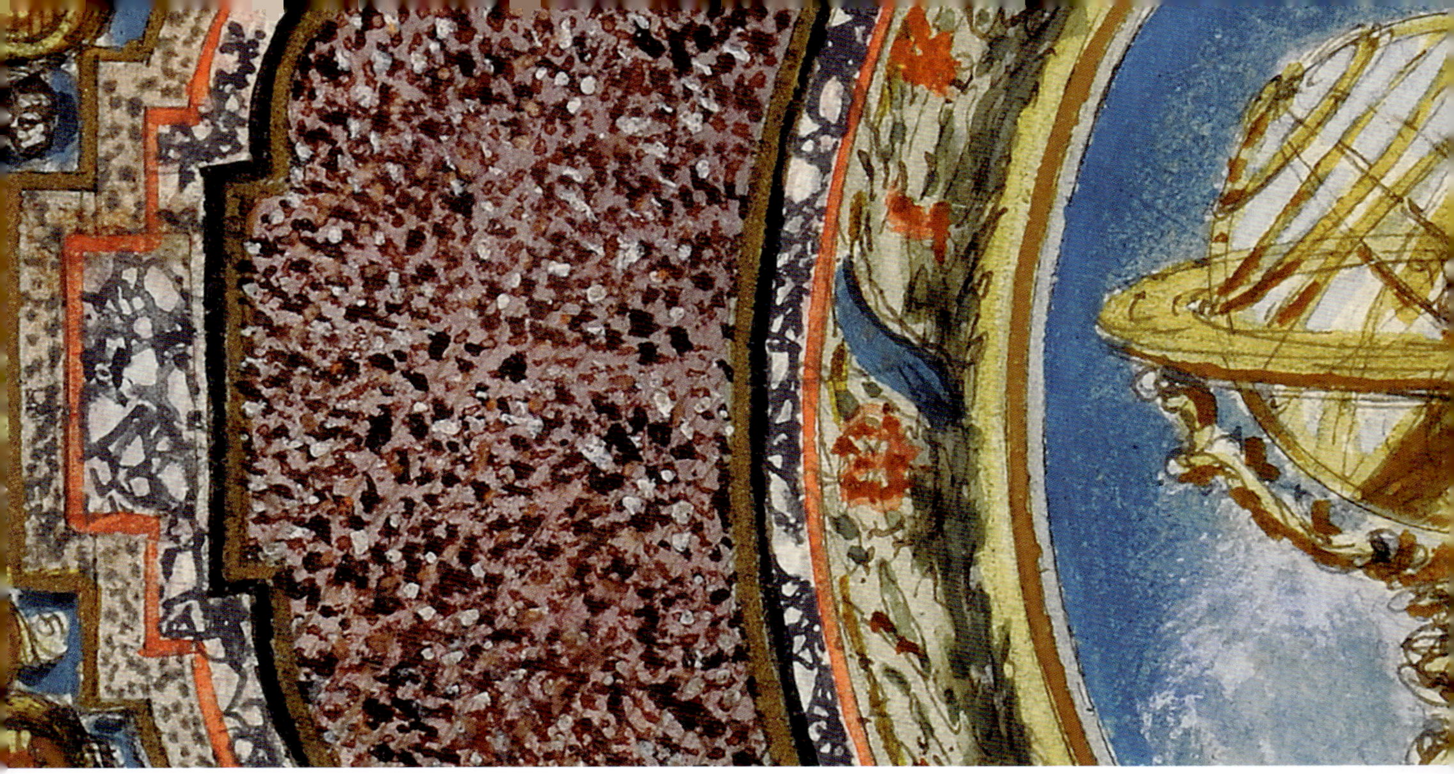

First published in 2017 by
Scala Arts & Heritage Publishers Ltd
10 Lion Yard
Tremadoc Road
London SW4 7NQ, UK
www.scalapublishers.com

In association with
Santa Casa da Misericórdia de Lisboa
Largo Trindade Coelho
1200-470 – Lisboa
Portugal

ISBN 978-1-78551-103-5

Scientific and editorial coordination (SCML): Teresa Leonor M. Vale (ARTIS – Institute of History of Art, School of Arts and Humanities, University of Lisbon)

Authors: António Filipe Pimentel, Carlo Stefano Salerno, Cristina Pinto Basto, Maria de Fátima Rezende Gomes, Magda Tassinari, Marialuisa Rizzini, Teresa Leonor M. Vale

Project management (Scala): Laura Lappin

Design: Luis Chimeno Garrido and José Domingues

Translated from Portuguese to English by Catriona Clayton for First Edition Translations Ltd, Cambridge

Printed in Spain

10 9 8 7 6 5 4 3 2 1

Photographic acknowledgements

Front and back covers
Cintra & Castro Caldas, L.da

Part I
Archivio Fotografico della Fondazione Torino Musei, Turin (fig. 5)
Biblioteca da Ajuda, Lisbon (fig. 6)
Biblioteca Nacional de Portugal, Lisbon (figs 2, 7)
Cintra & Castro Caldas, L.da (fig. 1)
DGPC/ADF (Coord. – Alexandra Encarnação. Inv. – Tânia Olim. Ed. – Alexandra Pessoa, Luísa Oliveira and José Paulo Ruas): Luísa Oliveira, Alexandra Pessoa (fig. 4), José Paulo Ruas (fig. 3), Vítor Branco (fig. 8)

Part II, Chapter 1
Antonio Gentile – Soprintendenza BAPSAE Caserta e Benevento (figs 9, 17)
Cintra & Castro Caldas, L.da (fig. 16)
DGPC/ADF (Coord. – Alexandra Encarnação. Inv. – Tânia Olim. Ed. – Alexandra Pessoa, Luísa Oliveira e José Paulo Ruas): Luísa Oliveira and Alexandra Pessoa (figs 13–15)
Fototeca della Soprintendenza Speciale per il PSAE e per il Polo Museale della Città di Napoli (figs 10–12, 18)

Part II, Chapter 2
Cintra & Castro Caldas, L.da (figs 19–23, 26–29)
DGPC/ADF (Coord. – Alexandra Encarnação. Inv. – Tânia Olim. Ed. – Alexandra Pessoa, Luísa Oliveira and José Paulo Ruas): Pedro Ferreira (fig. 24)
Soprintendenza Speciale per il Patrimonio Storico, Artistico ed Etnoantropologico e per il Polo Museale della città di Firenze (fig. 25)

Part II, Chapter 3
Beaux-arts de Paris/prise de vue Jean-Michel Lapelerie (figs 32, 34, 36, 38, 41)
Cintra & Castro Caldas, L.da (figs 30, 31, 33, 35, 37, 39, 40, 42–44)

Part II, Chapter 4
Beaux-arts de Paris/prise de vue Jean-Michel Lapelerie (figs 46, 49, 51, 55, 57)
Cintra & Castro Caldas, L.da (figs 45, 47, 48, 50, 52–54, 56, 58)

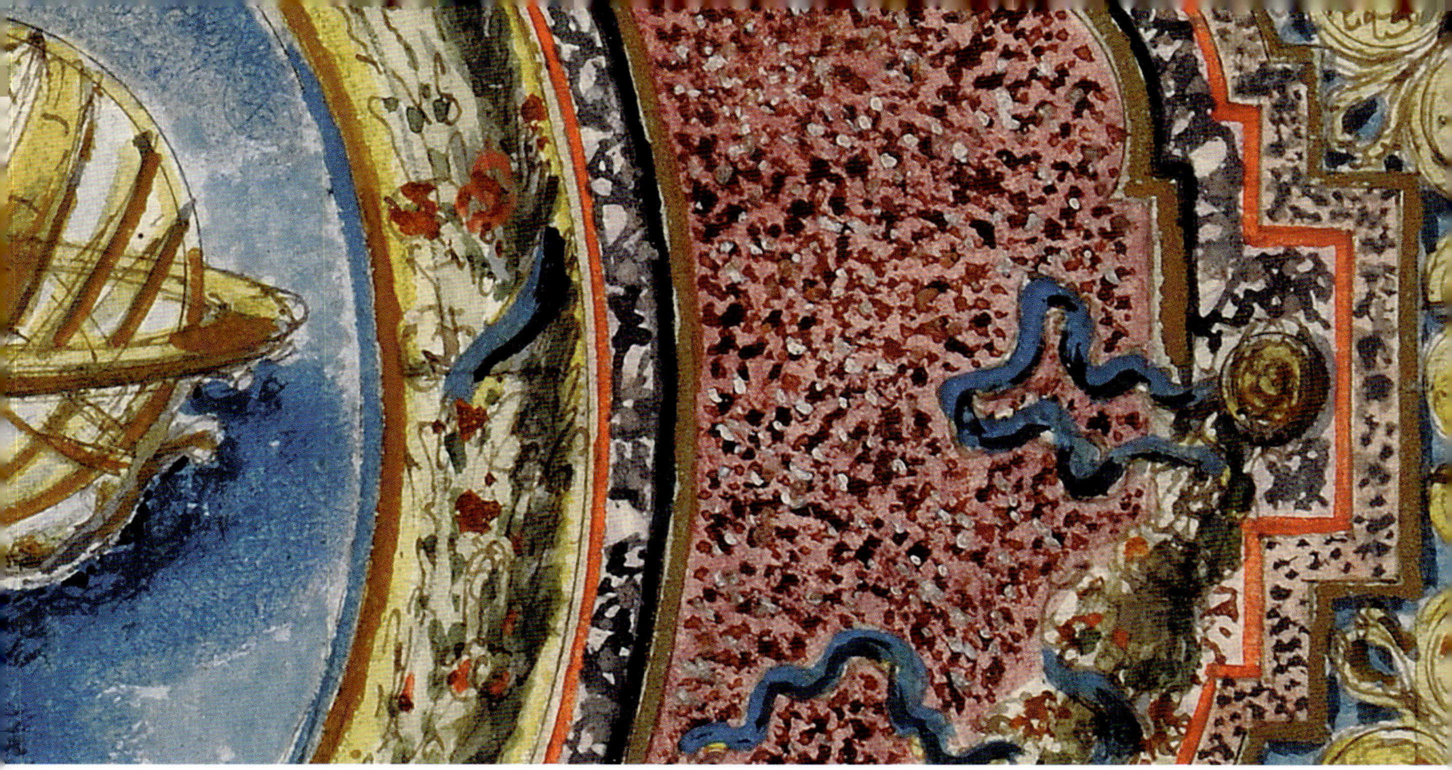

Part III, Chapter 1
Beaux-arts de Paris/prise de vue Jean-Michel Lapelerie (figs 59, 62, 64, 69, 71, 82–84)
Cintra & Castro Caldas, L.da (figs 60, 61, 63, 65–68, 70, 72–81)

Part III, Chapter 2
Cintra & Castro Caldas, L.da (figs 85, 88–94)
Núcleo de Audiovisuais e Multimédia da SCML: Carlos Sousa (fig. 87)
Servizio fotoriproduzioni, Museo di Roma – Roma Capitale, Sovrintendenza Capitolina ai Beni Culturali (fig 86)

Part III, Chapter 3
Archivio Fotografico della Fondazione Torino Musei, Turin (fig. 97)
Archivio Segreto Vaticano, Vatican (fig. 100)
Cintra & Castro Caldas, L.da (figs 96, 98, 99, 101, 102)
Fondazione Principi di Vicovaro, Rome (fig. 95)

Part III, Chapter 4
Cintra & Castro Caldas, L.da (pp. 148–149, figs 103–106, 108–110)
Cristina Pinto Basto/Biblioteca da Ajuda, Lisbon (fig. 107)

Part III, Chapter 5
Cintra & Castro Caldas, L.da (figs 111–112)

Acknowledgments
Biblioteca da Ajuda, Lisbon
Biblioteca Nacional de Portugal, Lisbon
Direção-geral do Património Cultural, Lisbon
École Nationale Supérieure des Beaux-arts, Paris
Fondazione Principi di Vicovaro, Rome
Fondazione Torino Musei, Palazzo Madama – Museo Civico d'Arte Antica, Turin
Museo di Roma – Roma Capitale, Soprintendenza Capitolina ai Beni Culturali
Soprintendenza BAPSAE Caserta e Benevento
Soprintendenza per il Patrimonio Storico, Artistico ed Etnoantropologico e del Polo Museale della città di Napoli, Naples
Soprintendenza Speciale per il Patrimonio Storico, Artistico ed Etnoantropologico e per il Polo Museale della città di Firenze, Florence

Frontispiece
Relief of St John the Baptist Preaching in the Desert (detail), with little angels and festoons
Bernardino Ludovisi
Carrara marble
(See fig. 39)

pp. 4–5
Detail of Christ's hand from the Baptism of Christ mosaic (main altar)
Mattia Moretti
(See fig. 20)

pp. 6–7
Armillary sphere (detail)
Luigi Vanvitelli, 2nd project,
Drawing no. 26 of the *Weale Album*, f. 35
Bibliothèque de l'École Nationale Supérieure des Beaux-arts, Paris [Library of the National Higher School of Fine Arts], Paris (Ms. 497)
(Beaux-arts de Paris/prise de vue Jean-Michel Lapelerie)

pp. 8–9
Decoration of the panel of the Baptism of Christ (detail)
Antonio Arrighi
Gilded metal
(Cintra & Castro Caldas, L.da)

pp. 10–11
Detail from monumental candlestick of angels surrounding the Portuguese coat of arms
Giuseppe and Leandro Gagliardi
Rome, 1751–52
Silver and gilded bronze
(inv. MPr. 1 and MPr. 2)
(Cintra & Castro Caldas, L.da)

pp. 12–13
Detail of angels from the Annunciation mosaic
Mattia Moretti
(See fig. 19)

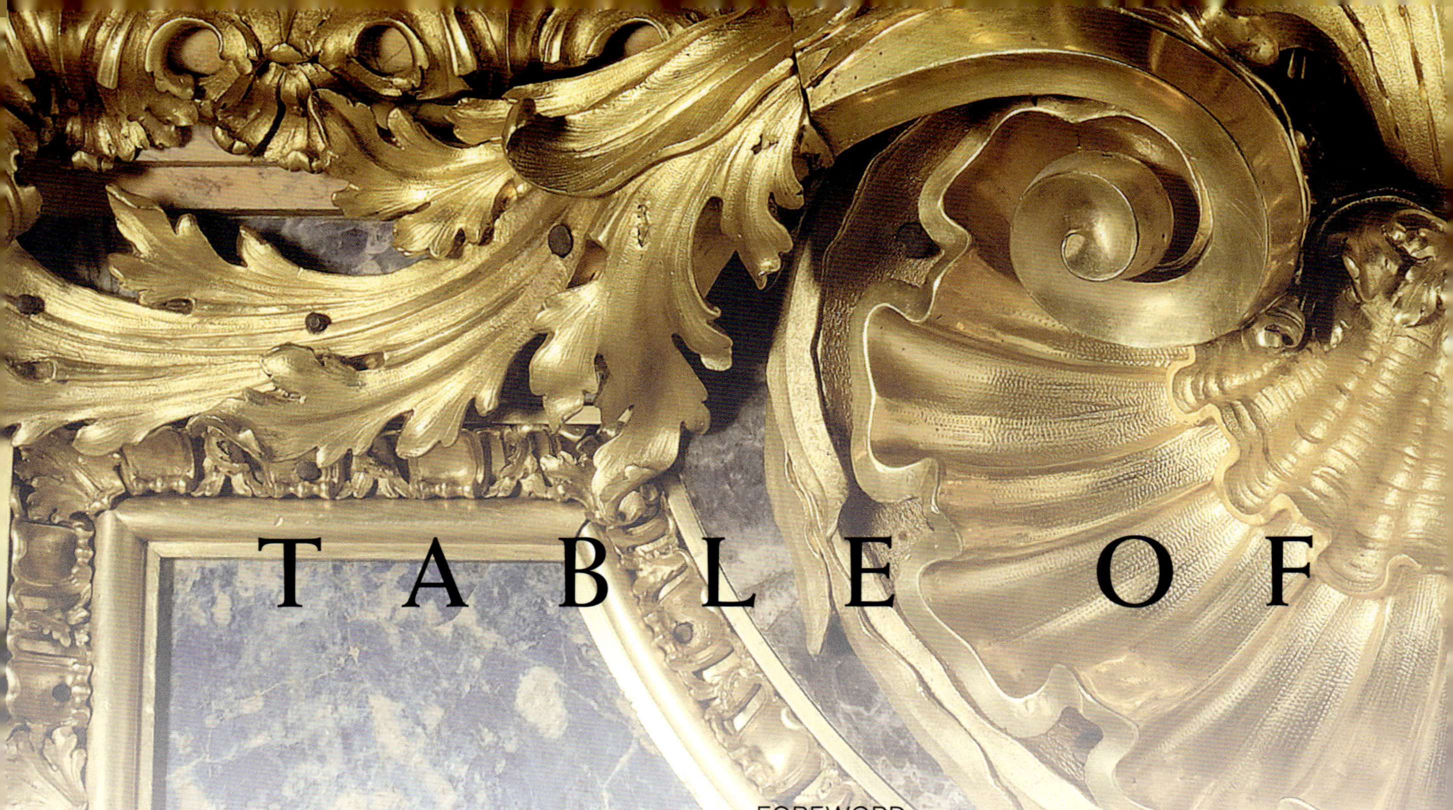

T A B L E O F

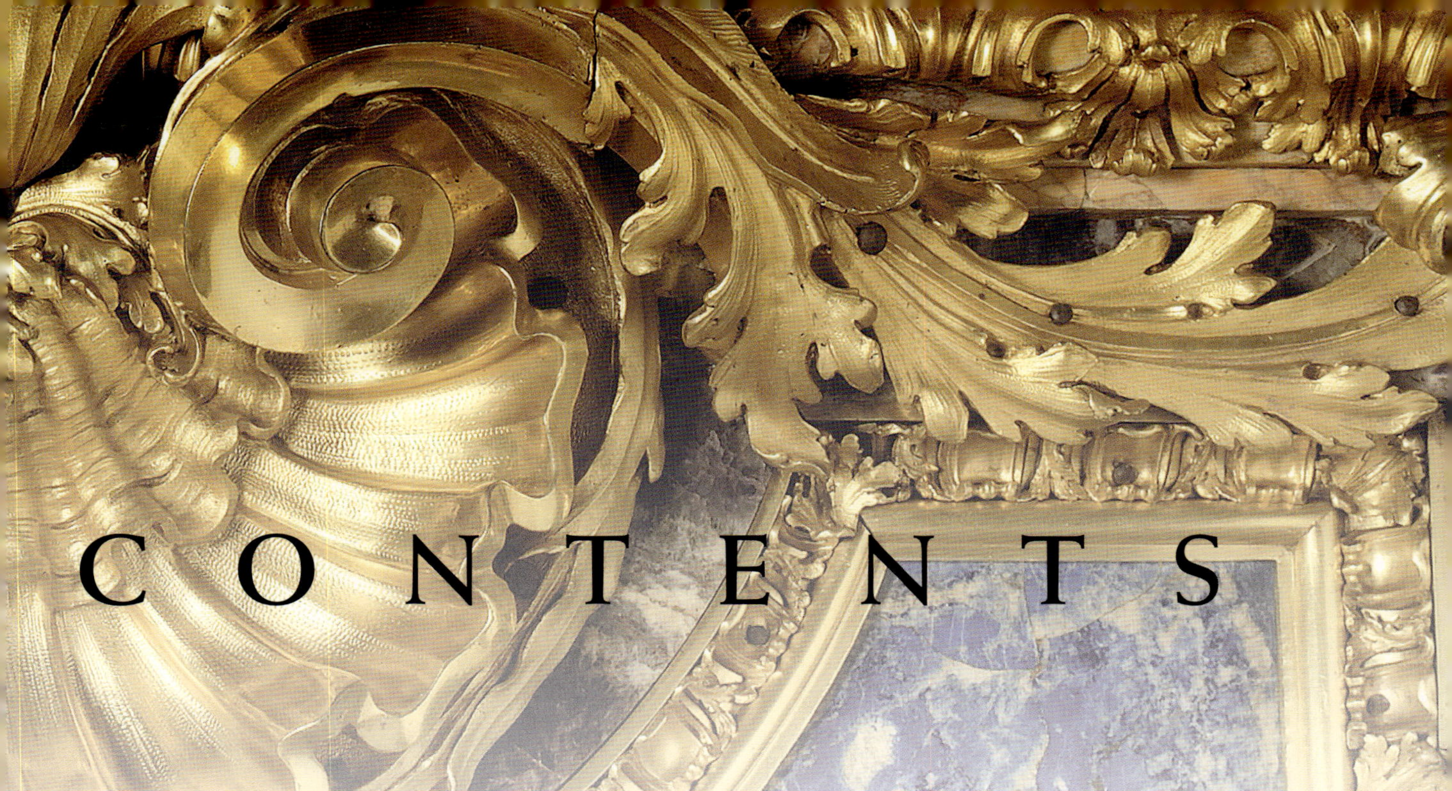

C O N T E N T S

PART III
THE COLLECTIONS

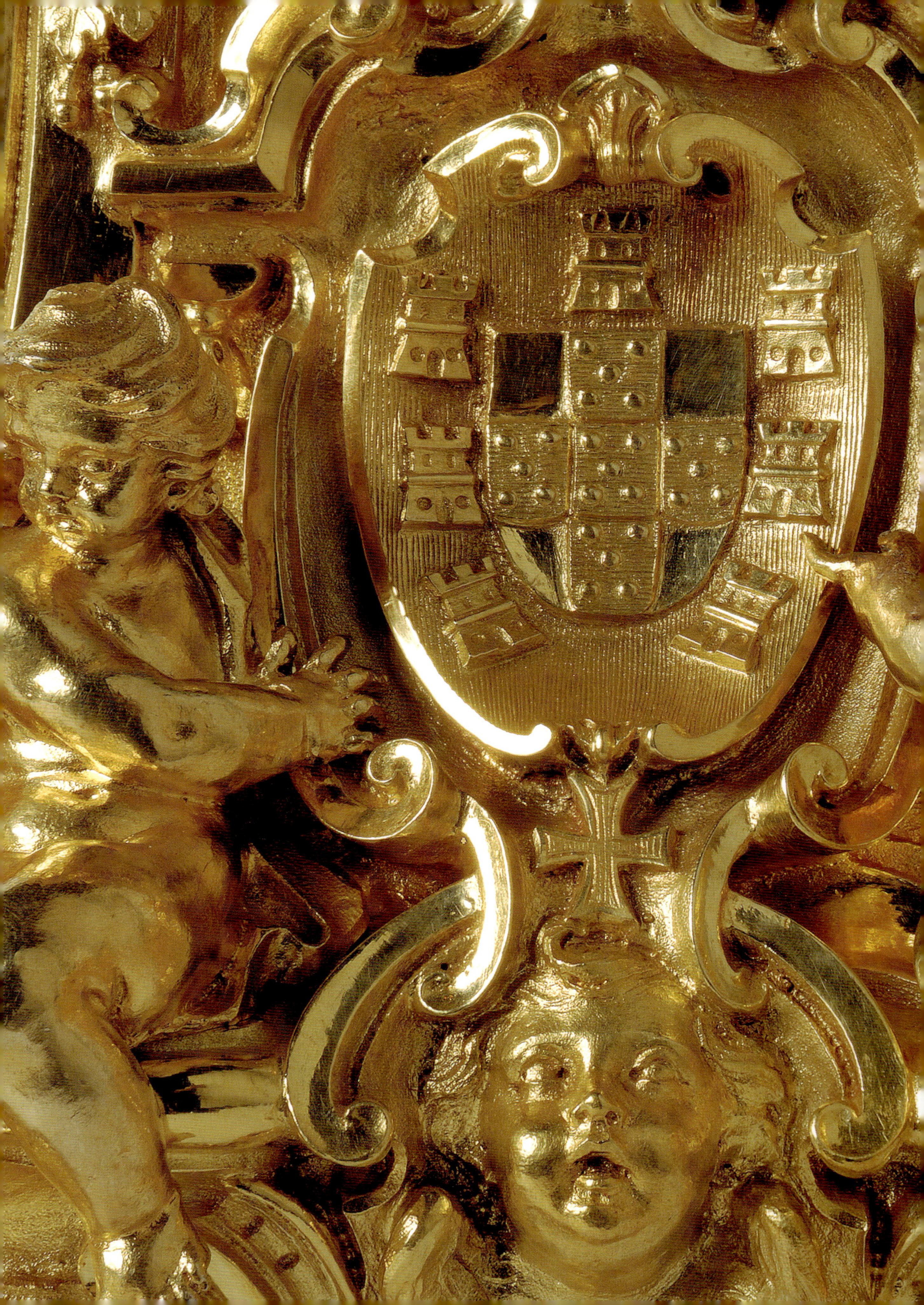

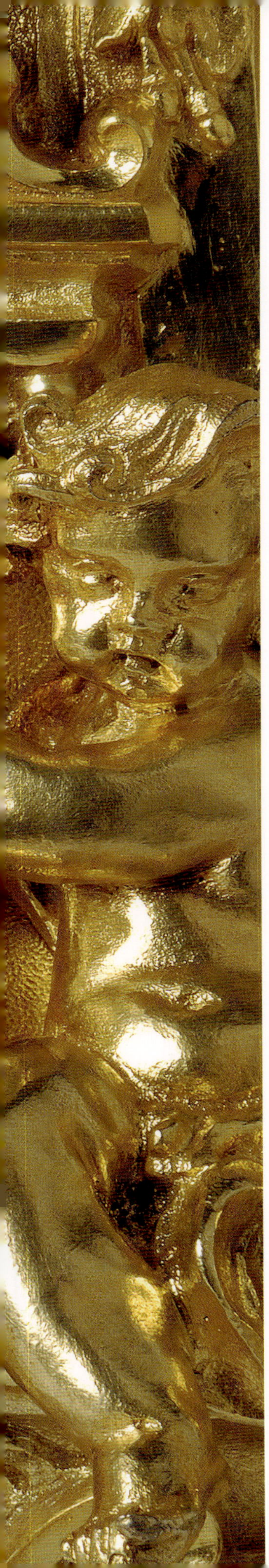

Foreword

Portugal can take pride in having bridged the world and brought its peoples and continents closer together without fear of distances, oceans or differences. Once a small, peripheral kingdom, it became an immense trading empire with direct links to Asia, Africa and America. But the transformation wrought at the turn of the fifteenth to the sixteenth century was not a matter of unalloyed wealth and prosperity. The great influx of population into the capital eventually gave rise to social problems including poverty and exclusion.

It was in this historical context, at a time of intense and dynamic change, that the Santa Casa da Misericórdia or Holy House of Mercy was founded in Lisbon in 1498. It was a brotherhood under the direct protection of the king, created with the aim of providing assistance to the most disadvantaged. Within a short time, similar institutions were established throughout the kingdom and overseas, from Rio de Janeiro to Macao. The Portuguese Houses of Mercy were the first social assistance network to extend their activities across the world, and even today they continue to play a vital role.

In Lisbon, the metropolis where most social problems were concentrated, the activity of the Santa Casa da Misericórdia was so significant that it remains one of the most important institutions in the country to this day, with a multifaceted support network that has shown itself able to adapt to new and constantly changing social demands.

For this reason, the Santa Casa da Misericórdia de Lisboa has always enjoyed the protection of the State. When its buildings were destroyed by the earthquake of 1755, it was re-housed in the building that the Jesuits had made their headquarters, which also included the Church of São Roque. Today this area lies in the heart of the city's historical centre, between Bairro Alto and Chiado, and is among the most highly prized for its architectural beauty and vibrant cultural life.

The Jesuit house was already one of the greatest monuments in the capital at the time, not only because it was the seat of a major religious order but also because it contained a collection of the best of Portuguese art from the sixteenth to eighteenth centuries. The Royal Chapel of St John the Baptist is one of the outstanding features of its interior, commissioned in Rome by the Portuguese monarch John V. Together with its fabulous treasure of gold, silver and liturgical vestments, this was the origin of the São Roque Museum founded in 1905.

The Santa Casa da Misericórdia de Lisboa has invested every effort in enhancing and displaying our patrimony to its best advantage ever since, most recently in the form of a far-reaching project to completely re-examine, restore and create an exhaustive record of the Chapel of St John the Baptist with a programme of research, restoration and promotion of our heritage.

The present volume contains a summary of the study recently published in Portuguese, aiming to bring the latest information about this baroque monument into the public sphere and thus, in an echo of the original historical goal of the great royal commission itself, to bridge different cultures, times and kinships and bring them closer together.

Pedro Santana Lopes
Trustee of the Santa Casa da Misericórdia de Lisboa

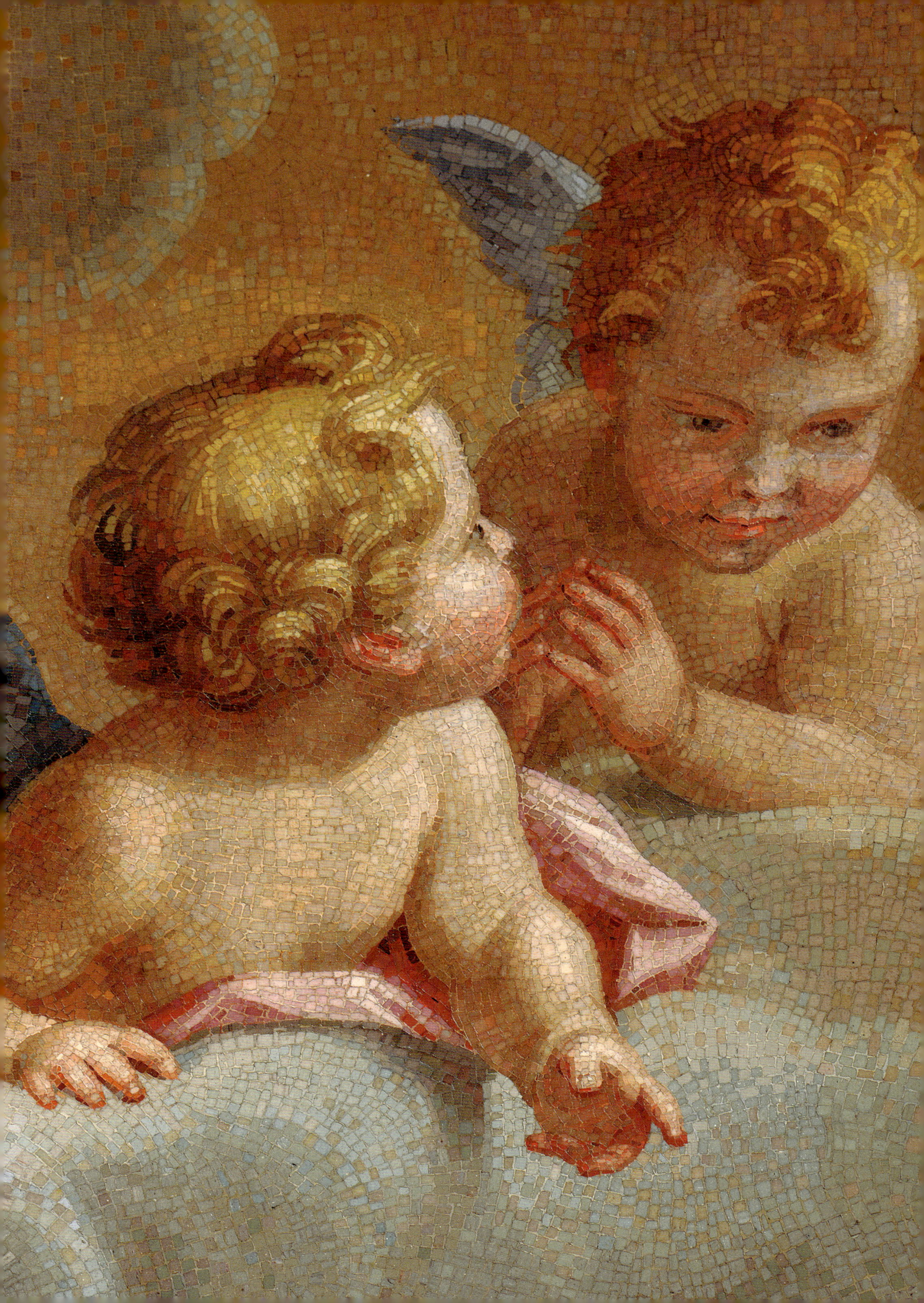

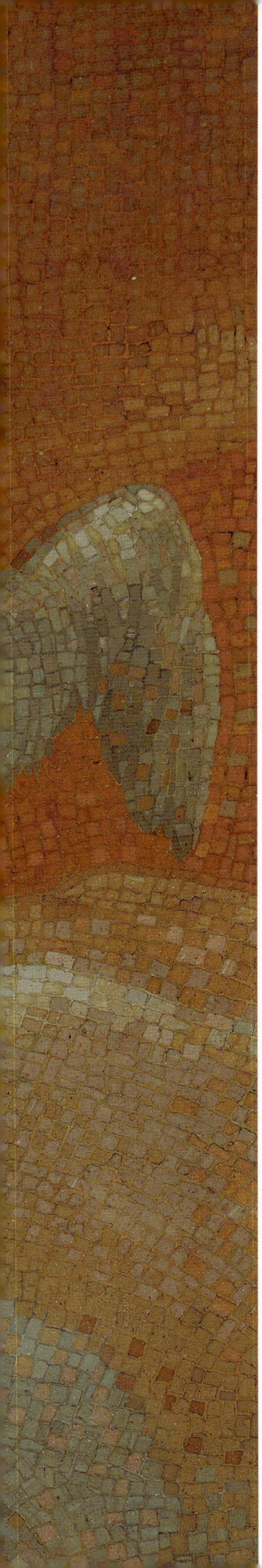

Introduction

In 2006, the Museum of São Roque belonging to the Santa Casa da Misericórdia in Lisbon initiated a project whose goal was the complete and comprehensive study of the Chapel of St John the Baptist. The project therefore included a number of different elements and encompassed not only scientific research – leading to a deeper and more complete understanding of the extraordinary work of art that is the chapel, reflected in a subsequent publication – but also an extensive campaign of conservation and restoration of the many and varied facets of the monument, which also helped to enrich our knowledge of it.

The two interconnected initiatives – the research project and the campaign of restoration – resulted in a detailed monograph published in 2015 and constituting the most complete and comprehensive study ever undertaken of the Chapel of St John the Baptist in the Church of São Roque in Lisbon, addressing not only the process of commissioning the chapel and the work of constructing it, but also the collections that belong to it.

The Chapel of St John the Baptist was constructed in its entirety in Rome in the 1740s, in execution of a commission from the Portuguese monarch John V. Its enormous significance in historical, cultural and artistic terms, both on a national and international level, unquestionably deserves to be reflected in the publication of this in-depth study, an organised corpus of the information available on the chapel. The scope of the present study significantly expands upon earlier publications, particularly noteworthy among which are the pioneering work of Sousa Viterbo and Vicente de Almeida (*A Capella de S. João Baptista Erecta na Egreja de S. Roque. Fundação da Companhia de Jesus e Hoje Pertencente à Santa Casa da Misericordia. Noticia Historica e Descriptiva* – The Chapel of St John the Baptist Built in the Church of S. Roque. Founded by the Company of Jesus and Now Belonging to the Santa Casa da Misericordia. A Historical and Descriptive Record) published in 1900 and that of Maria João Madeira Rodrigues printed in 1989 (*A Capela de S. João Baptista e as suas Colecções* – The Chapel of St John the Baptist and Its Collections).

Under our scientific and editorial supervision, this book brings together and integrates studies by a number of highly regarded Portuguese and Italian researchers, specialists in the many different artistic fields in which the chapel and its collections offer outstanding examples: architecture, sculpture, mosaics and metalwork; gold and silver; textiles, lace, furniture and books among others.

Magnificently illustrated with an outstanding selection of photographs, the present publication is a synthesis of that study and maintains the same scientific approach and rigorous standards in all its content, ensuring that a comprehensive understanding of the Chapel of St John the Baptist will be disseminated and promoted not only to a specialised audience in the form of the scientific community, but also to the general public, who will not fail to be captivated by the extraordinary beauty of this unparalleled architectural and artistic creation.

Teresa Leonor M. Vale

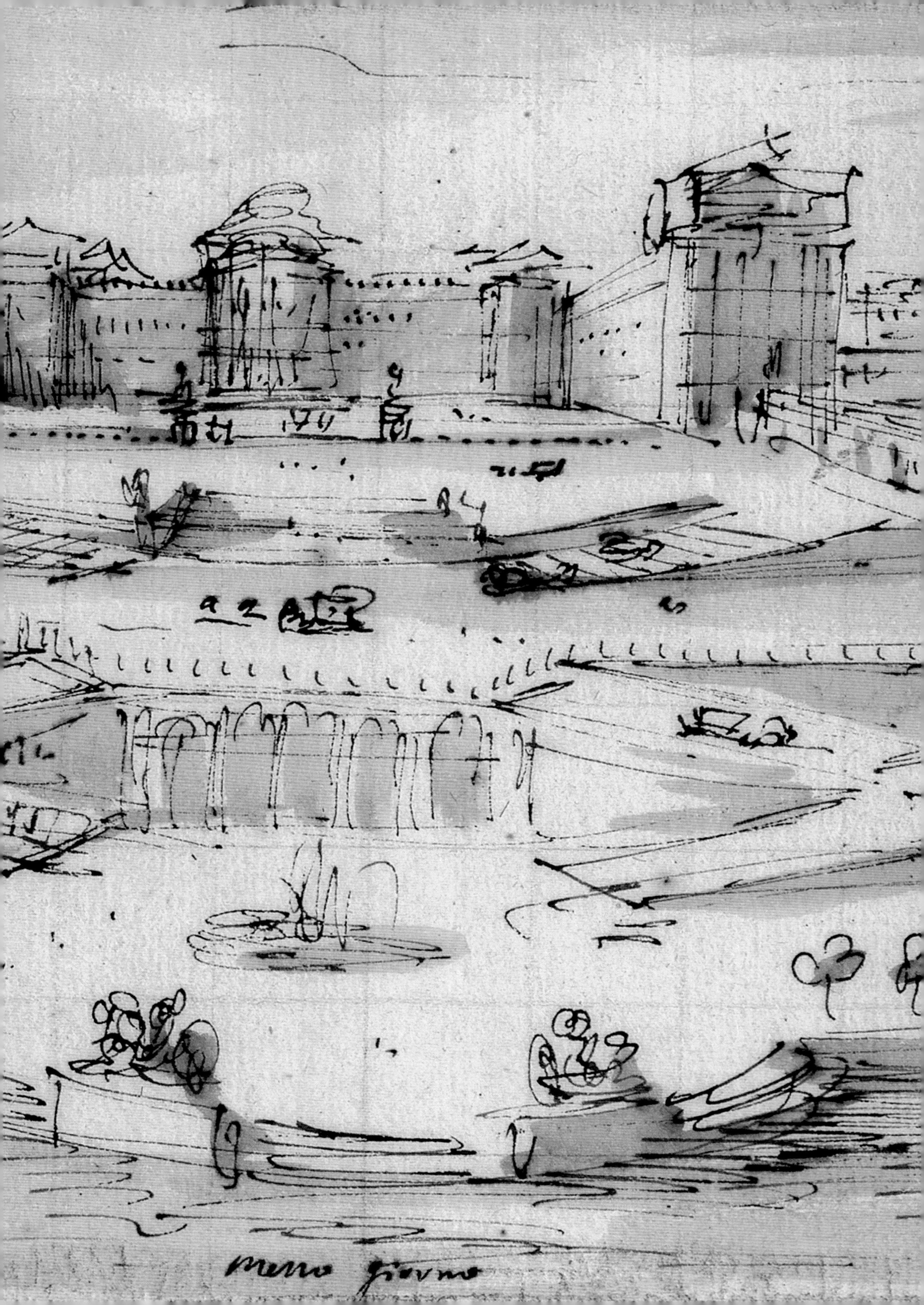
Mezzo giorno

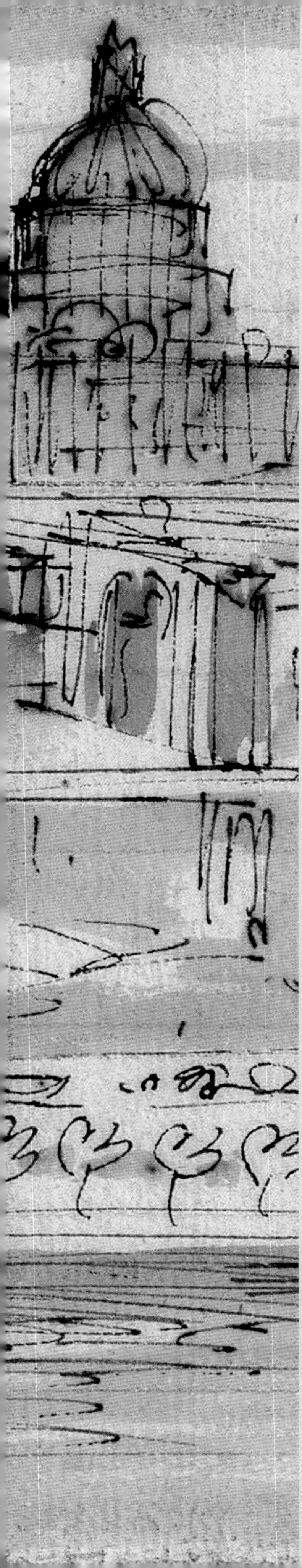

PART I
THE COMMISSION

A chapel for the king of Portugal: the controversial history of a truly prodigious commission

António Filipe Pimentel

1. History, legend and historiography

The story of the Chapel of St John the Baptist began in 1742 with the following message, sent to the Portuguese ambassador in Rome: 'His Majesty desires that a design be made as soon as may be, by the finest architect, who is presently to be found in Rome'[1] and culminated in 1747 when the work itself was shipped, together with its treasure.[2] It was recognised at an early date that this was an artistic ensemble of unquestionable value,[3] but despite that its history was soon obscured by legend based on the references contained in Brother Cláudio da Conceição's *Gabinete Histórico* (Cabinet of Historical Curiosities) dating from the early nineteenth century.

According to Brother Cláudio, when the monarch visited the old Jesuit church (fig. 1) he is said to have noticed the contrast between the luxury displayed in most of the chapels and the impoverished appearance of that dedicated to St John the

pp. 14–15
Sketch for the Royal Palace and Patriarchal Church of Lisbon
Filippo Juvarra, 1719
(See fig. 5)

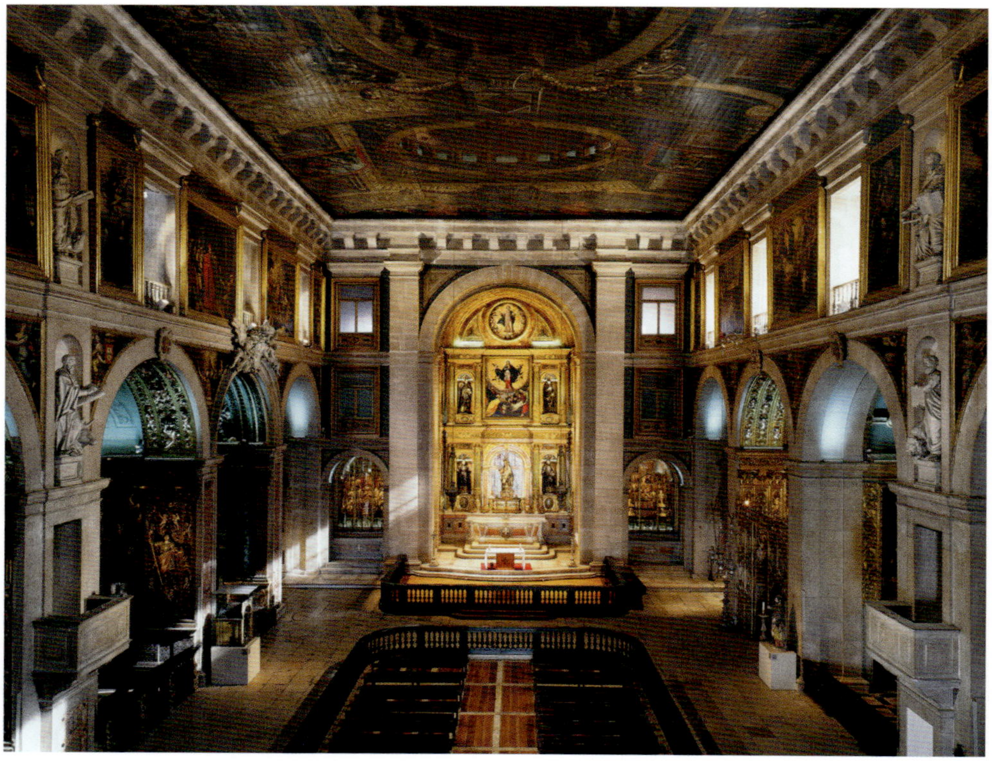

Fig. 1
Church of São Roque
(general view)

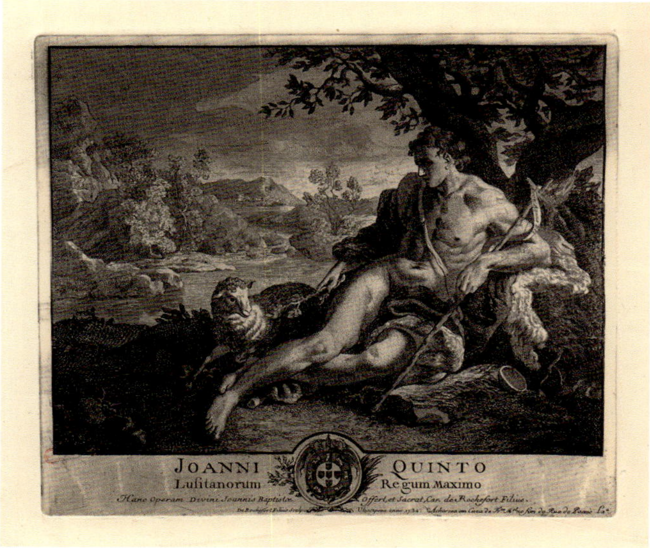

Fig. 2
Allegory of King John V (St John the Baptist)
Charles de Rochefort (engrav.), Pierre-Antoine Quillard (inv.) [author of original drawing], engrav. Lisbon, 1732
Etching, black and white
Biblioteca Nacional de Portugal [National Library of Portugal], Lisbon
(ref. E.693A)

Baptist. As this was his own patron saint, the king apparently decided to take it under his direct care and protection. Once the relevant maquette had been made and approved, the design was executed, assembled and consecrated in Rome, with a mass celebrated in the chapel by the pope himself. It was then dismantled and sent to Portugal, where it was erected on the site intended for it and unveiled to the public for the first time in 1751 – too late for John V, who had died almost six months before (fig. 2).[4]

The chapel has excited admiration ever since, not only for its inimitable luxury and the mastery of its execution[5] but because it is prized as a 'creation unique in the context of Portuguese art',[6] 'a monument that foreshadows Neoclassicism'[7] or even a thoroughgoing illustration of the aesthetic clash between Portugal's conservative, traditional baroque style and the reforming, classicising principles that dominated artistic creation in Rome at that time.[8]

In recent years, in fact, the Chapel of St John the Baptist has once more come to receive renewed critical attention.

2. Politics, diplomacy and devotion

The pious account given by Brother Cláudio, however, does not stand up to critical reading. It contains numerous controversial elements, none more so than the one that constitutes the very bedrock of the narrative: the fact that the chapel was supposedly dedicated to the monarch's patron saint.[9] This was hardly going to escape the notice of the chapel's first great historian, Sousa Viterbo, and it is in fact quite clear from the documentation that the chapel was dedicated to the Holy Spirit.[10] Given this, it seems clear that associating the chapel with the king's miraculous namesake was the result of a royal decree and done with a view to enhancing the king's prestige – much as his grandfather Manuel I had set out to do two centuries earlier.[11]

In fact this metaphorical allusion to the sovereign was to form part of a deliberate process of exalting royalty itself, of which the architectural design of the chancel of the Royal Basilica of Mafra[12] (figs 3 and 4) also constituted a fundamental stage. With this in mind we must therefore view the complex process of constructing this sumptuous chapel, and the choices made in doing so, in a different light.

One fact, nonetheless, seems beyond question today: the traditional insistence that this was a 'creation unique in the context of Portuguese art'[13] is wrong. In reality, the chapel was part of a larger undertaking at the epicentre of the symbolic and ideological system under the reign of John V: the Patriarchal Basilica established in 1716 and centred on the royal chapel in the palace of Ribeira. What is known today of this

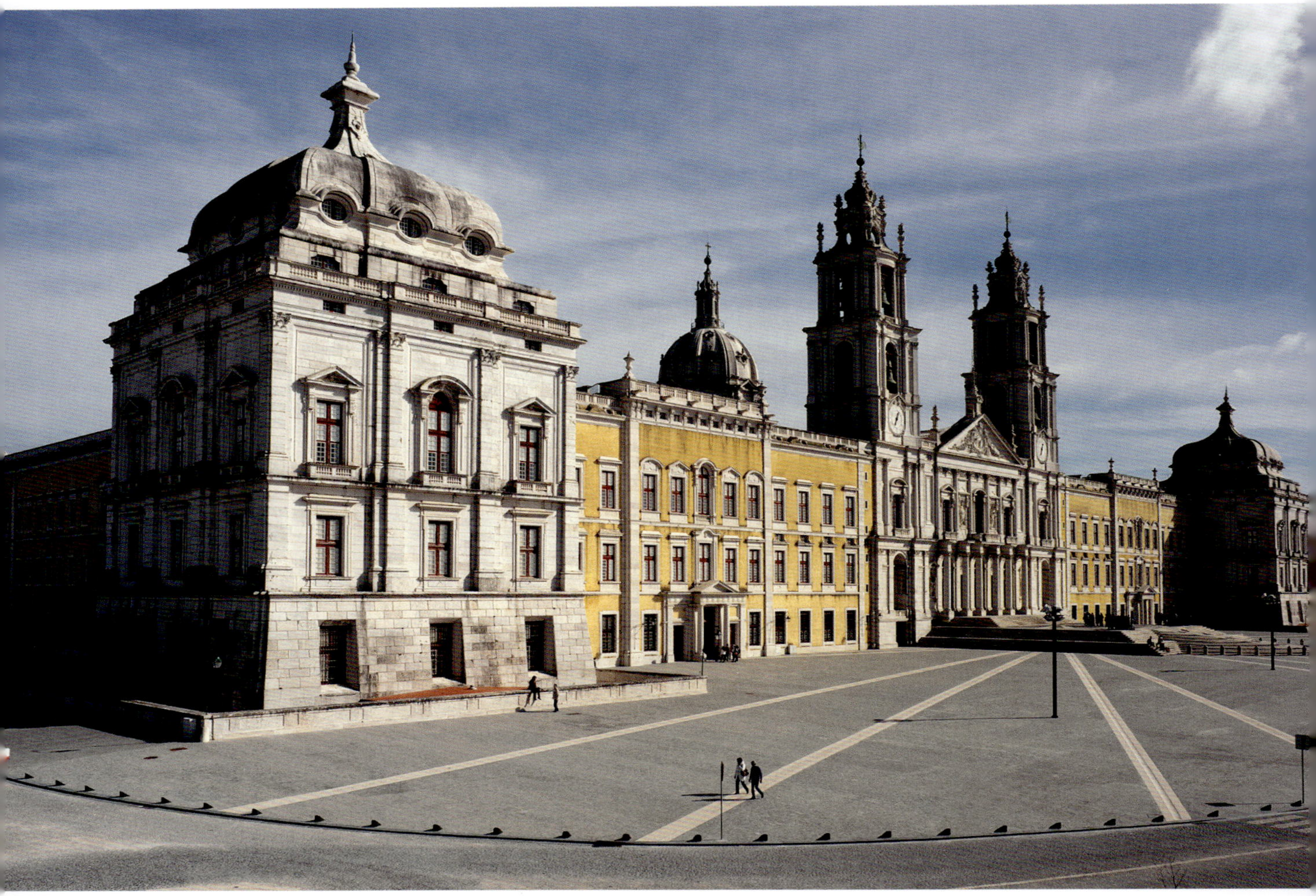

great undertaking demands – in the light of their aesthetic similarity[14] and the vastly greater scale of the latter – that the Chapel of St John the Baptist be recognised as constituting an appendix or subordinate phase[15] of the Patriarchal Basilica.

Fig. 3
Royal Palace of Mafra
(View of the façade)

The first patriarch of Lisbon himself, Tomás de Almeida – an admitted intellectual disciple of the Jesuit fathers[16] – sought to recreate in Lisbon the same ceremonial link as that established in Rome between Il Gesù (the central church of the Jesuit Order) and the Papal Basilica, an initiative of obvious significance given the ideological context in which he consecrated his own Lisbon jurisdiction under the epithet of the 'Rome of the West'.

The commissions involved in both projects combined both political and liturgical business dealings, running in parallel in the Eternal City via the same diplomatic channels and addressed to the same circle of artists. And they were intended for the same purpose: for the Patriarchal Basilica project, under the direction of João Frederico Ludovice.[17] Nicola Salvi and Luigi Vanvitelli, the Roman architects who designed the chapel, were also responsible for the commissions intended for the patriarchate; here too the process was marked by the same repeated episodes of

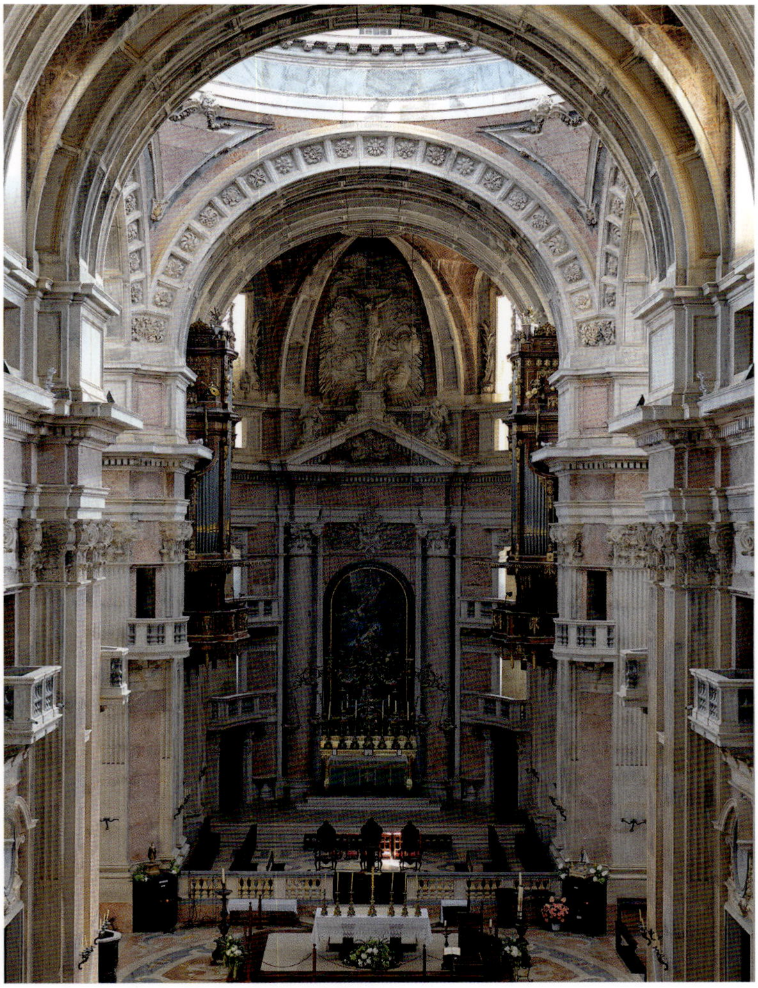

Fig. 4
High altar of the Royal Basilica of Mafra

criticism and refusal of designs sent from Rome that were characteristic of the process of work on the chapel: a very particular 'dialogue in design' between Lisbon and the Papal city.[18]

The choice of Rome for this commission was doubtless influenced by its centre-stage position in international diplomacy, particularly with regard to the Catholic powers. From the very first this city played a central role in the efforts invested abroad in terms of diplomacy under the Aviz or Johannine dynasty and, consequently, in diplomacy in artistic spheres as well. This investment was reflected in the importation of works of art and of artists involved in domestic projects, which were swiftly and unequivocally positioned as a tool of national affirmation and propaganda.[19] Relationships – and the resulting tensions – of a strictly political and diplomatic nature were thus inextricably intertwined with more specifically cultural and artistic relations.[20]

It is no coincidence that the triple commission (the Patriarchal Basilica, the Chapel of St John the Baptist and its treasure[21]) was set in motion at the time when the Portuguese sovereigns were granted the title of *Majestade Fidelíssima* (Most Faithful Majesty), and, particularly, just when rumours were spreading of a worsening decline in the income of the Portuguese Crown – rumours that it was becoming necessary to nip in the bud in Rome, the central forum of international diplomacy.

In this context, it is very likely that the decision to commission this fabulous chapel from the same workshops and with the same scheduling and administrative oversight as the impressive aesthetic reform of the Patriarchal Basilica, did indeed constitute a *programa anexo*, an appendix or subordinate scheme intended to reinforce the political and diplomatic effect so ardently desired by the government of John V: that of equipping the Lisbon court with a liturgical setting to match their ambitions, and at the same time to provide international affirmation of the status of the Portuguese Crown, aiming to make such a display of unlimited financial capacity as to dispel all doubt.

This, then, is the historical context – the intersection of interests and events – against whose backdrop an explanation can be found not only for the unique, complex and indeed quarrelsome process that surrounded the chapel's execution in Lisbon and in Rome, but also for the fact that this little 'Capella de Mosaico, o melhor que fosse possível' (chapel of mosaic, the best that may be possible) was transformed into an axis about which a veritable constellation of treasures, of gold, silver, jewellery, vestments and liturgical accoutrements, comprised 'one of the most important museums of the Italian decorative arts of the age'.[22]

3. From the Patriarchal Basilica to the Royal Chapel of St John the Baptist

For the reasons referred to above, it is important to trace the process whereby the royal chapel was transformed during the later elevation of the church to collegiate status in 1710 and to Patriarchal Basilica in 1716, together with the great transformation that was to culminate in 1746 in its re-consecration.

In a country where social status was measured by ecclesiastical standards, in fact, the spectacle of the court – whose actors had to perform their role in a physical setting that was itself without any grandiose proportions – could not resist appropriating liturgical pomp for its own benefit in a process that was facilitated by the obvious affinities between religious and courtly ceremony.[23] The staging of great religious ceremonies would thus enable the monarch to conduct the daily life of the court in brilliant style, without having to make too many concessions to the aristocracy – while at the same time ensuring the allegiance of a church flattered by its royal connection even as it was increasingly subordinated to royalist policies.

Indeed, it was in the dramatic context of the restoration of independence in 1640, and the Gallicanist theories that agitated the French Church in the sixteenth and seventeenth centuries, that the possibility was first raised in Portugal of organising the national ecclesiastical hierarchy in a way that was administratively independent of Rome's pastoral authority. The intention was to place the Portuguese Church under the authority of a patriarch, subordinate to the Apostolic See only in matters of dogma and moral questions.[24] Half a century later, the issue arose again – now in the context of reinforcing the absolute authority of the monarch. The Patriarchal Basilica was established in the royal chapel of the palace of Ribeira and placed under the authority of the patriarch, effectively endowing the new capital city of West Lisbon with the religious apparatus of a miniature version of the Vatican.[25] The years just prior to this had not been particularly conducive to grandiose endeavours, however. Portuguese involvement in the Spanish War of Succession and all the attendant economic difficulties and social instability this brought in its wake had created permanent obstacles to the monarch's cherished re-building plans, and it is probable that the reforms carried out suffered from a lack of coordination imposed by the circumstances.

This process proved beneficial to the concurrent project of works at the convent of Mafra built under Ludovice's direction: the project was launched in the years in which the religious status of the royal chapel was elevated, and by 1721–22 the convent underwent a radical reconfiguration, quadrupling the built-up area to create an unusual synthesis of royal palace, royal basilica, a pantheon for the monarchical dynasty, a convent, college and library. Here, the very architecture of royal power as John V was to shape it was realised in concrete form, embracing both secular and ecclesiastical elements in a harmonic and original synthesis.[26]

After the failure of Filippo Juvarra's plans for a sumptuous royal residence to be erected on the Tagus – designed with high theatricality, surrounded by magnificent gardens and encompassing, in a single architectural complex, both the patriarchal see and the residence of the metropolitan prelate – the monarch returned his attentions to the palace of Ribeira. Here, in the years that followed, the reforms took on new life and energy, drawing between 1728 and 1732 on the collaboration of another Italian architect: Antonio Canevari (fig. 5).[27]

In 1729 Mafra would once again occupy the sovereign's attention with the aim of proceeding, in October of the following year, to its consecration. Once this had been achieved, however, the frenzy of building work on this great monument ebbed and, little by little, the palace of Ribeira – which was, after all, the true centre of political life and served to represent the country – once again became the focus of the king's energies. Until the end of his reign, the royal residence on the Largo da Patriarcal continued to be embellished with new additions, culminating in 1749 with the apartments of the princess of Beira and her sisters (overseen by Ludovice alone after Antonio Canevari returned to Rome in the middle of 1732).

The two floors that offer a record of the patriarchal building project – the only surviving testimony of the extensive remodelling carried out in this area of the palace (figs 6 and 7)[28] – show that the body of the old church would have remained

Fig. 5
Sketch for the Royal Palace and Patriarchal Church of Lisbon
Filippo Juvarra, 1719
Pen-and-ink drawing in brown ink, pencil quadriculation
Palazzo Madama – Museo Civico d'Arte Antica [Civic Museum of Ancient Art], Turin (inv. 1859/DS, vol. 1, f. 96, dr. 157)

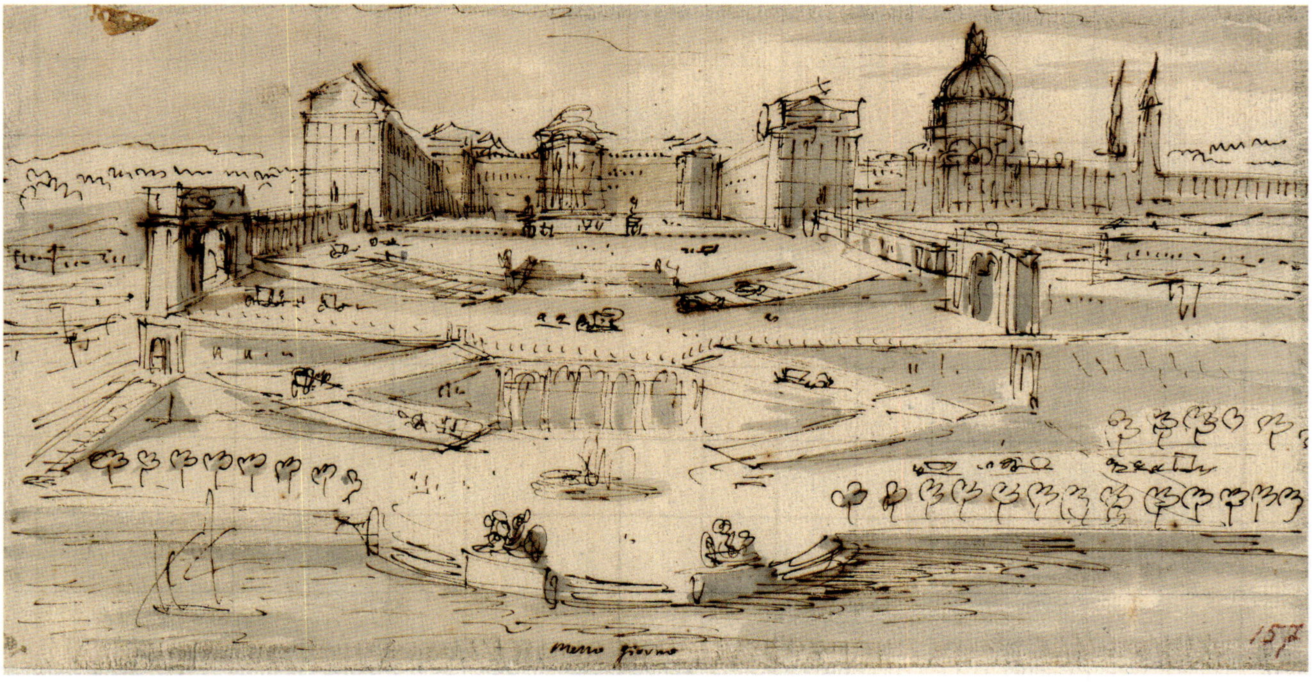

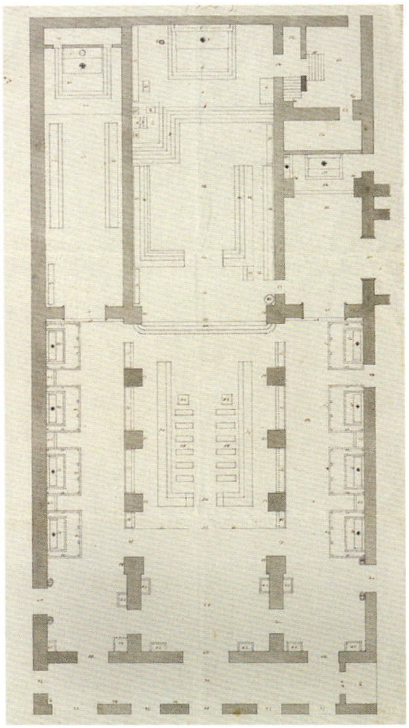

Fig. 6
Floor plan of the Patriarchal Basilica (post. 1755)
Drawing in Indian ink, grey wash
Biblioteca da Ajuda ['Assistance' Library], Lisbon (Ms. 54-XI-38, docs 17 and 17b)

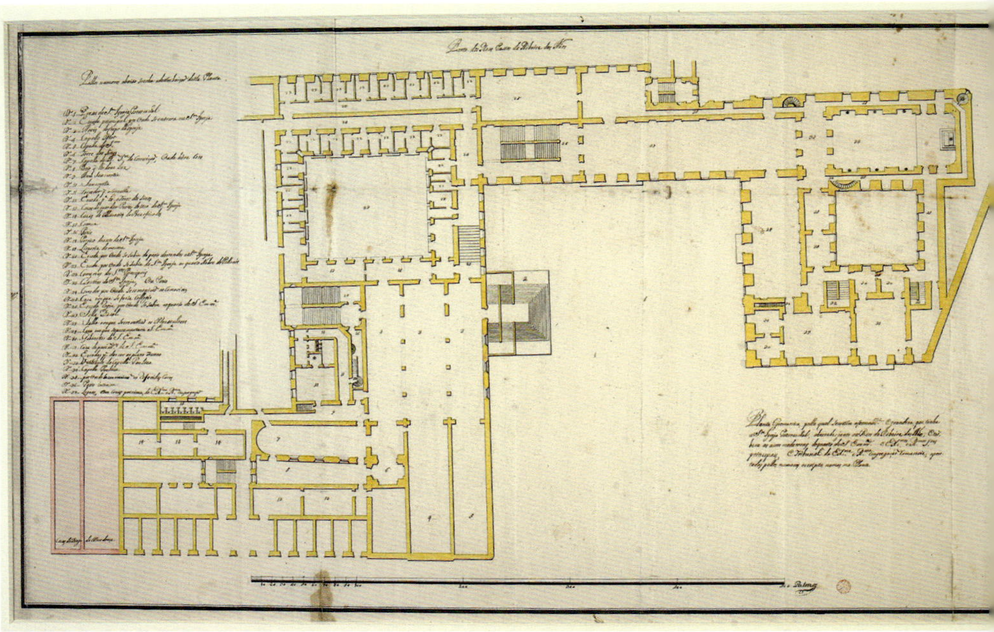

Fig. 7
Floor plan of the First Patriarchal Church
c. 1775 (?)
Drawing in Indian ink, washes
Biblioteca Nacional de Portugal [National Library of Portugal], Lisbon (D. 13R)

essentially unscathed. The projects of work carried out in 1712 and 1713 focused mainly on the chancel, making it possible to incorporate neighbouring buildings and extend the complex of the Patriarchal Basilica. The chancel was extended so far during the first phase of these works that it reached exactly the same length as the nave. The Evangile or 'gospel side' chapel on the left was dedicated to the Blessed Sacrament, and the one on the opposite side to the Holy Family; the latter extended only halfway back, leaving room in the rear for the *casa do tesouro* or treasury.

Perpendicular to this and opening directly onto it was the exceptionally rich Chapel of the Immaculate Conception, round which there extended a veritable labyrinth of annexes and sacristies and so on. Here there stood, resplendent, a magnificent statue in silver of the Virgin, commissioned from Giovanni Battista Maini in 1744 in accordance with detailed plans drawn up by Ludovice and dispatched by the king's secretary, Father João Baptista Carbone.[29] At the opposite end of the church, three doors led to the palace by way of a gallery running round the Chapel Courtyard, and to the apartments of the metropolitan prelate, which were reached by a long staircase. On the Epistle (right-hand) side, another staircase[30] led from the nave to this courtyard on the ground-floor level and to other rooms and annexes on the upper level. The nave on the Evangile or gospel (left-hand) side, in its turn, opened onto the outside by way of the famous staircase of five flights leading to where the new atrium – which in 1719 was still being built – now stood like a vast, modern square; the Patriarchal church square was thus transformed by this access route into the dynamic nucleus of a programme of urban design that sought to bring a whole amalgam of disparate constructions together in an aesthetically coherent project (fig. 8).

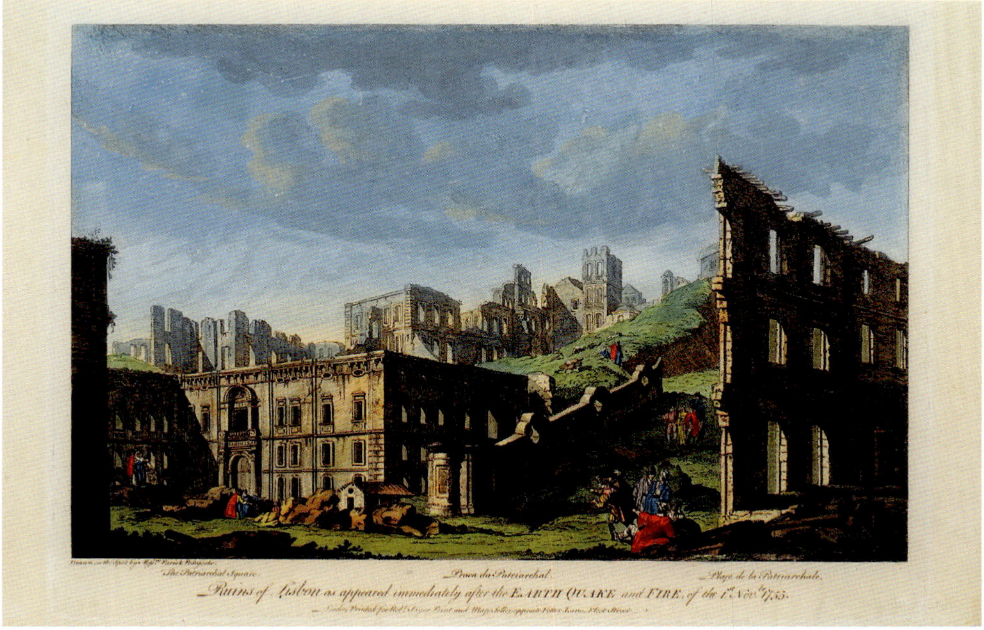

Fig. 8
Ruins of Patriarchal [Church] Square after the Earthquake of 1755
Jacques-Philippe Le Bas (engrav.), Miguel Tibério Pedegache Brandão Ivo (dr.), 1757
Watercolour engraving
Museu da Cidade [City Museum], Lisbon (inv. RC. GRA. 0441)

As part of a renewed investment of both money and effort on the architectural and urban development front, the Royal Basilica underwent a systematic cycle of aesthetic renovation that was symbolically crowned by the re-consecration of 1746. To this end a methodical operation was undertaken to send in excess of 320 packing-cases from Rome containing paintings, sculptures, vestments, tapestries, silverware, books and decorative metalwork for the Chapel of São Roque; there were also samples of various types of stone – though the earliest consignments included wooden replicas on a 1:1 scale for the three altars for the basilica of São Pedro.[31] In the event, the hopes of extending the building or erecting a new one were dashed; the renovation of the Patriarchal Basilica focused entirely on systematically transforming its interior, which was fabulously enriched and embellished with regalia and accoutrements obtained from the Eternal City.[32]

The decision to use Roman labour (always working within the guidelines sent from Lisbon) expressed a conscious wish to adopt this method of achieving the most effective outward reflection of the art of the Portuguese court.

Just as in the Chapel of St John the Baptist, tensions arose – most particularly with regard to the involvement of Luigi Vanvitelli in the plans for the new baptistery in the royal chapel,[33] because this crucial element lay at the very heart of the entire project of works and Ludovice, in his role as overall coordinator, jealously reserved for himself the task of defining its conceptual aesthetic and sense of plasticity, determining the architectural direction of the entire undertaking.[34]

Careful analysis of the commissioning of the Chapel of St John the Baptist thus casts an objective light not only on the establishment of this extraordinary enterprise, but also on that of the Patriarchal Basilica, revealing the coherence and indivisibility of the two. ■

NOTES

[1] Francisco Marques de Sousa VITERBO and R. Vicente d'ALMEIDA, *A Capella de S. João Baptista erecta na egreja de S. Roque*, Lisbon, Livros Horizonte, 1997, p. 105 (1st edition 1900).

[2] *Ibid.* p. 148.

[3] José-Augusto FRANÇA, *Lisboa Pombalina e o Iluminismo*, Lisbon, Bertrand, 1987, p. 49 (1st edition 1983).

[4] Frei Cláudio da CONCEIÇÃO, *Gabinete Histórico*, vol. XI, Lisbon, Impressão Régia [Royal Press], 1827, pp. 38–42.

[5] Francisco Marques de Sousa VITERBO and R. Vicente d'ALMEIDA, *op. cit.*, p. 8.

[6] Maria João Madeira RODRIGUES, *A Capela de S. João Baptista e as suas colecções*, Lisbon, Inapa, 1988, p. 17.

[7] José-Augusto FRANÇA, *op. cit.*, p. 49.

[8] Paulo Varela GOMES, *A Cultura Arquitectónica e Artística em Portugal no Século XVIII*, Lisbon, Editorial Caminho, 1988, pp. 97 ff.; *idem*, *A Confissão de Cyrillo*, Lisbon, Hiena, 1992, pp. 101 ff.

[9] Frei Cláudio da CONCEIÇÃO, *op. cit.*, vol. XI, pp. 38–42.

[10] Francisco Marques de Sousa VITERBO and R. Vicente d'ALMEIDA, *op. cit.*, p. 12 and note 1, referring to vol. 2 of the work by Father Baltazar Teles, *Chronica da Companhia de Jesus* (pp. 124 ff.), which contains information on the original chapel, its dedication to the Holy Spirit and its founders, who had a crypt or ossuary there.

[11] Paulo PEREIRA, *A Obra Silvestre e a Esfera do Rei, iconologia da arquitectura manuelina na Grande Extremadura*, Coimbra, 1990, especially chs. 3 and 4; Paulo PEREIRA, 'A simbólica manuelina. Razão, celebração, segredo', in *História da Arte Portuguesa*, vol. II, Lisbon, Círculo de Leitores, 1995, pp. 128–36.

[12] António Filipe PIMENTEL, *Arquitectura e Poder. O Real Edifício de Mafra*, Lisbon, Livros Horizonte, 2002, p. 180; *idem*, 'Real Basílica de Mafra: salão de trono e panteão de reis', in *Boletim Cultural*, 93, Mafra, Câmara Municipal [Town Hall], Feb., 1994.

[13] Maria João Madeira RODRIGUES, *op. cit.*, p. 17.

[14] António Filipe PIMENTEL, 'Uma jóia em forma de templo: a Capela de São João Baptista', in *Oceanos*, no. 43, Lisbon, Jul./Sept., 2000, pp. 148–63.

[15] Marie-Thérèse MANDROUX-FRANÇA, 'La Patriarchale du Roi Jean V de Portugal', in *Colóquio-Artes*, 2nd series, no. 83, Lisbon, 1989, pp. 34–43; Marie-Thérèse MANDROUX-FRANÇA, 'A Patriarcal do Rei D. João V de Portugal', in *Triunfo do Barroco*, Lisbon, Fundação das Descobertas, 1993, pp. 39–53; Marie-Thérèse MANDROUX-FRANÇA, 'La Patriarcale del Re Giovanni V da Portogallo', in Sandra Vasco ROCCA, Gabriele BORGHINI (dir.), *Giovanni V di Portogallo e la Cultura Romana del suo Tempo (1707–1750)*, Rome, Edizioni Àrgos, 1995, pp. 81–92.

[16] cf. António Filipe PIMENTEL, 'D. Tomás de Almeida (1716–1754)', in C.A. Moreira Carlos AZEVEDO (coord.), *Os Patriarcas de Lisboa*, Lisbon, Centro Cultural do Patriarcado – Aletheia Editores, 2009, pp. 7–22.

[17] Marie-Thérèse MANDROUX-FRANÇA, 'A Patriarcal do Rei D. João V de Portugal', *op. cit.*, p. 45.

[18] *Ibid.* pp. 46 ff.

[19] With regard to the significance and extent of the Portuguese Crown's relations with the Eternal City in the first half of the eighteenth century, see the excellent account provided by the above-mentioned work *Giovanni V de Portogallo e la Cultura Romana del suo Tempo*.

[20] António Filipe PIMENTEL, 'António Canevari e a Arcádia Romana: subsídios para o estudo das relações artísticas Lisboa/Roma no reinado de D. João V', in Teresa Leonor M. VALE (coord.), *Lisboa Barroca e o Barroco de Lisboa*, Lisbon, Livros Horizonte, 2007, pp. 31–38.

[21] António Filipe PIMENTEL, 'Nobre, séria e rica: a encomenda da capela lisboeta de São João Baptista em São Roque e a controvérsia Barroco *versus* Classicismo', in Sónia Gomes PEREIRA (org.), *Anais do VI Colóquio Luso-Brasileiro de História da Arte*, vol. I, Rio de Janeiro, unnumbered, 2004, p. 118.

[22] José-Augusto FRANÇA, *op. cit.*, p. 49.

[23] Norbert ELIAS, *A sociedade de corte* [Court Society], Lisbon, Estampa, 1987, p. 92, note 1; Jacques LEVRON, *La vie quotidienne à la cour de Versailles aux XVIIe–XVIIIe siécles*, 3rd edition, Poitiers-Ligugé, Hachette, 1986, p. 65; Emílio OROZCO DÍAZ, *El teatro y la teatralidad del Barroco*, Barcelona, Planeta, 1969, pp. 101–2.

[24] Luís Reis TORGAL, *Ideologia política e teoria do Estado na Restauração*, vol. I, Coimbra, Biblioteca Geral da Universidade, 1981, p. 255, note 1.

[25] António Filipe PIMENTEL, *Arquitectura e Poder, op. cit.*, p. 98.

[26] See *ibid.* pp. 141, 154–55, 176–88, and António Filipe PIMENTEL, 'O Real Edifício', in António Filipe PIMENTEL (coord.), *A Encomenda Prodigiosa. Da Patriarcal à Capela Real de St John the Baptist* (exhibition catalogue), Lisbon, Museu Nacional de Arte Antiga [National Museum of Ancient Art] – Museu de São Roque – Imprensa Nacional-Casa da Moeda, 2013, pp. 60–61.

[27] cf. António Filipe PIMENTEL, 'António Canevari e a Torre da Universidade de Coimbra', *Artistas e artífices e a sua mobilidade no mundo de expressão portuguesa*, Actas [Minutes], VII Colóquio Luso-Brasileiro de História da Arte, Oporto, Faculdade de Letras da Universidade do Porto, 2005, pp. 49–58; António Filipe PIMENTEL, 'De Lisboa ao Caia: em torno do programa politico e artístico da *Troca das Princesas*', in Teresa Leonor M. VALE, Maria João Pacheco FERREIRA and Sílvia FERREIRA (coord.), *Lisboa e a Festa: celebrações religiosas e civis na cidade medieval e moderna*, Actas [Minutes], Colóquio de História e de História da Arte [History and History of Art Colloquium], Lisbon, Câmara Municipal de Lisboa [Lisbon City Hall], 2009, pp. 65–84.

[28] cf. António Filipe PIMENTEL (coord.), *A Encomenda Prodigiosa. Da Patriarcal à Capela Real de S. João Baptista, op. cit.*, pp. 94–95.

[29] Teresa Leonor M. VALE, 'A estátua de Nossa Senhora da Conceição da Patriarcal de Lisboa e a eleição de modelos pictóricos para obras de escultura num texto de João Frederico Ludovice', *Artis*, Revista do Instituto de História da Arte da Faculdade de Letras de Lisboa [Journal of the Institute of History in the Lisbon Faculty of Letters], nos. 7–8 (2009), pp. 317–32, and Teresa Leonor M. VALE, 'Di bronzo e d'argento: sculture del Settecento italiano nella magnifica Patriarcale di Lisbona', in *Arte Cristiana. Rivista Internazionale di Storia dell'Arte e di Arti Liturgiche* [Christian Art. International Review of the History of Art and of the Liturgical Arts], Milan, Year 100, no. 868, Jan.–Feb. 2012, p. 57–66.

[30] *Elogio fúnebre e histórico do muito alto ... Rei de Portugal, o Senhor D. João V* Lisbon, Regia Officina Sylviana, e da Academia Real, 1750, pp. 96–97.

[31] Teresa Leonor M. VALE, 'Roma em Lisboa: as artes decorativas no contexto das obras de arte enviadas da cidade pontifícia para a capital portuguesa no reinado de D. João V', *Revista de Artes Decorativas* [Review of Decorative Arts], Universidade Católica Portuguesa [Catholic University of Portugal], no. 5, Oporto, 2011, pp. 57–78; Teresa Leonor M. VALE, 'Ainda Roma em Lisboa: as réplicas de altares da basílica de S. Pedro do Vaticano, enviadas para a capital portuguesa entre 1741 e 1745', in Maria João Pacheco FERREIRA, Pedro FLOR, Teresa Leonor M. VALE (coord.), *Lisboa e os Estrangeiros | Lisboa dos Estrangeiros antes do Terramoto de 1755. Actas do Colóquio*, Lisbon, Câmara Municipal de Lisboa [Lisbon City Hall], 2013 (in press).

[32] cf. Marie-Thérèse MANDROUX-FRANÇA, 'Progetto di candelabro con le armi patriarcali' in *Giovanni V di Portogallo, op. cit.*, p. 102; Sandra Costa SALDANHA, 'Os apóstolos em prata para a Patriarcal de Lisboa: modelos de ourivesaria dos escultores José de Almeida (1708–1770) e Joaquim Machado de Castro (1729–1822), *Revista de Artes Decorativas* [Review of Decorative Arts], Oporto, Universidade Católica Portuguesa [Catholic University of Portugal], no. 2, 2008, pp. 45–62; Teresa Leonor M. VALE, 'Roman baroque silver for the patriarchate of Lisbon', in *Burlington Magazine*, vol. CLV, no. 1.323, Jun. 2013, pp. 384–89).

[33] António Filipe PIMENTEL, 'Luigi Vanvitelli (1700–1773). Pia Batismal', in António Filipe PIMENTEL (coord.), *A Encomenda Prodigiosa. Da Patriarcal à Capela Real de S. João Baptista, op. cit.*, pp. 112–13.

[34] Cf. José-Augusto FRANÇA, *op. cit.*, p. 49.

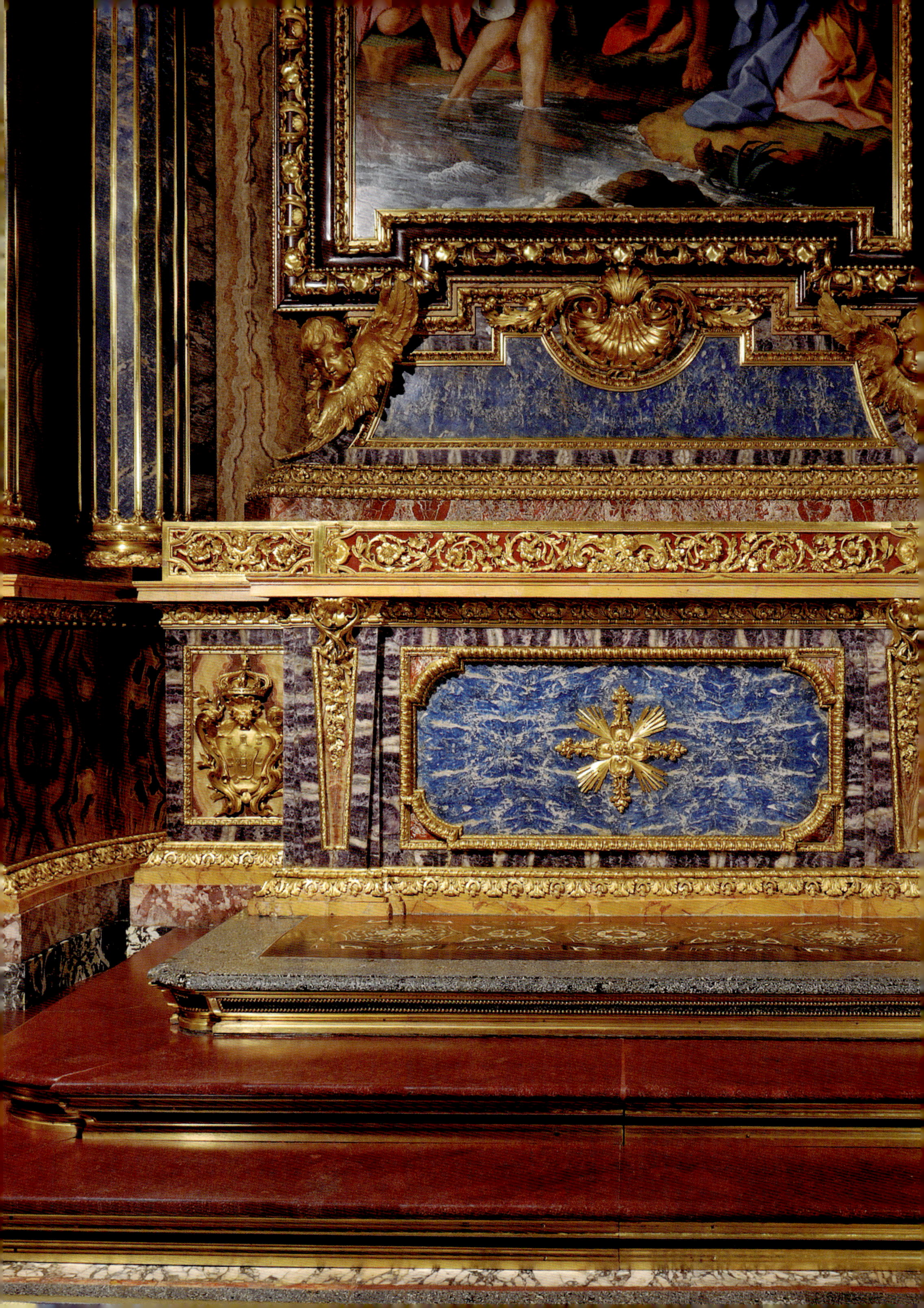

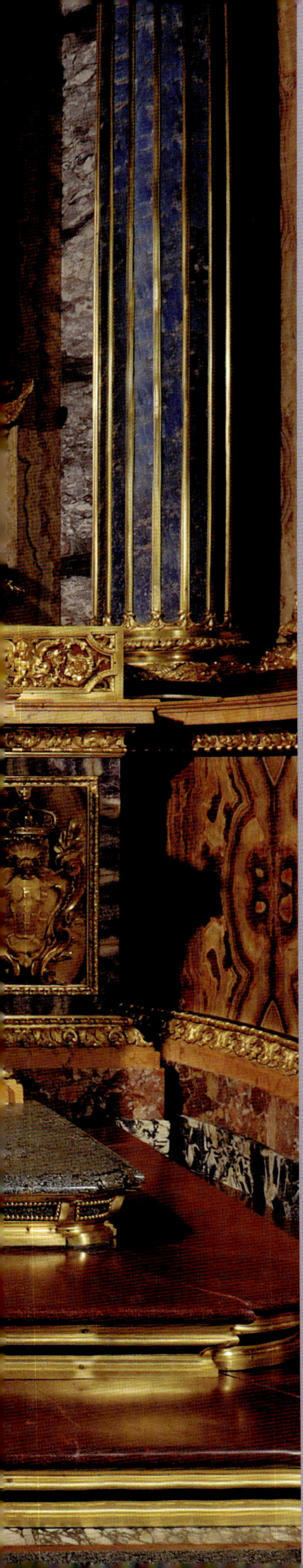

PART II

THE CHAPEL OF ST JOHN THE BAPTIST

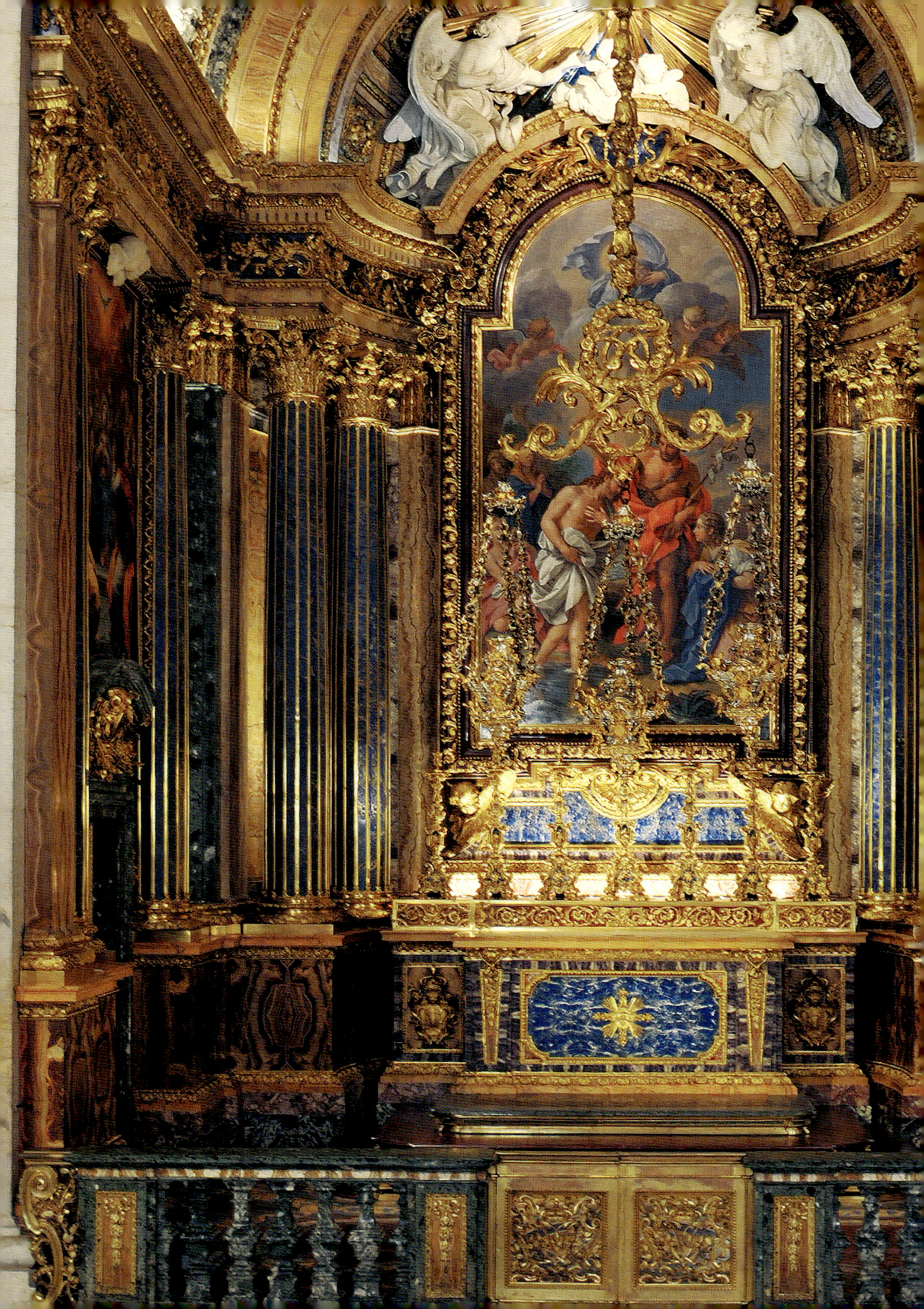

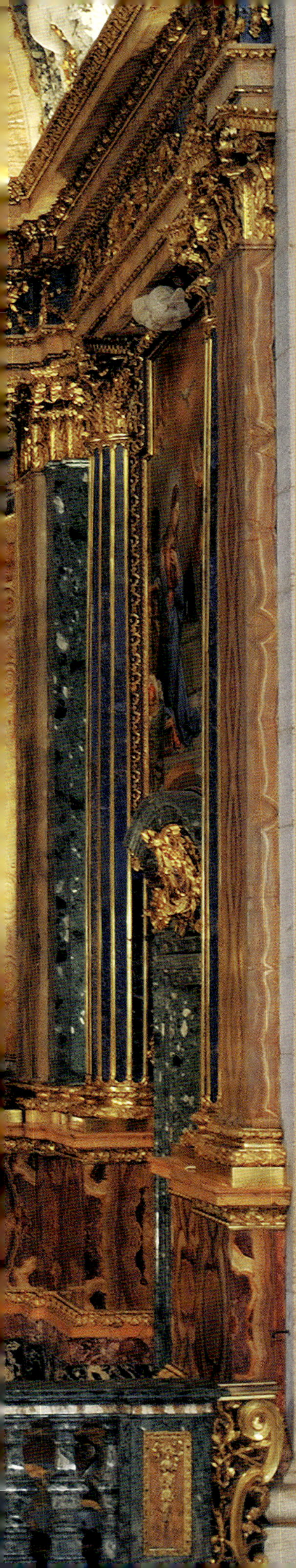

1. ARCHITECTURE

The Royal Chapel of St John the Baptist: a 'dialogue in design' between Lisbon and Rome

António Filipe Pimentel

1. The many forms of a singular commission

Once having grasped the complexity of the designs – aesthetic, symbolic, political and diplomatic – that were to govern the realisation of the Royal Chapel of St John the Baptist, it is important to go back and look at the commission's strict administrative process that began with a message sent on 26 October 1742 by Father João Baptista Carbone to Commander Manuel Pereira de Sampaio, the Portuguese ambassador in Rome.[1] The pious account of Brother Claudio da Conceição must also be taken as a primary source, even though it is already at some distance from the facts it reports.

The latter in fact states that the king had ordered measurements to be taken 'by his architects' and sent to Rome with a view to having a chapel made there: 'huma Capella de Mosaico, o melhor que fosse possível' (a chapel of mosaic, the best that may be possible'.[2]

Together with his message, Carbone sent plans and elevations. In the contents of the order itself there was written clarification to the effect that 'fica na liberdade do mesmo architecto usar de toda a casta de mármores mais raros e vistosos, assim dos antigos como dos modernos ... tendo amplo arbítrio de ornar tudo o mais nobremente e do melhor gosto que lhe fôr possível' (let the architect himself be free to use every rank and order of the rarest and most strikingly flamboyant kinds of marble, both the ancient and the modern ... having free rein to adorn the whole the most nobly and in the finest taste that he may)[3] – and yet it was recognised from the first that the king was directly involved in the process of commissioning the chapel,[4] with all the repercussions that this was to have with regard to aesthetic choices.

The artistic commission sent to Rome thus involved the production of an ensemble work (the chapel) which was addressed to the 'best architect, who is presently to be found in Rome'. The choice fell on a partnership consisting of Nicola Salvi (1699–1751) and Luigi Vanvitelli (1700–73).[5]

A disciple of Antonio Canevari[6] and a leading light in Roman aesthetics, at this time Salvi was absorbed in completing his celebrated masterpiece, the Trevi Fountain.[7] This may have brought him into contact with Luigi Vanvitelli, whom Benedict XIV had just put in charge of the *Fabbrica di San Pietro*[8] – the workshop complex at St Peter's which oversaw the construction and maintenance of the

pp. 26–27
Decoration of the altar table (frontal)
Antonio Arrighi
Gilded metal
(See fig. 50)

pp. 28–29
View of the Chapel of St John the Baptist (detail)
(See fig. 112)

building and its treasures – as both architects had entered the competitions for the fountain and for the façade of the basilica of San Giovanni in Laterano (St John Lateran).[9]

Ambassador Manuel Pereira de Sampaio's chosen architect(s) were to be offered both this commission and that of the baptistery of the Patriarchal Basilica. Historiographal analysis has now established Vanvitelli's authorial role,[10] but the documentation shows that payments were made to both artists[11] and the words of João Frederico Ludovice, their interlocutor in Lisbon, also testify to this.[12]

Nonetheless, the (quite natural) obligation laid down in Carbone's message – that the project had to be submitted for the monarch's prior approval – was to introduce a powerfully destabilising factor in the form of the king's artistic adviser, Ludovice. And it was not long before the project became embroiled in complications.

2. A (blazing) debate in design

The outlines that are known to us today – three drawings and a preliminary sketch, preserved in the Museum of San Martino in Naples and in the library of the Royal Palace of Caserta respectively (figs 9–12) – reveal an architecture strongly influenced by the Roman Baroque of Borromini, with sculpture taking on an explicitly dramatic role after the manner of Bernini.

In fact, the chapel was to be designed starting with a round or Roman arch (which already existed and therefore had to be accommodated) guarded by angel-candelabra with flying robes and flanked by hollow Corinthian pilasters at whose apex an armillary sphere was displayed, held up by fluttering *putti*, beneath the royal crown and a mantel of ermine from which hung festoons or garlands. The interior was to be composed of a rectangular space ending in a shallow recess that projected to form a frame around the altarpiece, and covered over with a vaulted ceiling of octagonal coffering. In this design the altarpiece or retable was seen emerging between densely clustered archivolts aligned with the two Corinthian pilasters that formed the intrados of the side arch and the half-columns that flanked the doorways leading onto the adjacent chapels on either side. On the side doors there were to be panels intended for the *Annunciation* and *Pentecost*, with an Ionic entablature running all round the top (without any frieze).

Within the area of the recess, amply highlighted by the placement of another side arch and also adorned with a coffering motif – though here the coffering is quadrangular in shape and arranged radially – the pilasters were to be repeated at the back; against these there would stand out four false or non-load-bearing columns arranged in an almost regular formation to frame the altarpiece. The altarpiece itself, which partially covers the central columns, was to be composed of a slightly tilted, elliptical panel crowned with cherubim and *putti* bearing a phylactery and dramatically supported by two angels posed as if carrying it: a motif that

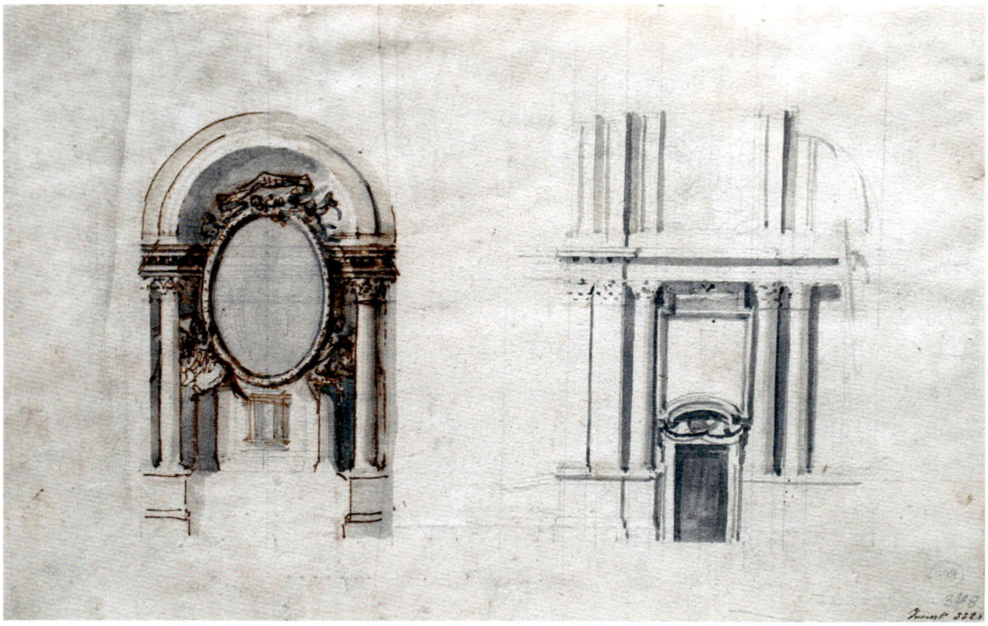

Fig. 9
Chapel of St John the Baptist for the Church of São Roque. View of the altar and section
Luigi Vanvitelli,
1st project, 1742
Drawing in brown ink, grey watercolour
Palazzo Reale [Royal Palace], Caserta, Campania
(no. 378 D, inv. 1951/52)

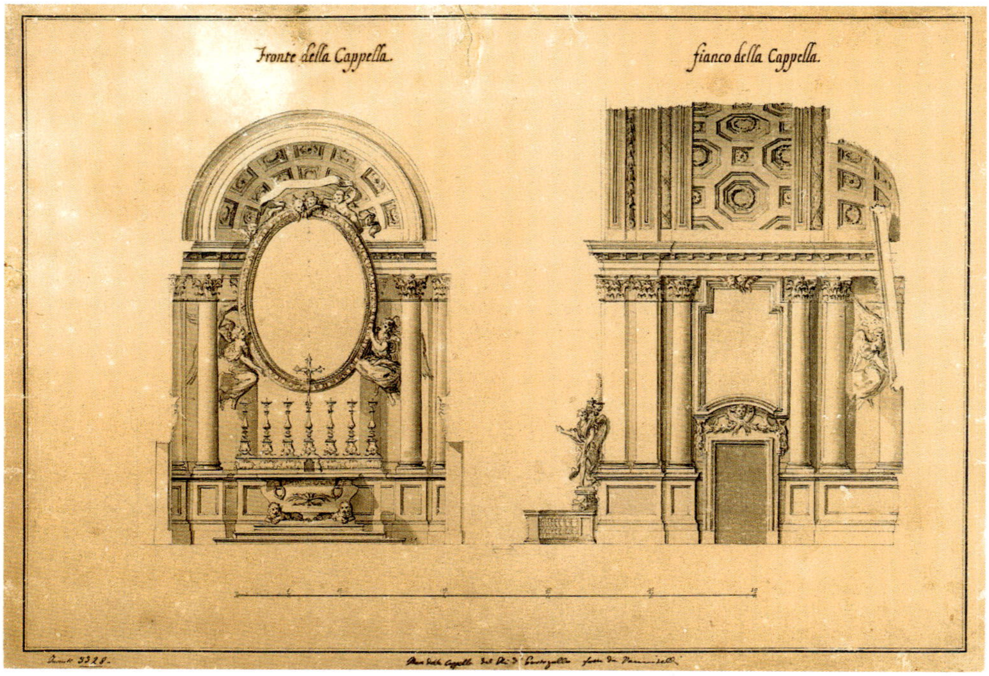

Fig. 10
Chapel of St John the Baptist for the Church of São Roque. Transverse and longitudinal sections
Luigi Vanvitelli,
1st project, 1742
Drawing in pencil and ink, watercolour
Museo Nazionale di San Martino [National Museum of San Martino], Naples
(inv. 3328/2)

Borromini had designed for the apex of the main façade of the Roman Church of San Carlo alle Quattro Fontane and which was in fact later made into an altarpiece. The altar table, comprised of an urn resting on two lions and styled to suggest antiquity, introduced an almost dissonant note, while the royal escutcheon stood out on the paved floor. The chapel was to be enclosed by a convex balustrade reached by ascending two steps. Obtaining approval for this design was to prove no easy matter.

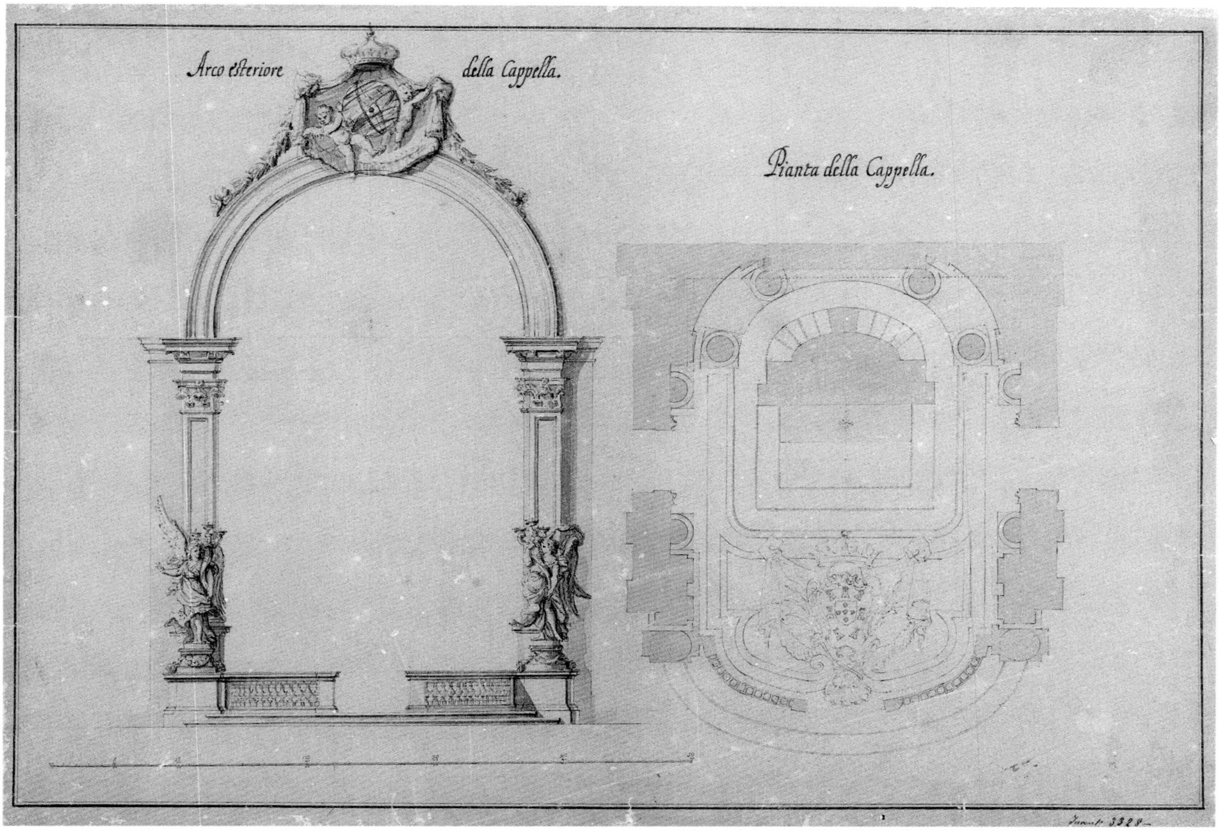

Fig. 11
Chapel of St John the Baptist for the Church of São Roque. Outer arch and plan
Luigi Vanvitelli,
1st project, 1742
Drawing in pencil and ink, watercolour
Museo Nazionale di San Martino [National Museum of San Martino],
Naples (inv. 3328/1)

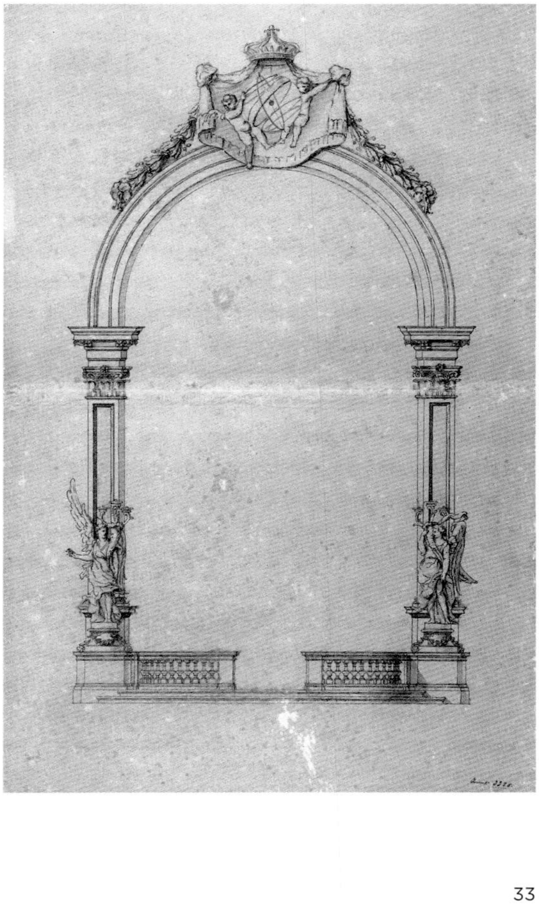

Fig. 12
Chapel of St John the Baptist for the Church of São Roque. Outer arch
Luigi Vanvitelli,
1st project, 1742
Drawing in pencil and ink, watercolour
Museo Nazionale di San Martino [National Museum of San Martino],
Naples (inv. 3328/4)

Indeed, a month and a half after the arrival of the Roman drawings, on 8 February 1743, Carbone returned them – now accompanied by criticisms and corrections drawn up in Lisbon, comprising an extensive memorandum which listed a series of amendments arising from the drawings. Attention was drawn to the fact that the chapel was a royal building, which demanded alterations to the cyma (an S-shaped decorative moulding), the altarpiece, the royal arms, the ceiling, the front façade of the outer arch, the altar, the predella (altar platform) and the tabernacle for displaying the Blessed Sacrament.[13]

Another memorandum, this time addressed to Agostino Masucci, was distinguished in sharp contrast to the above by the approval calmly granted to the painter's proposals.[14]

In a letter dated the seventh of the following April, Sampaio replied that 'the architects raised several questions about the instructions that came to me';[15] the ambassador dispatched this message to Lisbon, and on 28 July Carbone in turn sent him the reply[16] from the court architect with the suggestion that 'caprichos pittorescos, que não são admissiveis em huma Capella que se manda fazer de architettura nobre, séria e rica' (picturesque caprices, which are not admissible in a chapel that is ordered to be made with architecture that is noble, serious and rich) should be excluded, and enjoining that the memoranda be adhered to (fig. 13).[17]

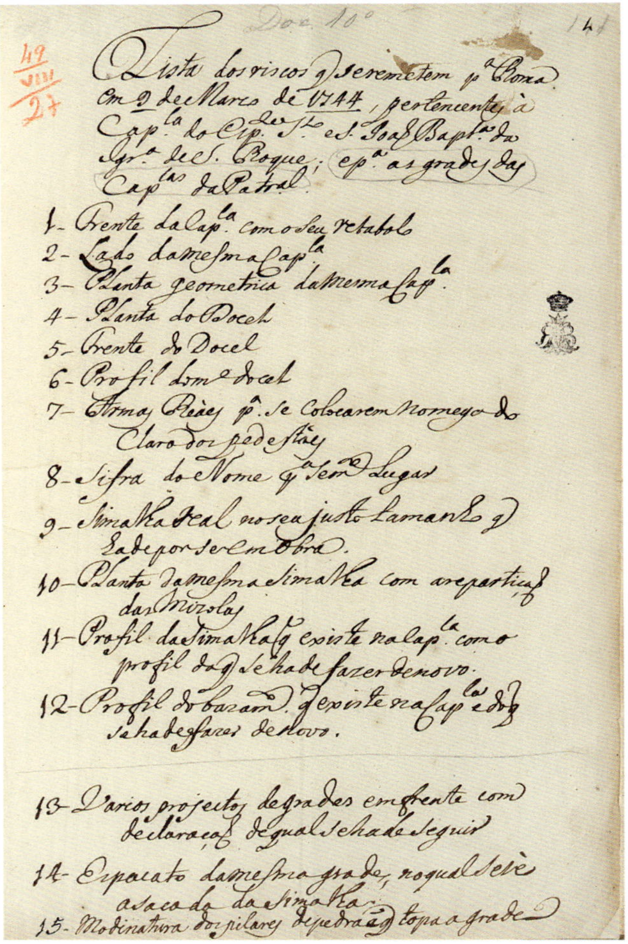
Doc. 10° 141
49 VIII 27
Lista dos riscos q se remetem p.a Roma em 2 de Março de 1744, pertencentes à Cap.la do Glor. S.to e S. João Baptista da Igr.a de S. Roque; e p.a as grades das Cap.las da Patriarcal
1- Frente da Cap.la com o seu retabolo
2- Lado da mesma Cap.la
3- Planta geometrica da mesma Cap.la
4- Planta do Docel
5- Frente do Docel
6- Profil do m.mo docel
7- Armas Reaes p.a se colocarem no meyo do claro dos pedestaes
8- Sifra do Nome q tem o Lugar
9- Simalha Real no seu justo tamanho q se ha de por ser em obra.
10- Planta da mesma simalha com a repartição das mizolas
11- Profil da simalha q existe na Cap.la com o profil da q se ha de fazer de novo.
12- Profil do bazam q existe na Cap.la e dos q se ha de fazer de novo.
13- Varios projectos de grades em frente com declaração de qual se ha de seguir
14- Espacato da mesma grade, no qual se vê a sacada da simalha
15- Modinatura dos pilares de pedra da topa a grade

Fig. 13
List of designs drawn for the project by João Frederico Ludovice for the Chapel of St John the Baptist (roll)
Biblioteca da Ajuda ['Assistance' Library], Lisbon (Ms. 49-VIII-27, f. 141)

On 1 August, Sampaio wrote that the order was 'repartida por infinitos Artífices, segundo as matérias de que ella consta' (divided between an infinite number of craftsmen, according to the materials of which it is composed) and, on 31 August, he continued in the same tone, reporting that 'Na Capella … se trabalha com muita diligencia, tendo-se adiantado de sorte, que concorre bastante gente por conta da curiosidade do Paiz, e Sua Santidade me intimou o querer vel-a antes que se embarque' (In the chapel ... work proceeds very diligently and has advanced so much that many people come flocking from across the country out of curiosity, and His Holiness has indicated to me that he wishes to see it before it is embarked).[18]

In the face, therefore, of criticisms and corrections that were merely literary, the work is thought to have continued and run over for many months, reaching such a point that Sampaio regularly increased the cost. The preamble was followed by minute instructions on every constituent part of this small but sumptuous temple, right down to the smallest detail: from the vaulted ceiling, whose archivolts were to

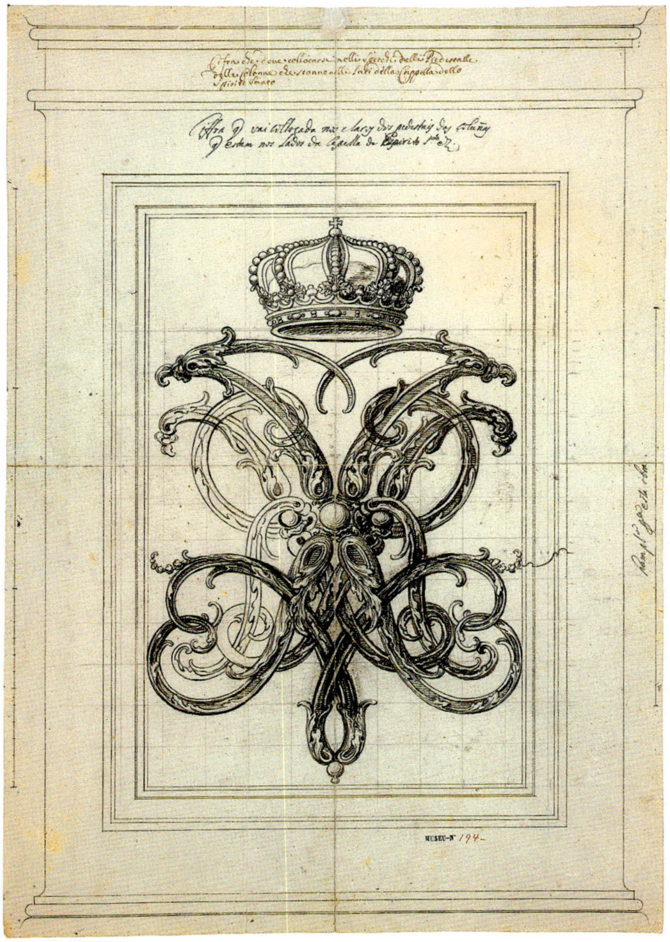

Fig. 14
Study of the royal monogram for the Chapel of St John the Baptist
João Frederico Ludovice, 1744
Drawing in black pencil, pen and watercolour wash in black and grey
Museu Nacional de Arte Antiga [National Museum of Ancient Art], Lisbon (inv. 194 Des. [Drawings])

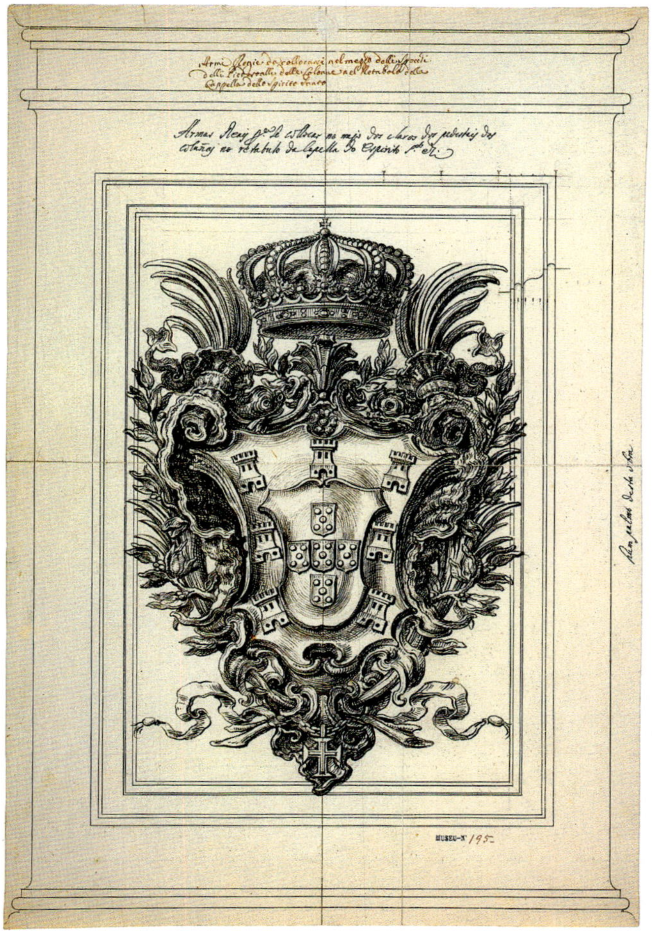

Fig. 15
Study for the Portuguese royal escutcheon for the Chapel of St John the Baptist
João Frederico Ludovice, 1744
Drawing in pen, ink, black pencil, India ink wash
Museu Nacional de Arte Antiga [National Museum of Ancient Art], Lisbon (inv. 195 Des. [Drawings])

Fig. 16 (overleaf)
Capital
Francesco Giardoni
Gilded metal

follow the order of the pillars and columns, in light-coloured marble, with festoons or garlands of gilded brass; to the lunettes that it should have on either side; to the entablature and its ornamentation to the altarpiece and its frontispiece, the side doors, the footing and finally, to the royal arms and cyphers.[19]

Finally, on 9 March, there followed the complete drawings of the chapel showing the plan, the front and side elevations and the royal escutcheon and monogram (figs 14 and 15), together with the design of the cyma, with the plan and profile of the footing. On the same day there followed yet more detailed instructions on the structure of various elements of the chapel, such as corbels for the cruets to hold

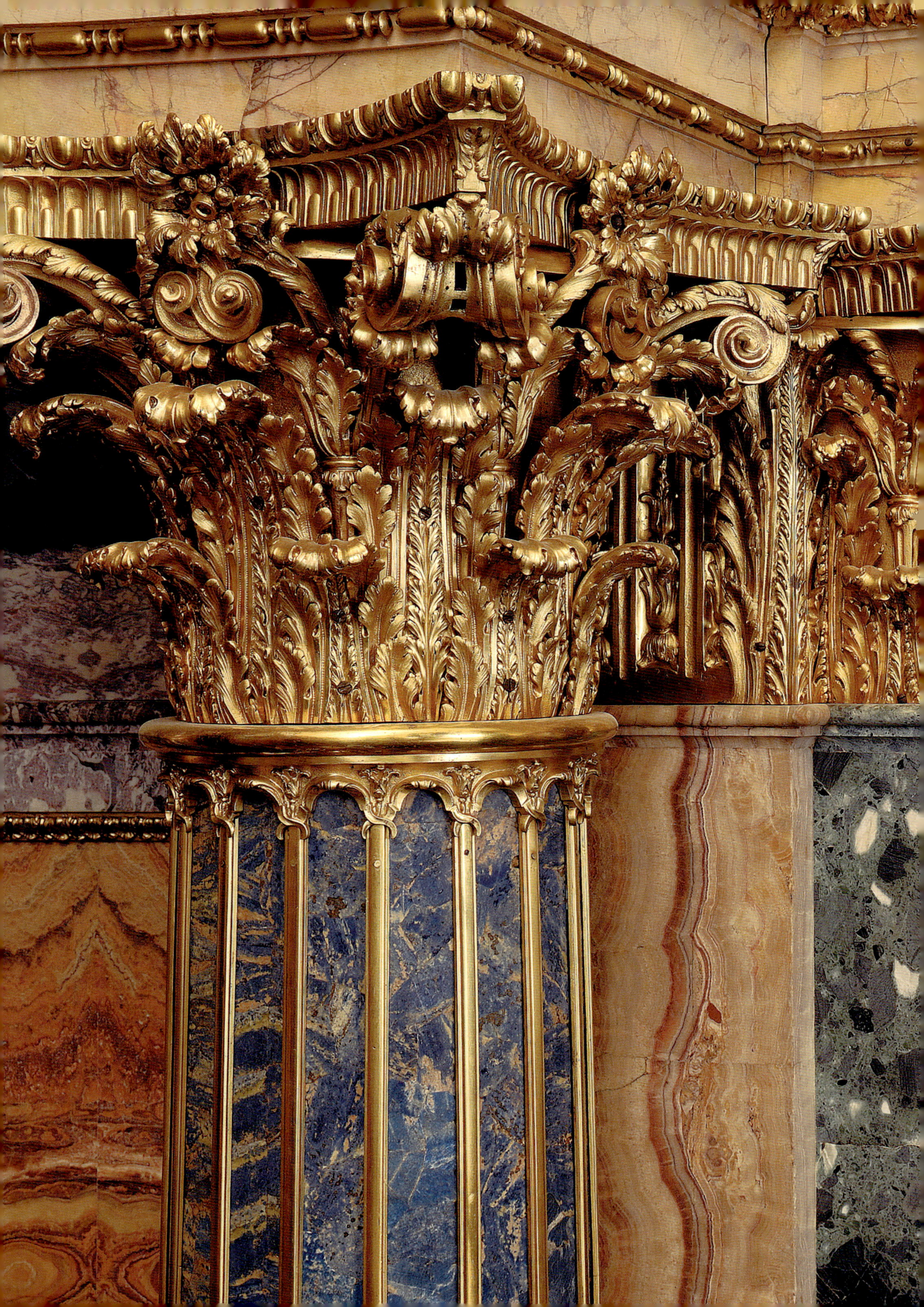

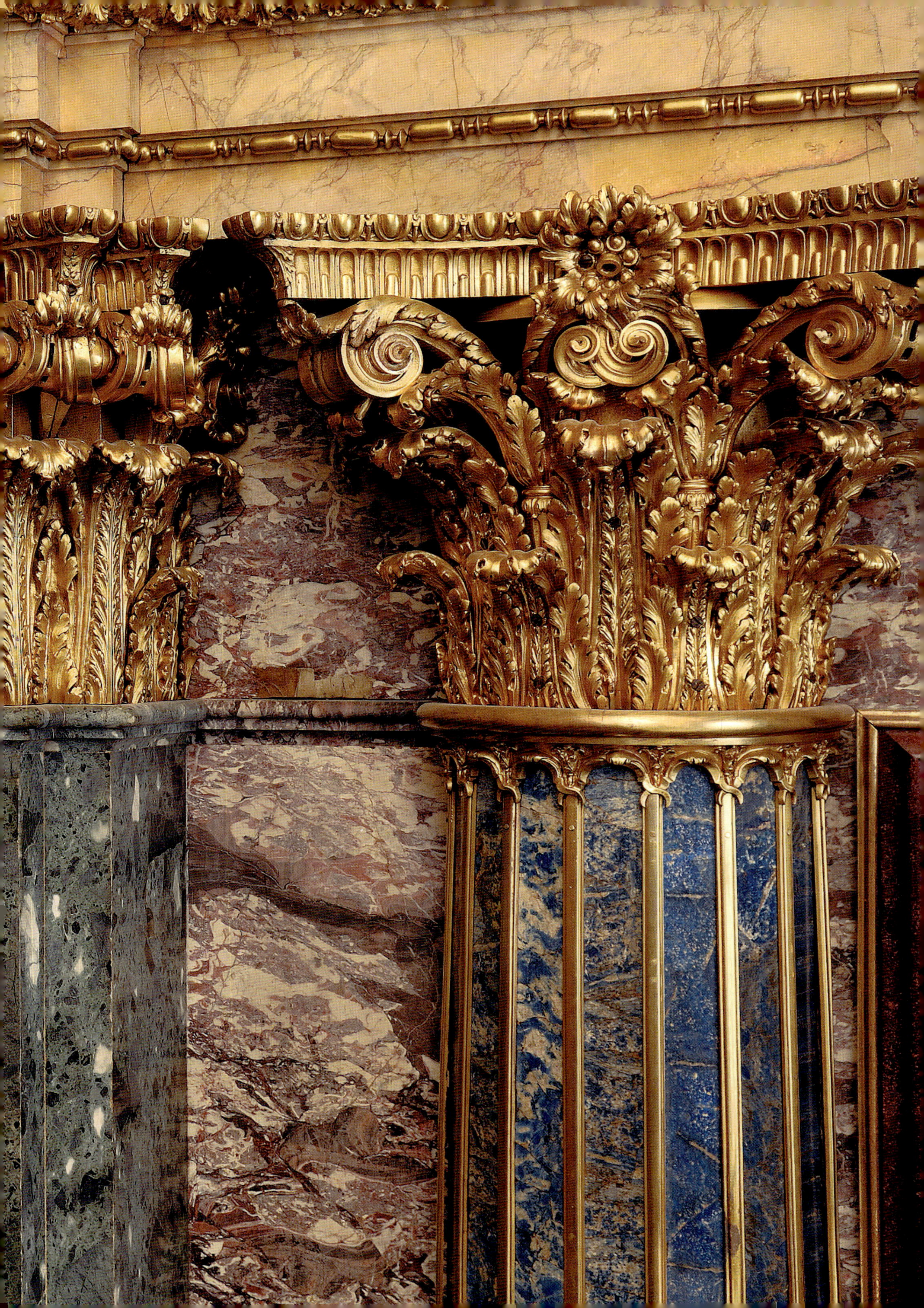

wine and water, confessionals, the gates of the balustrade and side doors, lamps and so on.[20]

The arrival in Rome of these papers and the drawings that accompanied them, at a time when – according to the ambassador – work on the chapel was already so far advanced 'de sorte, que ... Sua Santidade me intimou o querer ve-la antes que se embarque' (such that ... His Holiness intimated to me that he wished to see it before it is embarked) must have come as a bombshell. Immediately, then, on 12 April, Sampaio wrote to Lisbon acknowledging receipt of the papers and testifying to the surprise they had caused;[21] at the same time he did not fail to send the Roman architects' response to the alterations and instructions issued by the Lisbon architect.

If these papers, the schedule and their respective drawings drawn up in Lisbon caused astonishment in Rome, the impact of the response (now lost, but which apparently 'filled twelve sheets of paper'[22]) was no less great. An answer was not long in coming, and was expressed in terms of such vehemence as to call for explanation from Father Carbone.[23] The reply consists of a long and well-grounded dissertation in defence of the *centinado*; that is to say, the use of a curved line set against a straight line, specifically understood as the theoretical basis of this arrangement's compositional potential – at least in the sense in which it has been interpreted.[24]

But the truth is that we are entirely ignorant of the statements contained in the 12 pages of Vanvitelli's manifesto, whose loss leaves us in the dark with regard to the actual question to which Ludovice was responding.

3. One (master)piece and three authors

Whatever the facts, it remains inescapable that somewhere between the drawings being sent to Lisbon in December 1742 and the final work there was a metamorphosis, brought about by applying the instructions sent from Lisbon and, above all, the drawings that accompanied them. This is the only way to understand the execution of the two successive models.[25]

Ludovice's decisions were imposed by means of drawings on the entirety of Vanvitelli's project: the exterior elevation (whose design and appearance were to be completely changed by eliminating the Corinthian pilasters, the angel-candelabras and the convex balustrade) as well as the apex (where the royal escutcheon flanked by angels was to replace Vanvitelli's proposed panoply with the royal mantle extended above an armillary sphere held up by guardian spirits). It is interesting to compare the shield with the design moulded in bronze intended to be applied on the sides of the altar, and the way the arch is interrupted at the base of the shield by the curlicues of its corresponding frame. Other changes included the distribution of pilasters and columns (and the number of flutes on each) in the internal elevations; the entablature, which was Corinthian, imposed in its entirety, and the decoration of its corresponding frieze; and the structure and decoration of the vaulted ceiling, with its lunettes set in the protuberant part of the side panels, to give 'matéria para se enriquecer' (matter for enrichment). This must have referred to the ovate bas-reliefs carved by Carlo Marchionni and Bernardino Ludovisi, as there could be no other lunettes in a vaulted ceiling necessarily without openings. Other changes included the mouldings framing the panels 'de bronze com bellos lavores dourados' (of bronze, with beautiful gilded working) and the adoption of gilded bronze for the column capitals and bases; the structure of the altar and its corresponding altarpiece (attached to the wall, with its rectilinear panel topped with a semicircle – a design that Ludovice had published in Portugal – flanked by four columns and with a sculpture centred on the apex); the steps of the altar; the decision to eliminate the royal escutcheon on the paved floor and to replace it, as in the Patriarchal Basilica, with mosaic tables with an armillary sphere and its attributes; and indeed the very design of the royal cypher that was to adorn the chancel, the side doors and, together with the escutcheon, the altar table below the upper edging of the pedestals 'por piedade e reverencia que o dono tem a tão sagrado lugar' (out of piety and the reverence that its owner bears to such a holy place)[26] (figs 17 and 18).

The same is true, furthermore, of the fabulous treasure, which was also clearly the subject of a *dialogue in design* – one of which, however, we have scarcely any surviving record. Yet here too, it will undoubtedly be worth pursuing the trail of the architect-goldsmith Ludovice.[27]

One conclusion can thus be clearly drawn: if the design of the chapel did ultimately take on a classical nature – which has led history to regard it as a turning point in the evolution of Portuguese architecture – this was not something imposed from Rome 'contra a opinião e o gosto expressos em Lisboa' (contrary to the opinion and taste expressed in Lisbon).[28] On the contrary, this was in fact at the strong insistence of those in Lisbon who determined the elements that defined the aesthetics of power – however much it might go against the prevailing winds that were blowing in Rome.

Indeed, execution of the Chapel of St John the Baptist can only be understood in relation to that other, parallel project – the remodelling of the Patriarchal Basilica. The obsessive referencing of all things Roman visible in the Johannine aesthetic cannot be separated from the very specific goal of converting this city on the Tagus into the Rome of the West. In fact, having these sumptuous commissions executed in the most prestigious workshops of the Eternal City was an integral part of a foreign policy designed to elevate the image of the Portuguese monarch and his kingdom. This policy was deemed all the more necessary because – at a time when the kingdom was in decline – the king was in fact no longer as fabulously wealthy as he once had been, and the construction costs were rising exponentially.[29] What was intended, then, was to endow the Lisbon court with a religious setting in keeping with its ambitions, in the service of a political programme intended to glorify the Portuguese Crown and involving both the Patriarchal Basilica and the Chapel of St

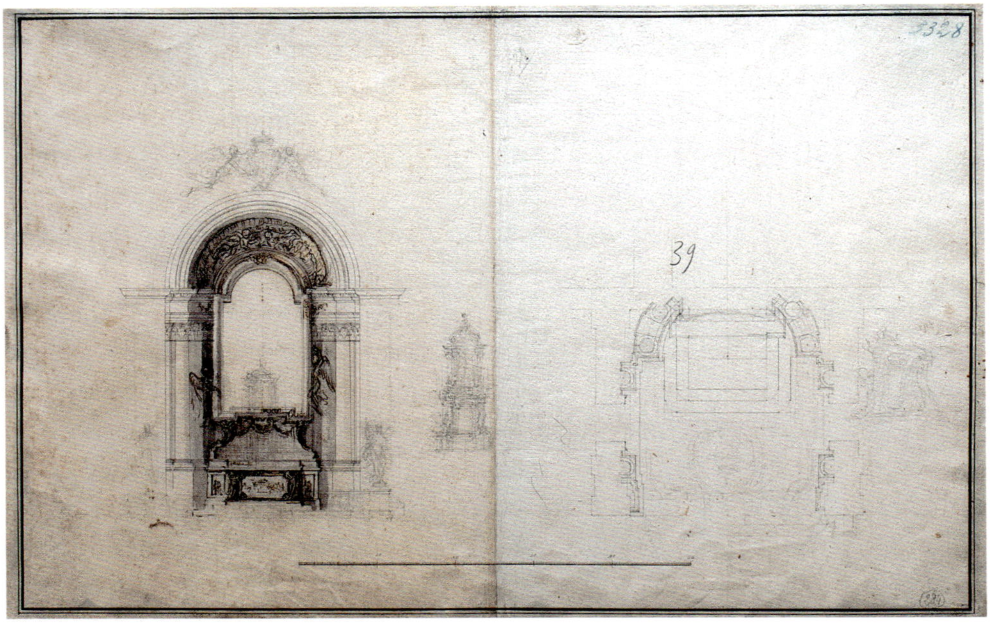

Fig. 17
Chapel of St John the Baptist for the Church of São Roque. View and plan
Luigi Vanvitelli, 2nd project, 1743–44
Drawing in pencil and brown ink, brown and white watercolour
Palazzo Reale [Royal Palace], Caserta (no. 248, inv. 1951/52)

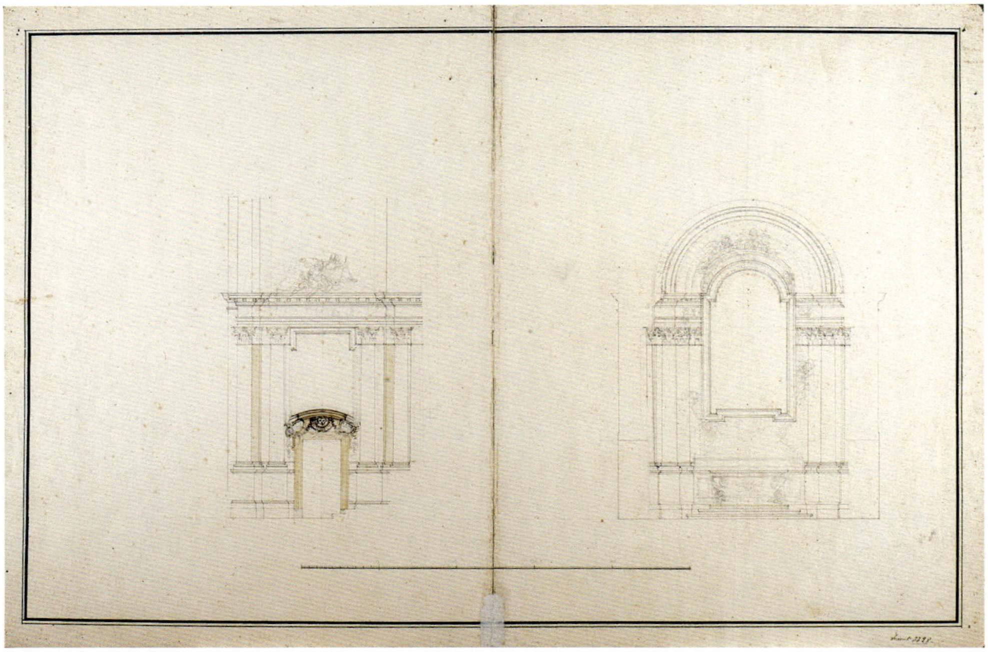

Fig. 18
Chapel of St John the Baptist for the Church of São Roque. Longitudinal and transverse sections
Luigi Vanvitelli, 2nd project, 1743–44
Drawing in pencil and ink, watercolour
Museo Nazionale di San Martino [National Museum of San Martino], Naples (inv. 3328/3)

John the Baptist, while at the same time making use of the specialised – but above all prestigious, and internationally renowned – labour force that Rome could offer (the fact that Vanvitelli was the architect of St Peter's would not have been irrelevant in the process of choosing him). The aim was to give the art of John V's court a visibility beyond the frontiers of Portugal, to which it could scarcely aspire if the project were confined within national borders from its conception to its execution, and at the same time to glorify the Crown as part of a plan to affirm its high status internationally – a plan that went far beyond these artistic commissions, and placed them at the service of a coherent image of power.

Meanwhile, work on the chapel was progressing. Sampaio conveyed the news to Lisbon that the pope had informed him he 'wished to consecrate the altar before it departs'[30] and in fact this consecration took place in the Church of Sant'Antonio dei Portoghesi.[31] Everything indicates, however, that only the altar was consecrated on this occasion and in fact the entire chapel was erected and exhibited to public admiration in the Capponi–Cardelli Palace during the course of that month – which was precisely one of the purposes it was intended to fulfil.

Seemingly indestructible, the Chapel of St John the Baptist, together with its treasure, survived even the great Lisbon earthquake; effectively it is a single, unified ensemble based on the intrinsic coherence of the final work, as if born of a single mind to whose brilliance (despite the acknowledgement that is of course due to all the many individuals who contributed to its execution) it ultimately offers the most eloquent and indisputable testimony.[32]

Let us therefore echo the words – no less fair an account for all that their author shrouds it in the haze of legend – of Brother Cláudio da Conceição, the first who sought to set down its history: 'uma das preciosidades mais raras, não digo só de Portugal, mas do Mundo inteiro' (one of the rarest treasures, not of Portugal only, say I, but of the whole world).[33] ■

NOTES

[1] Francisco Marques de Sousa VITERBO and R. Vicente d'ALMEIDA, *A Capella de S. João Baptista erecta na egreja de S. Roque*, Lisbon, Livros Horizonte, 1997, p. 105 (1st edition 1900); see also Pimintel's text in the present volume: 'Uma Capela para o Rei de Portugal: história controversa de uma encomenda prodigiosa', note 1.

[2] Frei Cláudio da CONCEIÇÃO, *Gabinete Histórico*, vol. XI, Lisboa, Impressão Régia [Royal Press], 1827, pp. 38–42; see also Pimintel's text in the present volume: 'Uma Capela para o Rei de Portugal: história controversa de uma encomenda prodigiosa', note 1.

[3] *Ibid.* p. 105.

[4] Francisco Marques de Sousa VITERBO and R. Vicente d'ALMEIDA, *op. cit.*, p. 130.

[5] *Ibid.* p. 130.

[6] Irisalva MOITA, 'O Aqueduto das Águas Livres e o abastecimento de água a Lisboa', *D. João V e o abastecimento de água a Lisboa*, vol. I (exhibition catalogue), Lisbon, Câmara Municipal de Lisboa [Lisbon City Hall], 1990, pp. 27–34.

[7] cf. Paolo PORTOGHESI, *Roma Barocca. Storia di una civiltà architettonica* , 2nd edition, Rome, Carlo Bestetti Edizioni d'Arte, 1967, pp. 429–34.

[8] Jörg GARMS, 'La Cappella di S. Giovanni Battista nella Chiesa di San Rocco a Lisbona', Sandra Vasco ROCCA and Gabriele BORGHINI (dir.), *Giovanni V di Portogallo (1707–1750) e la cultura romana del suo tempo*, Rome, Àrgos, 1995 pp. 113–14.

[9] cf. Gianfranco SPAGNIESI, 'Rome et sa culture à l'époque du voyage de Soufflot', in *Soufflot et l'Architecture des Lumières*, Actas [Minutes], École Nationale Supérieure des Beaux Arts, Paris, 2001, pp. 43–44.

[10] cf. Jörg GARMS, *op. cit.*, pp. 113–14 and António Filipe PIMENTEL, 'Uma jóia em forma de templo: a Capela de São João Baptista', in *Oceanos*, no. 43, Lisbon, July/September, 2000, p. 149.

[11] The documents in the Ajuda ('Assistance') Library do indeed specifically confirm a payment of 100 scudi romani or Roman escudos, in December 1742, 'à Nicola Salvi Architetto e suo compagno Vanvitelli per li disegni fatti per la Cappella dello Spirito Santo, e S. Giovanni Battista' (to Nicola Salvi, architect, and his companion Vanvitelli for the designs made for the Chapel of the Holy Spirit, and St John the Baptist) (Ms. 49-IX-22, f. 114); once more payments were made to both of them jointly, on 3 December 1744, 30 August 1745 and 22 December 1746, of 100, 200 and 120 escudos respectively (Ms. 46-XIII-9, f. 126); there were separate payments of 100 escudos made to each of the two architects in July 1745 (Ms. 49-IX-31, f. 119). On the other hand, Salvi's name appears alone on payments such as one of 386 escudos, on 15 July 1746, regarding the marble festoons for the vaulted ceiling of the chapel (Ms. 49-VIII-15, doc. 247), and another, the following December, concerning the work of the designers involved in making the maquette (Ms. 49-VIII-15, doc. 459). That would appear to shed light on his central role in the general overseeing and coordination of the commission, explaining the description of Vanvitelli as *suo compagno*, his companion (note that this does not contradict the latter's authorship of the surviving drawings; Vanvitelli performed a similar role in the *Fabbrica di San Pietro*). Such a situation was understandable in the context of a work site of such complexity.

[12] Francisco Marques de Sousa VITERBO and R. Vicente d'ALMEIDA, *op. cit.*, p. 128.

[13] Francisco Marques de Sousa VITERBO and R. Vicente d'ALMEIDA, *op. cit.*, pp. 108–11.

[14] *Ibid.* p. 112.

[15] *Ibid.* p. 132.

[16] *Ibid.* p. 134.

[17] *Ibid.* pp. 112–13.

[18] *Ibid.* p. 134.

[19] *Ibid.* pp. 115–16.

[20] António Filipe PIMENTEL, 'Uma jóia em forma de templo: a Capela de São João Baptista' ..., p. 154.

[21] Francisco Marques de Sousa VITERBO and R. Vicente d'ALMEIDA, *op. cit.*, pp. 136–37.

[22] *Ibid.* p. 120.

[23] *Ibid.* p. 137.

[24] cf. Paulo Varela GOMES, *A Cultura Arquitectónica e Artística em Portugal no Século XVIII*, Lisbon, Editorial Caminho, 1988, pp. 97 and ff; Paulo Varela GOMES, *A Confissão de Cyrillo*, Lisbon, Hiena, 1992, pp. 101 and ff.

[25] António Filipe PIMENTEL, 'Giuseppe Palms, Giuseppe Fochetti, Giuseppe Voyet e Genaro Nocoletti. Modelo para a Capela de São João Batista', in António Filipe PIMENTEL (coord.), *A Encomenda Prodigiosa. Da Patriarcal à Capela Real de S. João Baptista*, *op. cit.*, pp. 128–29.

[26] Francisco Marques de Sousa VITERBO and R. Vicente d'ALMEIDA, *op. cit.*, p. 127.

[27] The royal architect also sent minutely detailed 'instructions and advisories' to Rome concerning the items in gold, silver and jewellery – so detailed, in fact, that his role was close to being that of co-author. This is the case, in particular, for an extraordinary life-size statue of the *Virgin* (*Virgin of the Immaculate Conception*), modelled by Giovanni Battista Maini, about which Carbone wrote on 25 September 1744, 'here is a very long instruction indeed' (B.A., Ms. 49-VIII-41, f. 93v; see also Teresa Leonor M. VALE, 'Di bronzo e d'argento: sculture del Settecento italiano nella magnifica Patriarcale di Lisbona', in *Arte Cristiana. Rivista Internazionale di Storia dell'Arte e di Arti Liturgiche*, 100, no. 868, Jan.–Feb. 2012, pp. 59–62) and other references expressing astonishment, such as one, also addressed to Ambassador Sampaio, which the Jesuit included on 23 April 1745 when he wrote: 'I consign to Your Excellency the enclosed packet, which contains some advisory note on the cross of the altar of the new chapel, so that Your Excellency may have it executed by the craftsman, to whom the said work is committed' (B.A., Ms.49-VIII-41, f. 177).

[28] Paulo Varela GOMES, *A Cultura Arquitectónica*, *op. cit.*, p. 98. There is, however, a clear development in the author's position in his approach to this question, which can be seen between this ground-breaking essay – in which he maintains that the positions adopted in Lisbon were irrelevant to the final work, affirming that

Ludovice's text 'reveals from the first, from its very heading, that there was nothing to be done because Salvi and Vanvitelli had already gone ahead with their work' (p. 99) – and the argument he makes in his other (no less innovative) essay *A Confissão de Cyrillo*, in which he states that the chapel 'represents a de facto compromise between the ideas expressed in Rome and the demands of Lisbon', and seeks to draw up a balance sheet between the contributions made by Ludovice and those of the Roman architect(s) (pp. 91–98).

[29] It is well established, in fact, that the cost of the chapel commission reached exorbitant levels compared with initial estimates. Indeed, in a letter from Carbone to Sampaio dated 3 June 1747, he states that 'Of these commissions, no care was ever taken here that they should cost so much, since Frederico himself, who gave the instructions, understood that the whole work of the chapel would cost some half a million.' He returned to the subject on 27 June, saying, 'For Frederico, who was in Rome and saw the famous Chapel of São Ignacio, that cost 100,000 escudos, ruled that ours would cost no more than 200 thousand' (Francisco Marques de Sousa VITERBO and R. Vicente d'ALMEIDA, *op. cit.*, p. 13, note 1).

[30] *Ibid.* p. 138.

[31] *Ibid.* p. 139.

[32] Robert C. SMITH, 'João Frederico Ludovice, an eighteenth century architect in Portugal', in *Art Bulletin*, vol. XVIII, 3, 1936, p. 362.

[33] Frei Cláudio da CONCEIÇÃO, *op. cit.*, vol. IX, pp. 53–54.

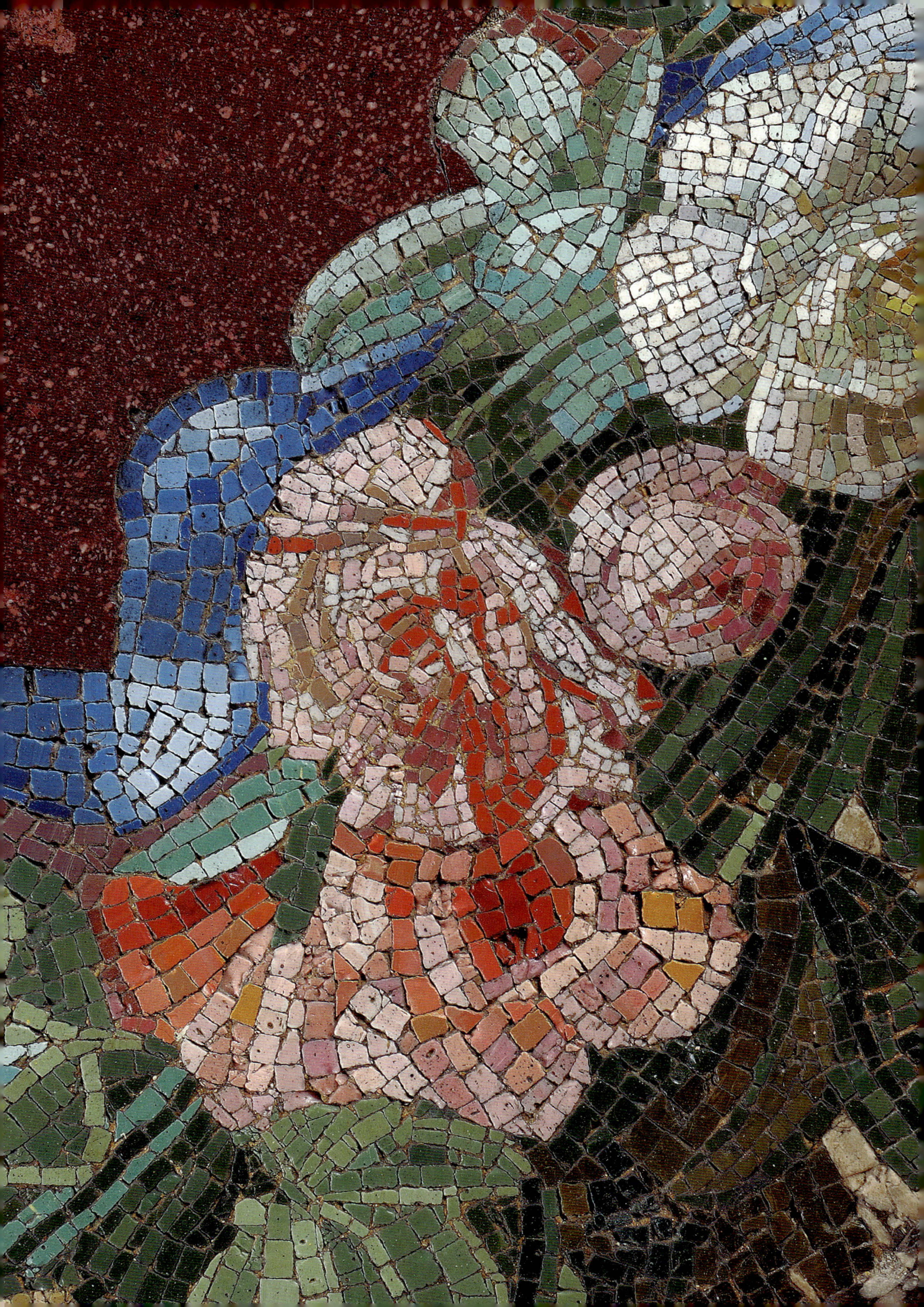

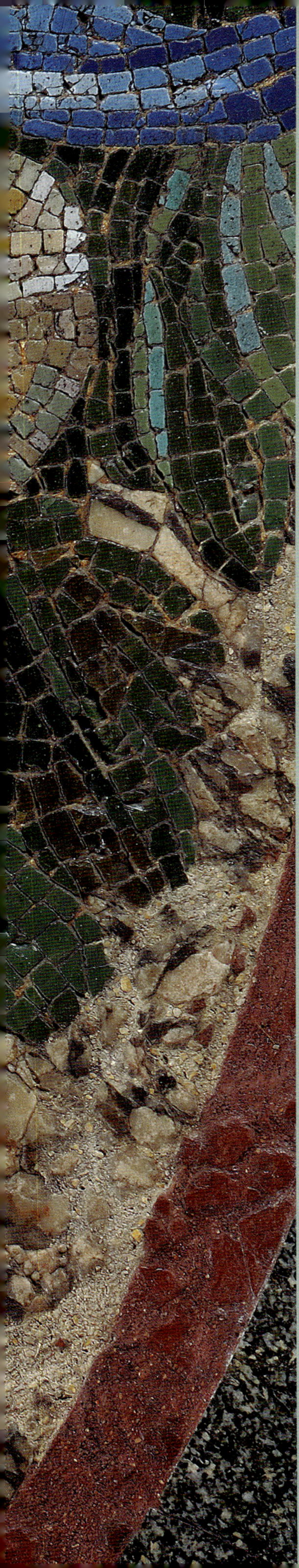

2. PAINTING AND MOSAICS

Paintings and mosaics

Carlo Stefano Salerno

From archived documents and from the examination made of the chapel during restoration work, it has been possible to gather information about the work done by artists belonging to the most important studio workshops in Rome in the first half of the eighteenth century – architects, painters, mosaic artists, sculptors, stonemasons, stone-cutters, smelters, silversmiths, ironworkers, wood-carvers, carpenters and labourers. Unusually, two architects were placed in charge of the work as co-directors: Nicola Salvi and Luigi Vanvitelli. The former – the elder of the two – was the well-known and accomplished director of the Accademia di San Luca and an institutional figure, representative of established Italian art. He was assisted by Luigi Vanvitelli, not in a subordinate role, as formerly suggested, but rather – I would say – with a substantial role in the planning, control and coordination of all stages of the project's execution. This is documented by a series of drawings for the various phases of execution of the chapel that Garms[1] has subjected to careful analysis. Less well known, however, were details of how the site and construction work were organised, and the fact that all the chapel accounts submitted by various artists and artisans over the course of many years were always signed by both architects, who were in charge of planning and design as well as of checking expenditure and ensuring the quality of work carried out at the construction site by the various trades and professions.[2] Analysing the various records of accounts relating to the chapel, such as that of Francesco Giardoni, who was commissioned to execute the architectural decorations in gilded bronze; or the accounts for the exorbitant costs of stone cladding by Cecilia Tedeschi, who belonged to a family of stonemasons and stone dealers; and stonemason Pietro Paolo Rotolone, we find that their acceptance was countersigned by Nicola Salvi, together with (as was customary) a suggestion that the costs be reduced.[3]

Agostino Masucci, the artist responsible for the three altarpieces, was the only artist who was able to work independently of the two architects and who designed his own work freely, discussing matters directly with the client.

Over the course of no fewer than ten years, Luigi Vanvitelli poured effort into the construction site and project of the Chapel of St John – in terms not only of his own original contribution but also of all the technical and organisational expertise he had acquired working in the *Fabbrica di San Pietro*.[4] Even the idea of building a chapel in parts, to be assembled and shipped by sea, has its precedent in St. Peter's – the high altar of Urbino Cathedral, which was built in Rome by Vatican craftsmen before being put in place on site.[5]

pp. 44–45
Floor (detail of armillary sphere)
(See fig. 26)

Agostino Masucci was chosen as painter with the full consent of King John V, who had admired his work on previous occasions and believed he would combine the requisite classicism with a certain grace that constitutes true artistic quality. The first drawings executed by Masucci are from very early in the process, and show the cornices of the first architectural design that was later modified at the request of the client in order to increase the size of the altarpieces.[6] He had already tackled the *Annunciation* and *Baptism of Christ* (figs 19–21), of which several versions are known,

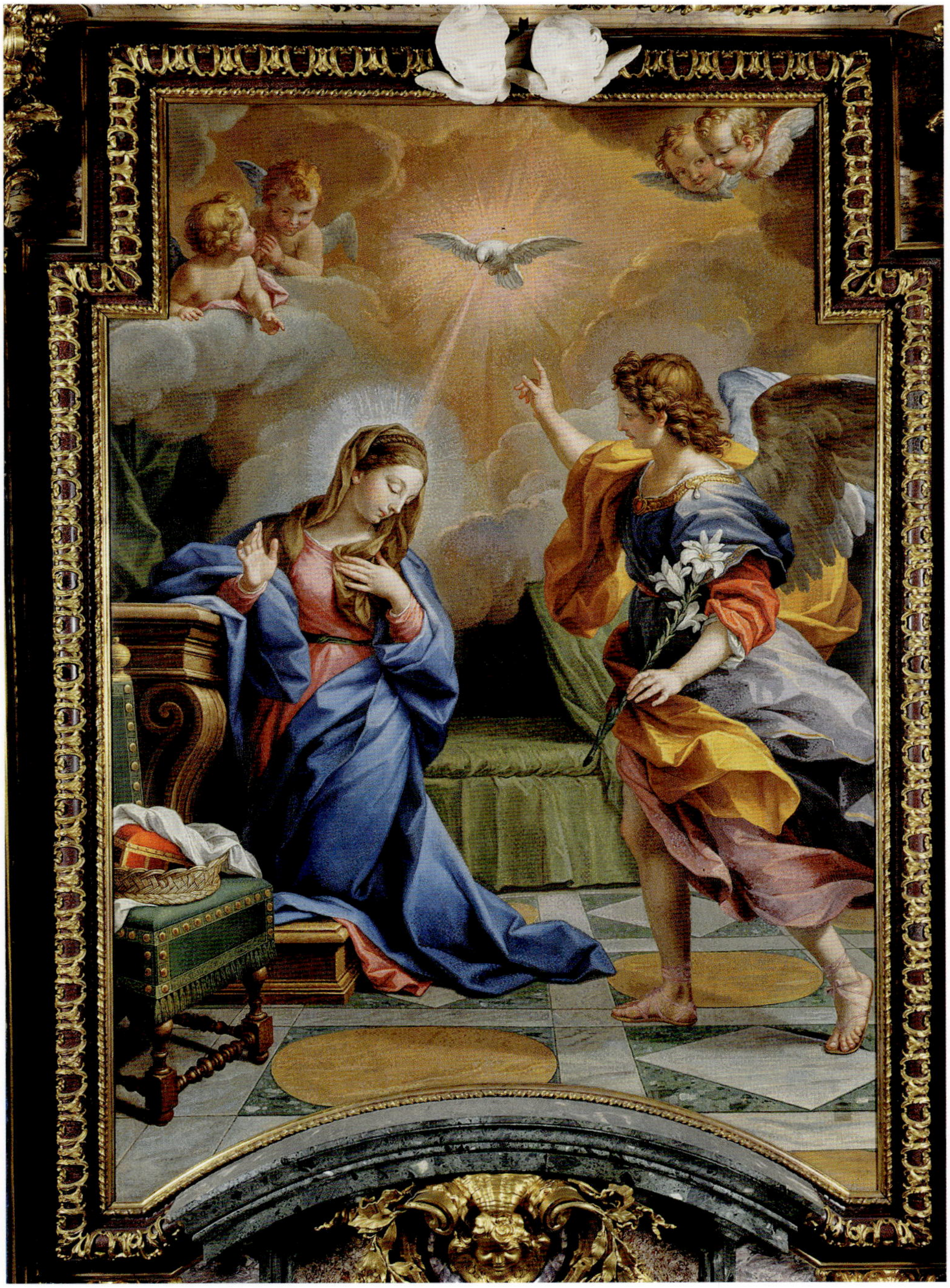

Fig. 19
Annunciation
Mosaic panel on the wall on the Epistle (right-hand) side
Mattia Moretti

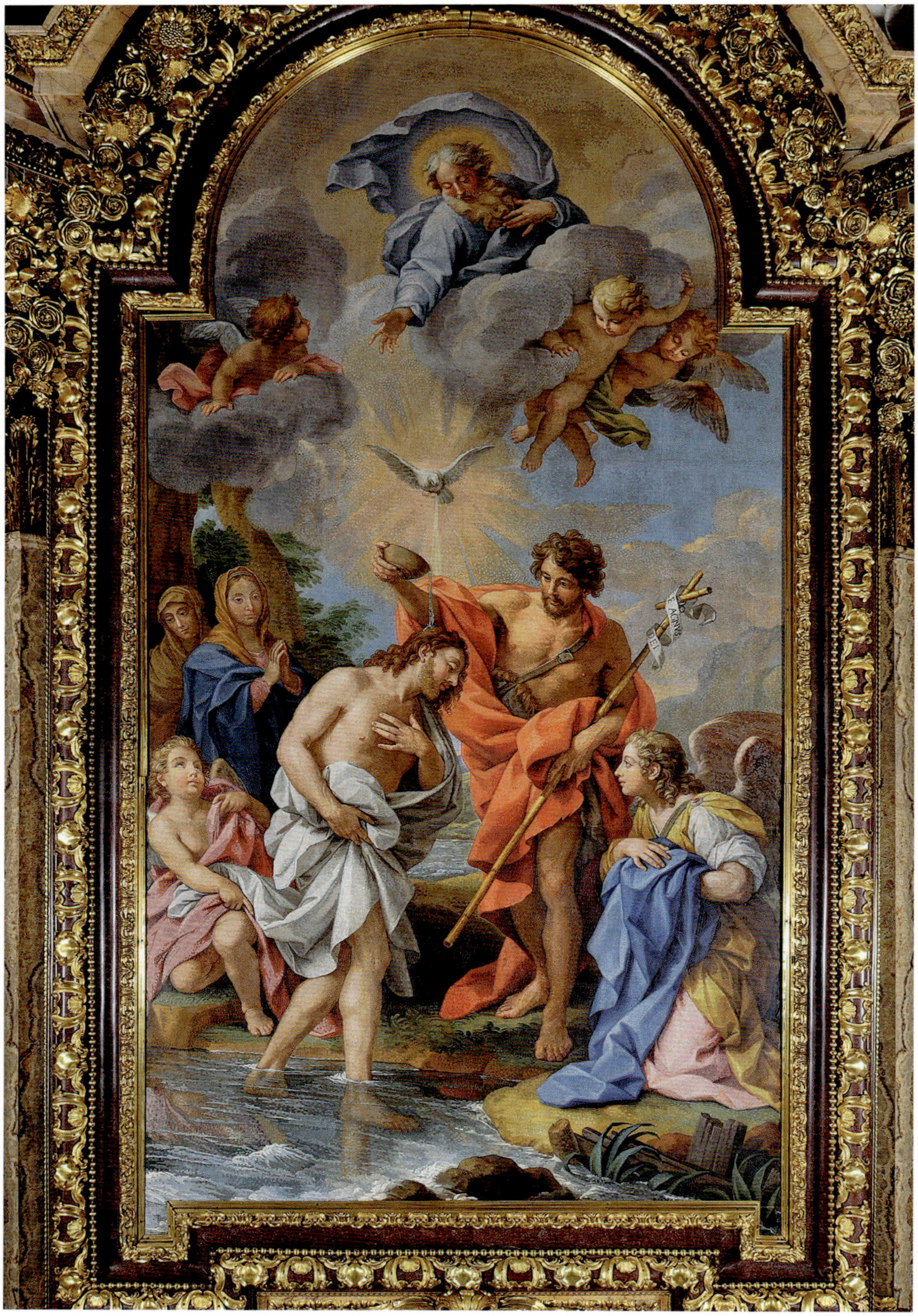

Fig. 20
Baptism of Christ
Mosaic panel over the altar
Mattia Moretti

Fig. 21
Detail of Christ's inclined head from the Baptism of Christ mosaic

in the Church of Santa Maria in the Via Lata between 1721 and 1724.[7] Compared to the previous versions these show only a few variations, some due to specific requests from the client.[8] For the third painting, the *Pentecost*, Masucci executed a new composition (figs 22 and 23). As may be deduced from the famous document *Advertencias para o Pinctor* (Advisories to the Painter) of 6 February 1743,[9] unlike in the case of the

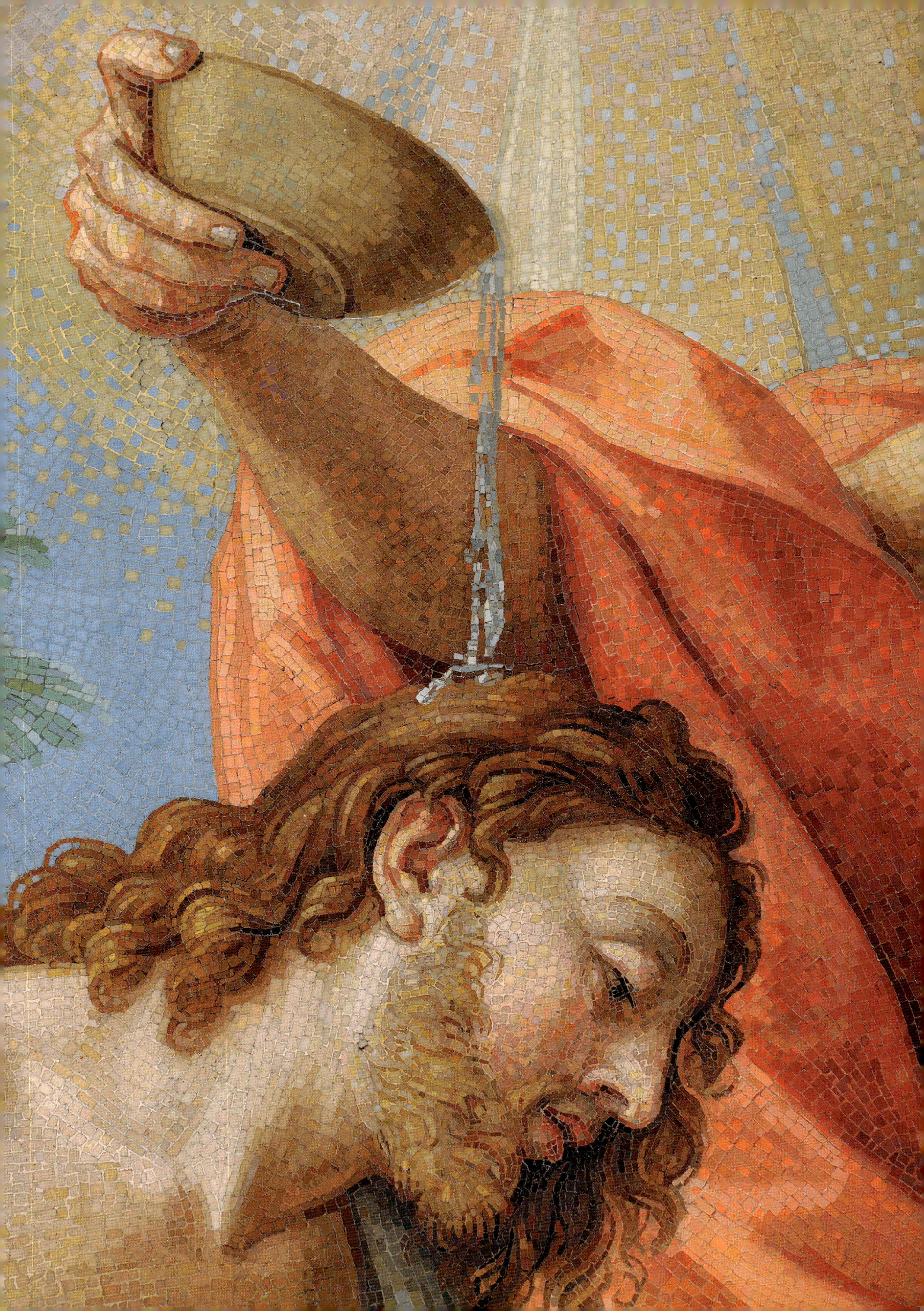

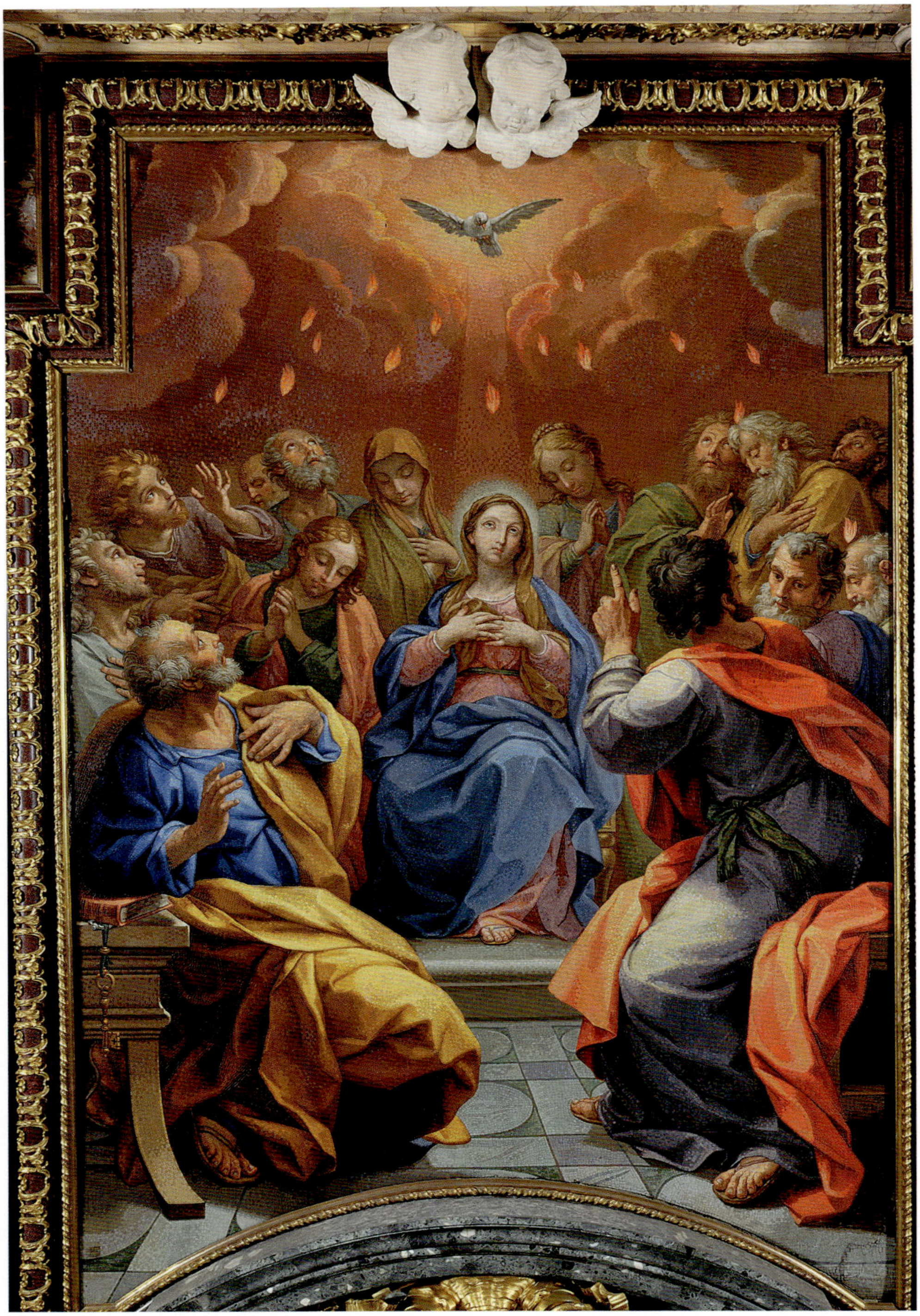

Fig. 22
Pentecost
Mosaic panel on the wall on the Gospel (left-hand) side
Mattia Moretti

Fig. 23
Detail of the Virgin Mary and two female figures from the Pentecost mosaic

architectural designs, these designs were immediately approved with enthusiasm – indicative of how perfectly the Roman painter had met the expectations of the sovereign and his adviser Father Carbone and, perhaps, of the court architect Ludovice himself. Models for the paintings were executed in oil on canvas, followed by – once more in oil on canvas – those required for their translation into the form of

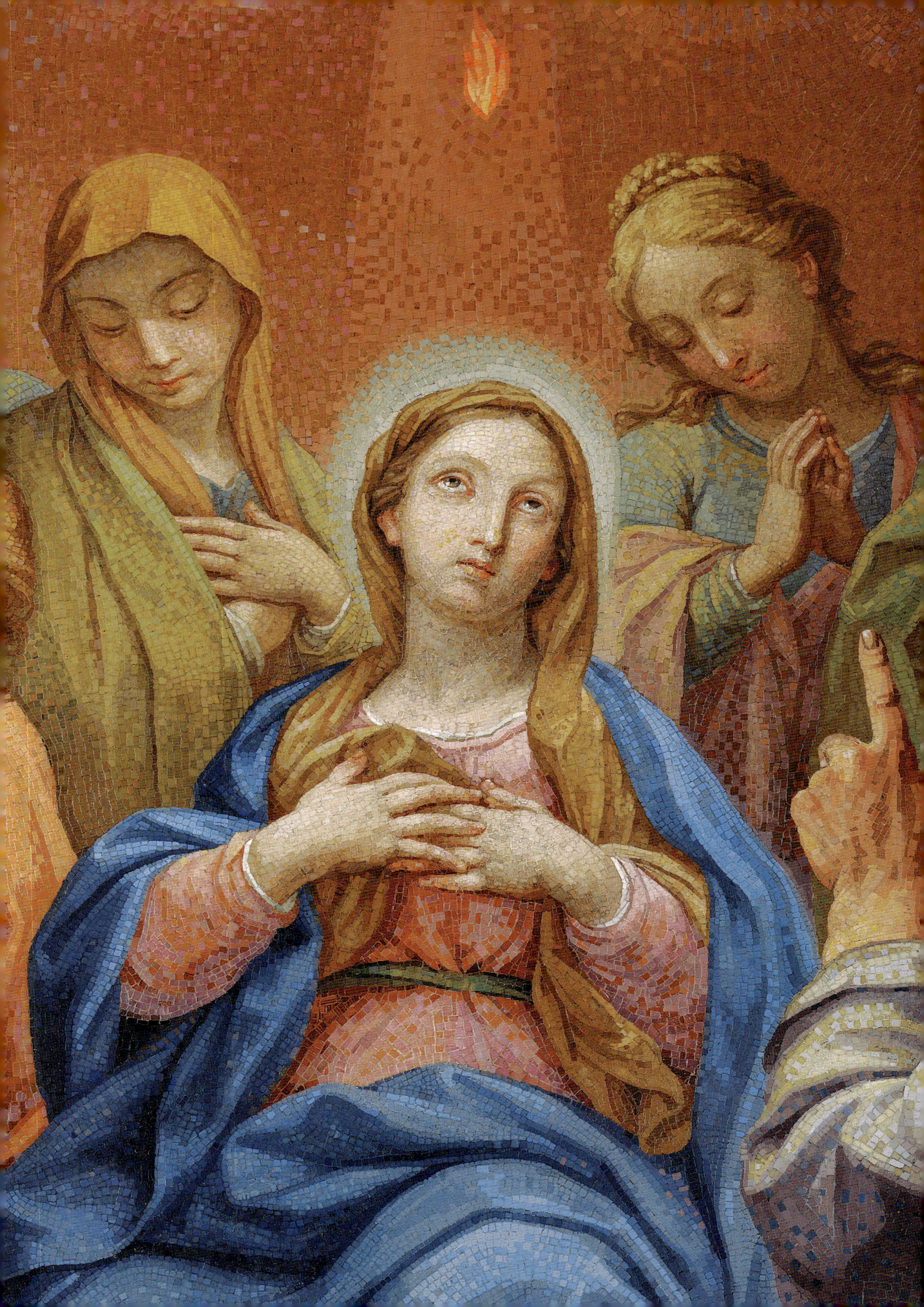

mosaics. Of the various versions preserved in the Aveiro Museum, one particularly worthy of consideration is the first design for the *Annunciation* sent to the client for approval (fig. 24).[10] The design was sent to Lisbon, but a copy was supposed to be executed in Rome to be delivered to the mosaic artists; this one was requested to be at least retouched by the master.[11] It is known that for the *Baptism of Christ* too, a painting was commissioned at a cost of 1,500 scudi to serve as a model for the final work as well as no fewer than two copies for which 1,000 and 600 scudi respectively were paid.[12] For the *Baptism*, the painting of the same subject by Carlo Maratta made for the Vatican Basilica[13] is rightly cited as a prototype; however there is also another even more important and authoritative model for this work: the altarpiece of the Baptistery of St John Lateran, painted about a century earlier by Andrea Sacchi, which is little known owing to its poor condition and to the fact that it has more lately been placed in the Vatican Pinacoteca (Gallery of Paintings).[14]

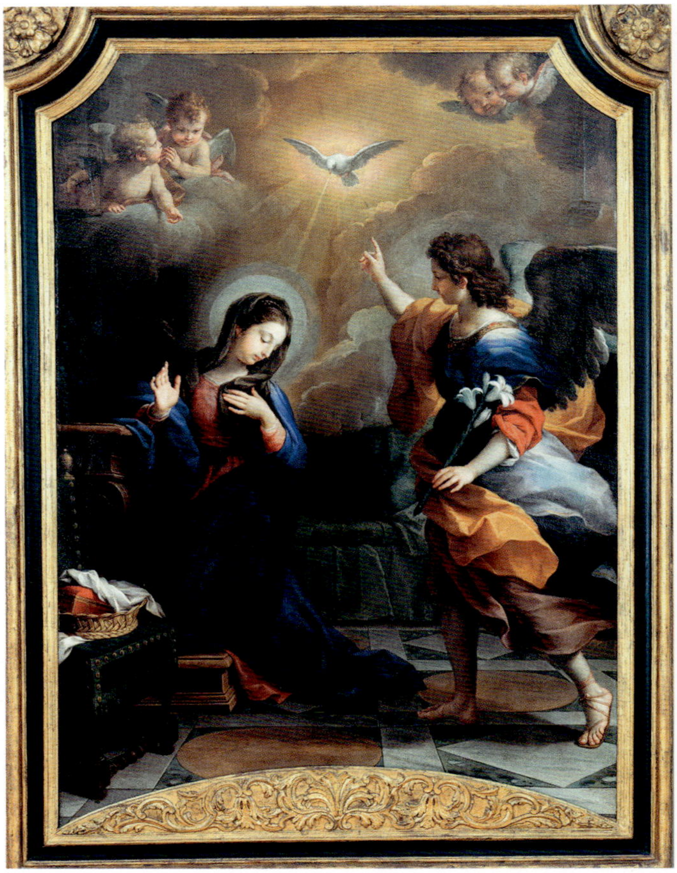

Fig. 24
Annunciation
Agostino Masucci, c. 1742
Oil on canvas
Museu Nacional de Arte Antiga [National Museum of Ancient Art], Lisbon, on loan to and exhibited in Aveiro Museum
(inv. 42411 TC)

The idea of translating the chapel altarpieces into the form of mosaics took shape at a very early stage; in a document dated 26 October 1742[15] there was already talk about this even though the decision had not yet been taken. This choice of technique highlights the direct conceptual link that the sovereign intended to establish with St Peter's Basilica, where mosaic had been given a central role as the art form used not only for vast wall decorations but also as the technique chosen to replace all the altarpieces. John V had direct knowledge of the mosaic technique; he had had a portrait executed by Pietro Paolo Cristofari depicting himself together with the queen consort Maria Ana of Austria from models by an unknown author, which have since been lost.[16] Finally, he was familiar with the works of Mattia Moretti, the mosaic artist who was to be chosen to translate the chapel's three altarpieces into mosaic form and who was the author of a portrait of remarkable quality – one depicting a sibyl, achieved using a different style and technique from those previously executed by Cristofari.[17] A document of great interest shows that Mattia Moretti submitted two estimates, one for making the mosaic after the manner of Cristofari's altarpieces and the other for making a mosaic of the *finezza* (fine quality) of his 'Sybil' (fig. 25). The significantly higher cost of the second estimate is due to the fact that in the Sibyl, the mosaic tiles are smaller and the consequent dissimilation of the mosaic technique is greater; the time required for its execution is therefore significantly longer,[18] raising the second quotation to the exorbitant sum of 20,000 scudi. The first option was based on the cost of the large portrait of Clement XII for the Corsini Chapel in St John Lateran, executed a short time earlier by Pietro Paolo Cristofari – a work measuring 100 square palms (a palm being a measurement representing approximately the distance between the tips of the thumb and little finger on an outspread hand). At 30 scudi a palm, the cost was 3,000 scudi for the work alone, excluding the cost of the materials. For the three altarpieces of the Chapel of St John, the first estimate anticipated a proportional cost of 9,210 scudi together with a cost of 1,228 for cutting and polishing, and therefore a total of 12,000 scudi. How the second quotation was worked out is clearly explained in the documents; they say that if the mosaic is to be 'più minuto del med.o della Cappella Corsini, et a similitudine della testa, e carni del quadro della mia Sibilla' (smaller than the same one of the Corsini Chapel, and with a similar head and body to that of the picture of my Sibyl), the cost rises from 35 to 46 scudi per palm, which makes 14,122; to this 2,043.55 is added for the *maggior sprego* or greater use of resources, and 3,840 scudi for four labourers for at least eight years.[19] It is explained that in this way, by adding up the listed items, the total comes to a figure of 20,002.55 scudi.

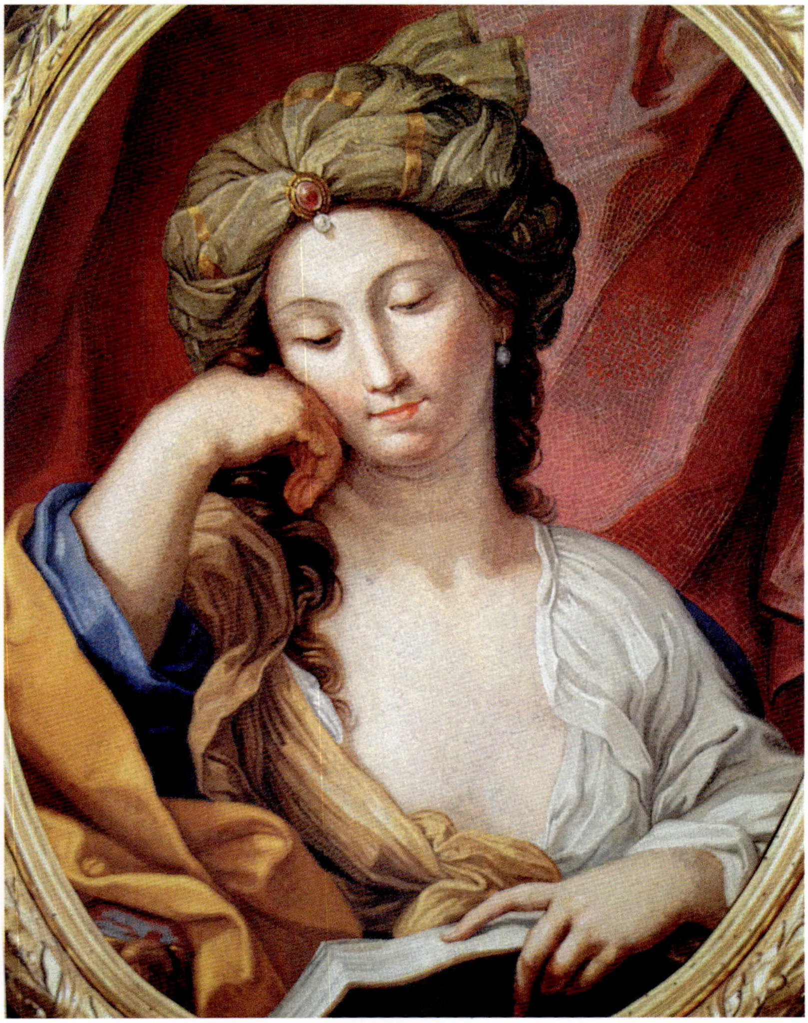

Fig. 25
Sibyl
Mattia Moretti, 1737
Mosaic
Uffizi Gallery (on loan), Florence (inv. 875)

Another important technical element which was also discovered during the recent restoration work is the fact that these mosaics are made with an extremely fine-grained texture that also requires the sides of the tiles to be ground before they are laid – an observation confirmed by the accounts of the labourers paid for the *taglio e rotatura* (cutting and grinding) of the tiles.[20] This is the only way, in fact, that it is possible to eliminate all irregularities and obtain a surface that is almost completely impermeable. It turns out that the supply of glass for the mosaic came from the famous *fornaciaro* or furnace-master Alessio Mattioli, the only one in Rome at that time capable of producing red-coloured glass in all its varieties, in tones of every shade from orange to yellow and particularly those colours considered the most difficult to make: the pinks and flesh tones. He was able to produce a highly prized type of glass known as *scorzetta* or 'orange-peel' glass owing to the formation of a fine layer of dark colour that forms on the surface of the glass during the cooling phases. Another important and highly prized characteristic for this type of glass is its opacity and evenness in colour – enabling it to imitate the effect of painting by making the mosaic tesserae conceal their actual nature as much as possible.[21]

Alessio Mattioli supplied not only glass in plates, as was customary, but also glass mosaic tiles *filato alla fornace* (drawn in the furnace), a technique that foreshadowed what was later destined to become famous as the Vatican micromosaic.[22] For every 9,684 pounds of coloured glass supplied in the form of *pizze* (sheets), there were just 461 pounds of drawn or 'spun' glass – that is to say, a proportion of about 20 to 1.[23] Only a modest amount was therefore crafted to specific dimensions and sections – perhaps triangular or rectangular – allowing the artists to use it for specific effects in creating figures and geometric compositions. These were not yet the glazes drawn or 'spun' in the crucible like those that Raphael and his team, and the other masters of the Vatican Mosaic Studio, were later to execute for their celebrated micromosaics; they were probably produced in the furnace, possibly using the 'drawing' technique, practised even today among some mosaic artists who are the heirs of that prestigious school.[24] At that time they were still made either using a more traditional technique of Venetian origin, that is to say *tirati in canna*, or 'rod-drawn' – stretched by simply lifting out some viscous molten glass with a rod and pulling the 'paste' while still in the plastic state with forceps until the glass itself forms a long cane or rod, much like what can be seen in the illustration plates in the *Encyclopédie* that show the tubes to be used for a barometer.[25]

Altogether, the costs and the amount of material needed for the three altarpieces and for the mosaic floor were extremely high; in total a good 9,692 pounds of glass were used, approximately equivalent to 3,200 kilograms.[26]

The surfaces of the mosaics, like those of the floor, were smoothed and polished using a technique thought to be typical, but of which very little detail is known today.[27] A 1748 document referring to the picture of St Basil by Pierre Subleyras in St Peter's Basilica tells us that it was laid down flat in order to grind and polish it, from which we learn that the pictures were ground and polished in the workshop and not when installed in their location.[28] The work of *rotatura*, or grinding and polishing, was not done by the mosaic artist but by a skilled labourer.[29] To grind the surface – that is to say, to obtain a perfectly polished floor – an emery powder was used that enabled the workers to abrade the surface until it was rendered perfectly flat, and to polish it gradually more and more finely until successive treatments with pumice allowed them also to remove even the shallowest scratches and grooves.[30] To carry out this operation they used an instrument called an *orso* (bear), a heavy stone of *peperino* – tuff or lava – with a handle that was moved back and forth, producing a movement likened to the pacing of a bear. By passing it across the surface over and over again, with water to keep the surface wet, the workers were able to obtain an extremely smooth surface that was finally polished with little pats of lead or lead sheets rubbed on the surface hour after hour with an ultra-fine abrasive paste of oxalic acid powder, a procedure modified today by the use of modern materials. A resin based on Greek pitch – colophony or natural pine rosin – had to be applied in order to protect the edges of the tiles from fracturing and to prevent the material removed from penetrating into the interstitial spaces during the grinding stage. After grinding and polishing, the workers proceeded to 'pinning' – using needles to remove the resin or residues of bedding putty or grout between the tiles. Some documents from the *Fabbrica di San Pietro* show that pinning was carried out using square needles – needles with a square cross-section that helped to make it easier to extract the material that was to be removed.[31] In this way it was possible to obtain a unified, even surface that was solid and durable. To join together the different parts that were executed on different supports – consisting of slabs of tuff for the stone parts, then those of mosaic and the strips of gilded brass – it was necessary to work round the edges *a forza di smeriglio e rotino* (using emery and a little wheel), until they were perfectly smooth and adhered to the brass strips.[32] In order to eliminate any irregularities that might still be visible due to any discontinuity in the tiles, the mosaic-makers once more adopted a technique similar to that used for the mosaic altarpieces of St Peter's Basilica in Rome: beeswax was applied to the surface, coloured so as to match the different shades of the tiles exactly. This technique was adopted not only for the altarpieces but also for the floor (fig. 26) – precisely the element most markedly enhanced by the recent restoration work – enabling us to restore its formal qualities and make it legible once more, as well as to rediscover its numerous historical and technical aspects, thanks to the study of the documents. This floor was the collaborative work of a team of stonemasons under the direction of Pietro Paolo Rotolone and including Guglielmo Paleat, Nicola Onofri and Giuseppe Ottaviani; their foreman or gangmaster appears to have been Enrico Enuò, and they were a proven and experienced team who had already worked on the Basilica of St Peter.[33] Rotolone also supplied the supports of *peperino* for the mosaics and all the individual parts for assembly.[34] The mosaic-workers had to deal with the technical difficulties of translating into mosaic form – for inclusion in the commissioned stonework – the designs that Luigi Vanvitelli had been able to draw and develop with a free hand, such as the 'fettuccia che finge svolazzare e scherzare sopra il detto fondo di porfido' (ribbon that seems to flutter and dance above the aforesaid background of porphyry).[35] The text goes on to refer to 'la degradazione de il commesso di porfido verde della de.ta fascia centinata, che gira a diminuzione e forma cartoccio dalla due parti laterali dell' ouato' (the gradual shading of the green porphyry commissioned for the aforesaid scalloped fascia, which curves as it diminishes, and forms a cartouche on either side of the oval) (fig. 27).[36] The mosaic floor is in my opinion particularly true to Vanvitelli

Fig. 26 (overleaf)
Floor
Mosaic, marble and gilded brass

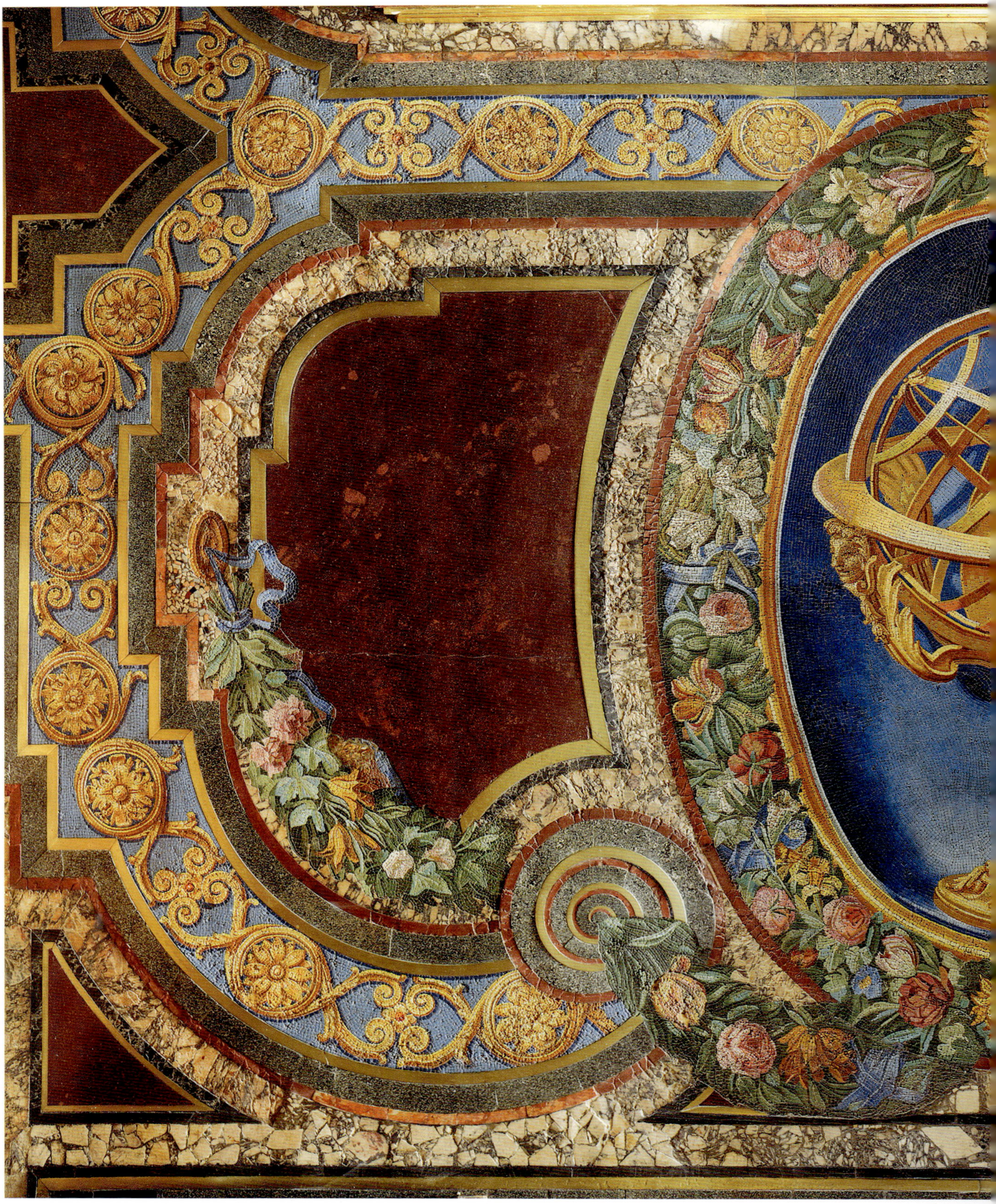

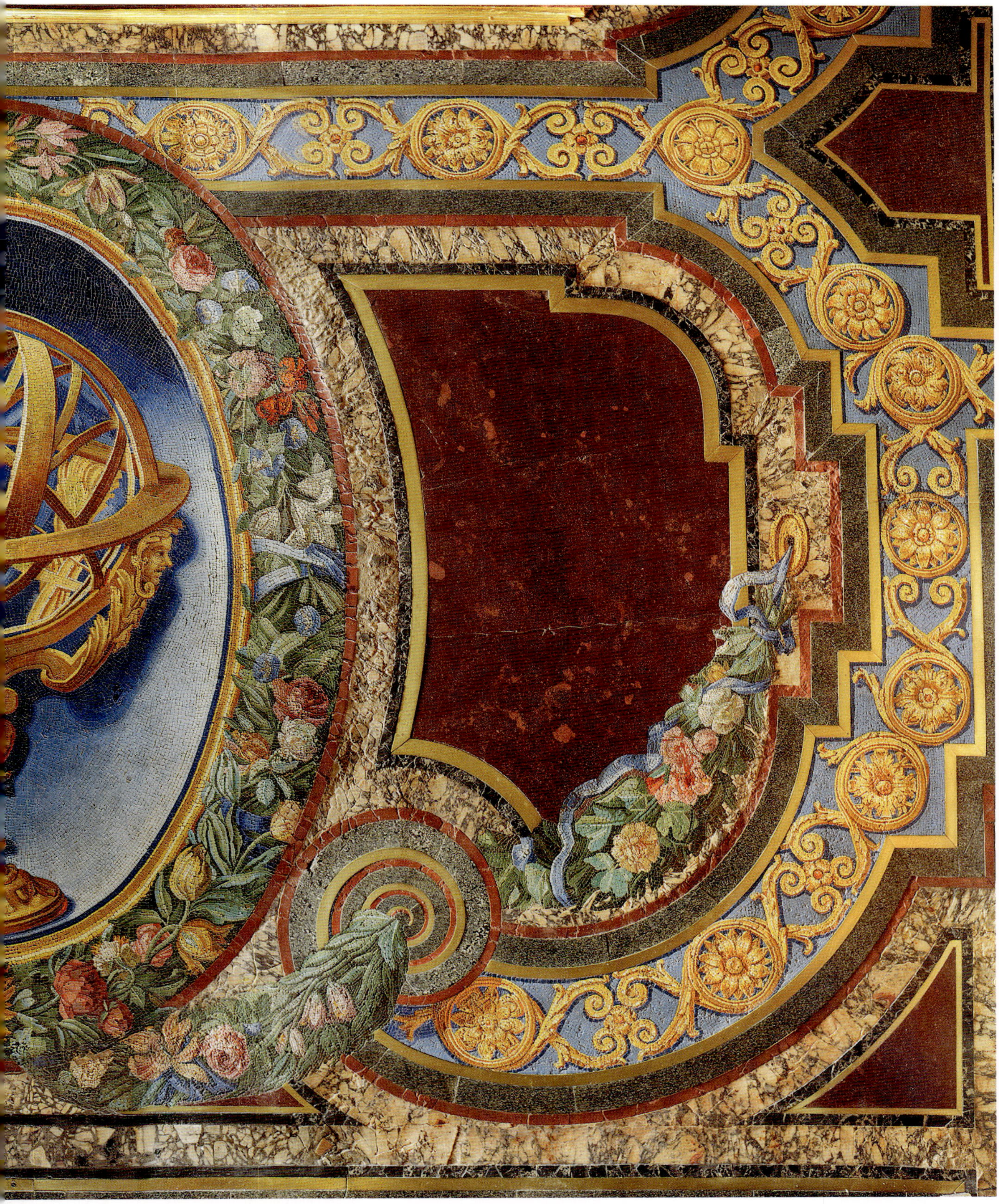

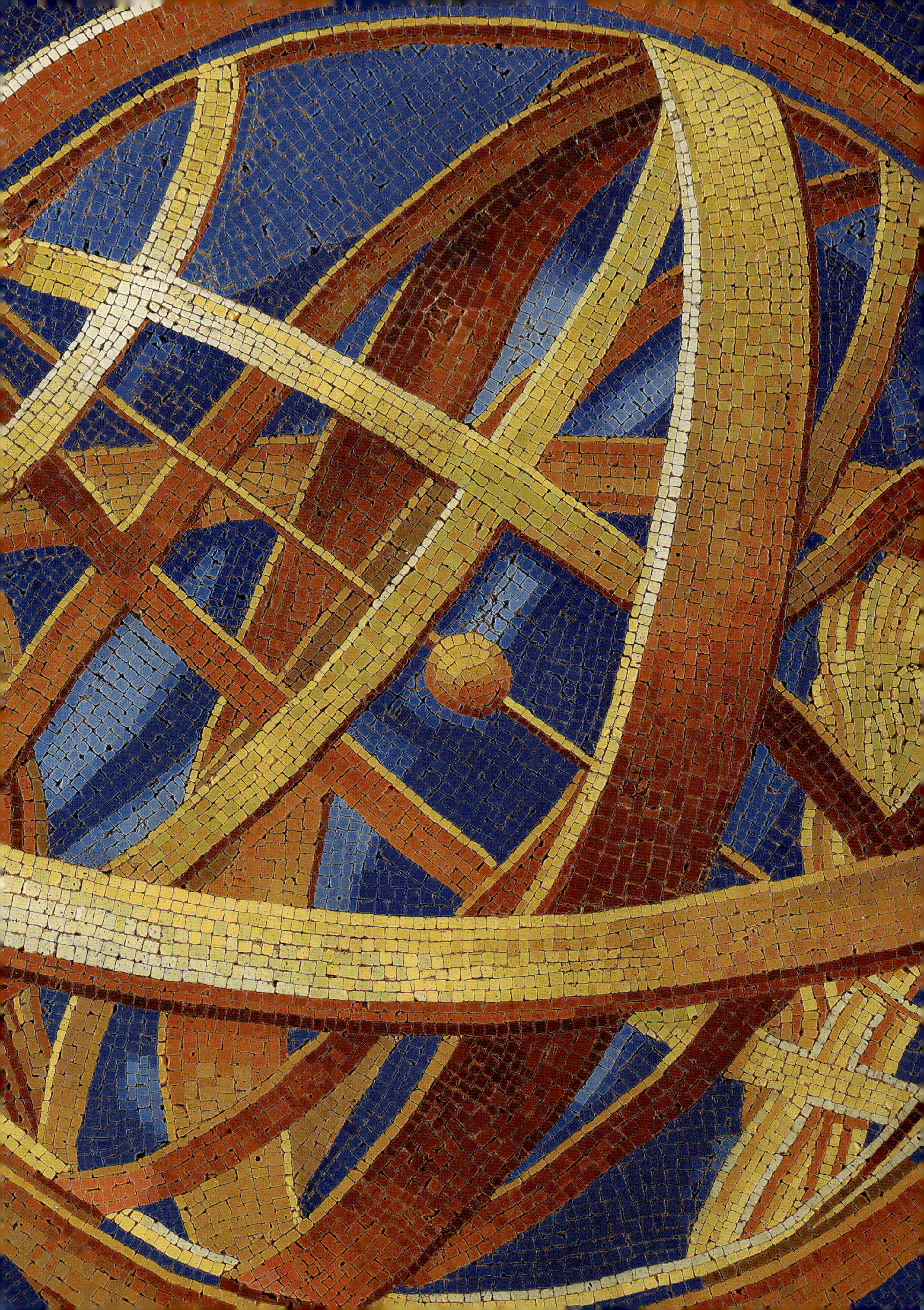

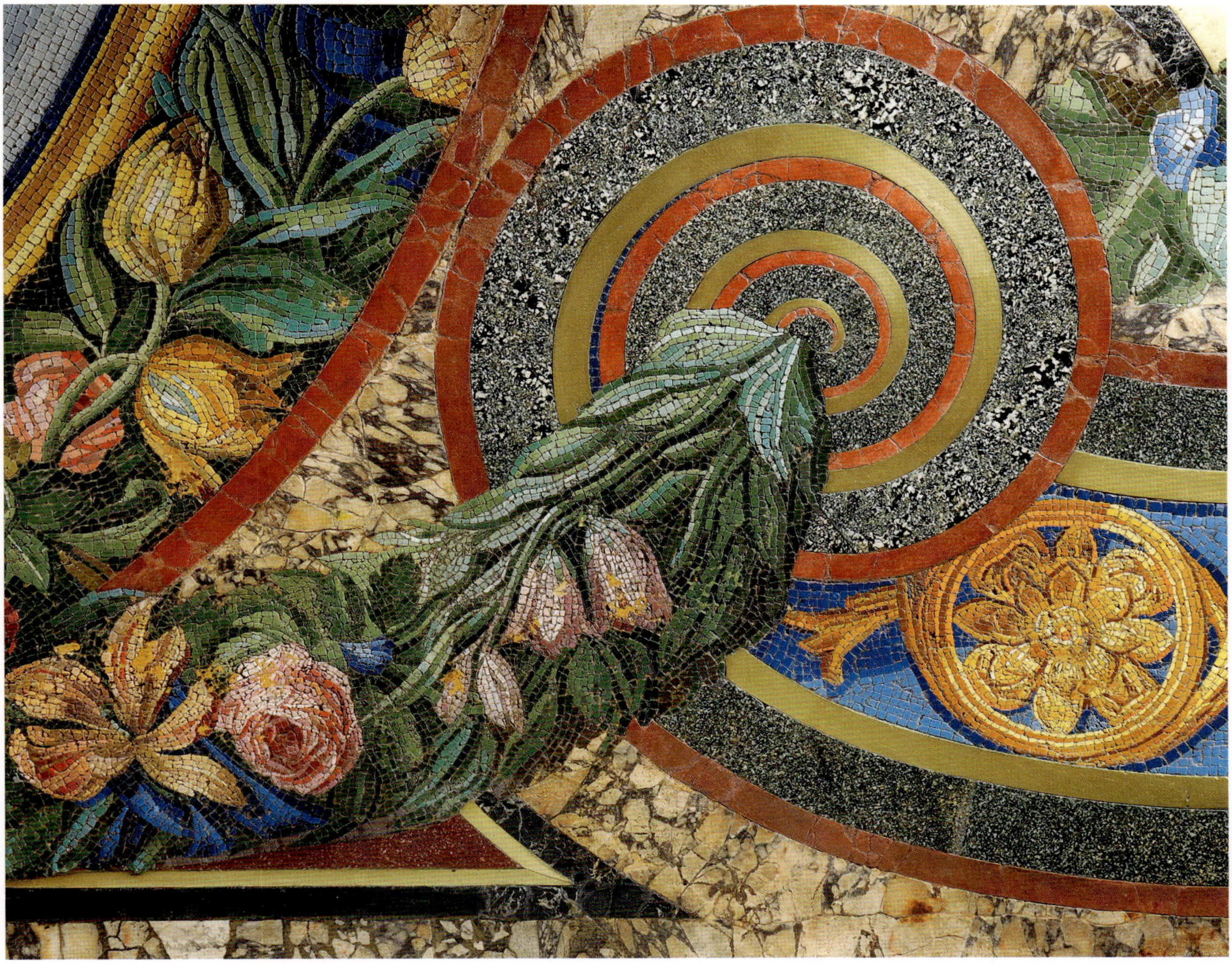

Fig. 27 (opposite)
Floor (detail of armillary sphere)

Fig. 28 (above)
Floor (detail of festoons with flowers, and of metallic friezes)

Fig. 29 (overleaf)
Floor (detail of armillary sphere)

in stylistic conception, and expresses a creativity conceived from the very first in full knowledge of the technique that was to be used to translate it into the finished work, through the complex process of cutting and working hard materials with very different characteristics – but all of which were precious and long lasting – which appear to be perfectly at one with the expression of its formal values. The novelty here, compared to earlier examples, lies in the figurative elements, starting with the astrolabe placed inside the oval – surrounded by garlands of flowers with festoons that spill over into the two large mirrored fields of porphyry – the polychrome marble frames in which bands of rosettes entwine, and especially the novel juxtaposition with gilded brass outlining, which gives a unifying effect to the entire chapel by linking the floor decoration to that of the walls while simultaneously constituting a truly unique and unprecedented result in their own right (figs 28 and 29).[37] The altar of Sant'Ignazio al Gesù in Rome is a crucial precedent, not only because it had been completed only a few years prior to 1742 and shared many technical aspects with the present work,

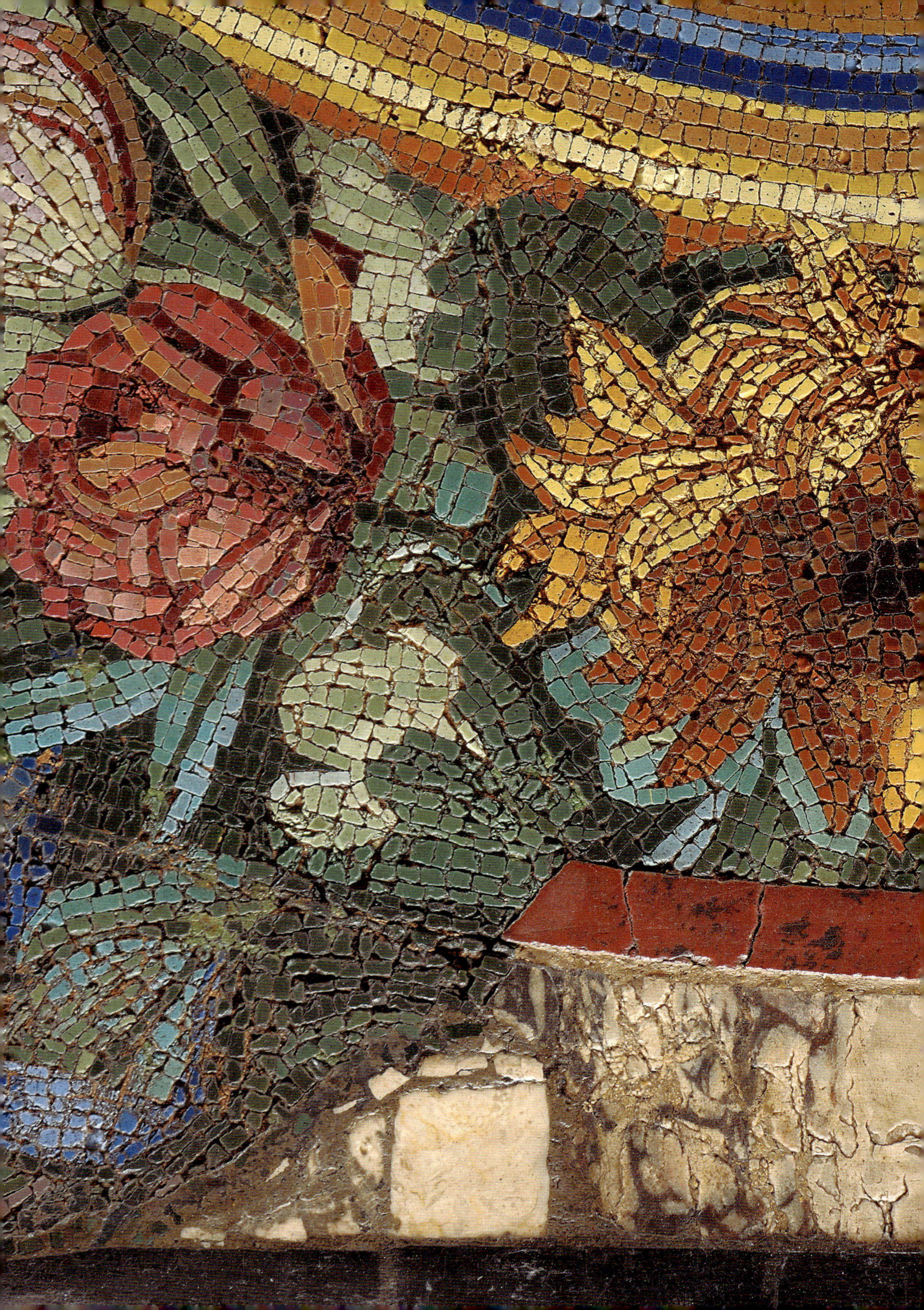

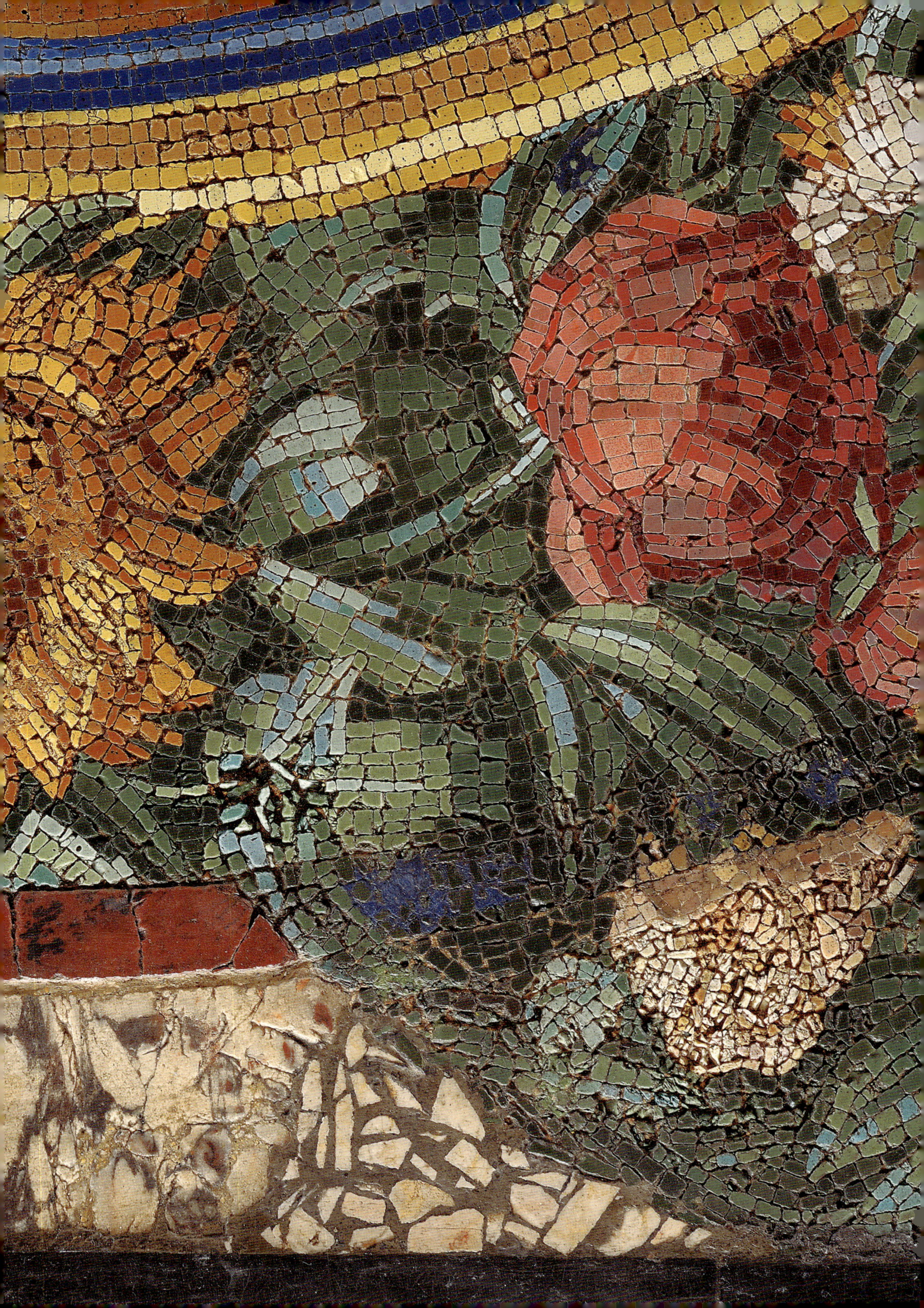

but also because it was commissioned by the Jesuits with the involvement for a long period of the German architect Ludovice, then working as a founder, who was very shortly afterwards to take on the role of court architect and direct the royal construction sites: those of the Convent of Mafra and the lost Patriarchal Basilica of Lisbon.[38]

The committee, comprising not only the king but also the court architect and the Jesuit adviser Father Carbone, met and had discussions regarding the creativity and technical expertise of the Roman architects, seeking to find a balance between the qualities of the precious materials to be used and the artistic quirks and peculiarities that were to be given expression – between artistic value and the intrinsic value of the materials, between matter and form. In fact they demanded explicitly that 'na dita capela respeldeça primorosamente o precioso da materia com a bizaria da arte' (in the said chapel, the preciousness of the material should shine forth as much as the curious whimsy of the art) and that they should be *mais ricas e de melhor gosto* (the richest, and of the finest taste).[39] Nor can the grandeur of the result be separated from another characteristic considered to be a key feature: the durability of the materials. This takes us back to the work site of the *Fabbrica di San Pietro* in Rome and the long technical discussion that lay behind hotly debated and dramatic decisions such as that of replacing the altarpieces, most of which were on canvas, with copies in glass mosaic in order to add durability to the formal quality and the preciousness of the materials. Despite the limitations of the medium and the changes suffered by the glass both in the Chapel of St John and in many of the altarpieces in St Peter's Basilica, the original colours of these mosaics can still be admired today and can help illuminate the paintings, many parts of which have darkened and deteriorated due to the use of binding agents, varnishes and the vicissitudes of their conservation history.[40] ■

NOTES

[1] Jörg GARMS, 'La cappella di S. Giovanni Battista nella chiesa di S. Rocco a Lisbona', in Sandra Vasco ROCCA, Gabriele BORGHINI (eds.), *Giovanni V di Portogallo e la Cultura Romana del suo Tempo (1706–1750)*, Rome, Àrgos Edizioni, 1995, pp. 113–22; Mario ROTILI, *La vita di Luigi Vanvitelli*, Naples, Società Ed. Napoletana, 1975, p. 106; Anna GIANNETTI, 'Luigi Vanvitelli', in Cesare DE SETA (ed.), *Luigi Vanvitelli e la sua cerchia* (exhibition catalogue), Caserta, Comitato Nazionale per le Celebrazioni del III Centenario della Nascita di Luigi Vanvitelli (1700–2000), 2000, p. 32.

[2] Armando SCHIAVO, *La Fontana di Trevi e le altre opere di Nicola Salvi*, Roma, Istituto Poligrafico dello Stato 1956, p. 197, had suggested a secondary role for Vanvitelli, later recognised by Garms as being of greater significance.

[3] Several accounts are signed by Nicola Salvi only, such as one concerning the marble festoons for the vaulted ceiling of the chapel, for the unfinished marble statuary, and many other detailed items, for 386 scudi dated 15 July 1746, BIBLIOTECA DA AJUDA (Lisbon), Ms. 49-VIII-15, c. 247, and signed by Nicola Salvi on 9 August 1746. Another account signed by Nicola Salvi only is one concerning the drawings for the small wooden model that the designers were instructed to execute, obliging them to go to the different locations where the works were being executed in order to copy them B.A., Ms. 49-VIII-15 c. 459 (1746).

[4] Nicoletta MARCONI, '"La prestigiosa collazione delle macchine del Zabaglia" e la "scuola" di meccanica pratica della Fabbrica di San Pietro', in Angela MARINO (ed.), *Sapere e saper fare nella Fabbrica di San Pietro: 'Castelli e ponti' di maestro Nicola Zabaglia 1743* (Paolo Portoghesi edition), Rome, Gangemi, 2008, pp. 54–91.

[5] Elisa DEBENEDETTI, 'Gli Altari in Duomo e altri altari urbinati', in Giuseppe CUCCO (ed.), *Papa Albani e le arti a Urbino e a Roma 1700–1721*, Rome, Marseilles, 2001, p. 318.

[6] The first known document relating to the commission, the letter of 26 October 1742, Francisco Marques de Sousa VITERBO, R. Vicente d' ALMEIDA, *A capella de S. João Baptista erecta na Egreja de S. Roque*, Lisbon, Livros Horizonte, 1997, p. 105 (1st edition 1900).

[7] Vittorio CASALE, in Sandra Vasco ROCCA, Gabriele BORGHINI (eds.), *op. cit.*, p. 360.

[8] Sandra Vasco ROCCA, 'Le committenze pittoriche di Giovanni V', in Sandra Vasco ROCCA and Gabriele BORGHINI (eds.), *op. cit.*, pp. 318–21. For a more detailed discussion of the development of the designs from their earliest versions to those executed for the chapel, see also Carlo Stefano SALERNO, 'A preciosidade da matéria e a "bizzaria da arte": projecto, organização, direção dos trabalhos, coordenação dos mesteres e encomenda', in Teresa Leonor M. VALE (ed.), *A Capela de São João Batista da Igreja de São Roque. A encomenda, a obra, as coleções*, Lisbon, Imprensa Nacional Casa da Moeda-Santa Casa da Misericórdia de Lisboa, 2015, pp. 92–98.

[9] S. Francisco Marques de Sousa VITERBO and R. Vicente d'ALMEIDA, *op. cit.*, p. 112.

[10] For analysis of the models, see Vittorio CASALE, *op. cit.*, p. 351, and Carlo Stefano SALERNO, *op. cit.*, pp. 92–98.

[11] Francisco Marques de Sousa VITERBO, R. Vicente d' ALMEIDA, *op. cit.*, p. 112, *Advertencia* of 6 February 1743.

[12] B.A., Ms. 49-VIII-22, no. 109.

[13] Vittorio CASALE, *op. cit.*, p. 360.

[14] Claudia TEMPESTA, 'Le storie del Battista in San Giovanni in Fonte', in R. BARBIELLINI AMIDEI, L. CARLONI, C. TEMPESTA (eds.), *Andrea Sacchi 1599–1661* (exhibition catalogue), Rome, Ed. De Luca, 1999, p. 45; Ann Sutherland HARRIS, *Andrea Sacchi*, Oxford, Phaidon, 1977, pp. 82–84, 84–89; Carlo Stefano SALERNO, *op. cit.*, p. 94.

[15] Francisco Marques de Sousa VITERBO, R. Vicente d' ALMEIDA, *op. cit.*, p. 105.

[16] See Paola Ferraris in Sandra Vasco ROCCA, Gabriele BORGHINI and Paola FERRARIS (eds.), *Roma Lusitana Lisbona Romana* (exhibition catalogue), Rome, Àrgos Edizioni, 1990, p. 59; citing only T. Espanca, *Inventario Artistico de Portugal*, Lisbon, Academia Nacional de Belas-Artes, 1966, pp. 30–31.

[17] The mosaic is located in the Museo degli Argenti in the Palazzo Pitti in Florence, and was left in Sampaio's will to Cardinal Neri Corsini (Alvar GONZÁLEZ-PALACIOS, 'Provenzale e Moretti: indagini su due mosaici',

in *Antichità viva*, XV, no. 4, Dec. 1976, pp. 29–30, 32–33, and Paola Ferraris in Sandra Vasco ROCCA, Gabriele BORGHINI and Paola FERRARIS (eds.), *Roma Lusitana, Lisbona Romana*, *op. cit.*, p. 60.

[18] B.A., Ms. 49-VIII-19, no. 152–55 (1750). The information is derived from a late document, a revision of the 1743 contract which was imposed on the mosaic artist in order to reduce costs; after the death of Manuel Pereira de Sampaio he was succeeded in 1750 by the priest Antonio Cabral with the task of reducing the exorbitant costs faced in previous years. Once again the agreements were countersigned by both Salvi and Vanvitelli.

[19] B.A., Ms. 49-VIII-19, no. 155 (1750).

[20] Those instructed to carry out this work were Giovan Battista Davini and his *compagni*, Gio' Maria Marini, Filippo Piccirilli and Lorenzo Valle; B.A., Ms. 49-VIII-13, no. 396.

[21] On Alessio Mattioli, see Carlo Stefano SALERNO, *op. cit.*, p. 109; Cesare MORETTI and Carlo Stefano SALERNO, 'Contributi allo studio dei materiali e delle composizioni degli smalti per i mosaici della Basilica di San Pietro tra il XVI e il XVIII secolo', in *Quaderni Friulani di Archeologia*, XVI, no. 1, Dec. 2006, pp. 13–23. See also Maria Grazia D'AMELIO, Carlo Stefano SALERNO, 'Virtù e difetti degli smalti settecenteschi di Alessio Mattioli: la qualità delle tinte e la loro alterazione dalle prime critiche del chimico Alessandro Martelli alle indagini sui mosaici della Basilica Vaticana nel periodo dell'occupazione francese', in C. FIORI, M. VANDINI (eds.), *Ravenna Musiva. Conservazione del Mosaico Antico e Contemporaneo. Atti del Convegno*, Bologna, Ante Quem, 2010, pp. 521–32.

[22] B.A., Ms. 49-VIII-13, no. 188: payments for glazes in the form of plates or slabs; B.A., Ms. 49-VIII-13, no. 199: 'a Mattioli il giorno 27 luglio 1744 per smalti filati dati da me a tutto il 16 maggio per i quadri di mosaico'.

[23] B.A., Ms. 49-VIII-23, no. 289 (1753).

[24] In 1821 the term *filati alla fornace* 'furnace-drawn [glass]' was still being used. The glass-maker Silvestro Pericoli was paid for *Gialli filati alla fornace* (yellow furnace-drawn glass) and *gialli filati alla lucerna* (yellow lamp-drawn [glass]): Archivio della Reverenda Fabbrica di S. Pietro (Vatican), ARM. 12 G 14 B, c. 496 and c. 497. I obtained information about the technique of drawing using a die-plate or drawing machine from a late colleague, Elisabetta Anselmi, who belonged to a family of mosaicists working in the Vatican Mosaic Studio.

[25] See Denis DIDEROT, Jean D'ALEMBERT, *Encyclopédie ou Dictionnaire raisonné des Sciences, des Arts et des Métiers*, vol. X, pl. XXI, 'Verre en bois'; with regard to this technique, see Marco VERITÀ, 'La tecnologia vetraria veneziana e i contenuti dell'opera', in Luigi ZECCHIN (ed.), *Il ricettario Darduin: un codice vetrario del Seicento trascritto e commentato*, Venice, Arsenale Ed., 1986, p. 31.

[26] B.A., Ms. 49-VIII-15, no. 54 (1746) contains a 'Conto delli smalti diuersi consegnati nella monizioni della Reu.da Fa.a di S. Pietro dal Sig.r Alessio Mattioli dalli 3 Ottobre 1744 a tutti li 28 luglio 1745 ... per li quadri e pauimento della Reali Cappella di Portogallo'.

[27] We have scarce and widely varying information with regard to stone-polishing in Leon Battista ALBERTI, *L'architettura (De re aedificatoria), testo latino e traduzione a cura di Giovanni Orlandi* (introduction and notes by Paolo Portoghesi), Milan, Ed. Il Polifilo, 1966, vol. II, book VI, ch. X, p. 504; Agostino DEL RICCIO, *Istoria delle Pietre*, 1597 (facsimile edition by P. Barocchi), Florence, Studio per Edizioni Scelte, 1979. Depicted for the first time in the Zabaglia engravings there is an *orso* (bear) 'di peperino, o d'altra pietra ruvida, nell'incavo di cui, a quell'effetto fattovi, si ferma il bastone, o manico con una zeppa Manuale, che spiana il mattonato dopo che ha fatto presa, tenendolo sempre bagnato' (of peperino, or some other rough stone, in the hollow of which, made in it for the purpose, the stick, or handle with a hand wedge, is stuck fast, which levels the brick-paved surface after it has set, keeping it always well wetted), Angela MARINO, '"Castelli e ponti" di maestro Nicola Zabaglia', in A. MARINO (ed.), *op. cit.* , vol. XI, p. 6.

[28] ARCHIVIO R.F.S.P., ARM. 43, E, N. 90, 1748.

[29] ARCHIVIO R.F.S.P., ARM. 43, E, N. 90, 1749: 98 scudi were paid for the grinding and polishing work carried out by Tomaso Albertini for the canons' choir in St Peter's. This is a substantial amount, and it is interesting in any event to note that the grinder and polisher was not a mosaicist.

[30] A list of materials for grinding and polishing in ARCHIVIO R.F.S.P. of 1749 concerning the altarpiece of the choir; among the materials there appear wax for grinding and polishing, white scouring [powder], gypsum for

making the 'bears', pumice, needles and charcoal; here it would seem that the final polishing was done with wax. ARCHIVIO R.F.S.P., ARM. 43, E, N. 90 c.479.

[31] ARCHIVIO R.F.S.P., ARM.. 43, E, n. 92, ARM. 43, E, note 91.

[32] B.A., Ms. 51-X-32, no. 89.

[33] See Carlo Stefano SALERNO, *op. cit.*, p. 108.

[34] B.A., Ms. 51- X-32, no. 83, B.A., Ms 51. X. 32, no. 87.

[35] B.A., Ms. 51- X-32, no. 390.

[36] B.A., Ms. 51- X-32, no. 88.

[37] For a more detailed discussion of the attribution to Luigi Vanvitelli of the project and the models for the floor, see Carlo Stefano SALERNO, *op. cit.*, pp. 104–5.

[38] Bruno CONTARDI, 'L'altare di San Luigi Gonzaga in Sant'Ignazio', in Alberta BATTISTI (ed.), *Andrea Pozzo*, Milan–Trento, Luni Editrice, 1996, p. 97. For the altar of São Ignazio al Gesù, see Vittorio DE FEO, 'Le cappelle e gli altari', in Vittorio DE FEO and Valentino MARTINELLI (eds.), *Andrea Pozzo*, Milan, Electa, 1996, pp. 70–71, 114–43, 126, 114–43; Pio PECCHIAI, *Il Gesù di Roma*, Rome, Società Grafica Romana, 1952, p. 132.

[39] Francisco Marques de Sousa VITERBO and R. Vicente d' ALMEIDA, *op. cit.*, p. 105.

[40] Cesare MORETTI, Teresa MORNA, Teresa MEDICI, Carlo Stefano SALERNO and Marco VERITÀ, 'Glass weathering in eighteenth century mosaics: the São João Chapel in the São Roque Church in Lisbon', *II International Conference on Glass Science in Art and Conservation. Supplement*, Valencia, no. 9 (Dec. 2008), pp. 37–40.

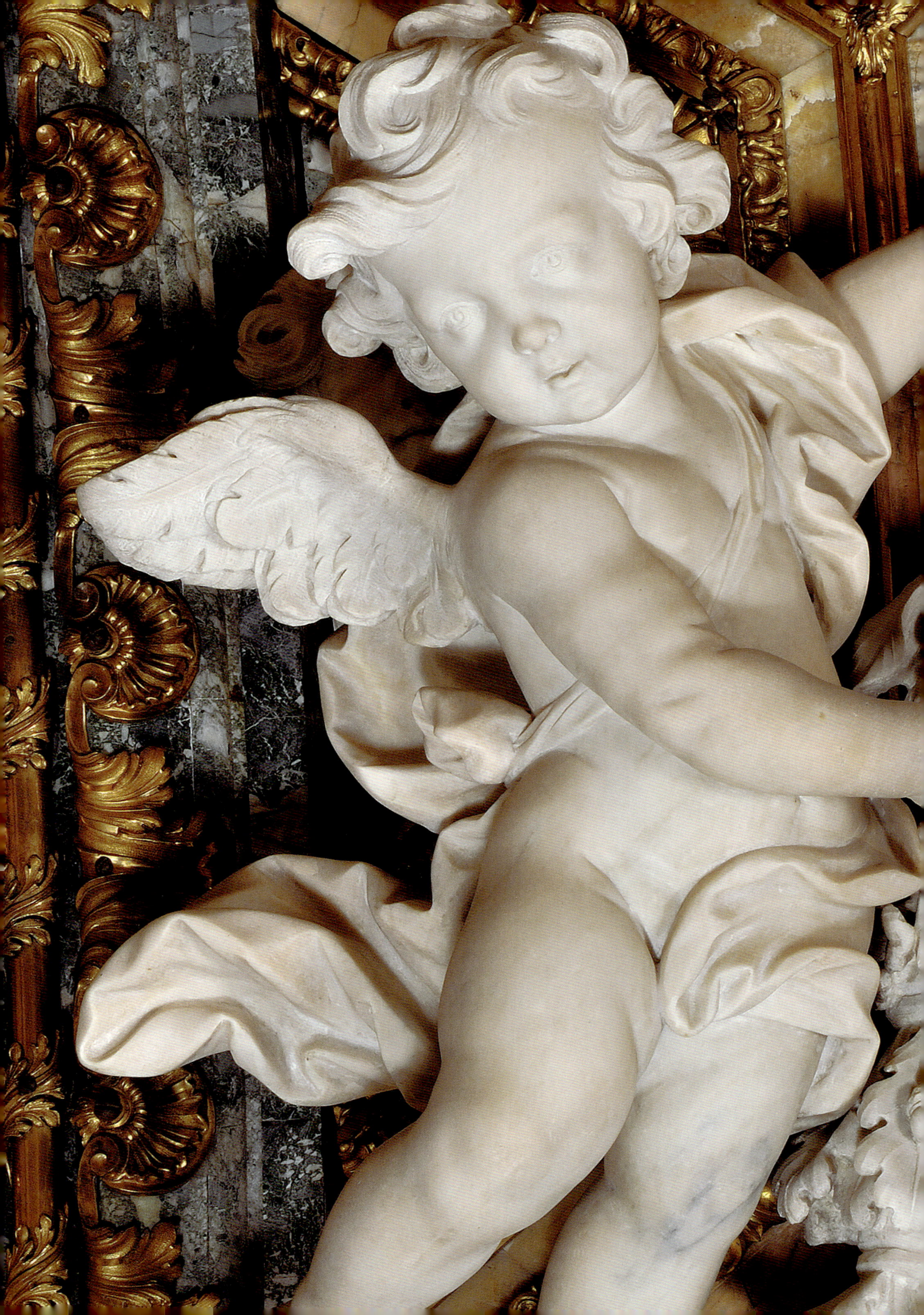

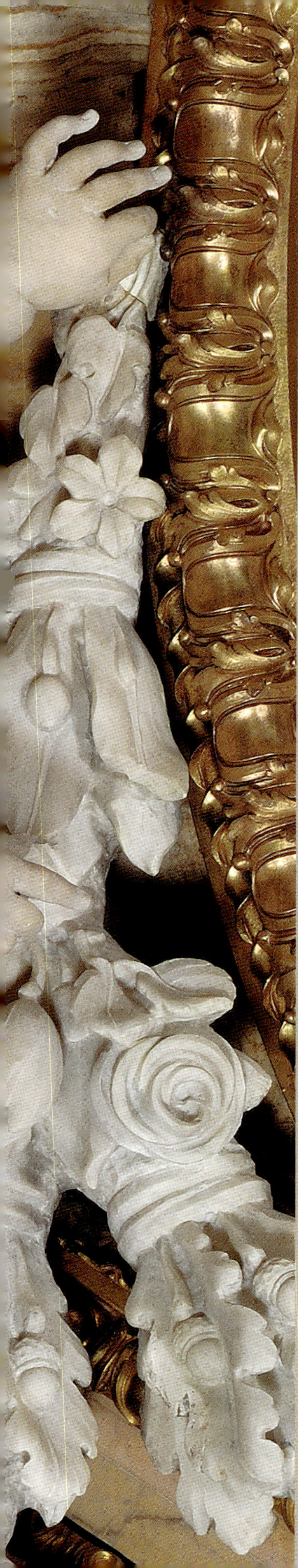

3. SCULPTURE

The sculptural elements of the Chapel of St John the Baptist: the status and function of sculpture in the overall ensemble of the work

Teresa Leonor M. Vale

The earliest document ever to have come to light concerning the commissioning of the Chapel of St John the Baptist is the well known and frequently referenced royal letter written from Lisbon on 26 October 1742, in which the order is given that there should be made in Rome 'e ornar uma capella dedicada ao Espírito Santo e a São João Baptista que esta na casa e para que o faça ajustado pelo sítio que ocupa a dita capella, se remete a sua planta alçada, exterior do emboco em toda a parede ate a cimalha da Igreja, outro alçado interior, e o espacato que mostra o seu lado e serventia e tribuna que esta sobre a mesma capella' (and adorned, a chapel dedicated to the Holy Spirit and to St John the Baptist, that is in our house; and in order that you should have it made to fit the site occupied by the said chapel, its floorplan has been sent, the exterior of the arch on the wall up to the cyma of the church, another drawing of the interior elevation, and the quadriculation that shows its side and the entrance, and the rostrum that is above the chapel itself).[1] This letter mentions nothing concrete with regard to the chapel's sculptures. Exactly the same is true of most of the correspondence on the subject exchanged between Ambassador Pereira de Sampaio and the Jesuit Father João Baptista Carbone; as far as the execution of the sculptural elements of the chapel is concerned, the information is much less rich and detailed than might be desired.

With regard to the chronology of the chapel's commissioning – which can be worked out based on analysis of the surviving correspondence and other materials produced for the purpose – there are two noteworthy references to the sculptural elements that have come into our hands:

9 March 1744 – A letter sent from Lisbon, containing multiple instructions regarding the execution of the chapel, among which the following passage refers to sculpture – and shows the high regard in which the court of Lisbon held the Lombard sculptor Giovanni Battista Maini (who had already executed works for Mafra and was to execute still more for the Patriarchal Basilica): 'Sobre o frontispicio do retabolo se collocou o Cordeiro adorado por dous anjos e pera maior riqueza se lhe poz hum grande resplendor com o qual se evita fazer-lhe o forro Lavoriozo; o dito Cordeiro e seu resplendor será de bronze dourado, e os Anjos de Marmore, advertindo que só se indica o Lugar das figuras, e o sentido dellas, porque a Escultura hade ser do Sr. Maine [*sic*], e de outros tão bons como elle, se os houver, não podendo elle fazer toda a que ha na Capella.' (On the frontispiece of the retable

pp. 66–67
Little angel and festoons from relief of St John the Baptist Preaching in the Desert (detail)
Bernardino Ludovisi
(See fig. 39)

Fig. 30
Relief of St John the Baptist Preaching in the Desert
(detail)
Bernardino Ludovisi
Carrara marble

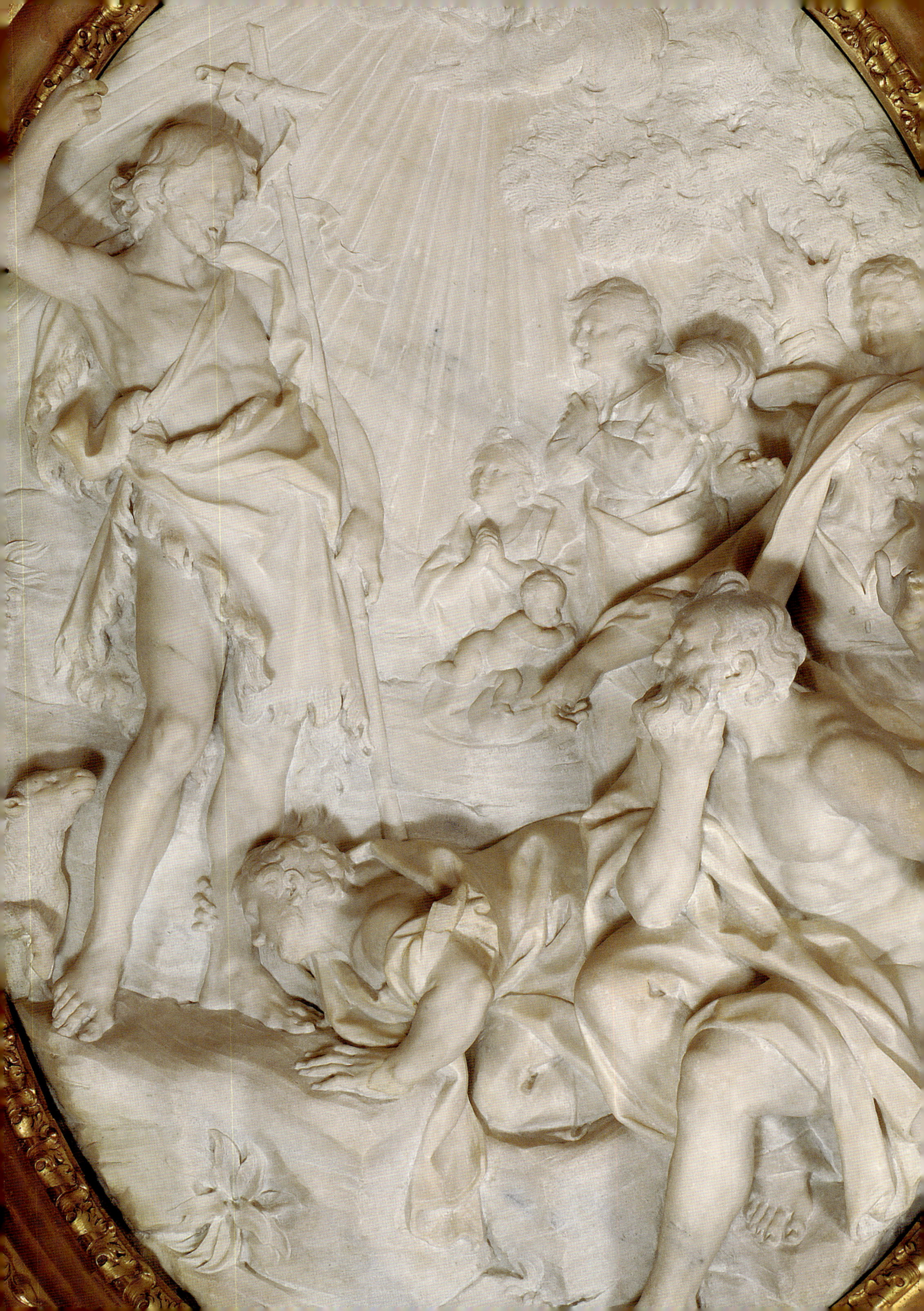

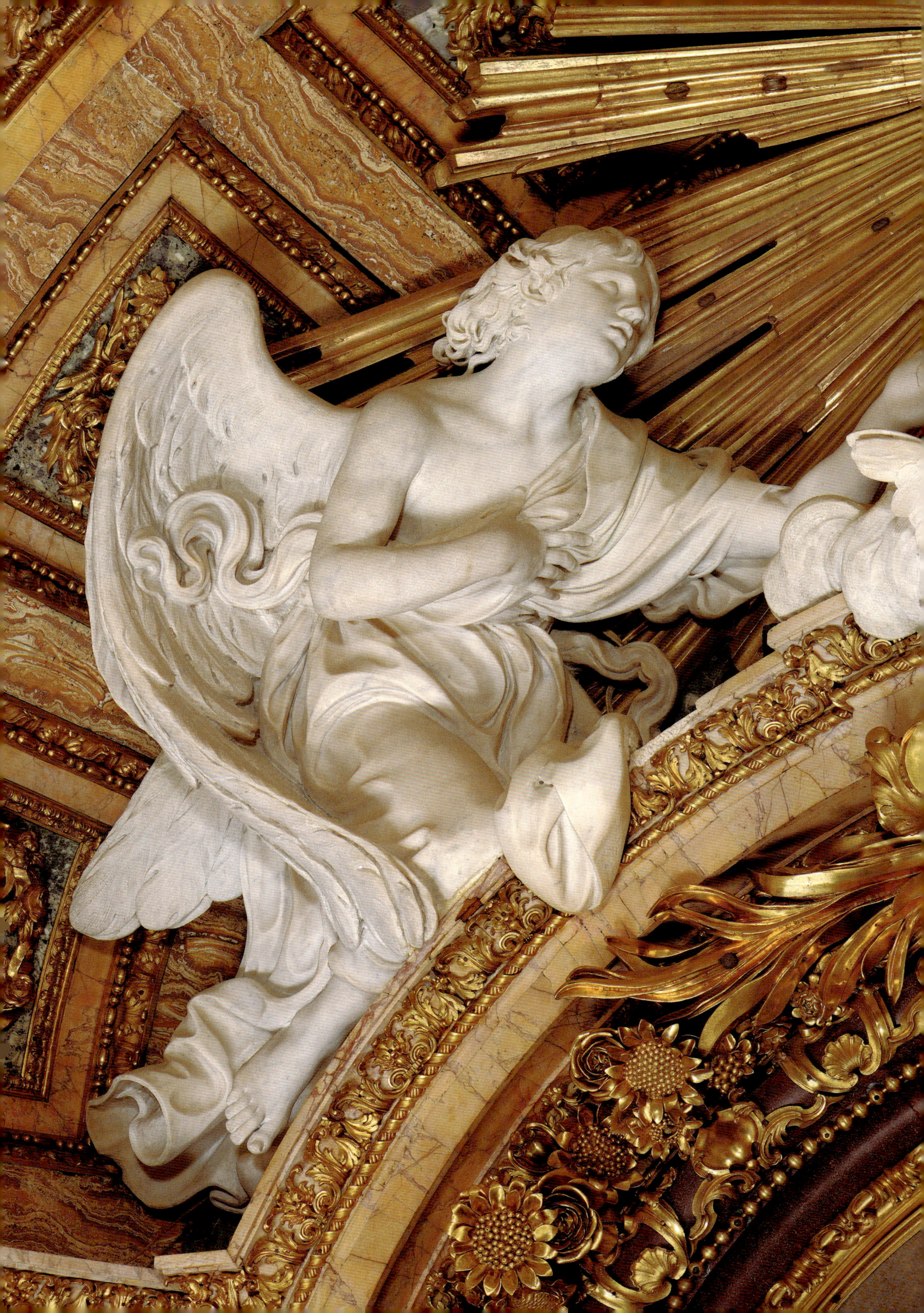

there was placed the Lamb adored by two angels, and to make it the richer this was given a great halo or nimbus which avoids the need to fill it which is laborious; the said Lamb and its halo will be of gilded bronze, and the angels of marble, with the warning that only the placement of the figures and their orientation is indicated, because the sculpture has to be by Signor Maine [*sic*], and by others as good as he, if any there be, as he cannot do all that there is in the chapel.)[2]

15 September 1745 – A letter written from Lisbon addresses an assessment of the cost of the various components of the chapel – an assessment that we believe to have been made by the architect and silversmith João Frederico Ludovice, according to information sent from Rome by Ambassador Manuel Pereira de Sampaio, since it says in the following passage: 'Tambem pelos nomes dos autores entendia [Ludovice] que não seria grande cousa algumas peças da Capella, como eram figuras de Anjos, Cherubins, etc. e melhor conceito formava das esculpturas de simples ornato.' (Also from the names of the artists [Ludovice] understood that some of the pieces for the chapel would not amount to much, as they were figures of angels, cherubim, etc., and he was forming a better opinion of sculptures simply adorned.)[3]

The relative lack of documentation ultimately reflects the role of sculpture in the overall ensemble of the work, as indeed the Chapel of St John the Baptist clearly constitutes a remarkable work of architecture that is merely set off with highlights in the form of sculpture. Unlike other works of a similar period, the chapel commissioned by John V for the Lisbon church of the Jesuits does not give sculpture any kind of leading role. In fact, Luigi Vanvitelli's project conceives of the chapel essentially as a work of architecture in which sculpture is included as an addition, albeit an integral one, within the scope of what we may consider to be the decorative elements. Application of the baroque concept of *bel composto* is still very much alive in the construction of the monument that is the chapel, but the role assigned to sculpture is mainly that of an element intended to enliven the architecture and contribute to the (quite simple) iconographic programme conveyed by the overall ensemble of the work.

From this point of view, the Chapel of St John the Baptist is not an isolated or exceptional case. Probably the last great chapel of the Roman *settecento* where it was possible to include a significant sculptural component was that of the Corsini family in the Basilica of St John Lateran, whose first stone was laid in 1732, the work being completed in early 1735; its consecration took place on 17 January of that year. However, neither the dimensions nor the architectural design – created by the Florentine architect and family protégé Alessandro Galilei (1691–1737) – nor the character of this chapel can be compared with those of the chapel executed in Rome for the Lisbon Church of São Roque. In fact, the architect of the Corsini Chapel, making reference to two other pontifical chapels chosen by Clement XII (Corsini) as a model (namely the Sistine and Paolina Chapels, built in the Roman Basilica of Santa Maria Maggiore) opted for a centralised floor plan (specifically, the Greek cross layout), whereas the much smaller Chapel of St John the Baptist has a

Fig. 31
Archangel flanking the cross at the top of the retable (detail)
Peter Anton von Verschaffelt
Carrara marble

rectangular floor plan. Furthermore, the fact that the Lateran Chapel was a family pantheon meant the presence of funeral monuments and, closely linked to these, an iconography centred on the virtues; this implied a sculptural component of greater importance, comprising statues in the round and reliefs, giving sculpture an even more significant role here than that which it had in the two pontifical chapels chosen as a model from which to work.

As the Chapel of St John the Baptist was built for devotional purposes, consideration should be given to other works with similar characteristics since the 1740s were no longer a particularly fertile period for such undertakings in Rome. In fact the examples that might be taken into consideration for this purpose are all slightly earlier ones – including particularly the remarkable Chapel of St Philip Neri (San Filippo Neri, or Antamoro) in the Church of San Girolamo della Carità, designed by Filippo Juvara (1676–1736) in 1707. Here the architect resolves the tight constraints of the small rectangular space by converting it into a lively ellipse and piercing the top wall with an oval oculus in front of which there stands the figure of *St. Philip Neri in Ecstasy*, by the sculptor Pierre Le Gros the Younger (1666–1719). Though differing architecturally regarding the choice of layout and the solutions adopted for lighting, as well as the resulting spatial qualities, the Antamoro Chapel of San Girolamo della Carità nevertheless has a significant affinity with the Chapel of St John the Baptist – specifically with regard to the presence of sculpture, especially at ceiling level. Both in the chapel of the Church of São Roque and in that of San Girolamo della Carità, it was decided to enliven the vaulted ceiling with sculpture; there are fluttering cherubim in both cases, and (also in both chapels) there are two particularly noteworthy reliefs alluding to their respective patron saints. Where in Lisbon there is a *Visitation of Our Lady to St Elizabeth* (by Carlo Marchionni) and a *Preaching of St John the Baptist in the Desert* (by Bernardino Ludovisi), in the chapel in Rome there are two reliefs depicting *St Philip Neri in the Catacombs of San Calisto* and *St Philip Neri Seeing the Souls of their Penitents Rising to the Heavens* (both by Pierre Le Gros) which are also placed on either side of the chapel.

Taking into account the aspects touched on above – which emphasise that sculpture in the Chapel of St John the Baptist cannot be seen as playing a leading role – it seems all the more important to approach these works of sculpture as we shall now seek to do: that is to say, specifically in the context of other more extensive works executed by the same artists, most of whom were well known sculptors in the context of the first half of the Roman *settecento*. Understanding the contribution of these artists to the Chapel of St John the Baptist in the light of their other work will, we believe, permit a better appreciation of the quality of the pieces made for the chapel of the Lisbon church; this will allow us to understand to what extent their work here was an important step in their artistic careers and to appreciate why they were chosen out of the numerous sculptors active in Rome at the end of the first half of the eighteenth century.

The Italian sculptors: their involvement and contribution

Not all the sculptors were Italian – the group responsible for the sculptural component of the Chapel of St John the Baptist included one French and one Belgian artist – but they were nonetheless all active in the context of Roman sculpture in the first half of the eighteenth century. As in the case of the vast order for Italian sculpture for the Basilica of Our Lady and St Anthony in Mafra, commissioned less than twenty years earlier, it would seem that the choice of sculptors to work on the Chapel of St John the Baptist depended principally on availability. The choice made by John V's agent in Rome, Manuel Pereira de Sampaio, was undoubtedly also based on the conviction that all of those chosen were artists of quality, capable of executing work for the king of Portugal, but the Portuguese ambassador certainly could not select the best sculptors active in Rome during this period. That was not only because some of them were involved in executing other works, but also because the commission was not particularly appealing to the great sculptors – bearing in mind that the sculptural component was not given a role of primary importance at all, seen in the context of the overall ensemble of the Chapel of St John the Baptist. And finally, once more considering the characteristics of the commission in sculptural terms (namely that it did not require the inclusion of any large statues or reliefs), it would not have been justified to spend large sums on renowned sculptors when the execution of the desired pieces could be entrusted to other, less costly artists. It should be noted that economising on costs was a constant refrain in the correspondence between Lisbon and Rome – much as had already been the case with the commissioning of sculpture for Mafra.[4]

On the other hand, it does appear that Ambassador Pereira de Sampaio sought to recruit sculptors whose work was already known and highly regarded in Portugal, such as Bernardino Ludovisi and Giovanni Battista Maini. Maini, whose participation in the project consisted of creating models for pieces in gold and silver, was held in very high esteem and much admired by the Portuguese court, as can clearly be seen from the letter of commission dated 9 March 1744 cited above – so even though his participation as a sculptor was essentially in the context of producing models for works pertaining to another field (that is to say, to the collection of gold, silver and jewellery) he could not fail to be included here in the chapter devoted to the sculptural work of the chapel.

One question that inevitably arises is the absence of the two most important figures from the world of sculpture in Rome in the eighteenth century: Pietro Bracci (1700–73) and Filippo della Valle (1698–1768) – both artists of recognised merit, who were already very well established at the time and who had already worked for Portugal (there are sculptures by both artists in Mafra).[5] In the case of della Valle this situation is all the less comprehensible as he is known to have executed the funeral monument for Ambassador Manuel Pereira de Sampaio himself, located in his Chapel of Our Lady of Conception in the Church of Sant'Antonio dei Portoghesi (even taking into account the fact that Cardinal Neri Maria Corsini, who would naturally have tended to choose a Florentine sculptor such as Filippo della Valle, might have played a decisive role in that choice).

We believe, however, that the absence of Bracci and della Valle from the group of sculptors responsible for the statuary of the Chapel of St John the Baptist is essentially explained by two factors. The first relates to the characteristics of the commission itself – the fact that the chapel's sculptural work was not planned to include statues or reliefs of significant size and that there was thus no justification (mainly from Lisbon's point of view) for spending large sums on famous sculptors since execution of the pieces could be entrusted to less expensive artists. A second possible explanation for the fact that Pietro Bracci and Filippo della Valle had no involvement in the Chapel of St John the Baptist is the availability of the sculptors. The 1740s were a period of intense activity for both men, as they were executing large and significant commissions.

In light of these considerations it can be readily explained and understood why these artists – already the two greatest sculptors active in Rome at the time – are not represented in the Chapel of St John the Baptist.

There were seven sculptors involved in the work for the Chapel of St John the Baptist – five Italians, and one French and one Belgian artist – both of the non-Italians being active in Rome at the time the chapel was executed. These artists and their works within the chapel are identified below:

Antonio CORRADINI (1668–1752):[6] two angels (marble), flanking the royal arms situated over the archway into the chapel; three heads of cherubim (marble), in the coffering of the vaulted ceiling (figs 32 and 33).

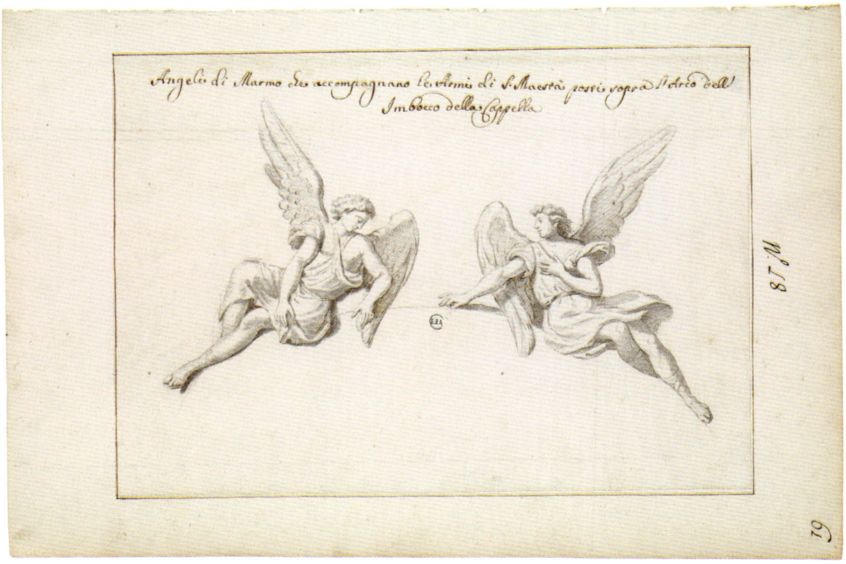

Fig. 32
Two angels intended to be executed by the sculptor Antonio Corradini
Drawing no. 18 of the *Weale Album*, f. 61
Bibliothèque de l'École Nationale Supérieure des Beaux-arts [Library of the National Higher School of Fine Arts], Paris
(Ms. 497)

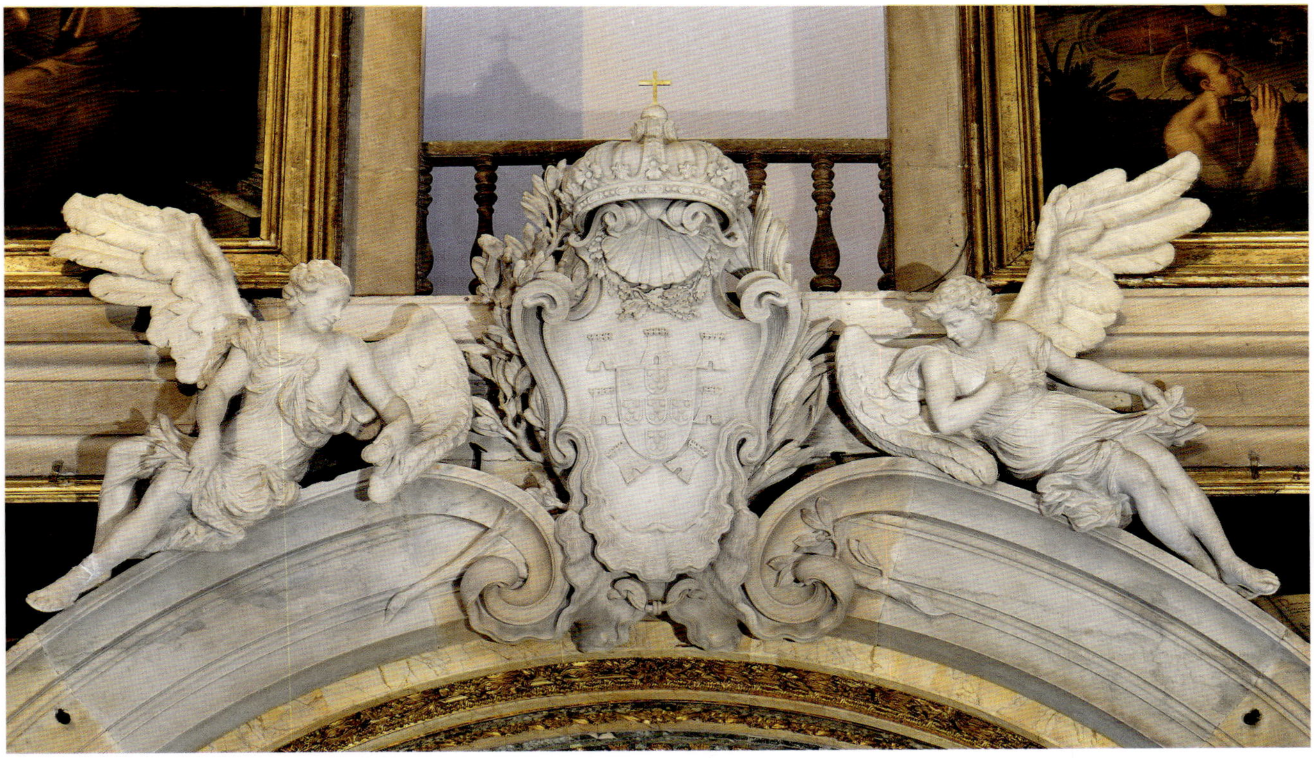

Fig. 33
Angels on the upper part of the archway into the chapel
Antonio Corradini
Carrara marble

Agostino CORSINI (1688–1772):[7] group of cherubim (marble), in the vaulting, on the Gospel (left-hand) side; two *putti* (marble), in the vaulting, flanking the relief on the Gospel (left-hand) side (figs 34 and 35).

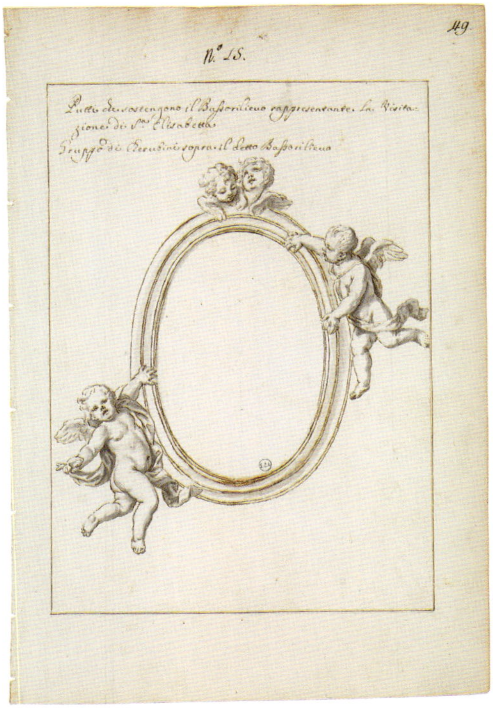

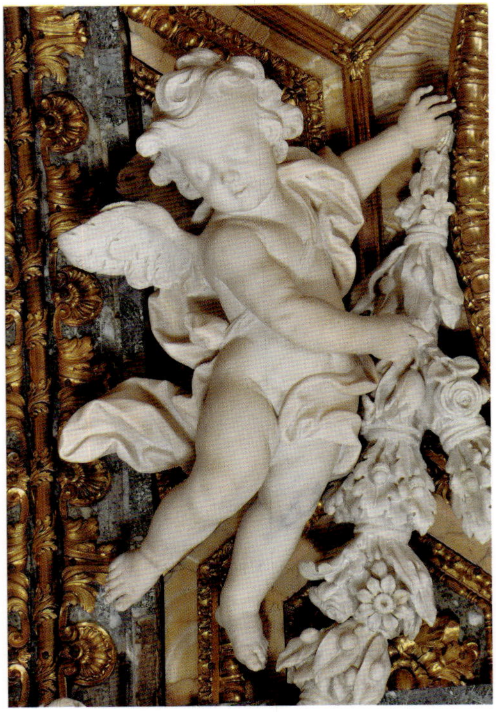

Fig. 34
Pair of little angels and two heads of cherubim
intended to be executed by the sculptor Agostino Corsini
Drawing no. 15 of the *Weale Album*, f. 49
Bibliothèque de l'École Nationale Supérieure des Beaux-arts [Library of the National Higher School of Fine Arts], Paris (Ms. 497)

Fig. 35
Little angel holding the relief of the Visitation of the Virgin
Antonio Corsini
Carrara marble

Domenico GIOVANNINI (active first half of the eighteenth century): royal escutcheon (marble) over the archway into the chapel and the corresponding models in plaster and in wax; festoons (marble) flanking the two reliefs in the vaulting; models (in plaster) of angels executed by Antonio Corradini. Domenico Giovannini seems to be an exception among the group of sculptors active in the work of the Chapel of St John the Baptist, but this is not in fact the case; although the presence of a sculptor who appears to have been responsible for no other work beyond that assigned to him in the chapel of the Church of the Society of Jesus in Lisbon seemed strange at first, the explanation for this emerged from the documentary research carried out. This revealed that Giovannini was not a sculptor but an *intagliatore di marmi* or *intagliatore di pietra* (a marble- or stone-carver),[8] being referred to as such in any and all payments even though these records always appear alongside those of sums owed to the sculptors.

Pierre de L'ESTACHE (c. 1688–1774):[9] two groups of cherubim (marble) surmounting the frames of the paintings on the side walls of the chapel; four heads of cherubim (marble), in the coffering of the vaulted ceiling (figs 36 and 37).

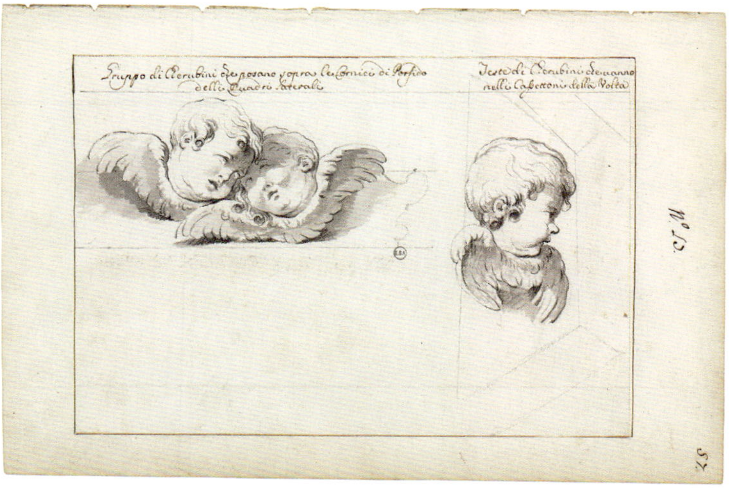

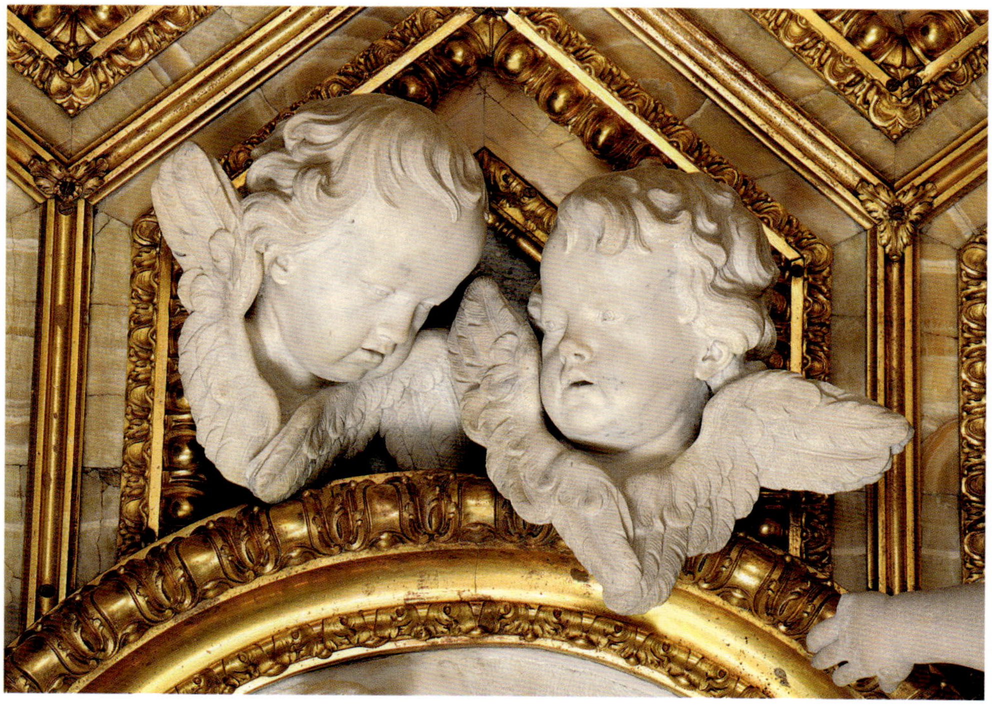

Fig. 36
Two groups of cherubim and four heads of cherubim
intended to be executed by the sculptor Pierre de L'Estache
Drawing no. 17 of the *Weale Album*, f. 57
Bibliothèque de l'École Nationale Supérieure des Beaux-arts [Library of the National Higher School of Fine Arts], Paris (Ms. 497)

Fig. 37
Pair of cherubim
above the relief of St John the Baptist Preaching in the Desert
Pierre de L'Estache
Carrara marble

Fig. 38
Relief of St John the Baptist Preaching in the Desert
intended to be executed by the sculptor Bernardino Ludovisi
Drawing no. 12 of the *Weale Album*, f. 39
Bibliothèque de l'École Nationale Supérieure des Beaux-arts [Library of the National Higher School of Fine Arts], Paris (Ms. 497)

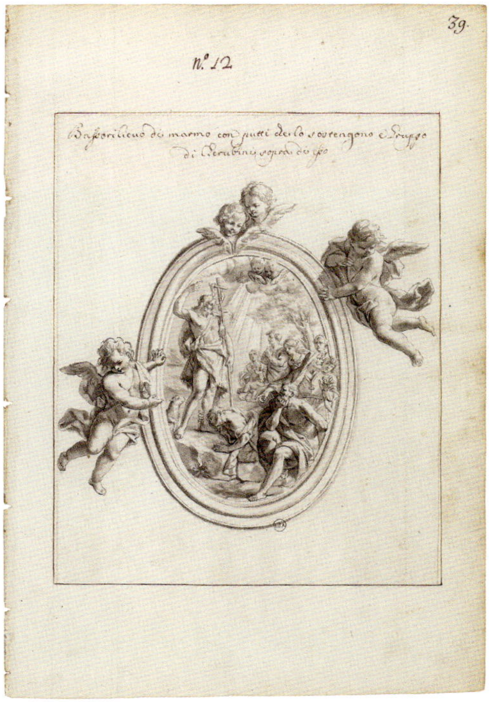

Bernardino LUDOVISI (1694–1749):[10] *St John the Baptist Preaching in the Desert*, 1743–44 (relief, marble), in the vaulting on the Epistle (right-hand) side; two *putti* and two heads of cherubim, 1744 (marble), flanking and above the frame of the above-mentioned relief; eight heads of cherubim, 1744 (marble), in the coffering of the vaulted ceiling; models of two *putti*, 1744 (later executed in silver by the silversmith Antonio Arrighi), flanking the frontal of the altar for high mass (figs 38 and 39).

Fig. 39
Relief of St John the Baptist Preaching in the Desert,
with little angels and festoons
Bernardino Ludovisi
Carrara marble

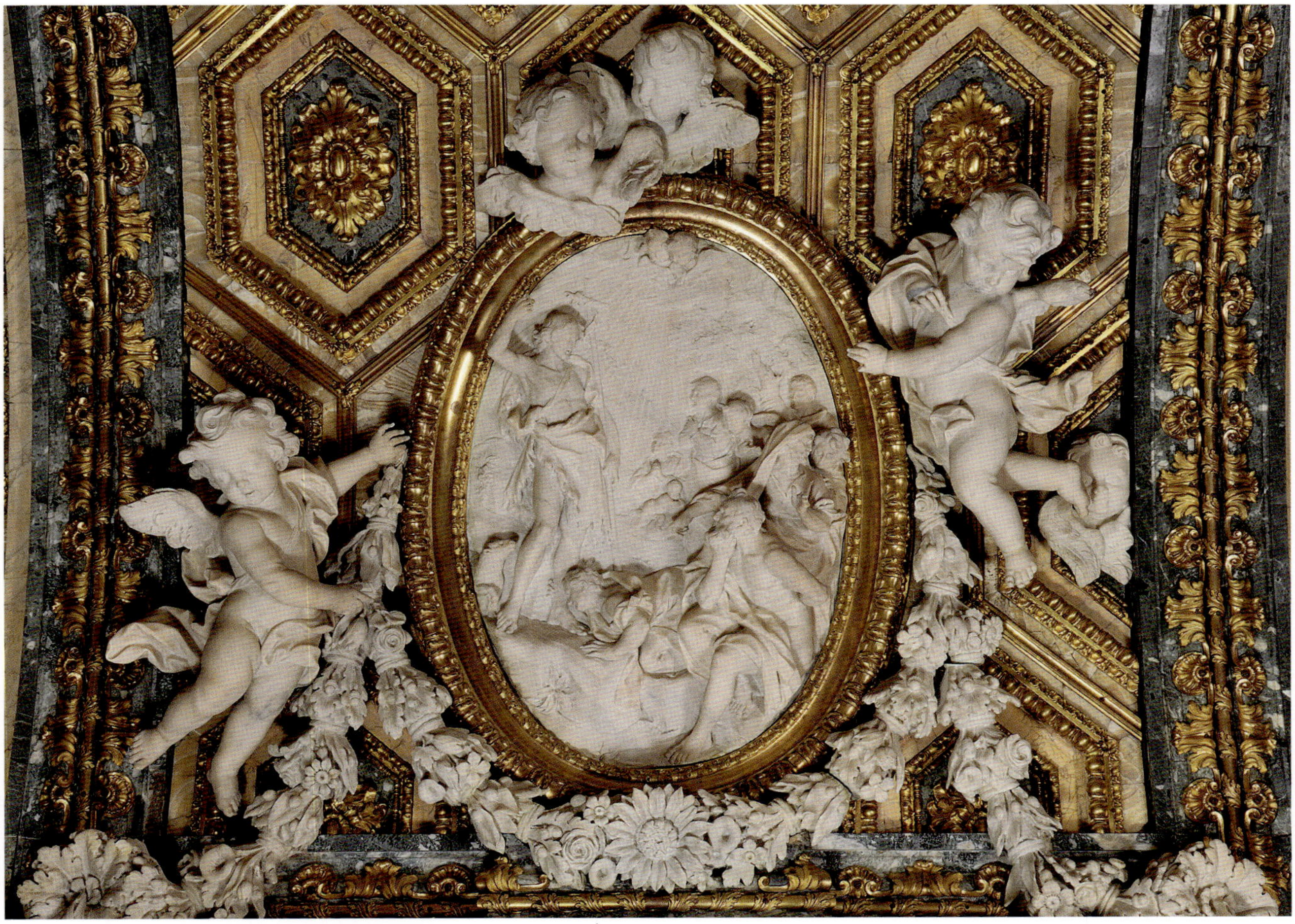

Carlo MARCHIONNI (1702–86):[11] *Visitation of the Virgin* (relief, marble), in the vaulting on the Gospel (left-hand) side (fig. 40).

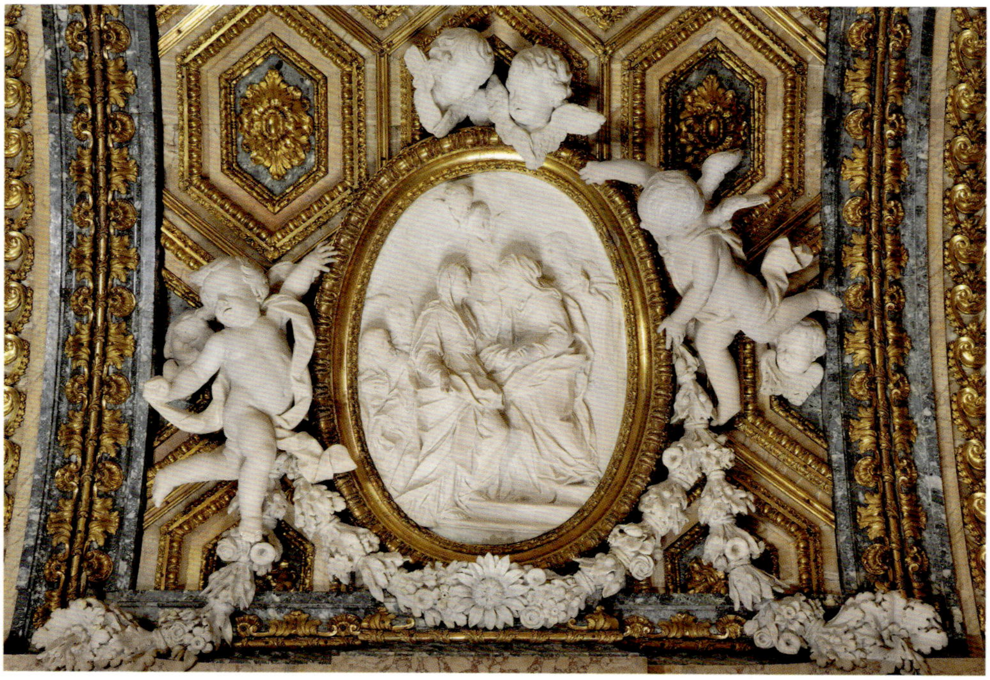

Fig. 40
Relief of the Visitation of the Virgin with little angels and festoons
Carlo Marchionni
Carrara marble

Peter Anton von VERSCHAFFELT (1710–93):[12] two archangels on the cyma of the frontispiece of the altar retable; group of cherubim, adorning the foot of the cross in metal on the frontispiece of the same retable, as well as the models for these pieces; the wax model of the relief on the frontal in silver and lapis lazuli (executed by the silversmith Antonio Arrighi); models for the groups of heads of cherubim to be placed over the side doors and those of a number of other decorative sculptural components of the chapel (figs 41–44). ■

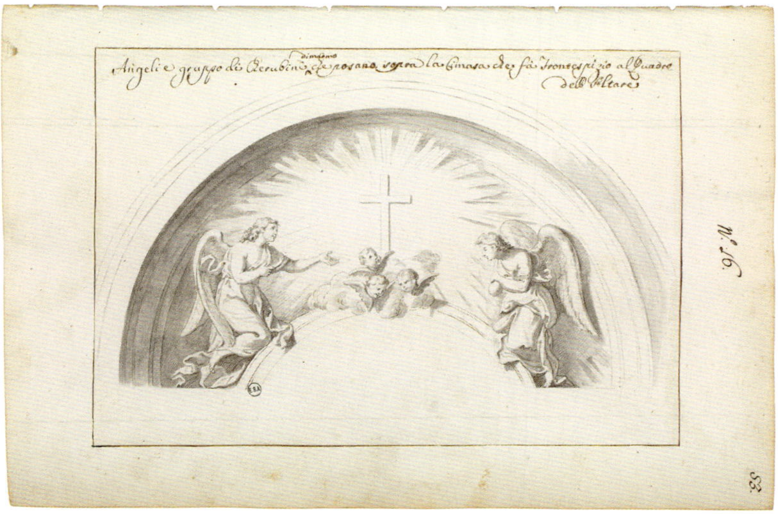

Fig. 41
Pair of archangels and group of cherubim intended to be executed by the sculptor Peter Anton von Verschaffelt
Drawing. no. 16 of the *Weale Album*, f. 53
Bibliothèque de l'École Nationale Supérieure des Beaux-arts [Library of the National Higher School of Fine Arts], Paris (Ms. 497)

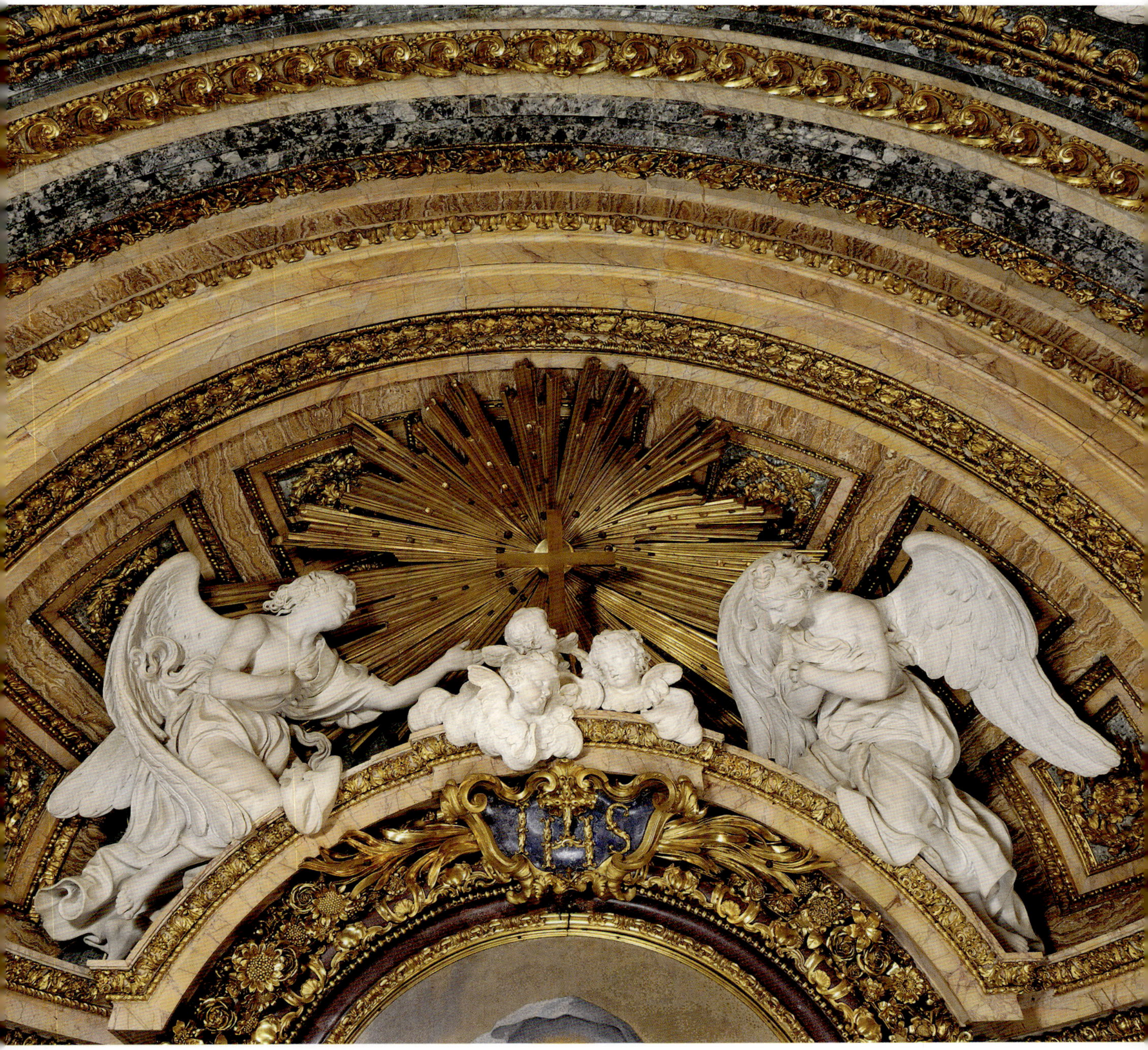

Fig. 42
Pair of archangels flanking the cross at the top of the retable
Peter Anton von Verschaffelt
Carrara marble

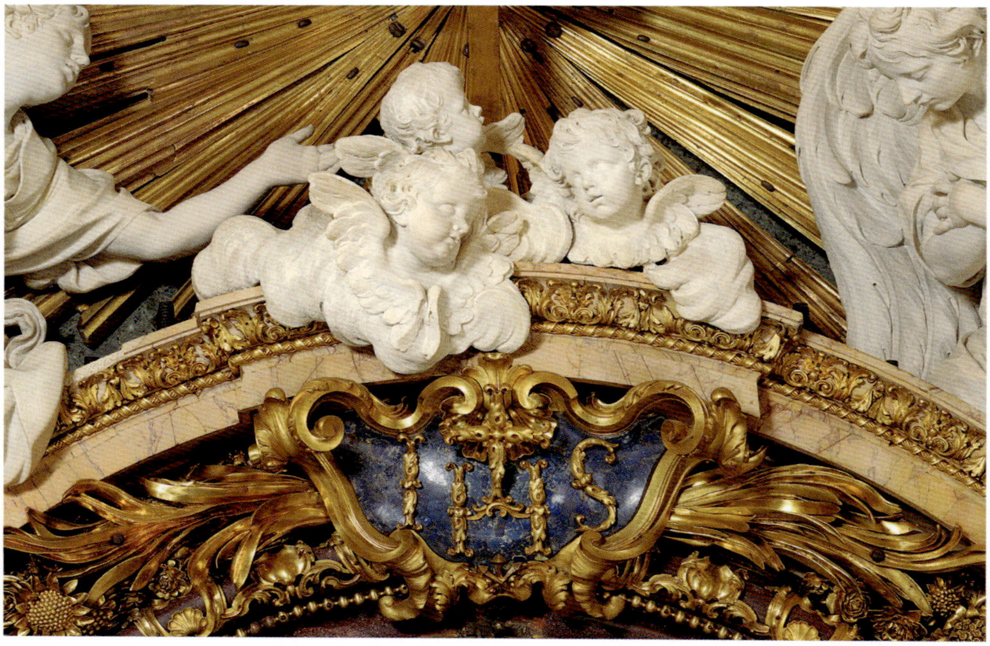

Fig. 43
Group of cherubim
at the foot of the cross,
at the top of the altarpiece
Peter Anton von Verschaffelt
Carrara marble

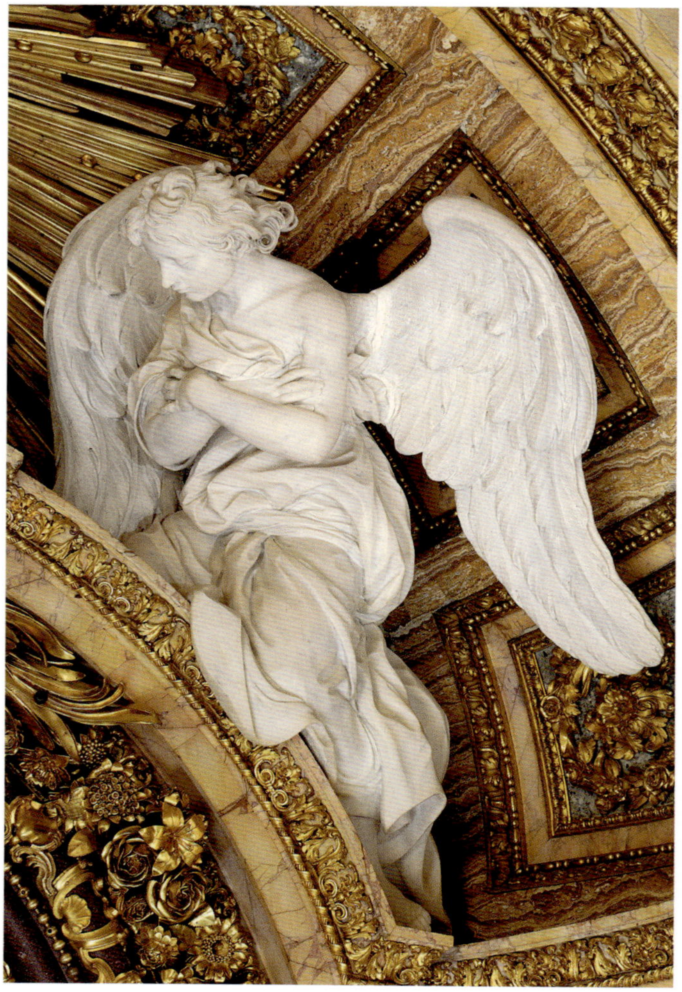

Fig. 44
Adoring angel, upper part
of the altarpiece
Peter Anton von Verschaffelt
Carrara marble

NOTES

[1] BIBLIOTECA DA AJUDA (Lisbon), Ms. 49-VIII-27, p. 1, §1.

[2] B.A., Ms. 49-VIII-27, p. 29; copy of this letter in B.A. Ms. 49-VIII-28 and Ms. 49-VIII-29, and it is included by Francisco Marques de Sousa VITERBO and R. Vicente d' ALMEIDA, *A Capella de S. João Baptista Erecta na Egreja de S. Roque*, Lisbon, Livros Horizonte, 1997, pp. 114–17 (1st edition 1900).

[3] B.A., Ms. 51-III-68, f. 185, pub. by Francisco Marques de Sousa VITERBO and R. Vicente d' ALMEIDA, *op. cit.*, p. 144.

[4] Teresa Leonor M. VALE, *A Escultura Italiana de Mafra*, Lisbon, Livros Horizonte, 2002.

[5] Bracci executed the statues of São Felix de Valois (1731) and of São Pedro Nolasco, both for the Galilee (entrance porch), while della Valle sculpted the *São Jerónimo* (St Jerome) (1733), intended for the interior of the basilica; the statue of São João da Mata (St John of Matha) is also attributed to him – cf. Teresa Leonor M. VALE, *A Escultura Italiana de Mafra*, Lisbon, Livros Horizonte, 2002, pp. 55–57, 71–73 and all the previous bibliography mentioned here.

[6] On Corradini cf. Monica De VICENTI, 'Piacere ai Dotti e ai Migliori. Scultori Classicisti del Primo "700"', in Giuseppe PAVANELLO (dir.), *La Scultura Veneta del Seicento e del Settecento. Nuovi Studi*, Venice, Istituto Veneto di Scienze, Lettere ed Arti, 2002, p. 236, which refers to the more extensive biography written by Bruno COGO, *Antonio Corradini Scultore Veneziano*, Este, Libreria Gregoriana Estense, 1996, pp. 36–39, 60–62, which remains the most significant work on this artist; cf. also Antonella PAMPALONE, 'Il progetto di Ferdinando Fuga per un busto di Benedetto XIV di Antonio Corradini: nuovi documenti sulla "Sapienza" di Roma', in Elisa DEBENEDETTI (dir.), *Studi sul Settecento Romano. Palazzi, Chiese, Arredi e Scultura*, vol. I, Rome, Bonsignori Editore, 2011, pp. 155–70, and by Anne-Lise DESMAS, *Le Ciseau et la Tiare. Les sculpteurs dans la Rome des Papes 1724–1758*, Rome, École Française de Rome, 2012, pp. 284–92.

[7] On Agostino Corsini cf. Jennifer MONTAGU, 'D. João V and Italian sculpture', in Jay A. LEVENSON (ed.), *The Age of Baroque in Portugal*, London – New Haven, Yale University Press, 1993, p. 84, and Jennifer MONTAGU, 'João V e la Scultura Italiana', in Sandra Vasco ROCCA and Gabriele BORGHINI (dir.), *Giovanni V di Portogallo e la Cultura Romana del suo Tempo*, Rome, Àrgos Edizioni, 1995, p. 398.

[8] cf. B.A., Ms.46-XIII-9, f. 194, Ms. 49-VIII-13, f. 247, no. 161, Ms. 49-VIII-14, no. 22, no. 70, no. 211, no. 334, no. 442, no. 541, Ms. 49-VIII-15, no. 8, no. 241, no. 338, Ms. 49-VIII-16, f. 207, Ms. 49-IX-22, f. 149, f. 175, f. 203, f. 213, f. 226, f. 229, f. 243, f. 256, f. 267, f. 298, f. 308, f. 316, f. 755, Ms. 49-IX-31, pp. 113, 126, 140, 175, 185, 196.

[9] On Pierre de L'Estache see particularly the website run by Anne-Lise DESMAS, www.lestache.com.

[10] On Bernardino Ludovisi cf. particularly the texts of Robert ENGGASS: 'Bernardino Ludovisi I: the early work', in *Burlington Magazine*, vol. CX (785), Aug. 1968, pp. 438–44, 'Bernardino Ludovisi II: the late work', in *Burlington Magazine*, vol. CX (786), Sept. 1968, pp. 494–501, 'Bernardino Ludovisi III: his work in Portugal', in *Burlington Magazine*, vol. CX (788), Nov. 1968, pp. 613–19, and 'Lo Stato della Scultura a Roma nella Prima Mettà del Settecento', in Sandra Vasco ROCCA and Gabriele BORGHINI (dir.), *op. cit.*, pp. 429–33 and the more recent contribution of Olga MINERVINO, 'Nuovi Contributi su Bernardino Ludovisi Scultore Romano' in Elisa DEBENEDETTI (dir.), *Sculture Romane del Settecento. La Professione dello Scultore*, vol. I, Rome, Bonsignori Editore, 2001, pp. 271–339.

[11] On Marchionni as a sculptor, see particularly Francesco PETRUCCI, 'Contributi su Carlo Marchionni Scultore', in Elisa DEBENEDETTI (dir.), *Sculture Romane del Settecento. La Professione dello Scultore*, vol. I, *op. cit.*, p. 37.

[12] cf. Joseph August BERINGER, *Peter A. von Verschafftelt*, Strasbourg, 1902; A. ANSELMI, 'La Decorazione Scultorea della Facciata di S. Maria Maggiore', in *Ricerche di Storia dell'Arte*, vol. XL, 1990; Antoine CAHEN, 'Les Prix de Quartier à l'Académie Royale de Peinture et de Sculpture', in *Bulletin de la Societé de l'Histoire de l'Art Français*, 1993 (1994), pp. 61–84; François SOUCHAL, 'Quelques Sculptures Retrouvées du XVIIIe Siècle', in *Bulletin de la Societé de l'Histoire de l'Art Français*, Paris, 1996 (1997), pp. 95–106.

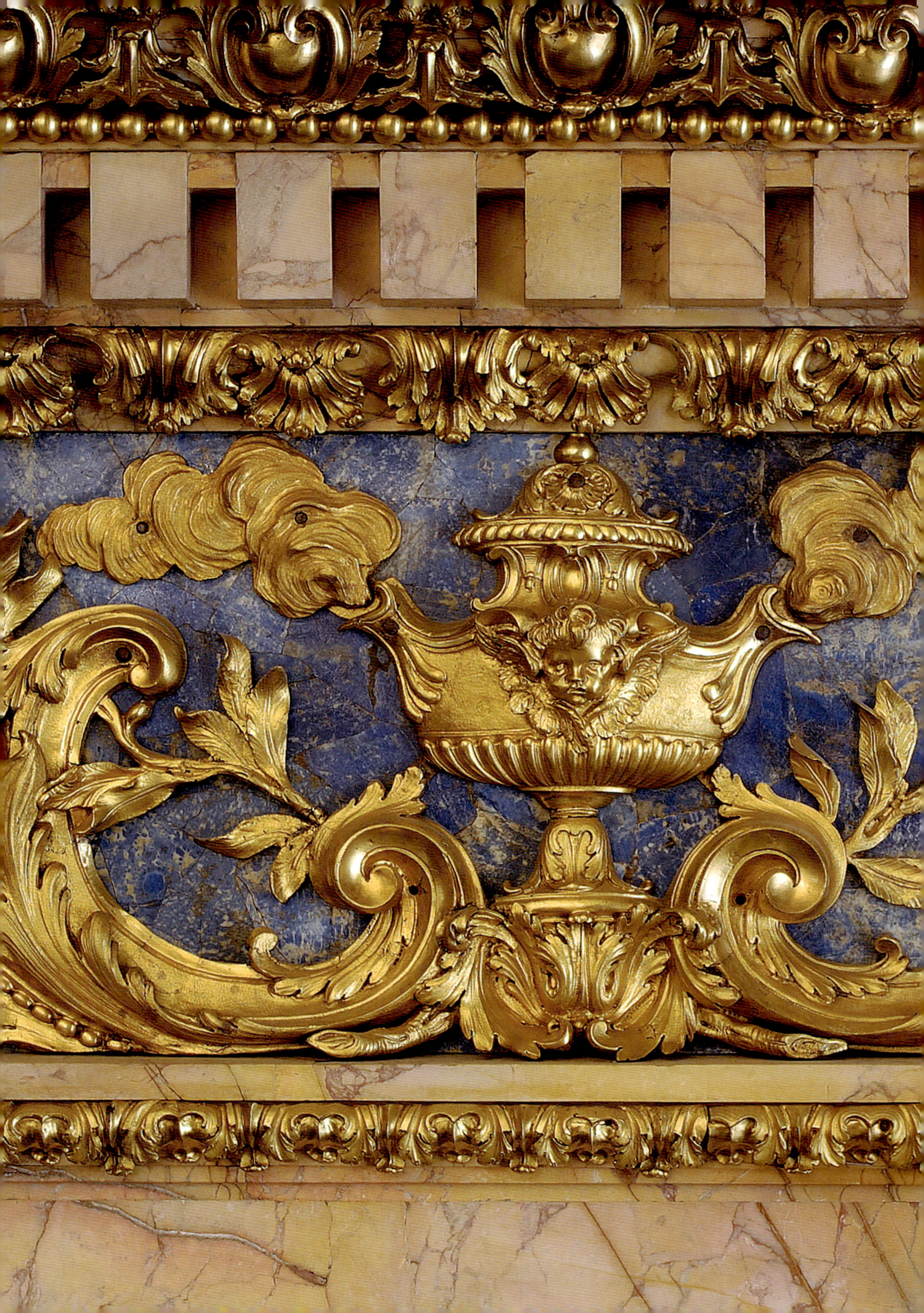

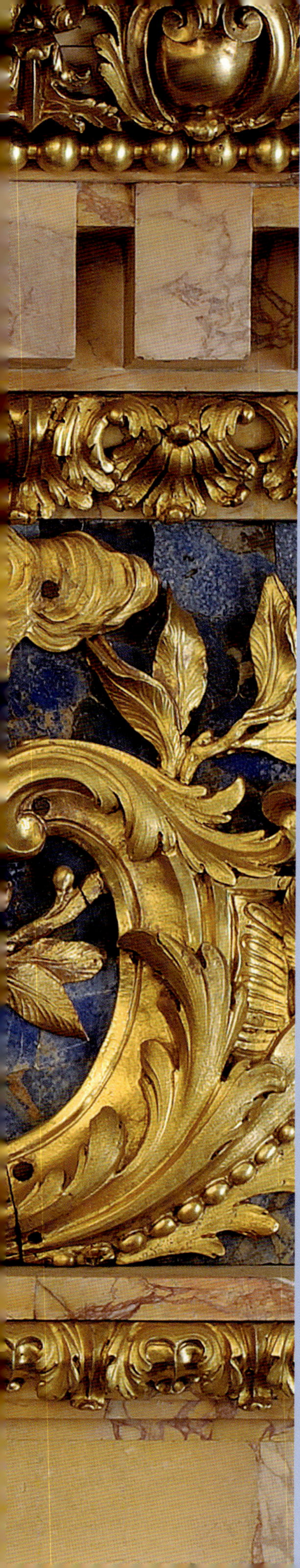

4. METALS

The gleam of gold highlighting the architecture

Teresa Leonor M. Vale

Every architectural surface in the Chapel of St John the Baptist is enlivened by the presence of metal, and the expressive elements comprising them are enhanced by these same metals (figs 45–47).

pp. 82–83
Decorations of the frieze on the architrave (detail)
Francesco Rosa
(See fig. 48)

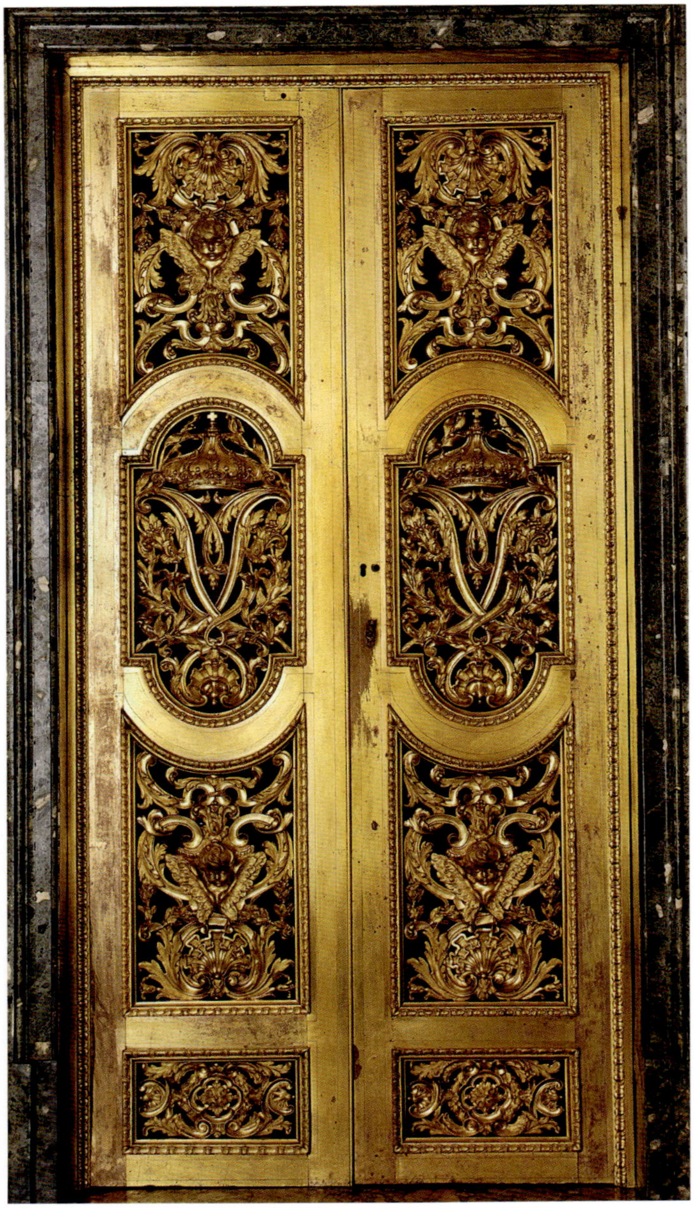

Fig. 45
One of the side doors
Silvestro Doria
Gilded metal

Fig. 46
Leaves of the side doors of the Chapel of St John the Baptist intended to be executed by Silvestro Doria
Drawing no. 40 of the *Weale Album*, f. 117
Bibliothèque de l'École Nationale Supérieure des Beaux-arts [Library of the National Higher School of Fine Arts], Paris (Ms. 497)

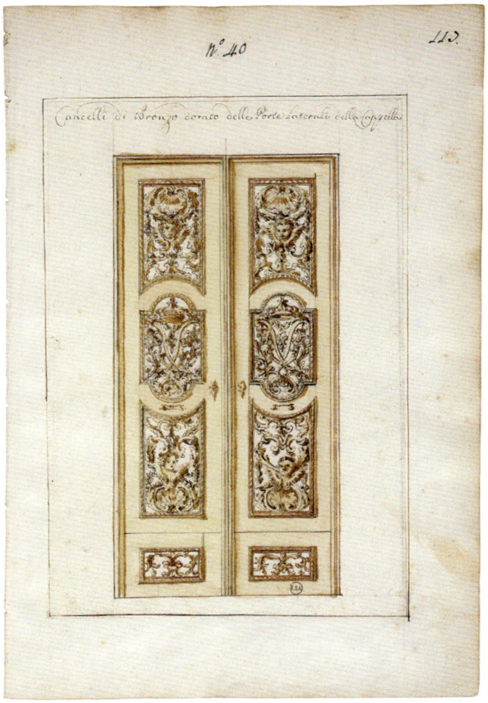

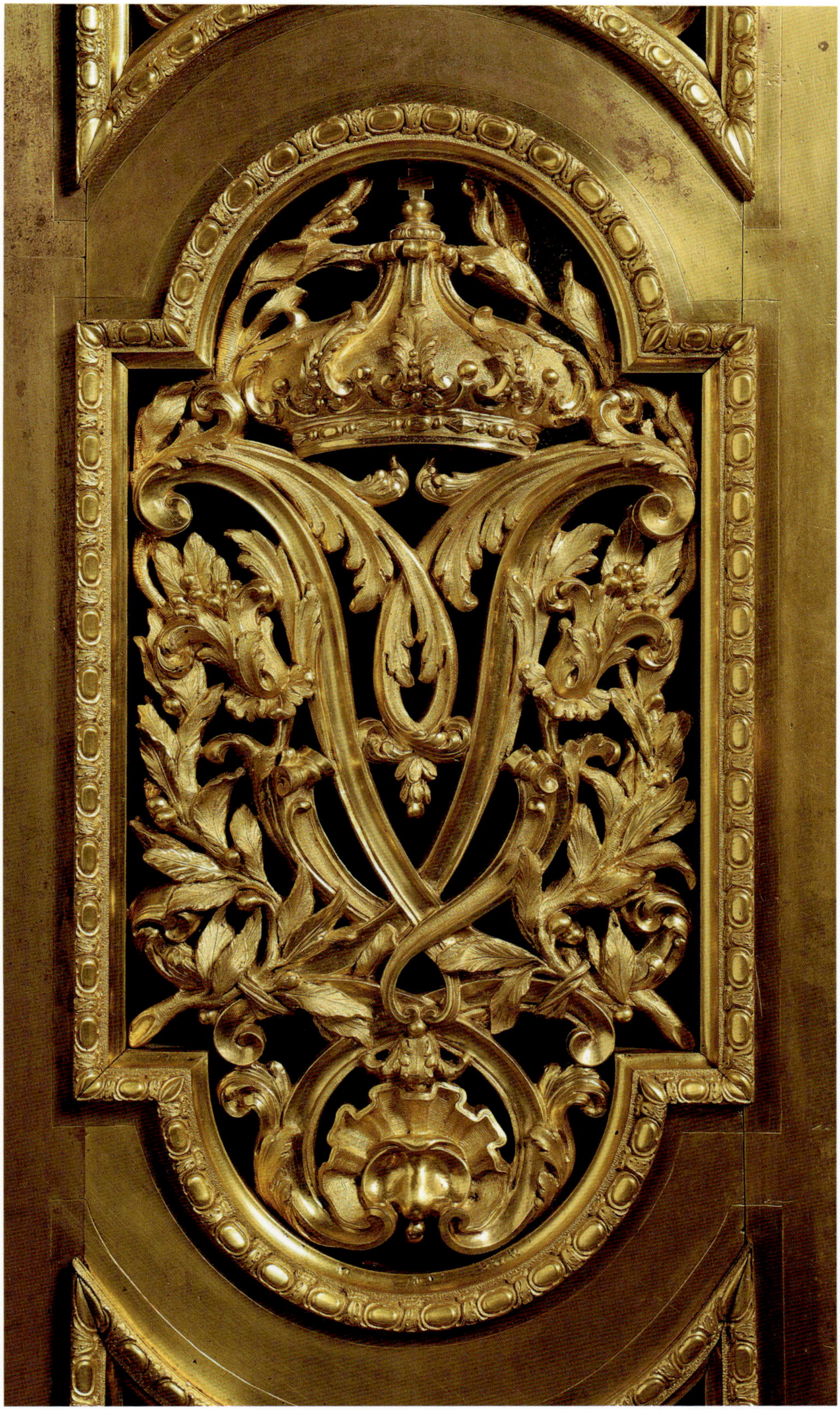

Fig. 47
Panel of side door
(central part)
Silvestro Doria
Gilded metal

The gleam of the gold that covers these metallic elements lends luminosity to the bases, shafts and capitals of columns and pilasters; it gives greater importance to friezes, archivolts and arches; and it is used on a panoply of ornamental details to enliven the intercolumns and other spaces that break up the expanse of the walls (figs 48–50).

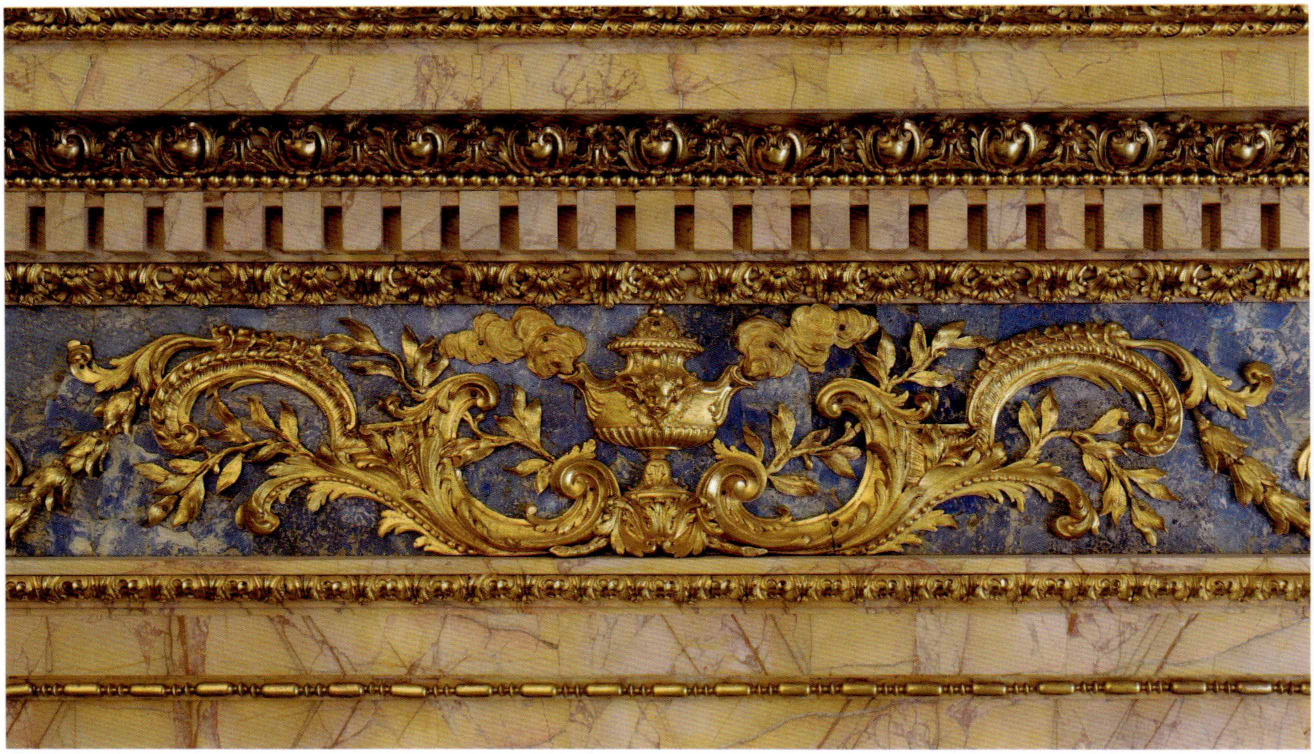

Fig. 48
Decorations of the frieze on the architrave
Francesco Rosa
Gilded metal

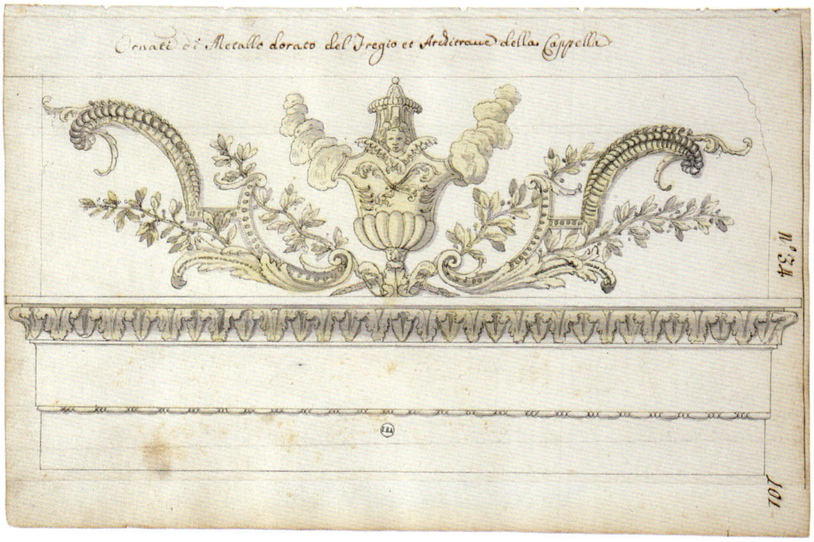

Fig. 49
Metal decorations for the frieze on the architrave, intended to be executed by Francesco Rosa
Drawing no. 34 of the *Weale Album*, f. 101
Bibliothèque de l'École Nationale Supérieure des Beaux-arts [Library of the National Higher School of Fine Arts], Paris (Ms. 497)

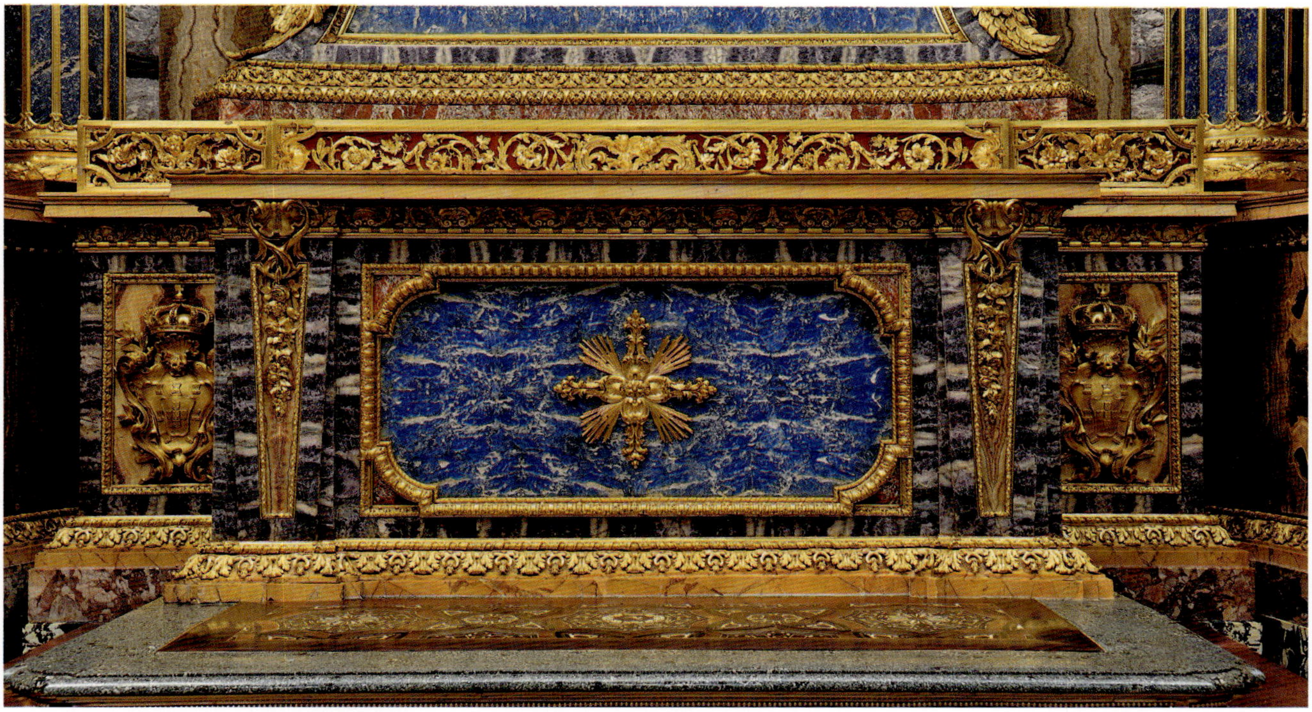

Fig. 50
Decoration of the altar table (frontal)
Antonio Arrighi
Gilded metal

A number of individuals from several professions related to metalworking all contributed to the making of the ornamental elements in metal for the Chapel of St John the Baptist. There were metalworkers, smelters and casters, as one might expect, but there were also silversmiths and even locksmiths and blacksmiths. This situation becomes more understandable if we consider how official works were organised with regard to metalworking in Rome in the first half of the eighteenth century, the context in which these pieces were made.

Indeed, it is often possible to identify workshops that were capable of providing a multidisciplinary set of solutions in the metal arts to an increasingly educated and demanding clientèle, and within a single workshop there would be individuals (often linked by family ties) with different skills and working in different areas of specialisation.[1] There would usually be one or more silversmiths, at least one of whom would have held a patent (i.e. official guild authorisation), and there would also have been other labourers and apprentices who worked under the guidance and supervision of the master. However, these silversmithing workshops usually also had a foundry area, necessary for creating the components of items in silver or gold, and it was by way of this area that a silversmith's workshop often expanded into working in non-precious metals as well; some other member of the family, who did not hold a silversmith's patent, would devote themselves to metalworking. It is also possible to identify another area within these workshops corresponding to another highly sought-after specialisation – and not only in the context of metalwork – which is gilding. These workshops, hives of industry, which flourished in Rome in the first half of the eighteenth century (though dating back to earlier times) thus

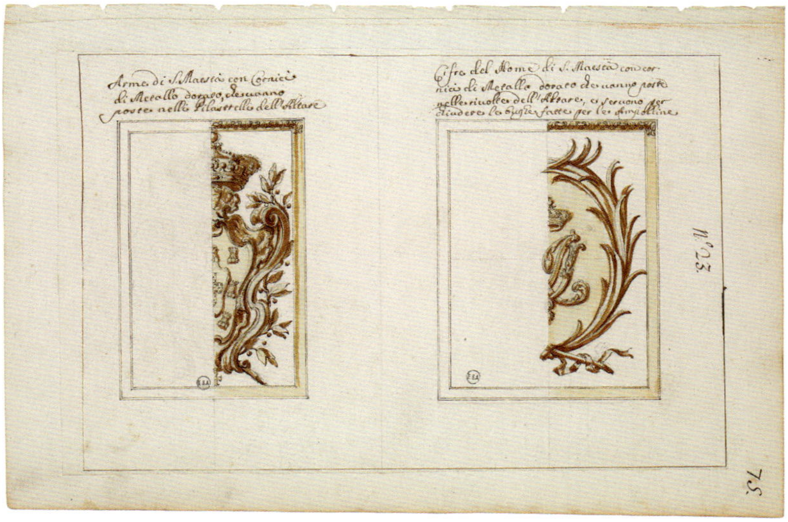

Fig. 51
Decoration for the altar table (lateral panels) intended to be executed by Antonio Arrighi
Drawing no. 23 of the *Weale Album*, f. 75
Bibliothèque de l'École Nationale Supérieure des Beaux-arts [Library of the National Higher School of Fine Arts], Paris (Ms. 497)

Fig. 52 (below)
Metal decorations (lateral panel of the altar)
Antonio Arrighi
Gilded metal

Fig. 53 (opposite)
Detail of panel showing the Portuguese coat of arms
Antonio Arrighi
Gilded metal

housed a range of specialised professionals who appeared to differ widely in their practice – silversmiths, metalworkers and brassworkers[2] – but often came together around a single piece and collaborated in order to ensure its proper execution.

It is not surprising, then, that we can see the labour of many hands in the metal elements of the works created for the Chapel of St John the Baptist – metalworkers, smelters and casters, brassworkers, silversmiths and also locksmiths and blacksmiths. Those experts in the art of working non-precious metals – whom we will designate by the inclusive term of metalworkers for convenience's sake – include Francesco Annibaldi, Silvestro Doria, Giovanni Paolo Kaiser, Pietro Mascelli, Angelo and Giuseppe Ricciani, Francesco Rosa and Agostino Valle. There were also five silversmiths involved in the work on non-precious metals: Antonio Arrighi, Francesco Giardoni, Francesco Guerrini and the brothers Francesco and Gaetano Smiti (figs 51–56).

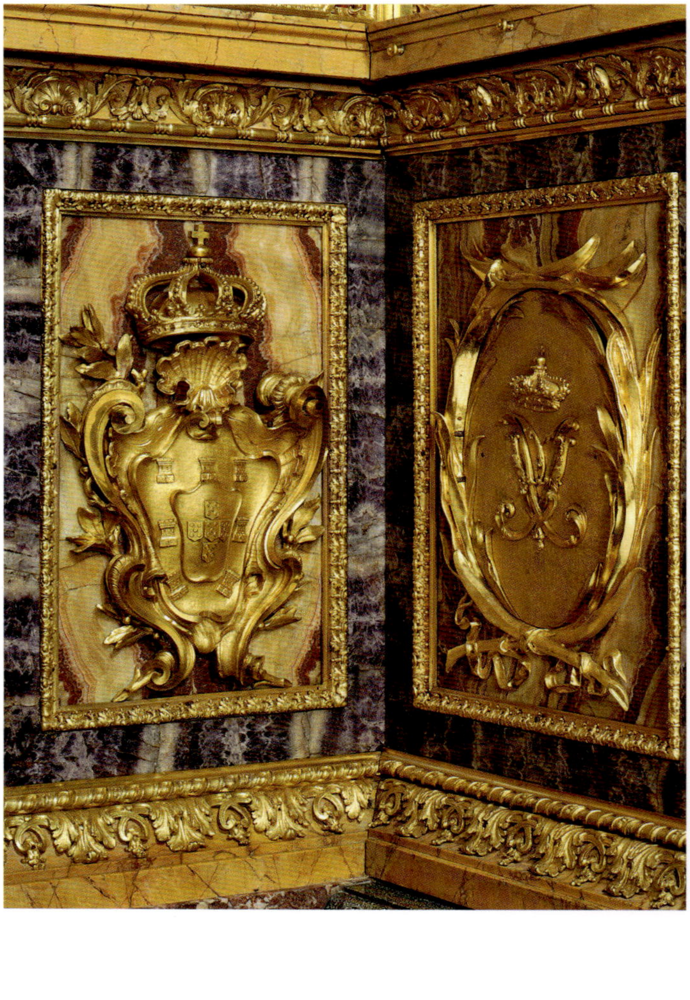

These metalworkers were mentioned from the first by Sousa Viterbo and Vicente d'Almeida,[3] although with a certain degree of imprecision inasmuch as these authors identified their activities with less accuracy. This is the case for Giovanni Paolo Kaiser and Giuseppe Ricciani, who were referred to as brassworkers but were in fact metalworkers, who fashioned works for the chapel on a par with those of the other professionals whom the authors identify as metalworkers.

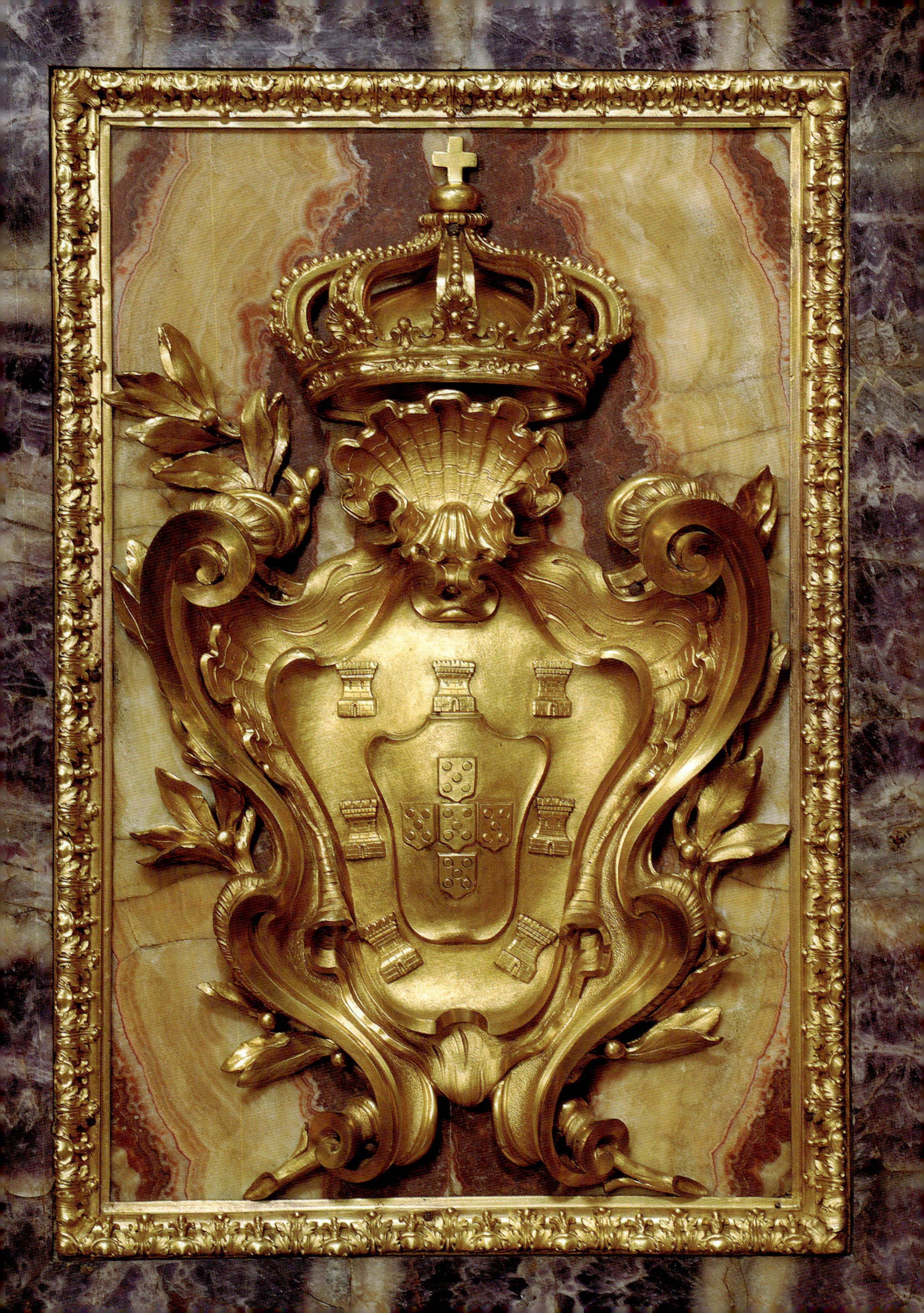

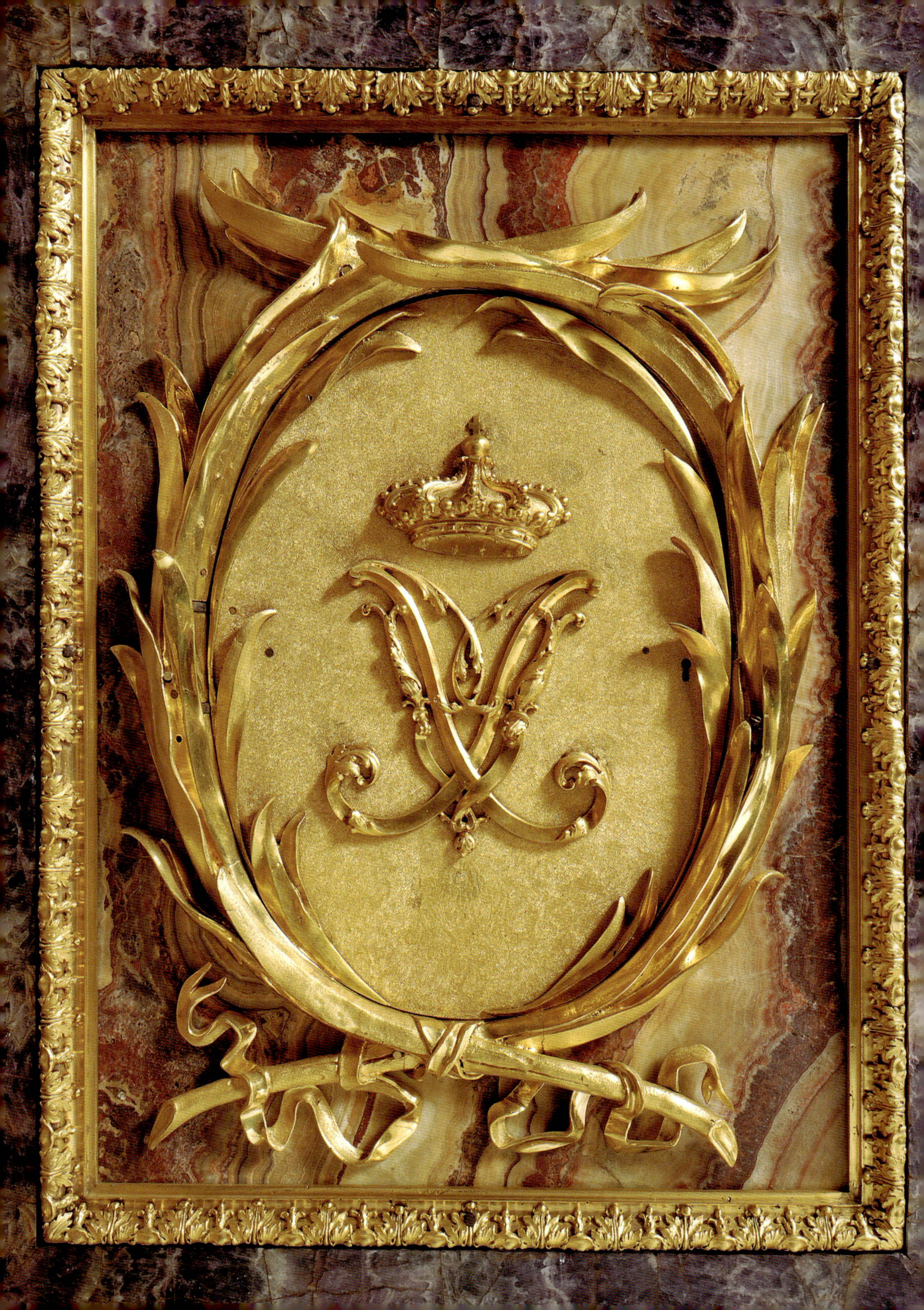

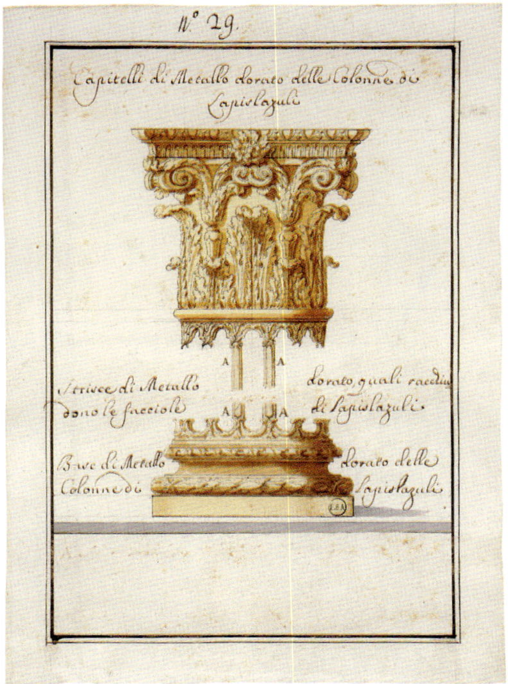

The information available about these individuals actively working on the chapel is generally scarce. While they were highly qualified professionals with significant technical expertise, though not artists, these individuals were not considered as deserving of any great scholarly attention, and as a result such information as can be found comes mainly from primary sources. In addition to the documentation that provides evidence of their involvement in the form of the corresponding payments, which are recorded in the account books of the Portuguese embassy in Rome, there is another type of document that offers a further possible avenue in some cases – namely the registers of the various parishes of Rome in the first half of the seventeenth century (which were drawn up every twenty-fifth or 'jubilee' year: in 1700, 1725 and 1750). These were the so-called *Stati delle Anime* (records of souls) in which the various members of family groups were registered together with their ages and professions, and which constitute a precious source of information about the population of Rome at the time (figs 57 and 58).

Fig. 54 (opposite)
Detail of panel showing the letters J and V
Antonio Arrighi
Gilded metal

Fig. 55 (above)
Capitals and bases for columns intended to be executed by Francesco Giardoni
Drawing no. 29 of the *Weale Album*, f. 89
Bibliothèque de l'École Nationale Supérieure des Beaux-arts [Library of the National Higher School of Fine Arts], Paris (Ms. 497)

Fig. 56 (right)
Capital
Francesco Giardoni
Gilded metal

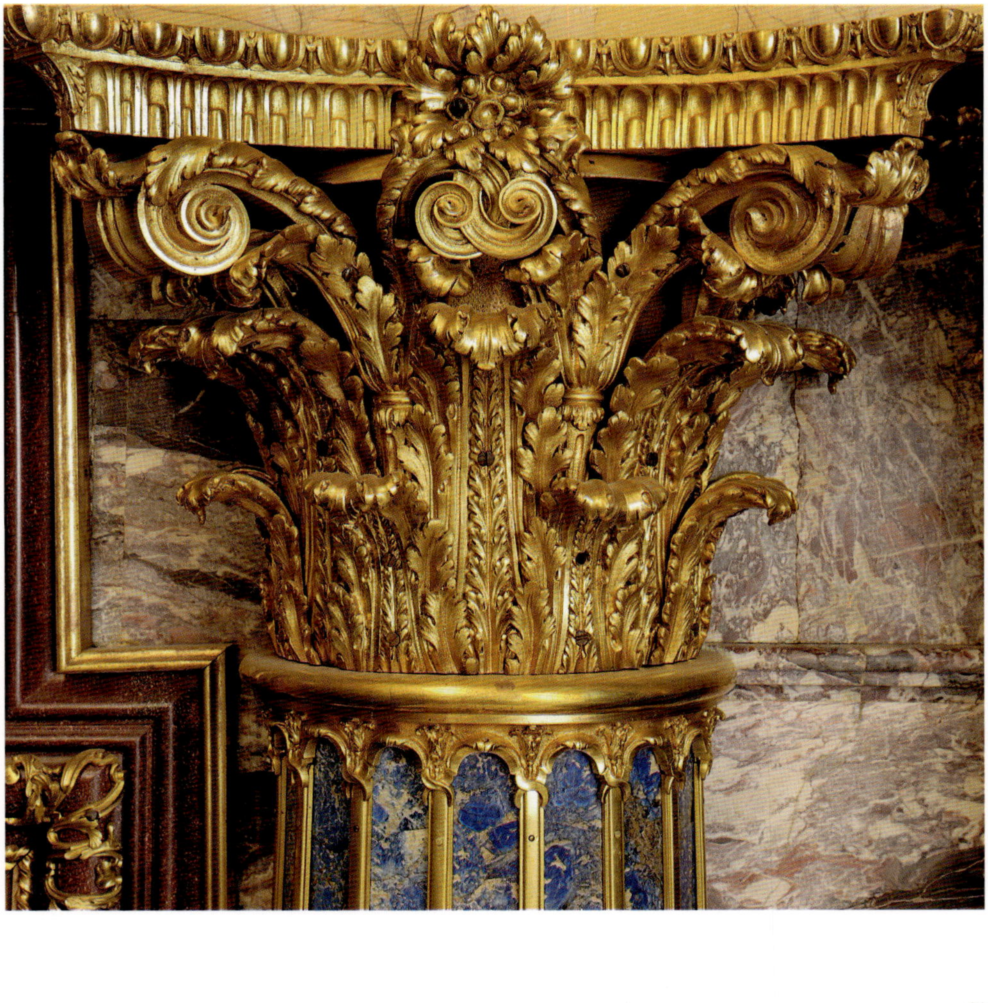

As mentioned above, it is clear that various silversmiths also played a significant part in the work in ordinary metal for the Chapel of St John the Baptist, and some of them were also entrusted with the specific gold and silver works commissioned for it. There are five silversmiths who can be identified in this context: Antonio Arrighi (1687–1776), Francesco Giardoni (1692–1757), Francesco Guerrini (1709–72?) and the brothers Gaetano (1711–55) and Francesco Smiti (1702–70). With regard to Francesco and Gaetano Smiti, it is worth mentioning that they have a number of different links to Portugal. First of all, their father – also a silversmith and originally

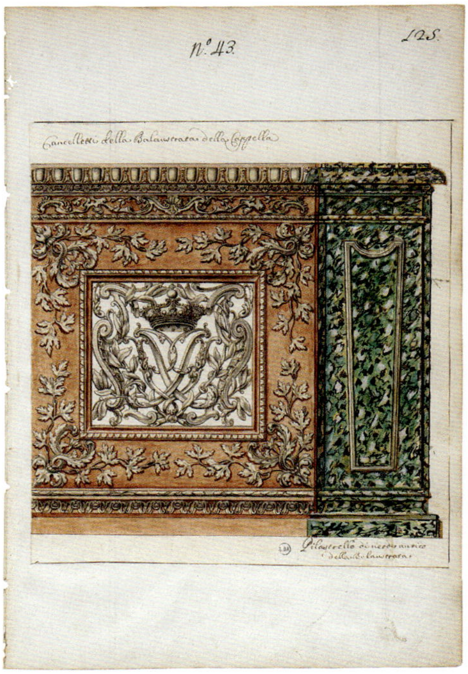

Fig. 57
Grilles of the balustrade
intended to be executed
by Francesco Guerrini
Drawing no. 43 of the
Weale Album, f. 125
Bibliothèque de l'École
Nationale Supérieure des
Beaux-arts [Library of the
National Higher School of
Fine Arts], Paris (Ms. 497)

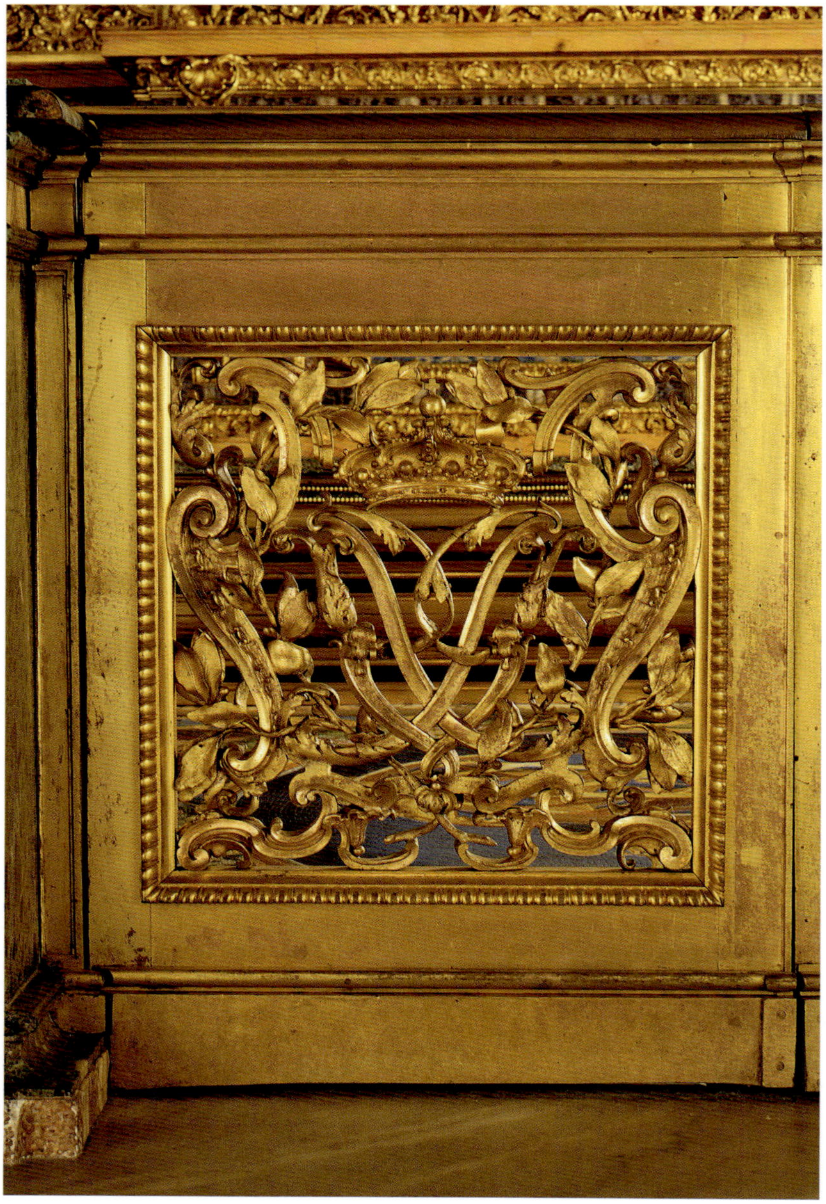

Fig. 58
Grille with royal monogram
(detail)
Francesco Guerrini
Gilded metal

from Antwerp – is known to have been in Portugal, where he arrived in 1700 from Rome, accompanying the German silversmith and founder Johann Friedrich Ludwig, then in the service of the Society of Jesus (Ludwig later became King John V's architect – the famous 'Frederico' who had his name changed to the Portuguese form of Ludovice). It is possible that their father's visit to Portugal played a part in the choice of the crest for their family's workshop, located on the via del Pellegrino, which is referred to as *insegna del'Arma del Portogallo*, the 'sign of the Arms of Portugal'.[4]

Both brothers worked as silversmiths, and it will have been in this capacity that both created gold and silver works for the chapel's collection; it is difficult to distinguish what each one did individually, given that they worked in the same workshop and made use of the same trademark, even though the payments are preferentially recorded in the name of Francesco.

This extremely brief journey through the ornamental elements fashioned in metal shows the very considerable extent to which these many and varied professionals in the metalworking arts, who realised the work in concrete form, contributed decisively to the total work of art that is the Chapel of St John the Baptist. Indeed, the presence of these metal elements, in harmonious dialogue with the polychromy of the marbles, not only contributes to but in some ways highlights the expression of opulence constituted by the ensemble of the chapel. ■

NOTES

[1] With regard to the organisation of the silversmithing (and metalworking) workshops in the eighteenth century, in Italy in general and in Rome in particular, the available bibliography is scarce. The following texts may be referred to: AAVV, *Le Botteghe degli Argentieri Lucchesi del XVIII Secolo* (exhibition catalogue, Museo Nazionale di Palazzo Mansi, Lucca, Jul.–Oct. 1981), Florence, Studio per Edizione Scelte, 1981, pp. 27–36; Franco FARANDA, *Argentieri e Argenteria Sacra in Romagna dal Medioevo al XVIII Secolo*, Rimini, Luisè Editore, 1990, pp. 19–33; Jennifer MONTAGU, 'The practice of Roman baroque silver sculpture', in *Silver Society Journal*, no. 12, Autumn 2000, pp. 18–25; Gabriele BARUCCA and Jennifer MONTAGU (dir.), *Ori e Argenti. Capolavori del '700 da Arrighi a Valadier*, Milan, Skira Editore, 2007, pp. 13–21 (ch. 'La bottega degli Arrighi').

[2] In the original Italian terms (as they appear in the payment books of the Portuguese embassy in Rome, which are preserved in the Biblioteca da Ajuda): *argentiere*, *metallaro*, *ottonaro*, respectively.

[3] Francisco Marques de Sousa VITERBO and R. Vicente d'ALMEIDA, *A Capella de S. João Baptista Erecta na Egreja de S. Roque. Fundação da Companhia de Jesus e Hoje Pertencente à Santa Casa da Misericordia. Noticia Historica e Descriptiva*, Lisbon, Livros Horizonte, 1997, pp. 88–89 (1st edition 1900).

[4] Elisa DEBENEDETTI, (ed.), *Artisti e Artigiani a Roma I, Degli Stati delle Anime del 1700, 1725, 1750, 1775*, (Studi Sul Settecento Romano, 20), Rome, Bonsignori, 2004, p. 384.

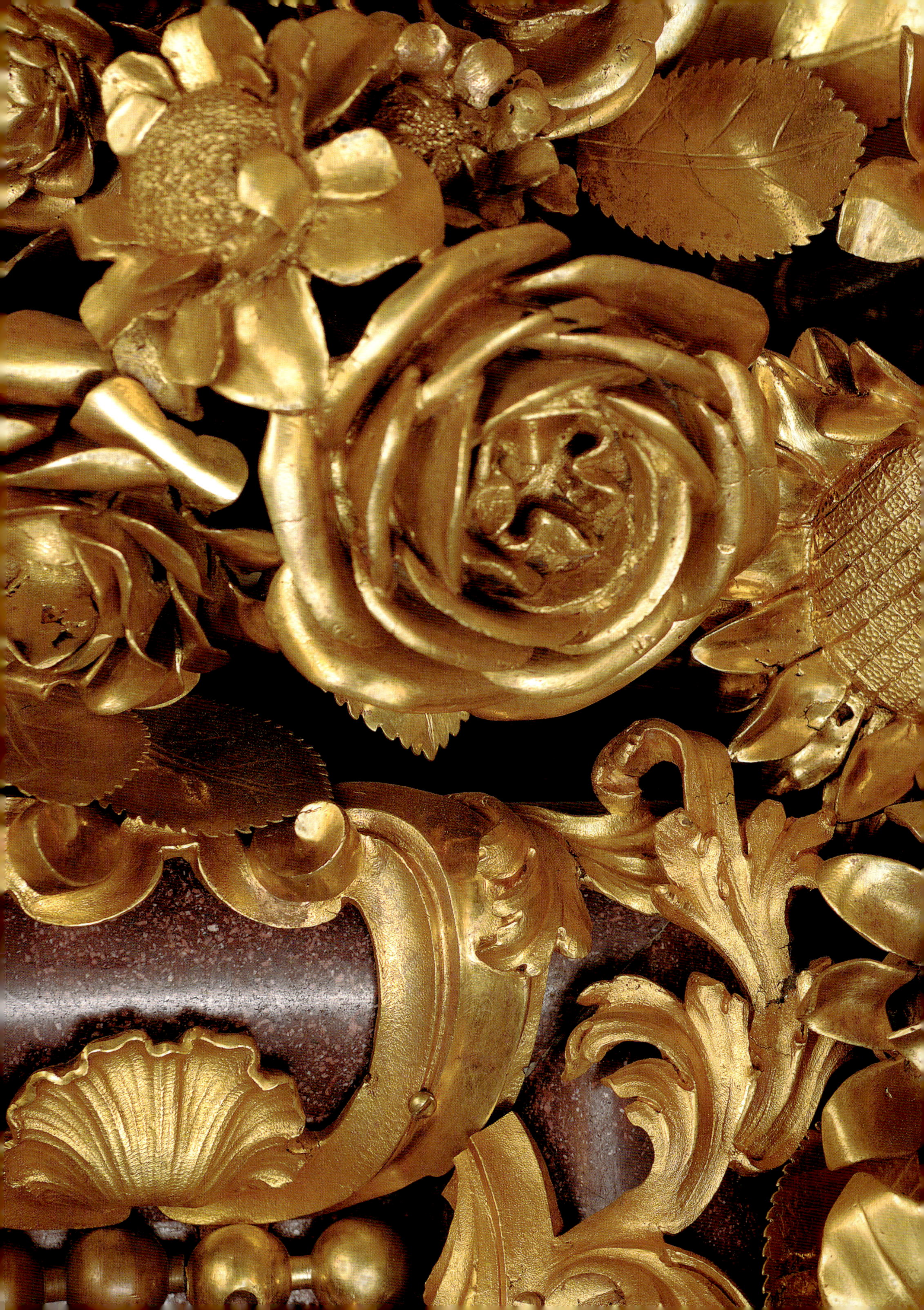

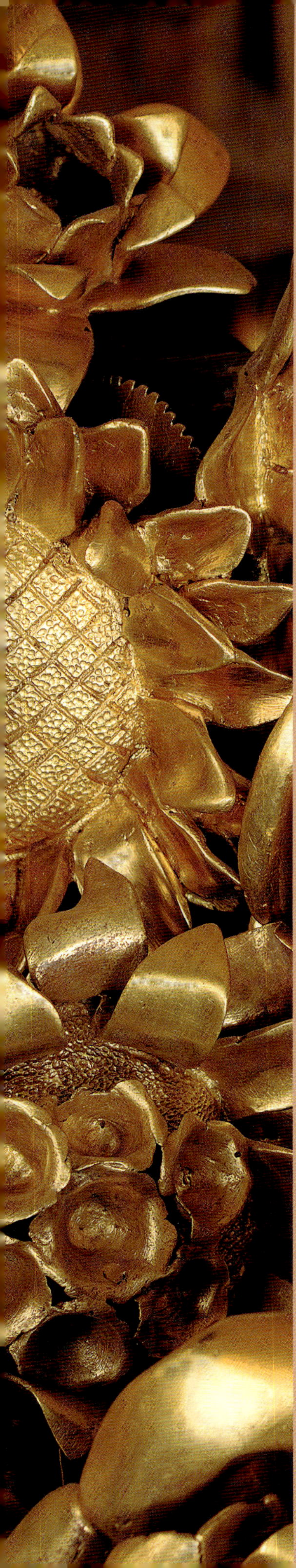

PART III

THE COLLECTIONS

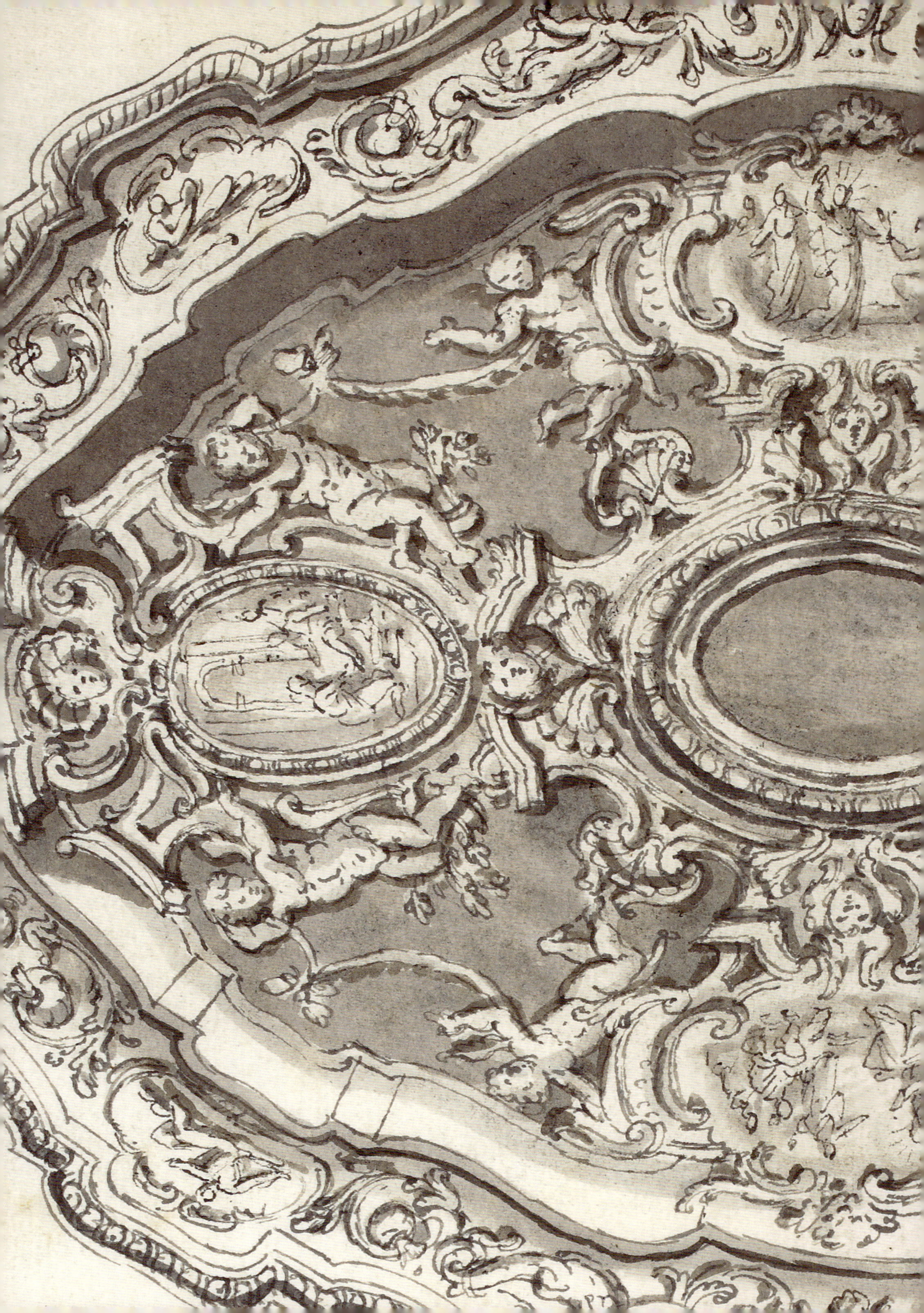

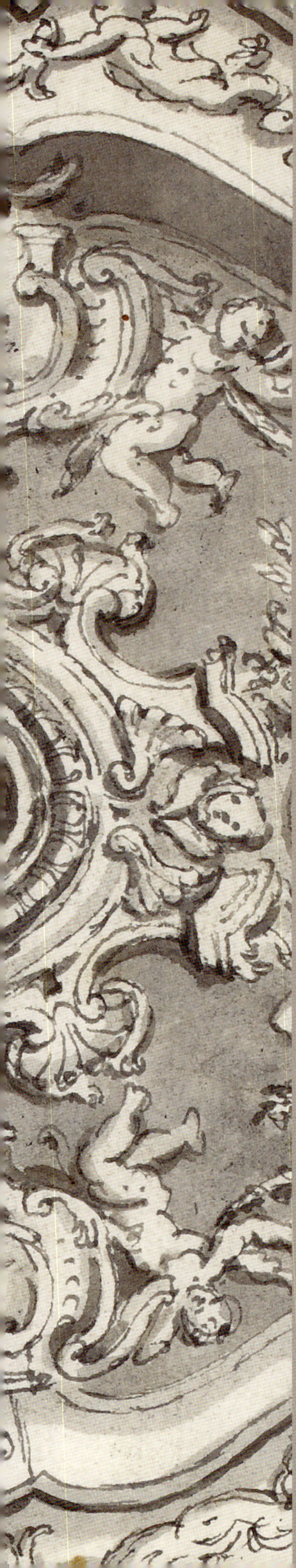

1. SILVER

The unique character of the silver collection of the Chapel of St John the Baptist

Teresa Leonor M. Vale

The exceptional silver collection of the Chapel of St John the Baptist

In a text published by an Italian author in the mid-1960s, it is argued that the collection of items in gold and silver belonging to the Chapel of St John the Baptist in the Church of São Roque was created as a coherent artistic ensemble 'di valore incalcolabile sia per ricchezza di materia che di perfezione di stile e di tecnica' (of incalculable value both for the richness of the materials and for the perfection of style and technique).[1] The author goes on to add that 'Nemenno in Italia, nè in Roma stessa – per strano che possa sembrare – si trova un complesso di oreficeria che raggiunga tale perfetta, armonica fusione di elementi artistici.' (Nowhere in Italy, not even in Rome itself – strange as it may seem – is there to be found a collection of silversmithing that achieves such a perfect, harmonious fusion of artistic elements.'[2] And in fact the collection of works in Italian baroque gold and silver that comprises the treasure of the Chapel of St John the Baptist does indeed prove to be unique. Any comparisons with contemporary works and/or works by the same artists – which would be vital to any comprehensive study and evaluation – can only be carried out on an individual basis. Of course there are contemporary works by the same artists, of exactly the same type and having obvious affinities in terms of morphology and decoration, to be found in Italy and Rome in particular; however, there is no other collection that is truly analogous, from the moment of its conception and design to its realisation in concrete form, which can serve as a point of comparison.

The nearest instance to this one – although in this case it is not truly a set (that is, conceived as such from the start), but rather a collection of pieces that are chronologically very close and which are even in part by some of the same artists who executed the collection of the Chapel of St John the Baptist – is that of the gold and silver works given by Pope Benedict XIV (Lambertini) to the Cathedral of San Pietro in his native city of Bologna.[3] In San Pietro's treasury there are indeed some pieces clearly related to those made in Rome for the Chapel of St John the Baptist; in fact it is even the case that a censer and an incense boat in this collection made by the silversmith Antonio Gigli were actually made for the Lisbon chapel but were later – by order of John V, put into effect by Ambassador Manuel Pereira Sampaio – given to the pope, who then in turn gave them to the cathedral in Bologna.[4]

pp. 94–95
Decoration of the altar (detail)
Antonio Arrighi
Gilded metal

pp. 96–97
Ewer and basin set (detail)
in gilded silver to be executed by the silversmith Vincenzo Belli
(See fig. 71)

We thus find ourselves faced with an exceptional set of pieces – perhaps the most important in both national and international terms of any in existence when taken as a whole, since the exceptionally rich contents of the Patriarchal Basilica of Lisbon were destroyed – of which we will seek to give the most comprehensive account that analysis of the works themselves and the available documentation will permit.

The commission

The process of commissioning the set of works in gold and silver that formed part of the vaster commissioning process of the entire Chapel of St John the Baptist was set in motion by one specific document, sent from Lisbon on 9 March 1744 and entitled 'Relação das pessas de Ouro, e prata, etc[a], que se mandam vir de Roma para Serviço da nobilissima Capella do Espirito Santo e S. João Baptista da Igreja de S. Roque, e cazo de não virem antes que a Capella, a devem acompanhar' (Account of the pieces in gold, and silver, etc., that are sent for, to come from Rome for the service of the most noble Chapel of the Holy Spirit and St John the Baptist in the Church of São Roque; and if they should not come before the chapel, they must accompany it).[5] This minutely detailed document mentions almost all the works that were in fact later to be produced, namely: the altar-ledge set referred to as the *muta nobile* or 'noble set' (six candlesticks together with their respective cross), the two credence table candlesticks, the pair of monumental candlesticks, three silver lamps, thirty candlesticks, eight reliquaries, a processional monstrance (in gold), a chalice and a pyx (also in gold), two purification vessels (one in white silver and one in gilded silver), a pair of cruets together with their respective lavabo dish (in gilded silver), a finger bowl, a thurible and an incense boat (with its spoon), another pair of cruets (in white silver), a sanctus bell, a box for wafers, a processional cross, four lanterns, six canopy poles and an altar frontal.[6] It was moreover recommended in this text that 'Todas as peças que contem esta encomenda … sejão obradas na ultima perfeição, e com a maior brevidade, e que todas venhão em caxas próprias e capazes de estarem nelas guardadas o tempo que não servirem' (All the pieces that are contained in this commission … are to be wrought to the highest perfection, and as soon as possible, and let all of them come in their own boxes and be able to be kept in them for the time they are not in use).[7] This document by no means concluded the commission, however, as on the following 21 May an advisory notice was sent from Lisbon concerning the March order, with particular instructions regarding the monstrance – more specifically, stipulating that the monstrance had to have a plinth that raised it higher when it was used to display the consecrated host but would not be excessively heavy when the same monstrance was carried in procession.[8]

With regard to this initial stage of the commissioning process, there are a number of noteworthy absences – that is to say, there are pieces that do not appear in either of these two documents dated March and May 1744 but on which work nevertheless began right away, as other documentation dated shortly afterwards shows, and which were executed at roughly the same pace as the pieces specifically mentioned in the commission.

This is the case for the altar cards – three in silver and three in bronze – made by the silversmith Antonio Vendetti. Although the two sets of altar cards were not mentioned in the two letters of March and May 1744, the fact is that as early as December 1745[9] Antonio Vendetti received a first payment for them – just as in the case of other silversmiths involved in executing the pieces that were listed in the order of 1744. Hence it may be plausibly assumed that the altar cards were commissioned at some time shortly after the dates of the two above-mentioned letters.

The execution of the pieces can later be traced in the correspondence exchanged between Lisbon and Rome, which is backed up by the (regular) payments duly recorded in the account books of the Portuguese embassy in Rome (of which the corresponding copies were made in order to send them to Portugal).

Fig. 59
Frontal of the altar
to be executed by the silversmith Antonio Arrighi
Drawing no. 55 of the *Weale Album*, f. 169
Bibliothèque de l'École Nationale Supérieure des Beaux-arts [Library of the National Higher School of Fine Arts], Paris (Ms. 497)

Depiction of the pieces

As we mentioned earlier with regard to the sculptural elements of the Chapel of St John the Baptist, so too are the pieces comprising the collection of gold and silver for the royal chapel represented in the set of drawings known as the Weale Album,[10] whose history is referred to above (figs 59–61).

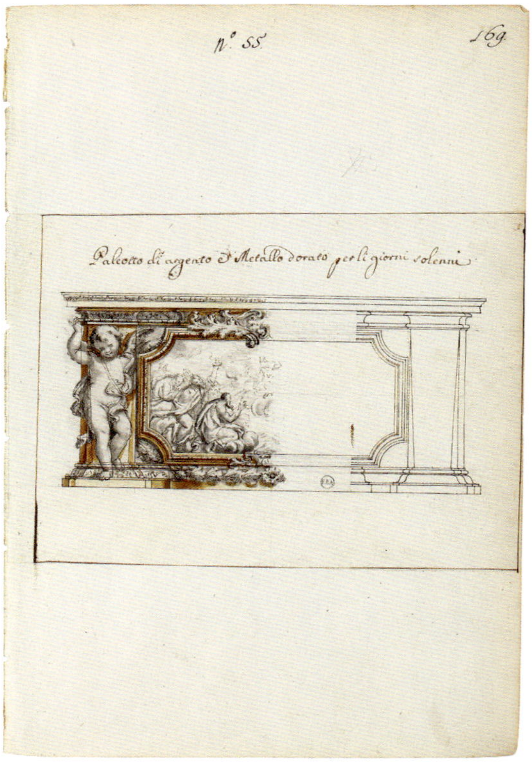

This is the most important source regarding the iconography of the gold and silver collection of the royal chapel in the Church of São Roque, and the only one that enables us to examine the pieces that have since been lost. In fact, it is only in the Weale Album drawings that we can see, for example, the 30 candlesticks produced for the ceremony of displaying the Blessed Sacrament, all of which have been lost to the vicissitudes of time and history, or the sole monstrance of the collection (made by the silversmith Tommaso Politi) or various other pieces executed in gold – such as a chalice and a pyx, by the silversmiths Lorenzo de Caporali and Francesco Princivale respectively. These drawings are therefore of the greatest importance – hence their reproduction here.

The presentation of the works in Rome

A final point worthy of mention in this section devoted to the collection of gold and silver – before proceeding to a systematic analysis of the works themselves – is the matter of their

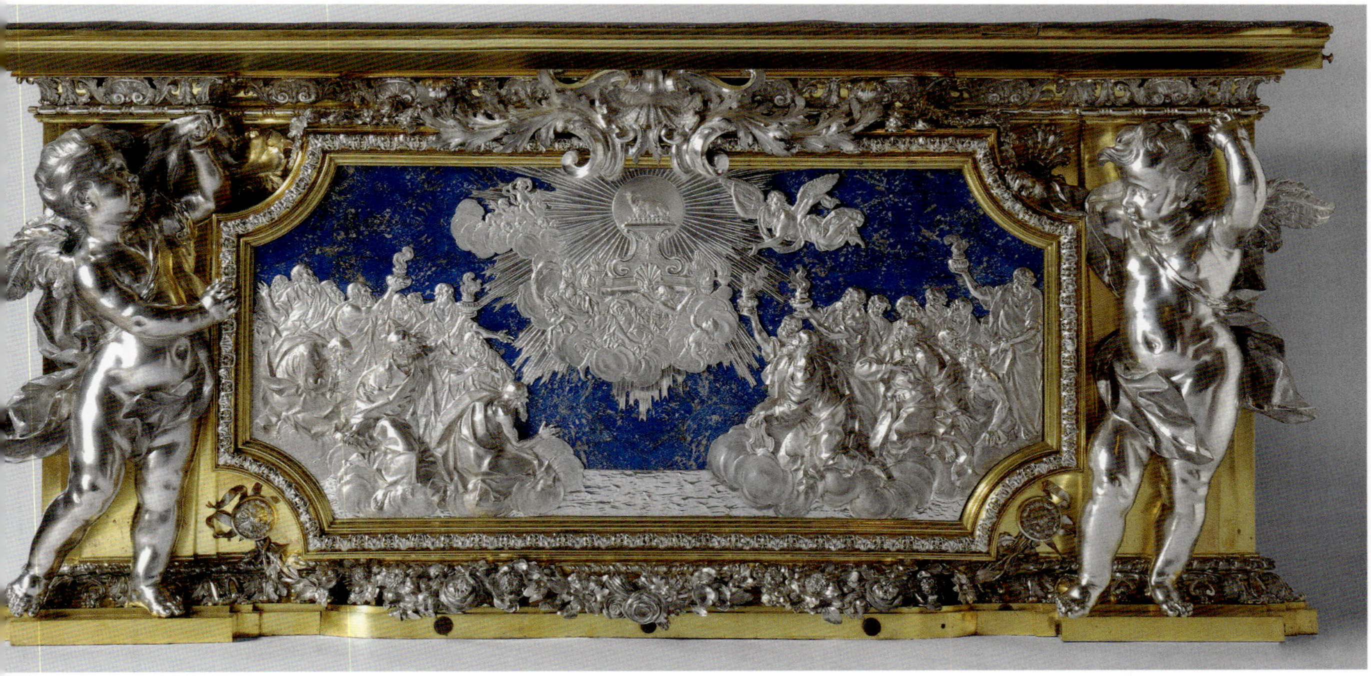

Fig. 60
Frontal of the altar depicting a scene from the *Apocalypse*
Antonio Arrighi
Rome, 1749–50
Silver and lapis lazuli
(inv. MPr. 10)

Fig. 61 (overleaf)
Frontal of the altar (detail)

presentation in Rome, before they were sent to Portugal. This action of the Portuguese ambassador, Manuel Pereira de Sampaio, was in fact perfectly in keeping with the Roman spirit but also with what we might call strategic image-building today; he was very well aware of how much it would help to disseminate the idea of the king of Portugal's wealth – and by implication his power – to display some of these remarkable pieces to the eyes of the Roman aristocracy, always admirers of beautiful things.[11] In April 1747, therefore, the ambassador proceeded to take a temporary lease on some rooms in the palace that then belonged to the Marquises Capponi, and commissioned a sumptuous décor for these interiors, the execution of which was entrusted to the *festarolo* or organiser of festivities Francesco Feliziani. The bookkeeping entry for the payments made to Feliziani can be found in the Biblioteca da Ajuda ('Assistance' Library).[13] Reading these manuscripts, which are made up of lists of tasks carried out and expenses incurred (such as the rental of the textiles used), enables us to grasp the sheer scale of the undertaking involved in building a setting and staging the display of the most remarkable and precious works of art intended for the Chapel of St John the Baptist (and also for the Patriarchal Basilica). We learn, for example, that on 23 April 1747 several rooms of the palace formerly belonging to the Marquises Capponi were decorated and some of the elements of the construction work and also individual pieces intended for the Chapel of St John the Baptist were arranged there. For this purpose, a tent was set up inside the space, beneath whose draperies various exhibits were displayed, ranging from the vaulted ceiling (or part of it) to a painting (undoubtedly one of Agostino Masucci's, which served as the basis for the mosaic compositions for the altar and the side walls) and including pilasters and so on.

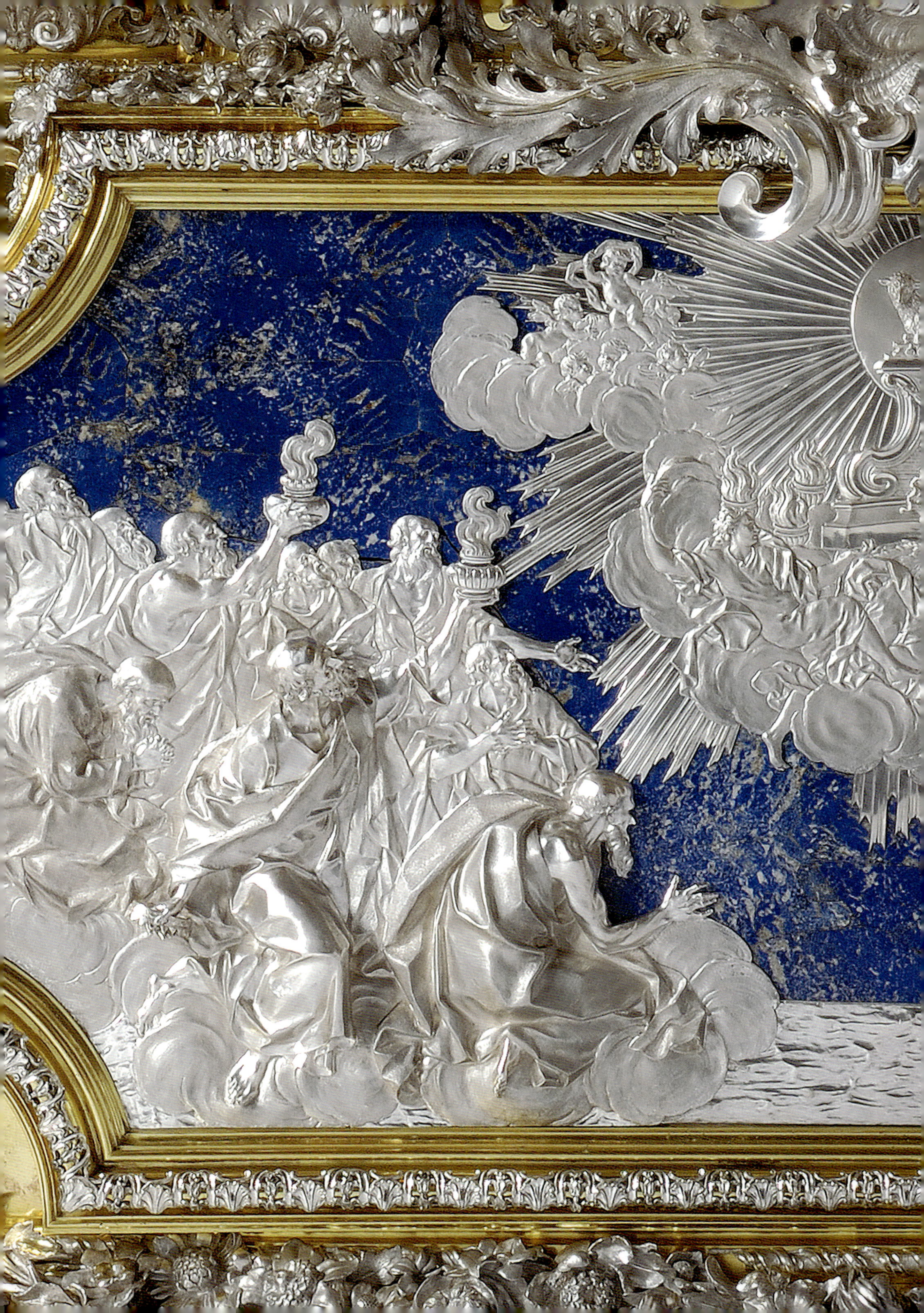

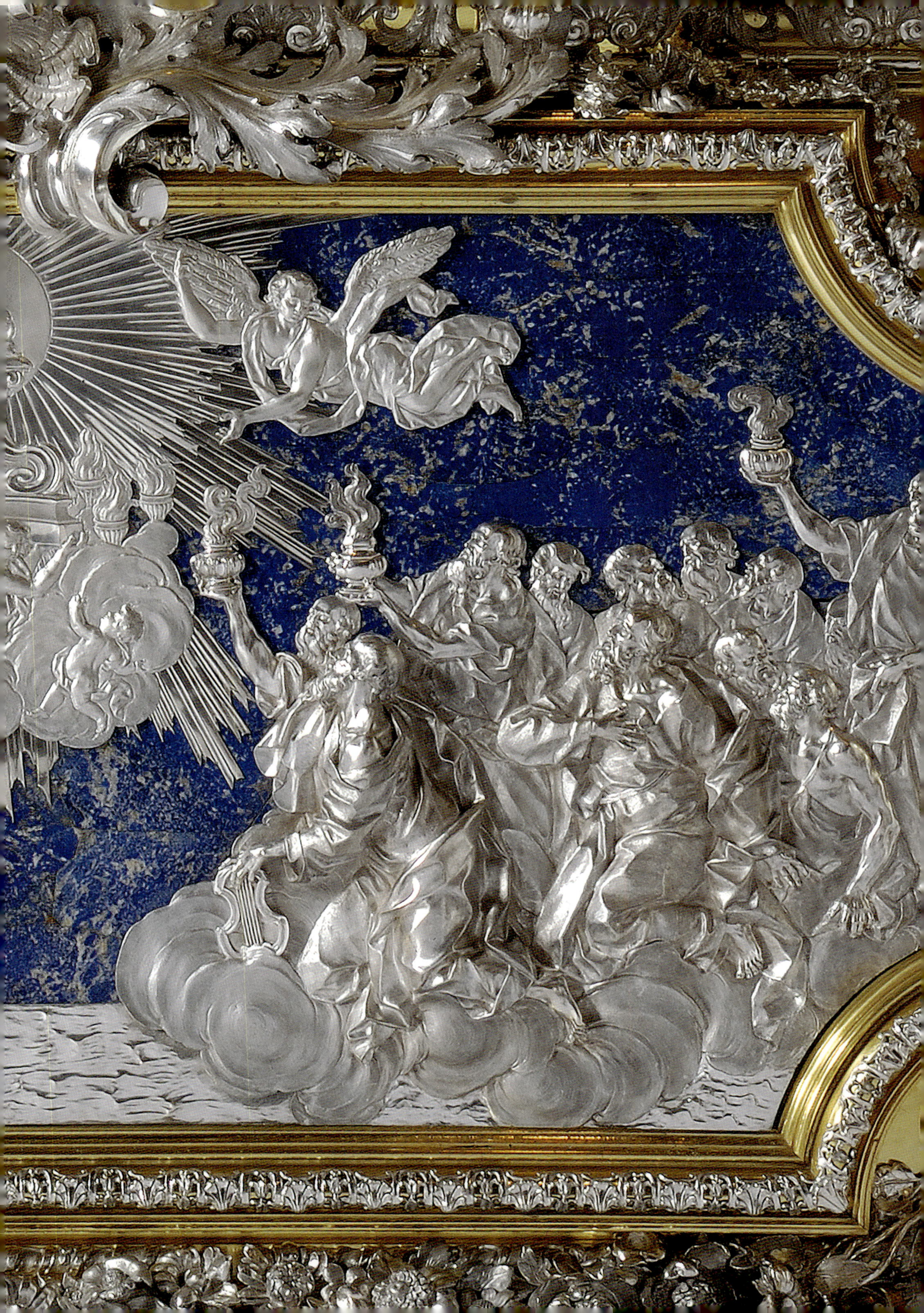

The Roman newspaper *Diario Ordinario del Chracas* could not fail to record this event and the edition of 29 April 1747 devoted well over five pages to it, praising the pieces and mentioning some of the artists responsible for their creation.[14]

Another exhibition of artworks intended for Lisbon took place on 10 September 1749, this time at the residence of the ambassador, the aforementioned palace on the Piazza della Pilotta. On this occasion a canopy was set up in order to properly display a life-size gilded silver statue of Our Lady of the Conception which was intended for the Patriarchal Basilica. It was transported from the Gagliardi workshop to the ambassador's palace, where the exhibition also included an entire altar-ledge set and other candlesticks arranged on a table under the canopy already present in the *stanza di Vdienza* or Audience Room,[15] and the tabernacle made by Antonio Arrighi for the Chapel of St John the Baptist. To mark the occasion, there was a *rinfresco dentro la stanza alla Cinese* – refreshments were served in the 'Chinese room' at the palace.[16]

The immense investment in these displays of pomp and ceremony, admirably orchestrated by Manuel Pereira Sampaio, was intended to show the Roman aristocracy and in particular the pope and papal court (with whom he associated) the power, artistic refinement and taste of the Portuguese Crown and of the king in particular.

Authorship: the silversmiths and sculptors involved in the execution of the works

In following the detailed directives from Lisbon, the role of Portuguese Ambassador Manuel Pereira Sampaio began in Rome with the by-no-means easy task of recruiting silversmiths – who had to be both available and sufficiently experienced – to fashion such a significant number of pieces. The ambassador naturally resorted to the services of the aforementioned Antonio Arrighi, a silversmith who had worked for the Portuguese Crown since at least the 1720s. Arrighi was joined by many other silversmiths, some already highly regarded and of established prestige in Roman circles – such as Angelo Spinazzi and Vicenzo Belli – and others less notable or well known, such as Antonio Gigli, Carlo Guarnieri, Tommaso Politi and Francesco Antonio Salci, among others.

One aspect that has been barely touched upon in relation to the gold and silver collection of the Chapel of St John the Baptist is that of the sculptors involved in its execution. It was in fact very common in Rome in the eighteenth century (as it also was in Naples, for example) for sculptors to make the designs and models for works to be executed by silversmiths.

Examining the silver collection of the royal chapel in the Church of São Roque reveals the involvement of at least four sculptors: the Italians Agostino Corsini (1688–1772), Bernardino Ludovisi (1694–1749) and Giovanni Battista Maini (1690–1752), and the Flemish sculptor active in Rome Peter Anton von Verschaffelt (*c.* 1710–93). The first of these executed the model for the relief on the frontal for the *muta nobile* (the altar cross and candlesticks set) later executed by Antonio Arrighi, while the second was responsible for the models of the angels that flank this same frontal. The third executed the model of the Crucified Christ for the altar-ledge cross of the *muta nobile* and took part in designing the monumental candlesticks; the last is traditionally considered to have been the author of the design for the chandelier and the three lamps intended for daily use in the chapel. It should be noted that all these artists also executed sculptures for the chapel (with the exception of Maini, who had however worked for Mafra in the previous decade).

The collection

The gold and silver collection of the Chapel of St John the Baptist, as it exists today, consists of the following pieces:

Altar frontal depicting a scene from the *Apocalypse*, Antonio Arrighi (1687–1776)
Pair of monumental candlesticks, Giuseppe Gagliardi (1697–1749) and Leandro Gagliardi (1729–1804) (figs 62 and 63)
Four reliquaries (with the relics of St Valentine and St Prosper, and of the martyred St Felix and St Urban), Carlo Guarnieri (1710–74?) (figs 64–66)
Altar cards (two sets of three altar cards, one in white and gilded silver and the other in gilded bronze), Antonio Vendetti (1699–1796) (fig. 67)
An altar set for high mass, Angelo Maria Spinazzi, Giovanni Felice Sanini (1727–87), Tommaso Politi (1717–96) and Francesco Antonio Salci (1715–66); model for the figure of *Christ* executed by the sculptor Giovanni Battista Maini (fig. 68)
An altar set for everyday use (six candlesticks and an altar cross in gilded bronze and lapis lazuli), Antonio Arrighi
Pair of credenza table candlesticks, Giovanni Felice Sanini (figs 69 and 70)
Ewer and basin (set), Vincenzo Belli (1710–87) (figs 71 and 72)
The 'service for mass' (pair of cruets and salver, chalice, Communion cup, sanctus bell, purificator vessel and candle snuffer), Antonio Gigli (*c.* 1704–61?) (figs 73–78)
Thurible, incense boat and spoon, Leandro Gagliardi (figs 79 and 80)
Wafer box, Francesco Smiti (1702–70) (fig. 81)
Chandelier and three lamps, Simone Migliè (1679–1752).

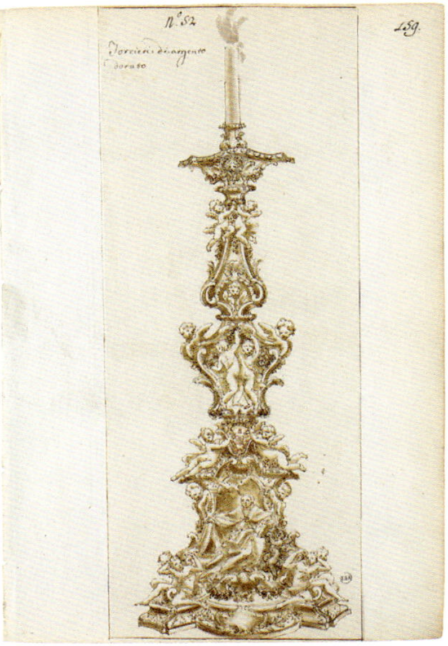

Fig. 62
Monumental candlestick
to be executed by the silversmith Giuseppe Gagliardi
Drawing no. 52 of the *Weale Album*, f. 159
Bibliothèque de l'École Nationale Supérieure des Beaux-arts [Library of the National Higher School of Fine Arts], Paris (Ms. 497)

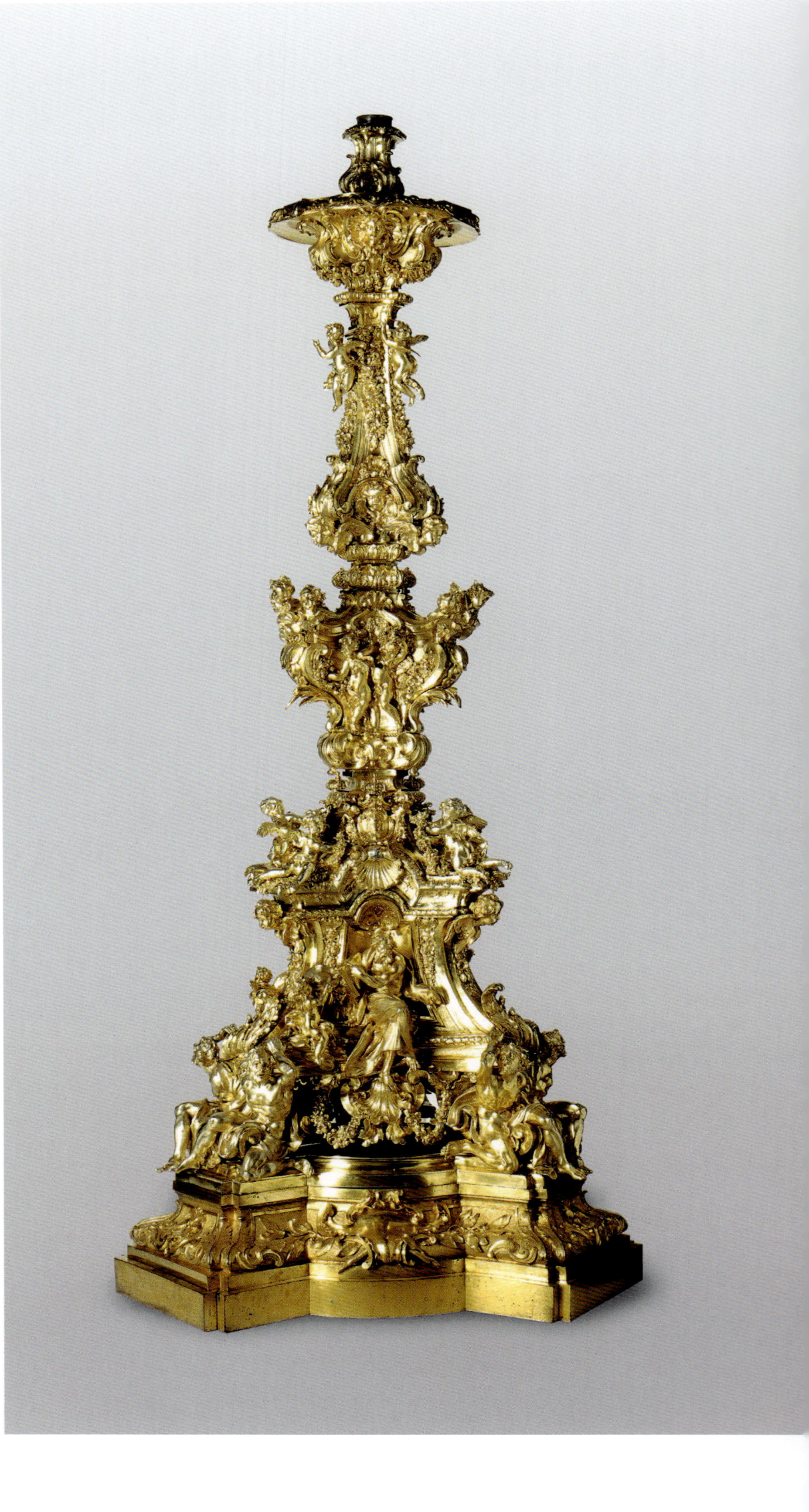

Fig. 63
One of a pair of monumental candlesticks
Giuseppe and Leandro Gagliardi
Rome, 1751–52
Silver and gilded bronze
(inv. MPr. 1 and MPr. 2)

Fig. 64
Reliquaries to be executed by the silversmith Carlo Guarnieri
Drawing no. 53 of the *Weale Album*, f. 163
Bibliothèque de l'École Nationale Supérieure des Beaux-arts [Library of the National Higher School of Fine Arts], Paris (Ms. 497)

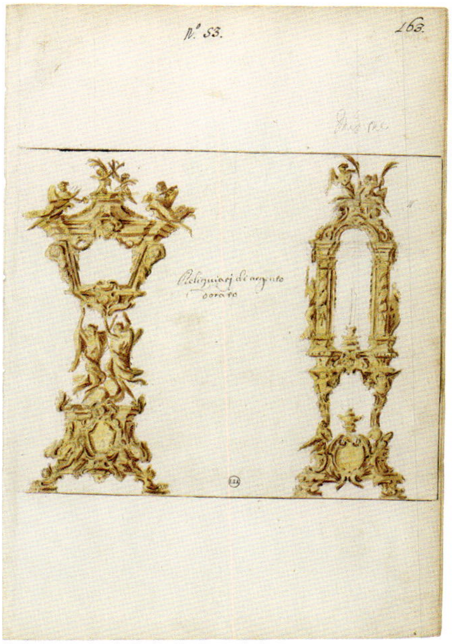

Fig. 65
Reliquary of St Valentine
Carlo Guarnieri
Rome, 1753–54
Silver and gilded bronze
(inv. MPr. 14)

Fig. 66
Reliquary of St Felix
Carlo Guarnieri
Rome, 1753–54
Gilded silver
(inv. MPr. 17)

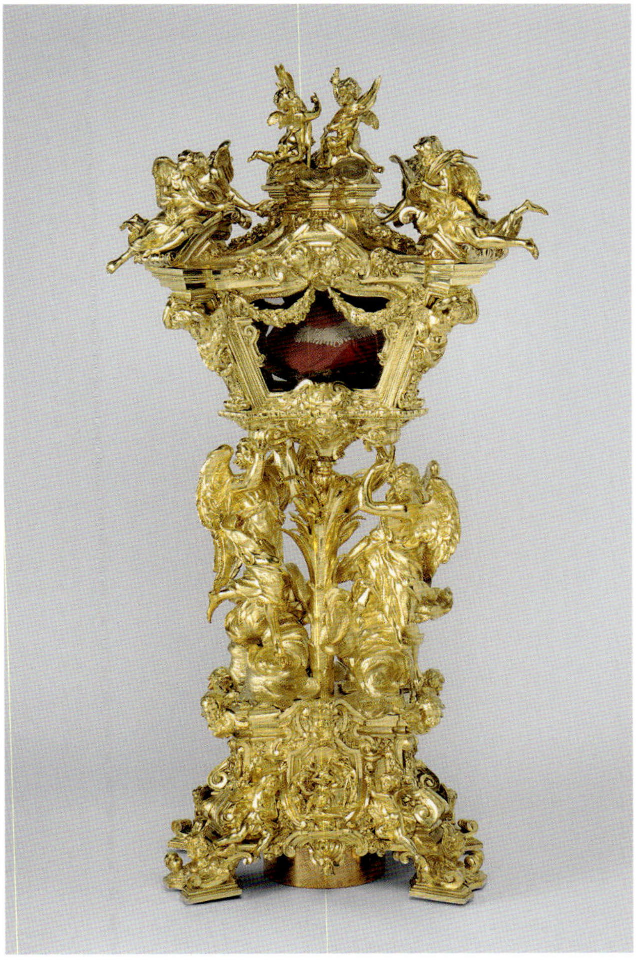

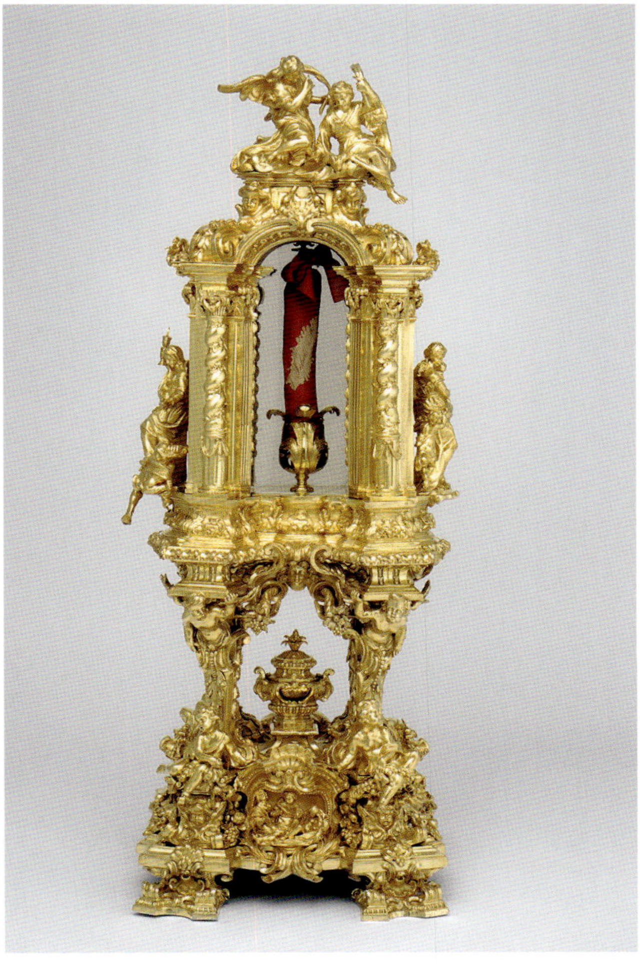

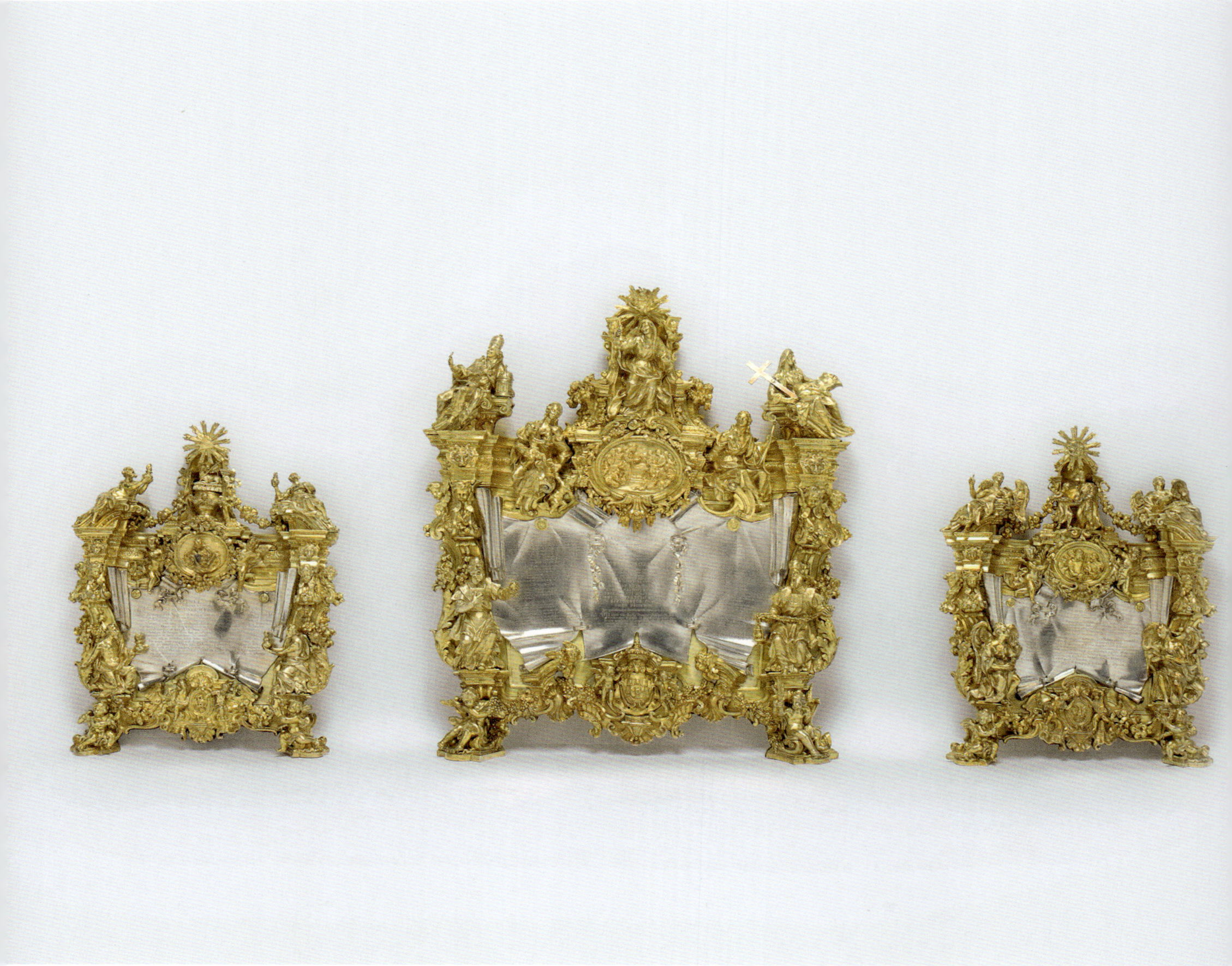

Fig. 67
Altar cards for high mass
Antonio Vendetti
Rome, 1737–60
White and gilded silver
(inv. MPr. 18, MPr. 19
and MPr. 20)

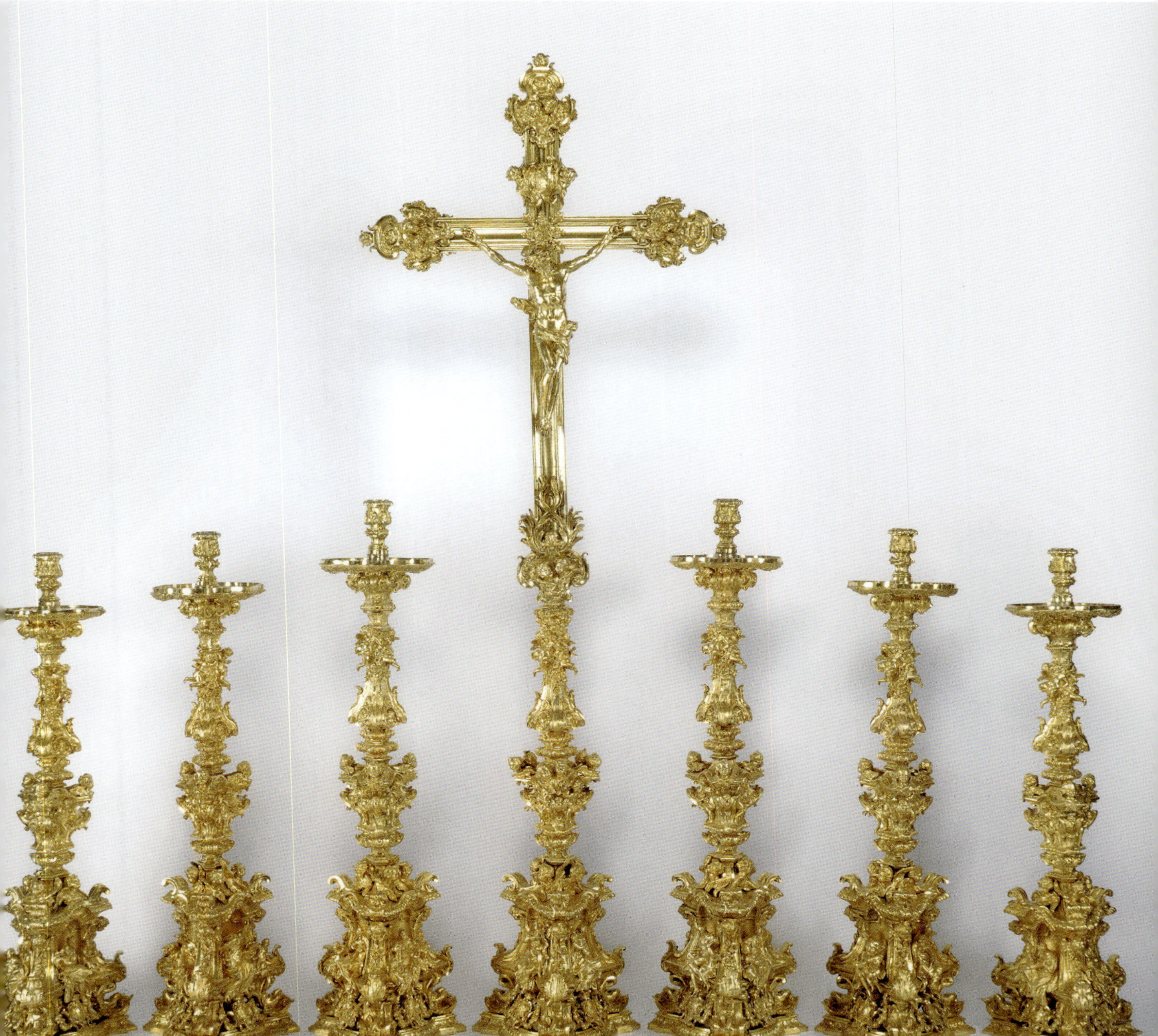

Fig. 68
Altar set (cross and six candlesticks for high mass)
Angelo Spinazzi (designer), Giovanni Felice Sanini,
Tommaso Politi and Francesco Antonio Salci (silversmiths),
Giovanni Battista Maini (sculptor)
Rome, 1749–50 (?)
Gilded silver
(inv. MPr. 3, MPr. 4, MPr. 5, MPr. 6, MPr. 7,
MPr. 8 and MPr. 9)

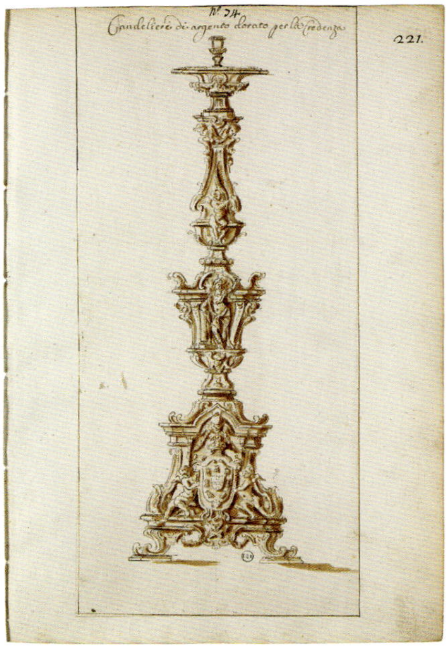

Fig. 69
Credenza table candlesticks
in gilded silver to be executed by Giovanni Felice Sanini
Drawing no. 74 of the *Weale Album*, f. 221
Bibliothèque de l'École Nationale Supérieure des Beaux-arts [Library of the National Higher School of Fine Arts], Paris (Ms. 497)

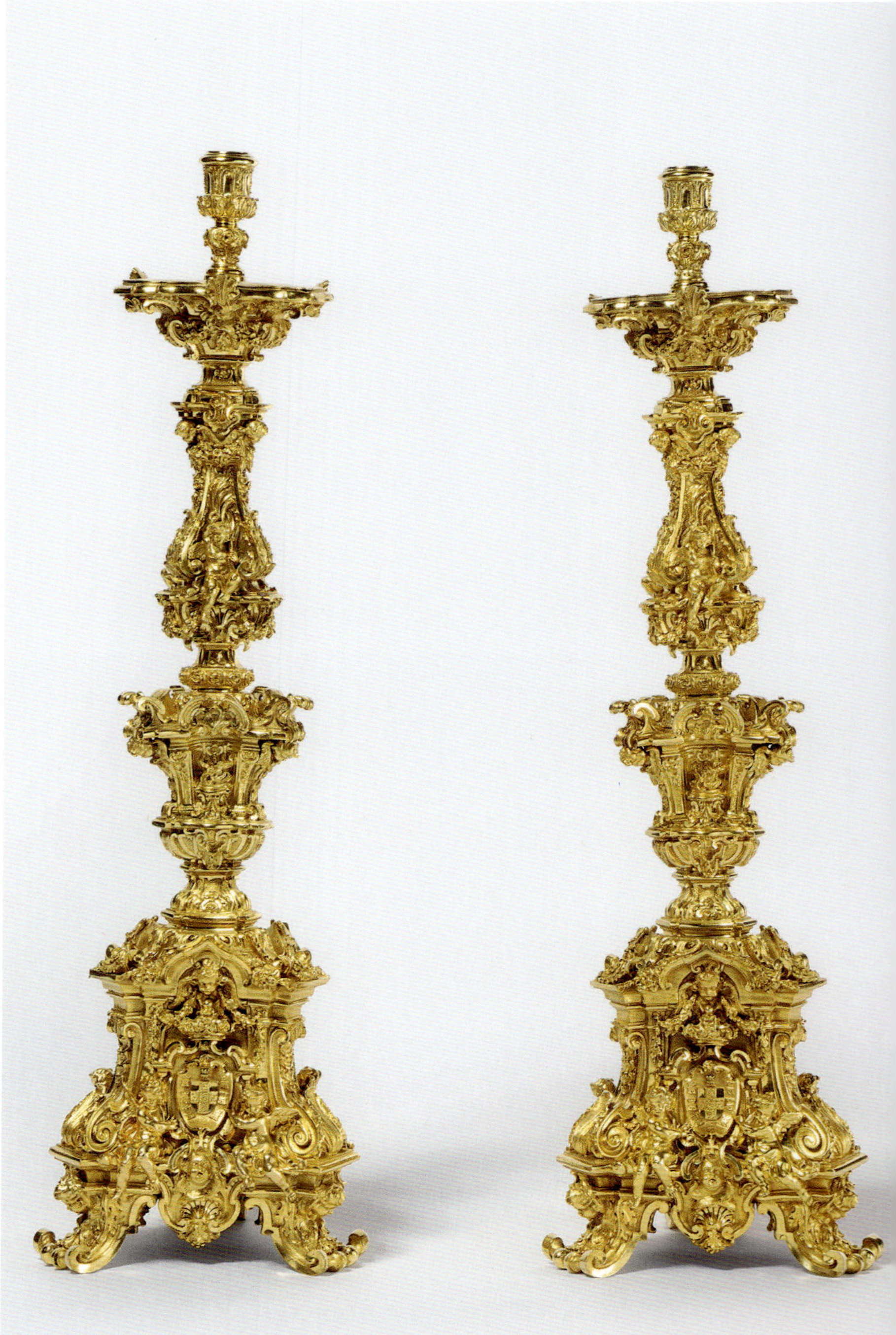

Fig. 70
Credenza table candlesticks
(pair)
Giovanni Felice Sanini
Rome, 1748 (?)
Gilded silver (inv. MPr. 12 and MPr. 13)

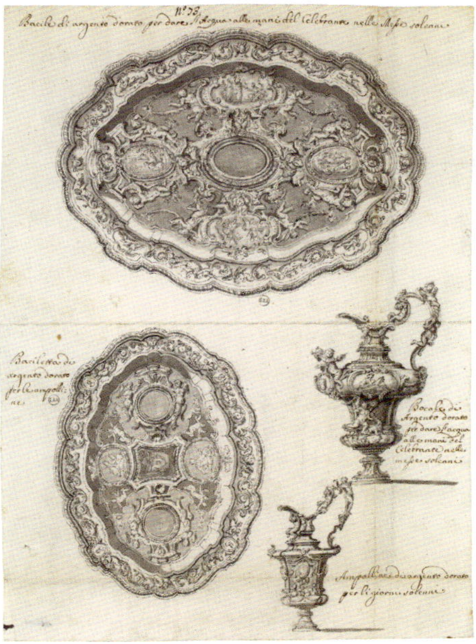

Fig. 71
Ewer and basin set in gilded silver to be executed by the silversmith Vincenzo Belli
Drawing no. 73 of the *Weale Album*, f. 213
Bibliothèque de l'École Nationale Supérieure des Beaux-arts [Library of the National Higher School of Fine Arts], Paris (Ms. 497)

Fig. 72
Ewer and basin set
Vincenzo Belli
Rome, 1746–47
Gilded silver
(inv. MPr. 27 and MPr. 28)

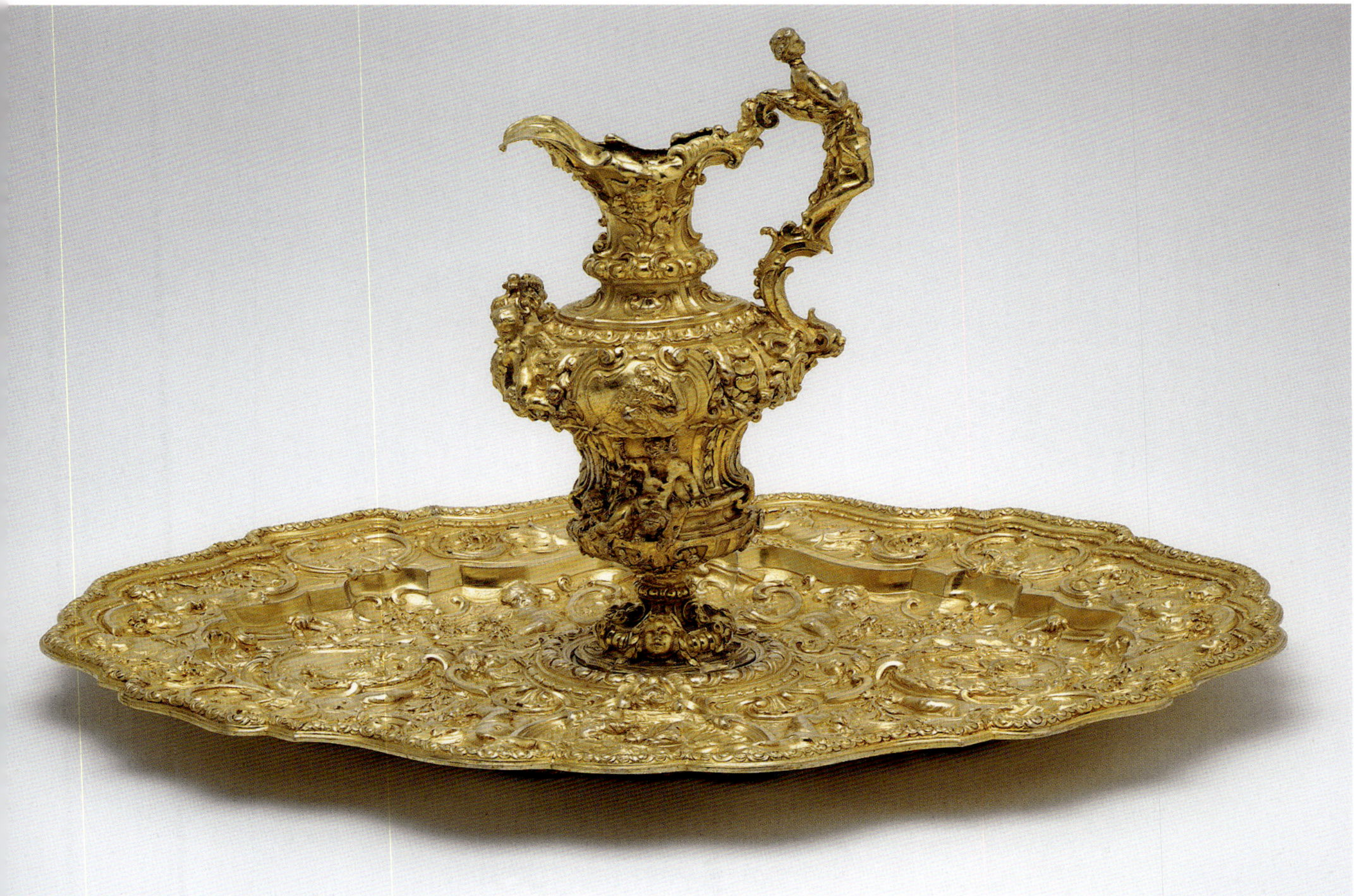

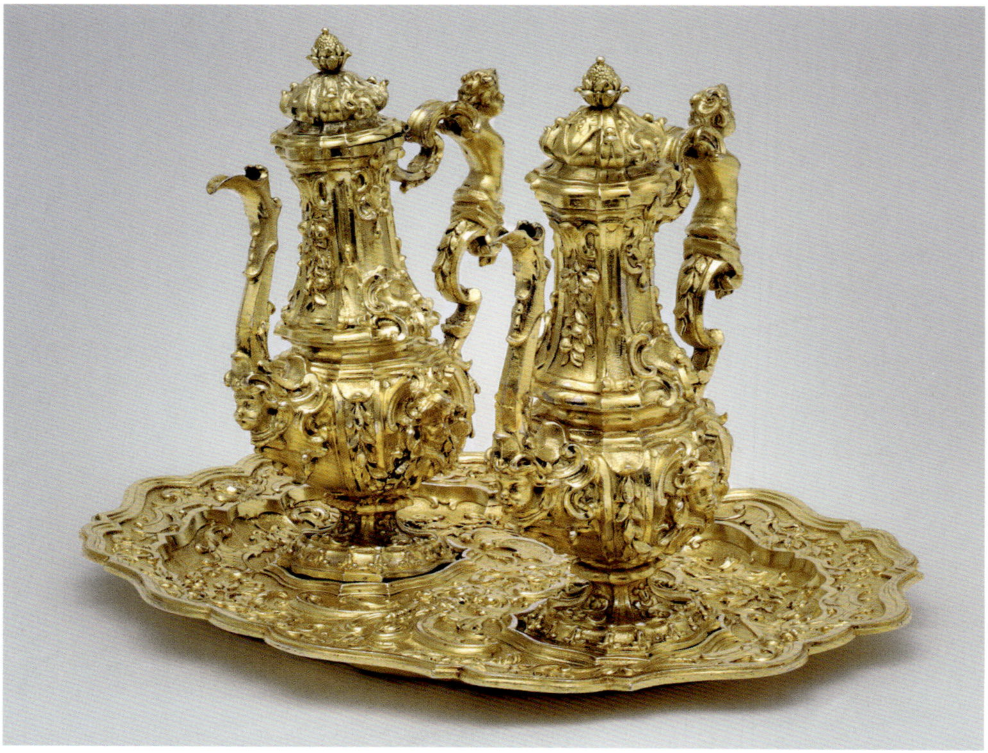

Fig. 73
Service for Mass: pair of cruets and salver
Antonio Gigli
Rome, 1746–51
Gilded silver
(inv. MPr. 24, MPr. 23, MPr. 25, MPr. 26 and MPr. 11)

Fig. 74
Service for Mass: chalice
Antonio Gigli
Rome, 1746–48
Gilded silver
(inv. MPr. 24)

Fig. 75
Service for Mass: Communion cup
Antonio Gigli
Rome, 1749–51
Gilded silver
(inv. MPr. 23)

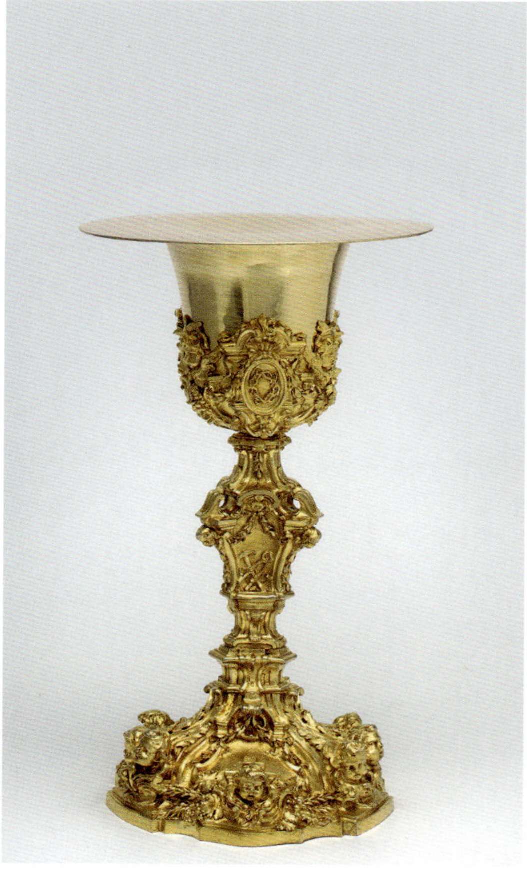

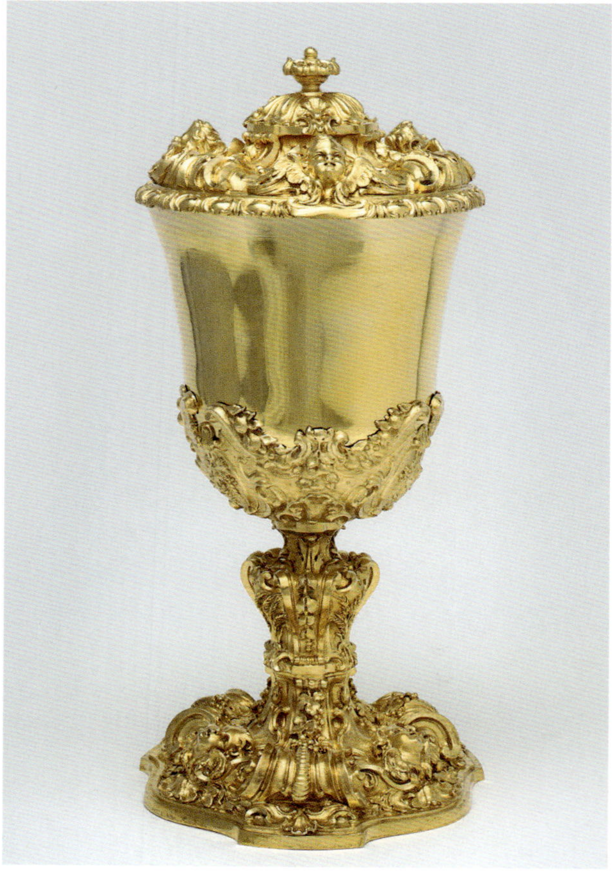

Fig. 76
Service for Mass: sanctus bell
Antonio Gigli
Rome, 1746–47
Gilded silver
(inv. MPr. 25)

Fig. 77
Service for Mass: purification vessel
Antonio Gigli
Rome, 1746–47
Gilded silver
(inv. MPr. 26)

Fig. 78
Service for Mass: candle snuffer
Antonio Gigli
Rome, 1746–47/1748–49
Gilded silver
(inv. MPr. 30)

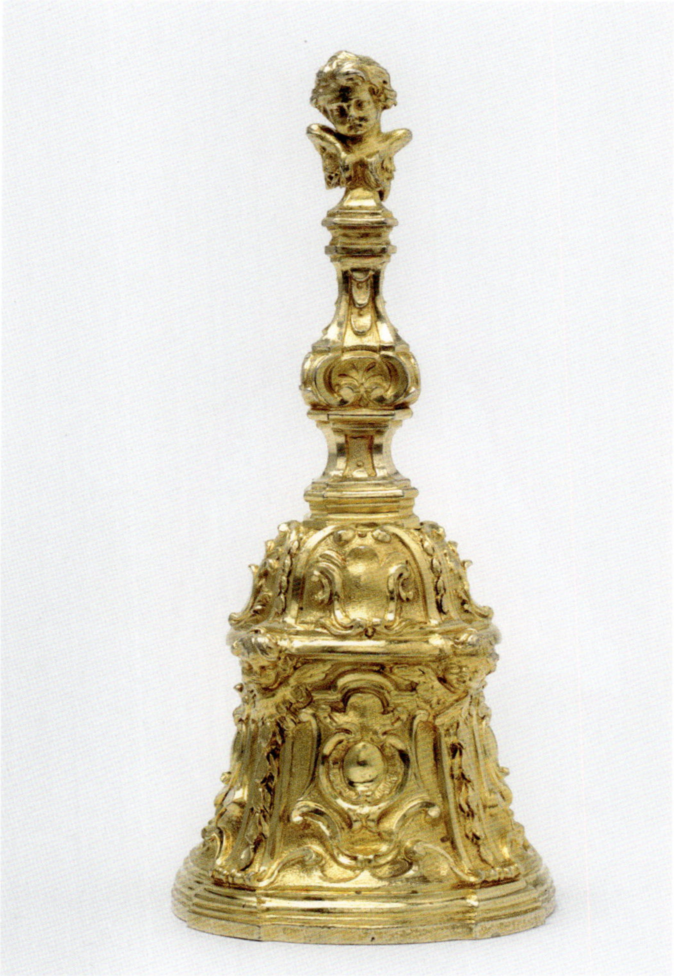

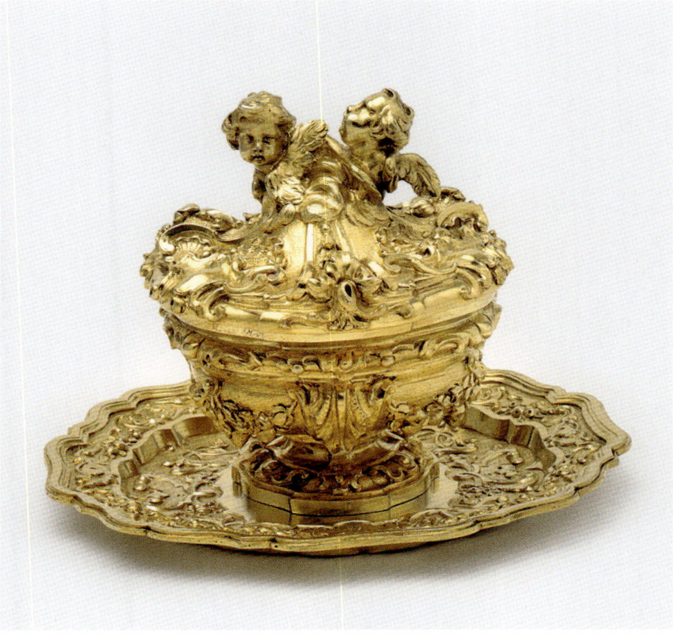

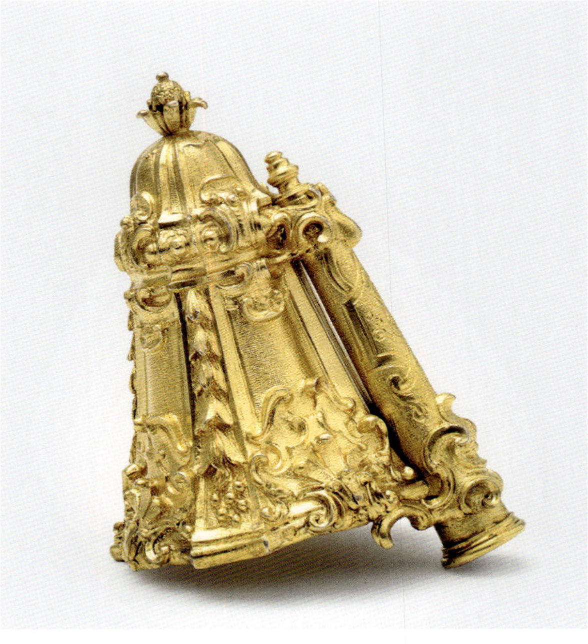

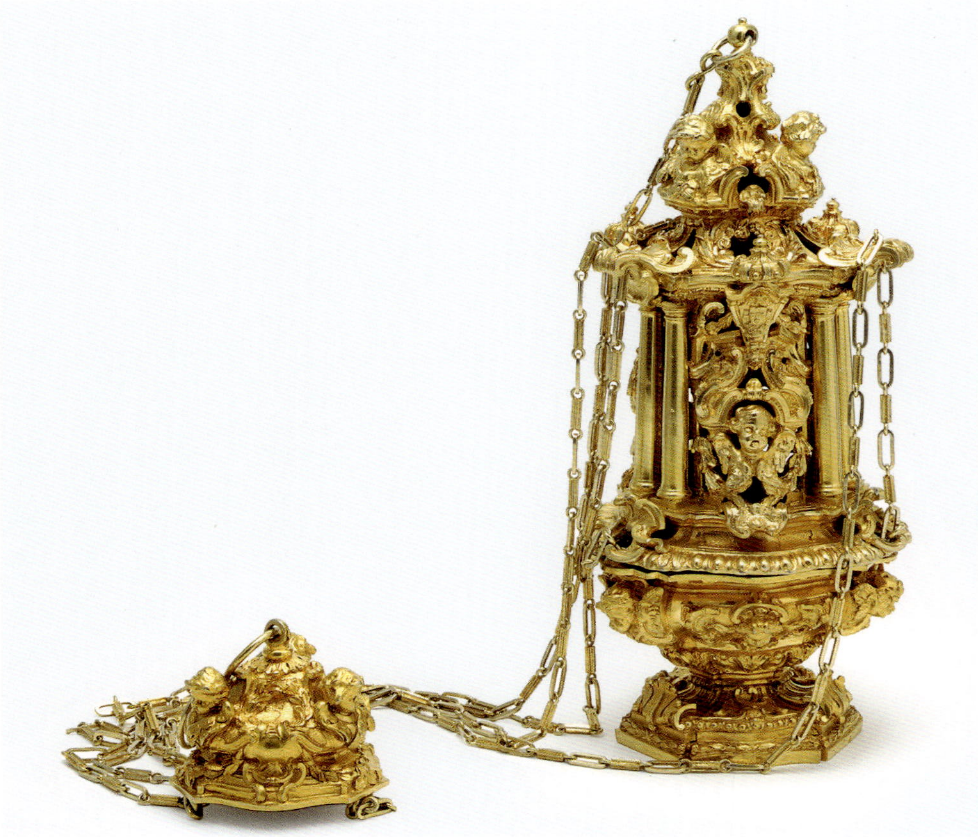

Fig. 79
Thurible
Leandro Gagliardi
Rome, 1749–50
Gilded silver
(inv. MPr. 21)

Fig. 80
Incense boat and spoon
Leandro Gagliardi
Rome, 1749–50
Gilded silver
(inv. MPr. 22)

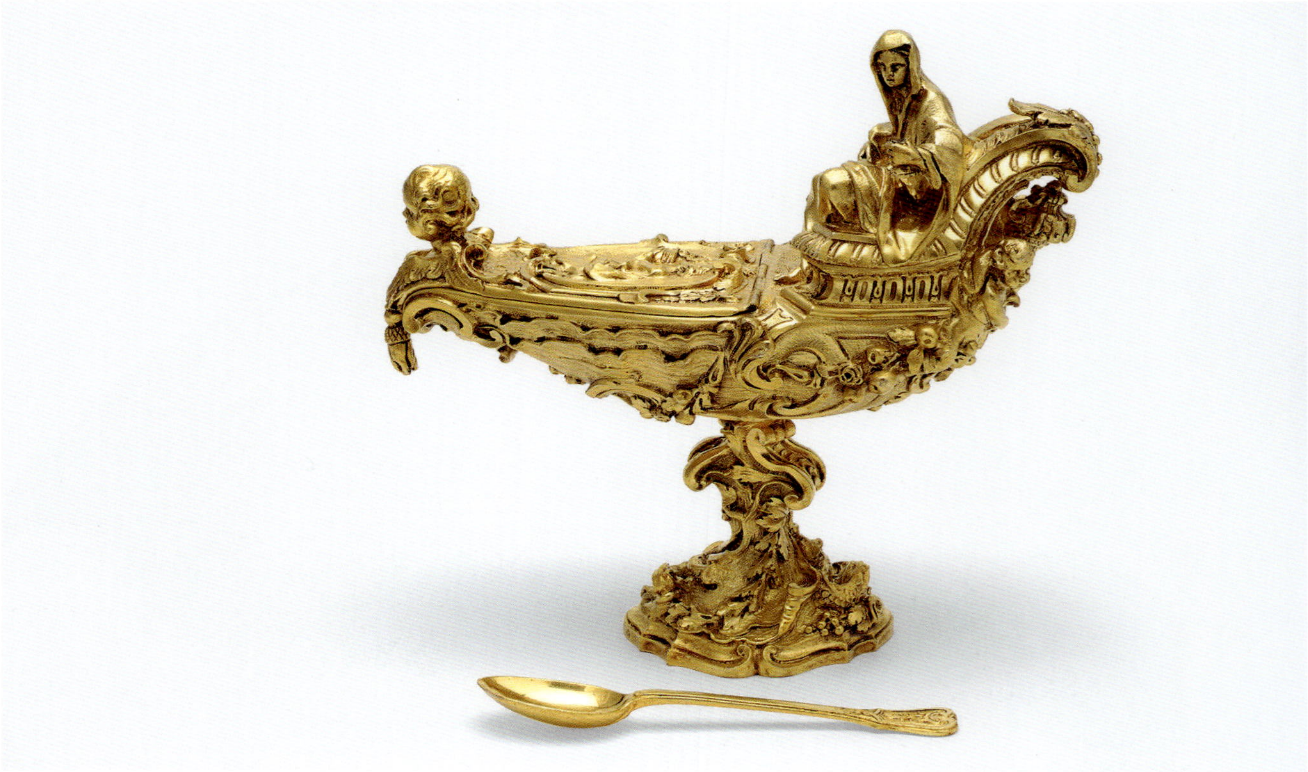

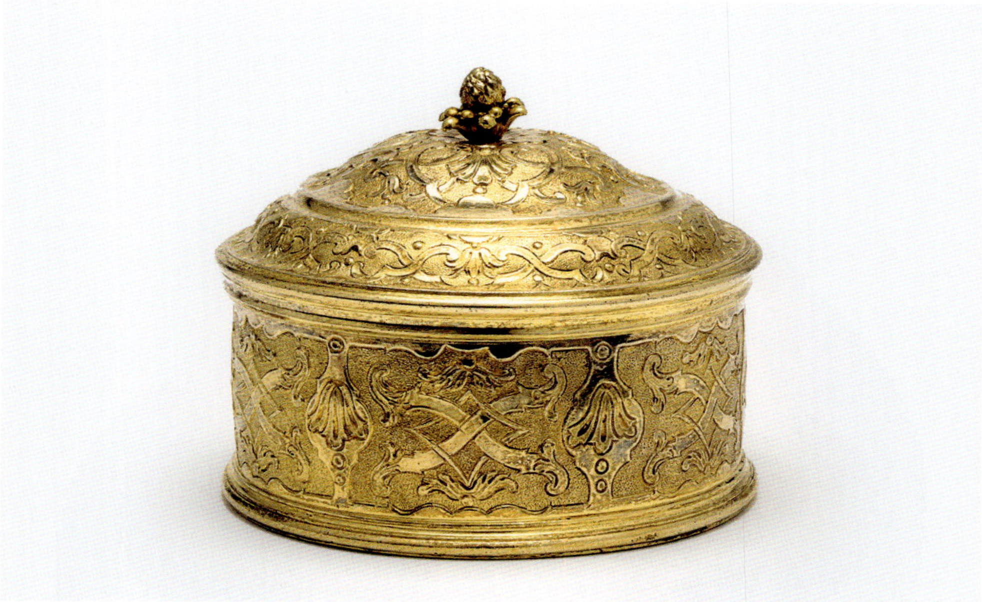

Fig. 81
Wafer box
Francesco Smiti
Rome, 1748
Gilded silver
(inv. MPr. 34)

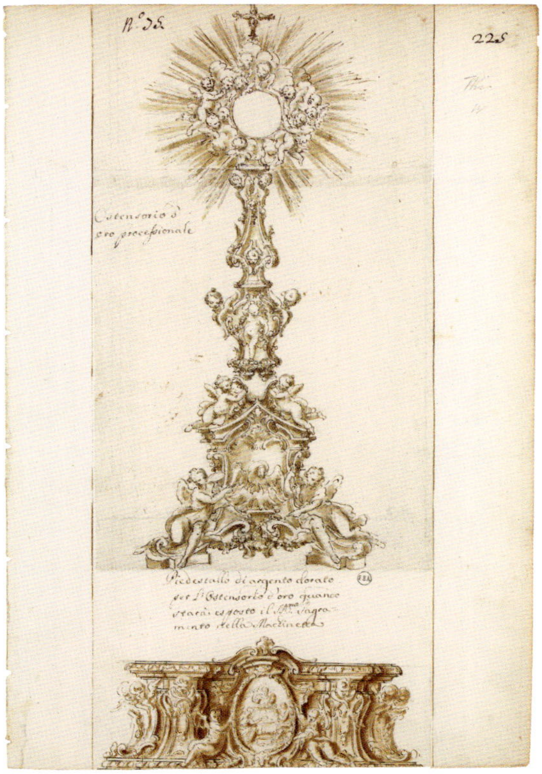

Fig. 82
Lost Pieces: monstrance
in gold (and corresponding base) to be executed by the silversmith Tommaso Politi
Drawing no. 75 of the *Weale Album*, f. 225
Bibliothèque de l'École Nationale Supérieure des Beaux-arts [Library of the National Higher School of Fine Arts], Paris (Ms. 497)

The lost pieces

In addition to the pieces already mentioned as belonging to the collection of the Chapel of St John the Baptist, there were originally others, three of them in gold (figs 82–84), which have since disappeared. These include some of the most important works, as can be seen from information already published in the work of Sousa Viterbo and Vicente de Almeida and later commented on in that of Maria João Madeira Rodrigues.[17]

How part of the gold and silver collection of the Chapel of St John the Baptist came to be lost is not clear from such information as can be obtained by documentary means, as there is little available. The oldest listing of the gold and silver pieces belonging to the royal chapel in São Roque after the expulsion of the Society of Jesus is believed to be that drawn up by order of Luís Francisco Xavier Telles de Mello, 'cónego da Santa Igreja Patriarcal, como Administrador da Real Capela de São João Baptista' (canon of the Holy Patriarchal Church, as

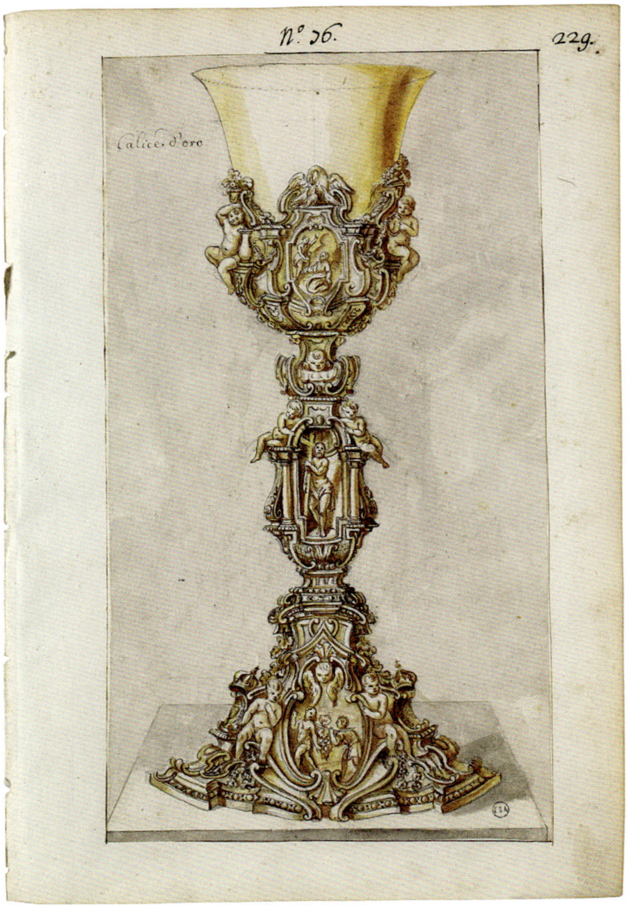

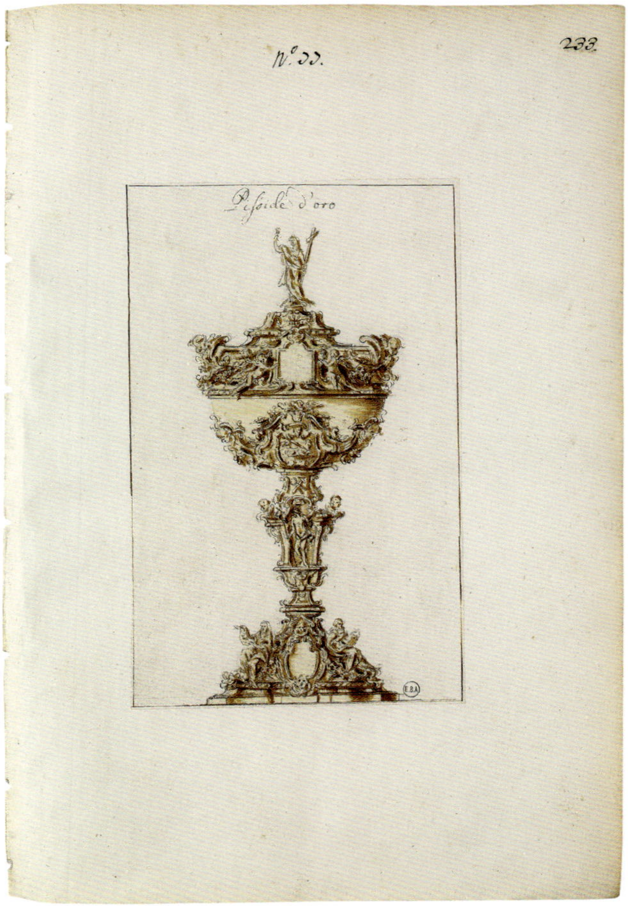

Fig. 83
Lost Pieces: chalice in gold to be executed by the silversmith Lorenzo de Caporali
Drawing no. 76 of the *Weale Album*, f. 229
Bibliothèque de l'École Nationale Supérieure des Beaux-arts [Library of the National Higher School of Fine Arts], Paris (Ms. 497)

Fig. 84
Lost Pieces: pyx in gold to be executed by silversmith Francesco Princivalle
Drawing no. 77 of the *Weale Album*, f. 233
Bibliothèque de l'École Nationale Supérieure des Beaux-arts [Library of the National Higher School of Fine Arts], Paris (Ms. 497)

administrator of the Royal Chapel of St John the Baptist) and dated 20 October 1781.[18] In this list, the works in gilded silver match those existing at present with the exception of the candle snuffers, of which there were still two at that time. There were also still eight reliquaries then – the four in gilded silver extant today, and four in white silver. These pieces – a candle snuffer in gilded silver and four reliquaries in white silver – were no longer in existence as early as 1812, when the same canon of the patriarchal church signed a declaration to this effect.[19] Other documentation from the same archive sheds some light on the fate of the snuffer and the four reliquaries; in fact a certificate dated 29 October 1808 attests to the delivery of these pieces to the mint – where they were melted down – by order of General Junot.[20]

As for the remaining missing works, it has not been possible to establish anything concrete. It should be noted, however, that Sousa Viterbo and Vicente de Almeida included the box for wafers made by Francesco Smiti among the missing pieces, because they had not then identified this silversmith's brand mark on the existing one. ■

NOTES

[1] Ana CANDIAGO, 'Um Tesoro di Oreficeria Romana del sec. XVIII a Lisbona: Gli Argenti di S. Rocco', in *Estudos Italianos em Portugal*, no. 24, 1965, p. 61.

[2] *Ibid.* p. 64.

[3] Franca VARIGNANA (ed.), *Il Tesoro di San Pietro in Bologna e Papa Lambertini*, Bologna, Minerva Edizioni, 1997.

[4] cf. *ibid.*, pp. 212–13, nos. 72 and 73 (illust. 95 and 96).

[5] BIBLIOTECA DA AJUDA (Lisbon), Ms. 49-VIII-27, Doc. 8 (pp. 45–52 of the numbering in pencil); this document was published by us in its entirety in Teresa Leonor M. VALE, 'Eighteenth-century Roman silver for the Chapel of St John the Baptist of the Church of São Roque, Lisbon', in *Burlington Magazine*, vol. CLII, no. 1.289, 2010, pp. 528–35.

[6] The pieces are referenced in exactly the order in which they appear in the manuscript – cf. B.A., Ms. 49-VIII-27, Doc. 8 (pp. 45–52 of the numbering in pencil).

[7] B.A., Ms. 49-VIII-27, Doc. 8, p. 50.

[8] B.A., Ms. 49-VIII-27, Doc. 11 (pp. 61–62 of the numbering in pencil), p. 61.

[9] cf. B.A., Ms. 49-IX-31, p. 142.

[10] Bibliothèque de l'École Nationale Supérieure de Beaux-Arts, Paris, Ms. 497.

[11] On these exhibitions, see Teresa Leonor M. VALE, 'Mettere in scena in lusso le mostre di opere d'arte commissionate da Giovanni V di Portogallo in due palazzi romani (1747 e 1749)', in Elisa DEBENEDETTI (ed.), *Studi sul Settecento Romano. Palazzi, chiese, arredi e scultura*, vol. I, Rome, Bonsignori Editore, 2012, pp. 259–272.

[12] The palace in question would be the one known as the Capponi–Cardelli Palace, on the via di Ripetta, near the land leased for the construction of the chapel on via della Penna – cf. Jörg GARMS, 'La Cappella di S. Giovanni Battista nella Chiesa di S. Rocco a Lisbona', in Sandra Vasco ROCCA and Gabriele BORGHINI (dir.), *Giovanni V di Portogallo (1707–1750) e la Cultura Romana del suo Tempo*, Rome, Àrgos Edizioni, 1995, p. 119.

[13] The payments to Francesco Feliziani (dated 8 December 1747) can be consulted in B.A., Ms. 49-VIII-16, ff. 394–97: 'Conto delli Lauori fatti per seruizio dell'Ecc.mo Sig.re Commendatore Sampaio al Palazzo dell'Ill. mo fù Marchese Capponi A di 23 Aprile 1747' and Ms. 49-VIII-16, ff. 400–1: 'Conto Delli Lauori fatti per seruizio dell'Ecc.mo Sig.re Commendatore Sampaio alla Cappella di Sua Maestà Rè di Portogallo A di 23 Aprile 1747'; see also B.A., Ms. 49-VIII-13, ff. 424–25 (unnumbered).

[14] cf. Luca Antonio CHRACAS, *Diario ordinario*, Roma, no. 4644, 29 April 1747, pp. 6–12.

[15] cf. B.A., Ms. 49-VIII-21, ff. 450–57.

[16] cf. B.A., Ms. 49-VIII-21, f. 457.

[17] cf. Francisco Marques de Sousa VITERBO and R. Vicente d'ALMEIDA, *op. cit.*, pp. 47–50, and Maria João Madeira RODRIGUES, *A Capela de S. João Baptista e as suas Colecções*, Lisbon, Inapa, 1989, pp. 244–45.

[18] cf. Arquivio Histórico da Santa Casa da Misericórdia de Lisboa (Lisbon), *Inventario da Fabrica da Real Capela de S. João Baptista* (SCML/IG/SJB/01/Liv. 001).

[19] A.H.S.C.M.L., *Inventario da Fabrica da Real Capela de S. João Baptista*, f. 6.

[20] cf. A.H.S.C.M.L., *Inventário de Bens. Tesouro da Real Capela de S. João Baptista*, ch. 8, Doc. 3 (Certidão da Prata Fundida na Casa da Moeda – certificate of silver melted down in the mint, 29 October 1808).

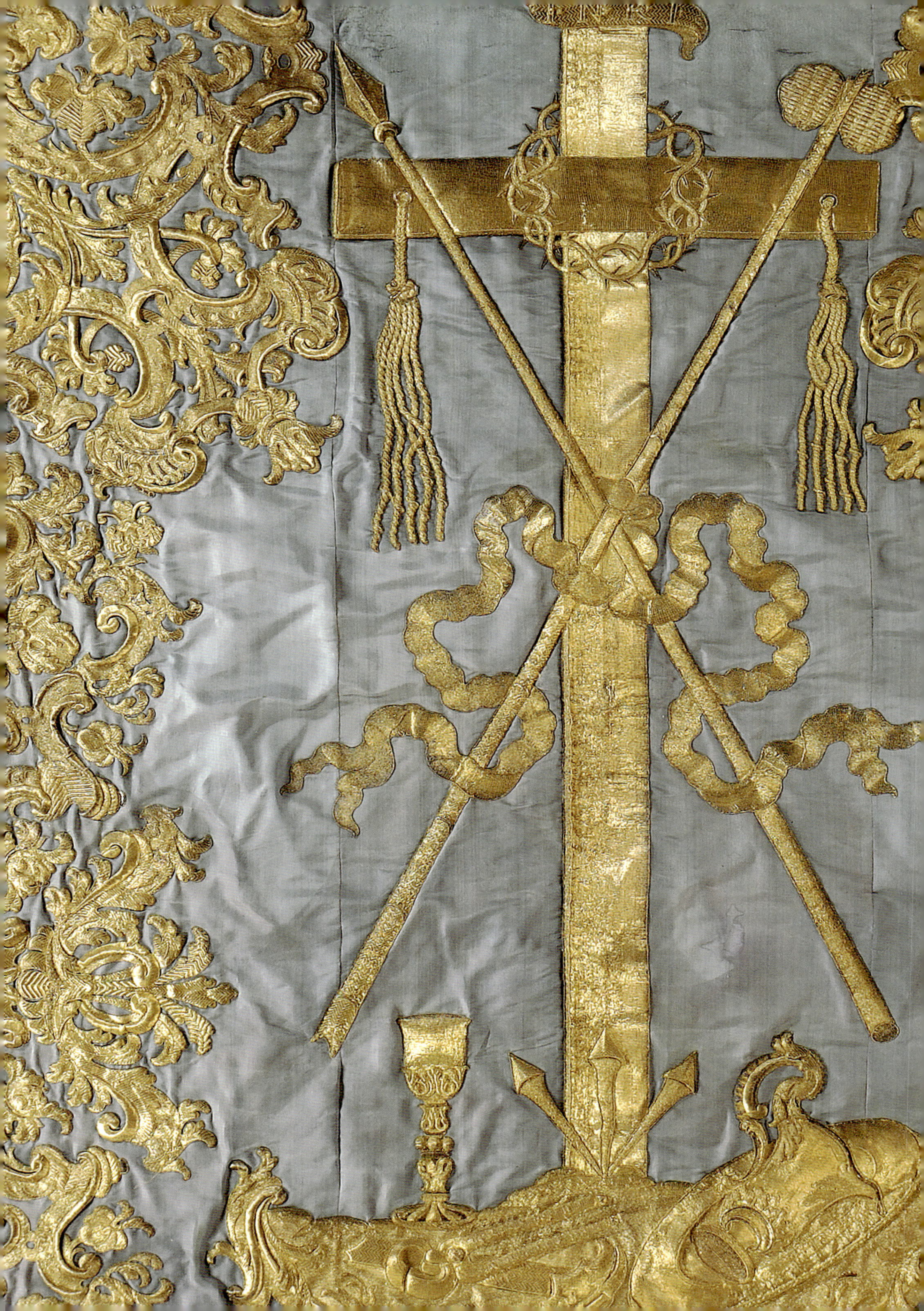

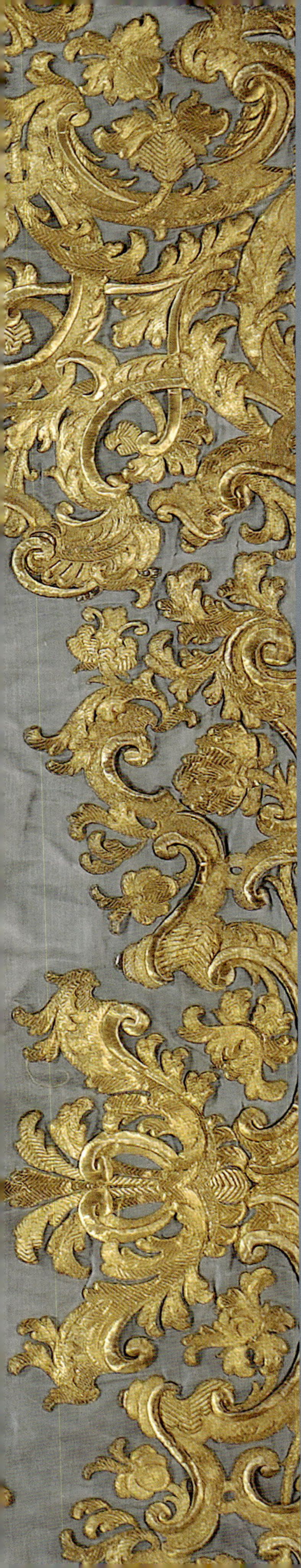

2. TEXTILES

Gold, gold, gold ... : the textiles collection of the Chapel of St John the Baptist

Magda Tassinari

pp. 118–119
Detail of the instruments of the Passion of Christ from the Curtain of the Passion
Filippo Gabrielli, Cosimo Patrenostro
(See fig. 92)

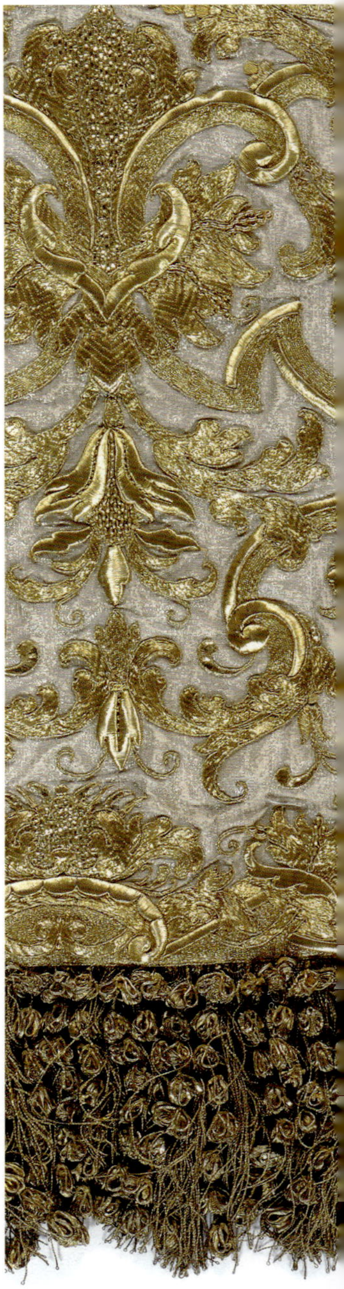

John V always showed a keen interest in and paid great attention to precious textiles, aware of the role they played – much like the figurative works of art and precious objects with which he enriched churches and palaces – as a means of 'externalising' his power in tangible form. In John V's hands artistic and cultural patronage and luxury were indeed effective tools – ones that he used to convey to his contemporaries an image of prestige fit to match that of the greatest sovereigns of the day, and to ensure that future generations would remember him. Although they are fragile and therefore limited to a short lifespan, textiles have qualities often superior to those of other precious objects in terms of communication, as they are easily transportable and can be adapted to various settings and requirements.

When it came to commissioning textiles, John V had always been a demanding patron who kept abreast of the latest fashions. He was also a man of good taste, elegant, refined and cultured,[1] and with a natural desire to be fashionable – which demanded that particular attention be paid to the superfluous, to everything that – precisely because it was not necessary – constituted a sign of wealth and magnificence. The job of emphasising and showing off this superfluity was largely entrusted to embroidery, which was used in almost manic abundance to spread its decorative web over any fabric intended for interior decoration, or to any and every part of a garment. Embroidery was highly prized as a commodity endowed with great economic and artistic value – all the greater if it made use of sophisticated designs, and demanded the use of precious materials and the greatest technical perfection of execution (fig. 85).[2]

Behind the production of such pieces for ritual use lay the implicit theological motive of which they were the tool: their purpose was to help the user enter into contact with mysteries – to contemplate divine beauty and to perceive the transcendence of the divinity with their own senses and by means of ritual. Both theological concepts and motives of political strategy underlie these prestigious commissions for the sumptuous ritual vestments with which the sovereign enriched the sacristies of many religious buildings in Portugal, particularly the basilica of Mafra and the Patriarchal Basilica. Of all the commissions, this last – the set of liturgical vestments intended for the Chapel of St John the Baptist in the Church of São Roque in Lisbon, dating from 1744 – is certainly the most important known to date. It represents the culmination of the sovereign's appreciation of Italian artistic genius that was manifest throughout his life and reign[3] to an extent that distinguishes John V from other powerful Europeans of

Fig. 85
Pulpit cloth
from the white vestments
for high days (detail)
Giuliano Saturni
Rome, 1744–49
(inv. MT. 028)

his time (who tended to be much more oriented towards the French makers of these objects).[4] His choices were certainly the result of suggestions from advisers attached to the clergy, as well as information acquired from the ambassadors representing the Crown in Rome, most of whom were educated and refined aristocrats who could not have been more at home in the ambience of the pontifical court whose lifestyle and tastes they had assimilated.[5]

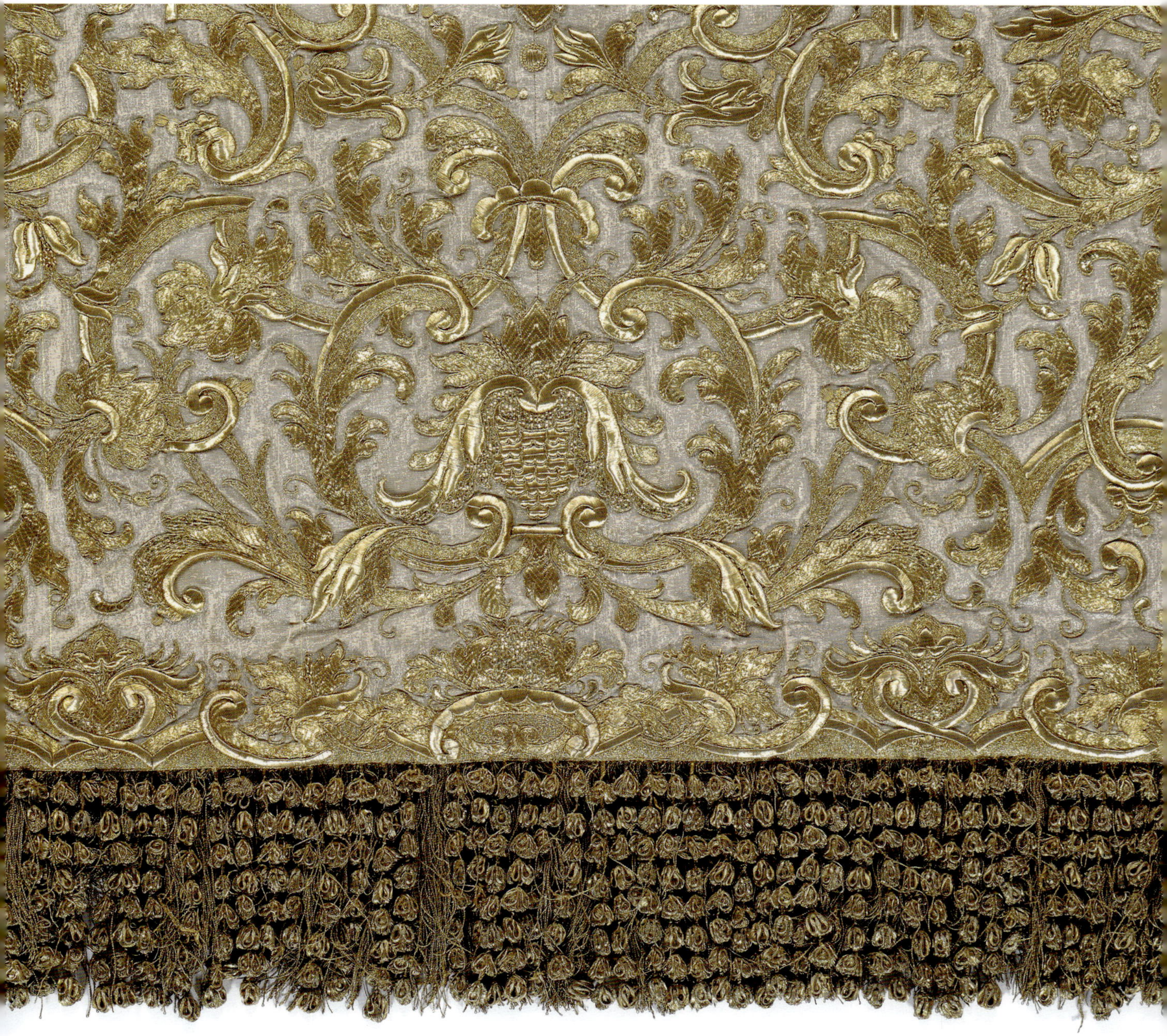

The commissioning of the embroidery

The list of the textile items, chosen in accordance with the king's wishes, to comprise the entire set of liturgical vestments for the Chapel of St John the Baptist appears for the first time in a detailed report sent from Lisbon to Rome, dated 9 March 1744.[6] The work must have begun shortly afterwards, since in the last months of that year there were already payments made *per ricami per servizio della cappella* (for embroidery for the service of the chapel)[7] which are duly recorded as such in the account books of the Portuguese embassy in Rome. In the year immediately following, the Roman workshops of the embroiderers involved in the execution of the commission issued a note – a kind of budget – in which the overall cost of the work was estimated; thanks to this document we know the names of the different craftsmen and the prices established, amounting to a total of 33,798 *scudi* and 89 Roman *baiocchi*.[8] The order dated 9 March 1744 begins by mentioning two sets of vestments for high mass, one white and one crimson, both complete and equally rich;[9] these are followed by five sets of vestments for holidays with chasubles, in the liturgical colours white, red, green, purple and pink, each with its corresponding altar frontal. The fabric to be used for the vestments for both high days and holidays was to be silk, 'gilded' (referred to in the manuscript as lamé) in silver and gold, and all the embroidery also had to be made of gold. Finally, the sets for everyday use were commissioned in the liturgical colours; they were to be made in silk, with the embroidery also in yellow silk, the colour of gold. In addition to the ritual vestments, together with their corresponding accoutrements and items intended for dressing the altar, there was yet more finery for the decoration of the chapel, including three 'veils' or curtains intended for covering up the chapel paintings during Holy Week. On perusal of the order document, what is most striking to the reader is the great insistence that the vestments must be 'conforme os mais ricos e de melhor gosto que se usarem em Roma' (just like the richest and those in best taste that may be used in Rome'.[10] The objective was clear: just as for the other works of art commissioned for the chapel, the textile component – never a secondary concern in the project of building up the royal image which, as mentioned above, was extensively realised in the form of liturgical spectacle in typical eighteenth-century fashion[11] – had to be modelled after the taste, style, pomp and grandeur of Rome.

'della maggior perfezzione, ricchezza e gusto possibile' – of the greatest possible perfection, wealth and taste

The unique – and very Italian – feature of this collection, coming from the best Roman workshops of the time[12] (fig. 86) is the unity that it maintains across a variety of decorative motifs. These are different in each set and there are no repetitions (since they were made by different artisans working independently), but

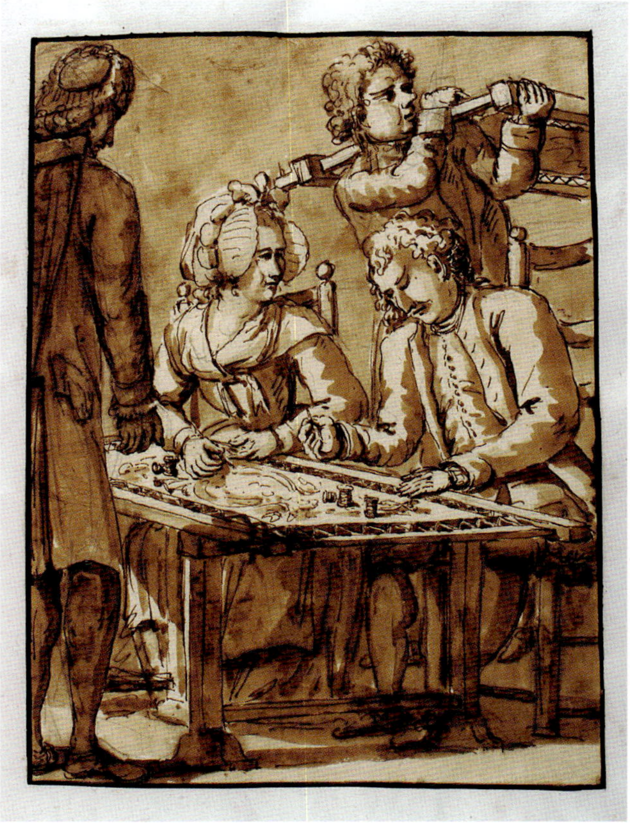

Fig. 86
Embroiderers working at the Loom
Giuseppe Barberi, 1790–99
Watercolour drawing
Museo di Roma, Rome
(inv. GS 2895 6)

Fig. 87 (overleaf)
White vestments for high days and holidays
Display of vestments in the Chapel of St John the Baptist collection, in the Museum of São Roque, Lisbon, 2008

at the same time they are all similar and correspond to a shared project in terms of their exuberance and inventiveness, while retaining control of the formal balance of the whole. They share a refined character which – thanks to a high level of technical expertise – prevents their sumptuousness from appearing excessive, no matter how clearly it is displayed by the splendour of the gold used. Also common across the collection is the way they are well matched to the architectural solutions of the chapel in which the embroidered fabrics were to be displayed, just as they were to be well matched and in perfect harmony with the other exceptionally rich liturgical accoutrements. The collection expresses a decorative vocabulary drawn from the varied and complex motifs available, produced by the exuberant creativity of Rome in the eighteenth century. Indeed, here we see *chinoiseries* – whimsical elements originating in the French taste for the Rococo and drawn from the rich repertoire of arabesques and grotesques that were then in circulation among workshops and academies, thanks to selections of engravings of works by the *maîtres ornemanistes* (from Audran to Gillot, and from Watteau to Berain to D. Marot). These were perfectly combined with the balance and naturalism typical of the classically inspired Italian Renaissance tradition, the latter aspects being interpreted and developed within the Baroque context and marked by the indelible influence of Bernini and his collaborators. One artist who came to stand out among these last was Giovanni Paolo Schor,[13] who spread the influence of models drawn from Bernini and Cortona into every sector of the applied arts. It should also be noted that in the last years of the seventeenth century and the first of the eighteenth, the designs of other Roman artists were increasingly adopted; this was the case for Filippo Passarini, who published his *Nuove invenzioni d'ornamenti* (new inventions in ornament) intended for use by artists and craftsmen in different branches of activity – among whom embroiderers are specifically mentioned.[14]

The most important of the 11 sets of liturgical vestments that make up the chapel's textile collection is undoubtedly the white vestments for high mass (fig. 87), intended for pontifical masses and exceptional not only for its remarkable decorative elements but also for the sheer number of elements that comprise it – of which 31 survive today, although there were originally more than fifty.[15] The craftsman Giuliano Saturni created some subtle and sinuous motifs in his pieces, which repeat and multiply both vertically and horizontally so as to completely cover the larger items, and appear in a simplified version on the

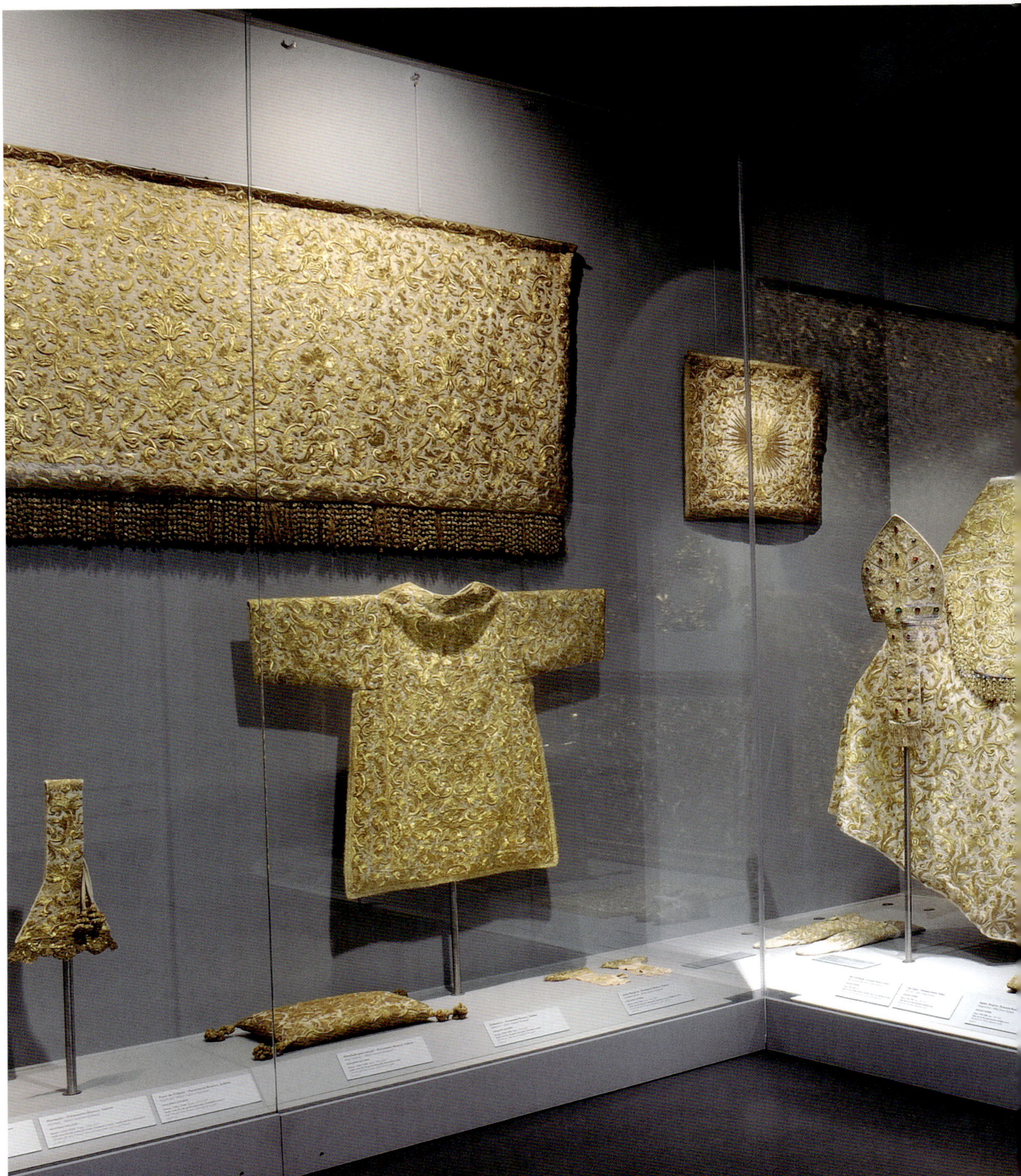

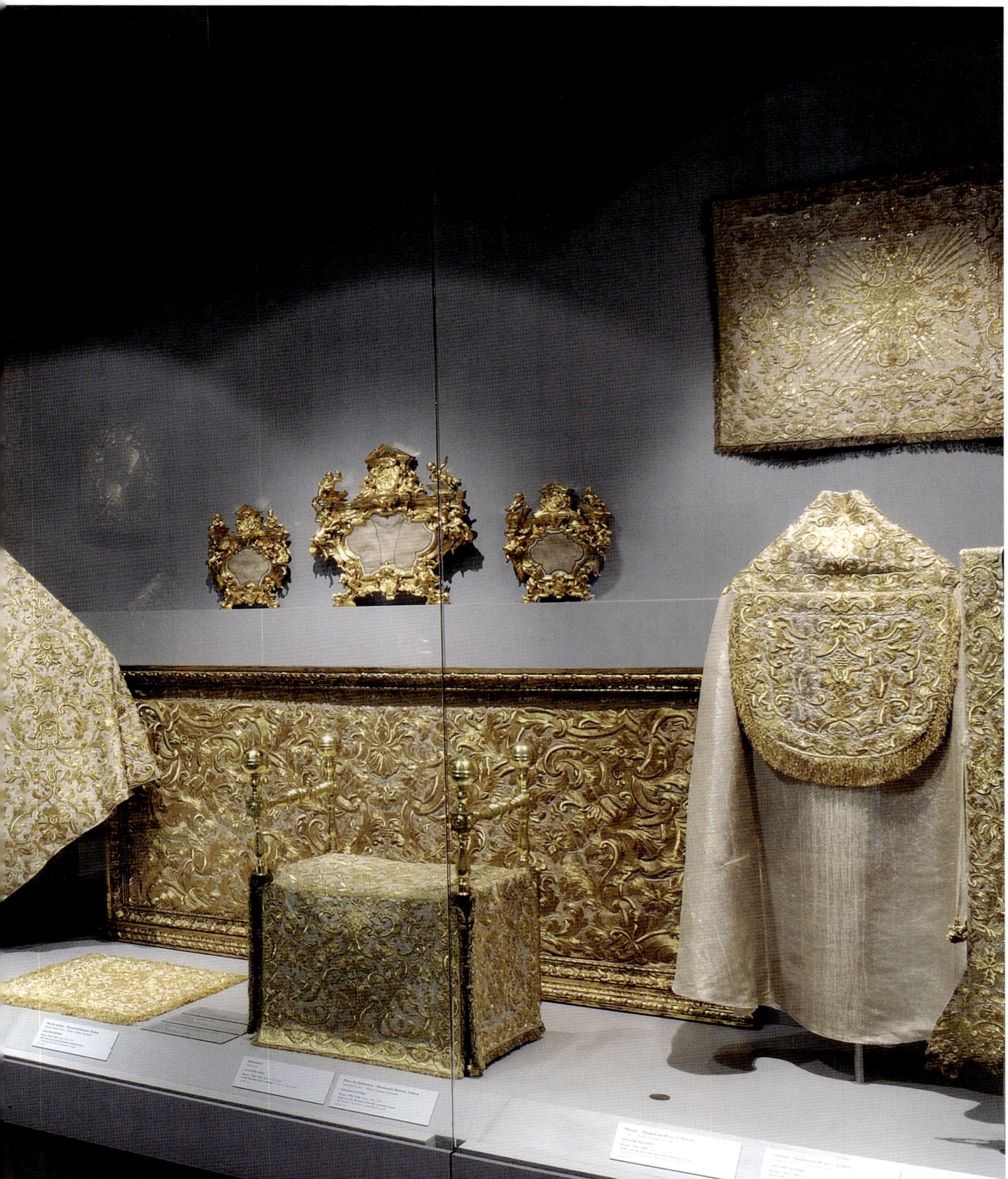

smaller items, creating frames or interlacing to form crosses or fan out in rays. The second of the sets for high masses, in crimson (figs 88 and 89), is composed of 27 elements; this was executed by Gerolamo Mariani, a master craftsman who employed a more full-bodied and incisive style than Saturni. Mariani tended more towards geometrical decoration and more obviously visible relief, characterised by his vigorous acanthus-leaf motifs flourishing across the surface, arranged 'candelabra-style' (as if growing out of small baskets, on the 'great' cope or *cappa magna*). The volutes alternate or interlace with more whimsical elements made up of asymmetric lines, broken and angular, belonging to a repertoire closely related to the Rococo. Of the sets for holiday masses, the white vestments embroidered by Nicolò Bovi have some unusual characteristics, both in terms of materials and decoration. Near the hems, which are embroidered in silver in a herringbone pattern that creates a shimmering play of light and dark, there are small floral compositions embroidered in gold and arranged in an orderly manner, according to an alternating scheme; while in the central part of the chasuble there are larger elements consisting of fanciful forms created by pairs of volutes facing one another. Another noteworthy feature is the particular effect that results from the presence of innumerable *paillettes* or sequins. The purple holiday vestments, embroidered by Cosimo Patrenostro (or Paternoster),

Figs 88 and 89
Cappa magna ['great' cope]
Red vestment for high days
Gerolamo Mariani
Rome, 1744–49
Silk and silver-gilt thread, embroidered in gold
(inv. MT. 3)

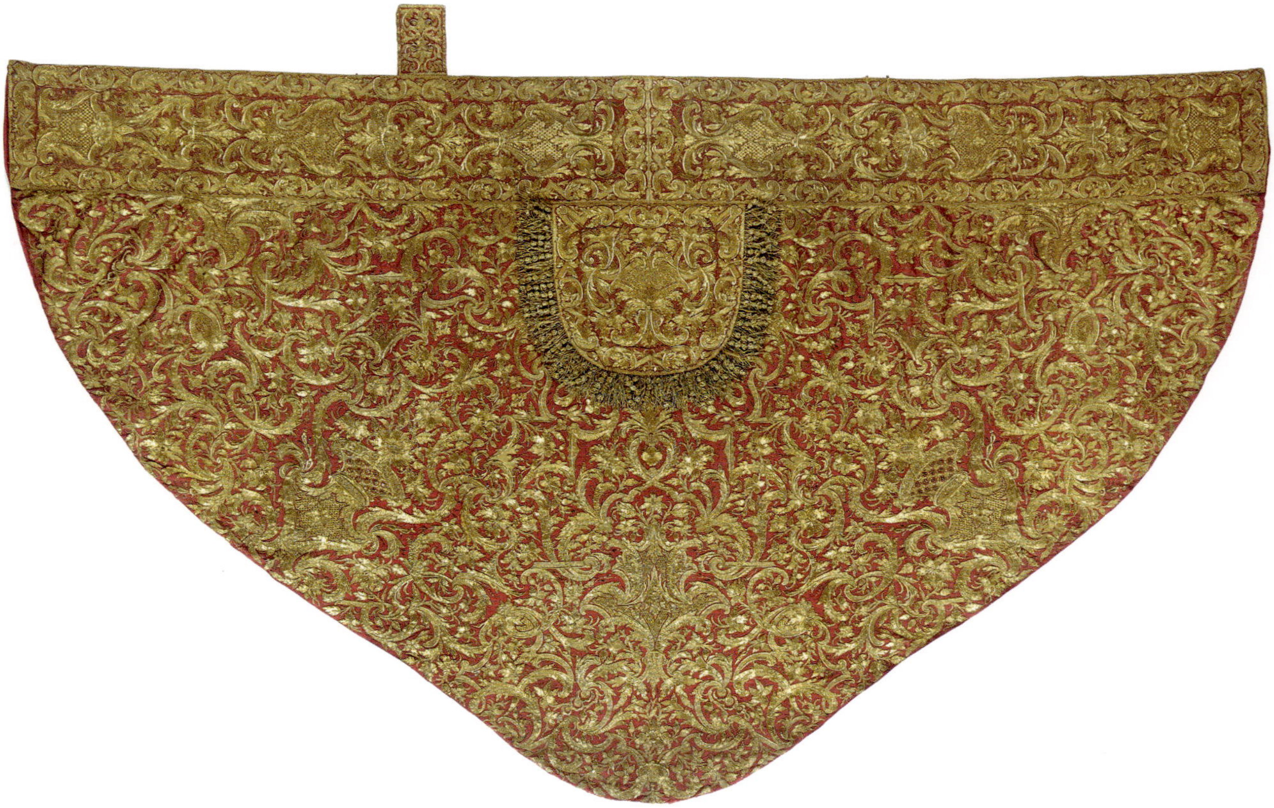

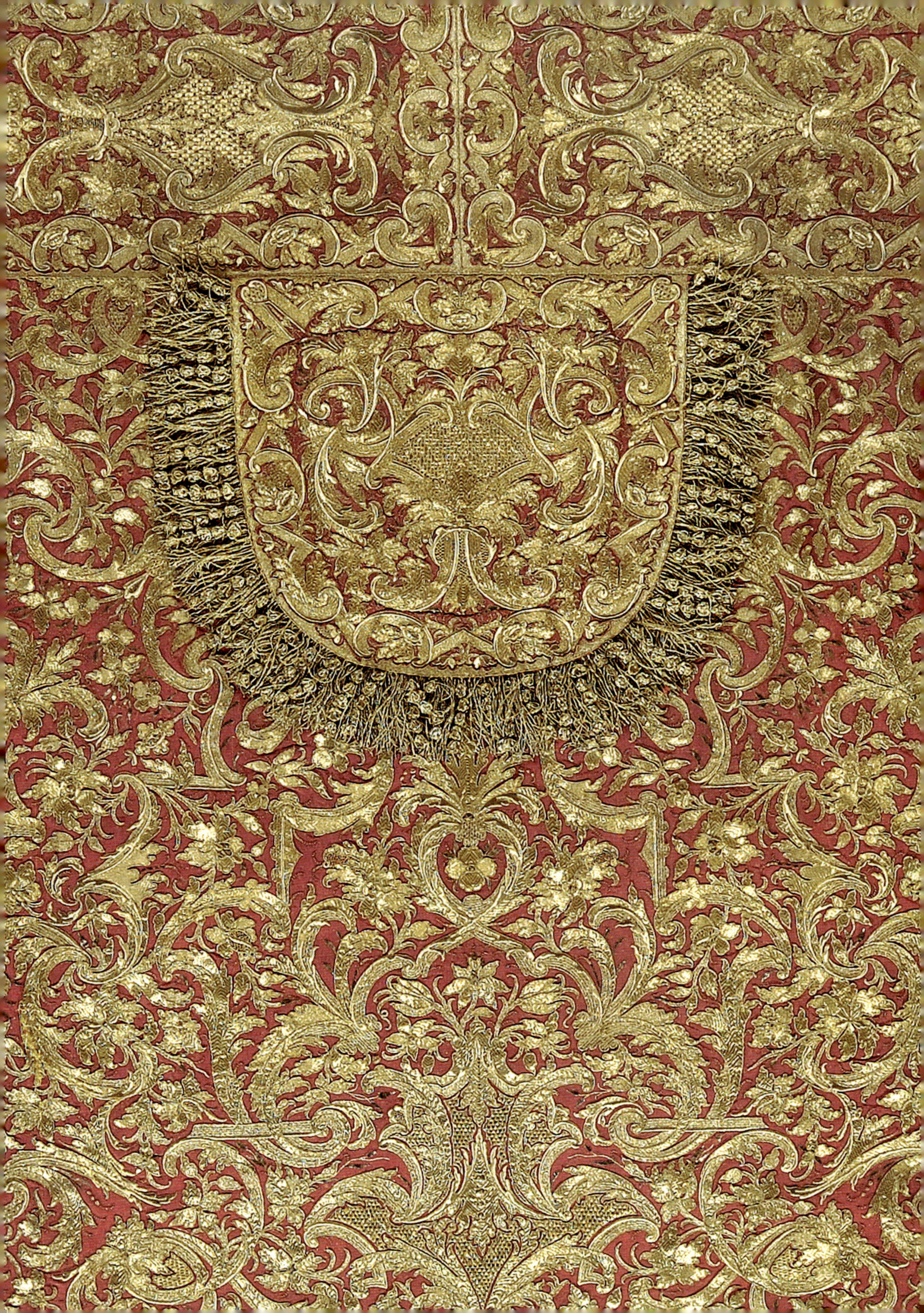

are perhaps the most sophisticated of the holiday ensembles, thanks to the happy contrast of the violet background with the yellow of the gold embroidery – a perfect synthesis between baroque tradition and rococo exoticism, between linearity and plasticity. The embroidery of these vestments is consistently of an extremely high quality. No lower in quality are the green holiday vestments executed by Filippo Gabrielli (figs 90 and 91).[16] Checking the payment receipts has enabled us to ascertain that the holiday frontals in white, purple and green do not appear in the accounts relating to the execution of the corresponding sets of vestments, but in the extensive list of works for which payment was made to Giuliano Saturni. They must therefore have been created by this master craftsman and not by Bovi, Gabrielli and Patrenostro, as previously thought.[17] Filippo Salandri was the craftsman responsible for the two holiday sets in red and pink (these are complete sets – that is to say, they include the corresponding frontals).[18] The embroidery comprising the chapel collection reaches its greatest heights of achievement with the so-called *veli della Passione* – the veils or curtains of the Passion (fig. 92). The size and the combination of straight and curved lines forming the shape of the three panels match the frames of the chapel's three mosaic pictures, for which they were made. They were intended to cover up the images during Holy Week as a token of mourning, as was Catholic ritual in those days (and still is, in some places), which called for the use of the colour purple. The instruments of the Passion of Christ are shown in relief in the embroidered motifs visible in the centre of the pieces, framed by a very rich and elaborate floral decoration enlivened with baroque volutes and rococo motifs. The execution of the three great cloths[19] was entrusted to Giuliano Saturni,[20] but in fact it was Filippo Gabrielli and Cosimo Paternoster who fashioned these very elaborate and prestigious pieces – the central curtain by the former, and one of the side curtains by the latter.[21] The cost of the other side curtain, paid to Saturni, was 711 *scudi*.[22] Giuliano Saturni was also entrusted with the production of three particularly precious objects, the bags intended for covering up the crucifixes as a sign of mourning during the days of the Passion of the Lord. These were perfectly

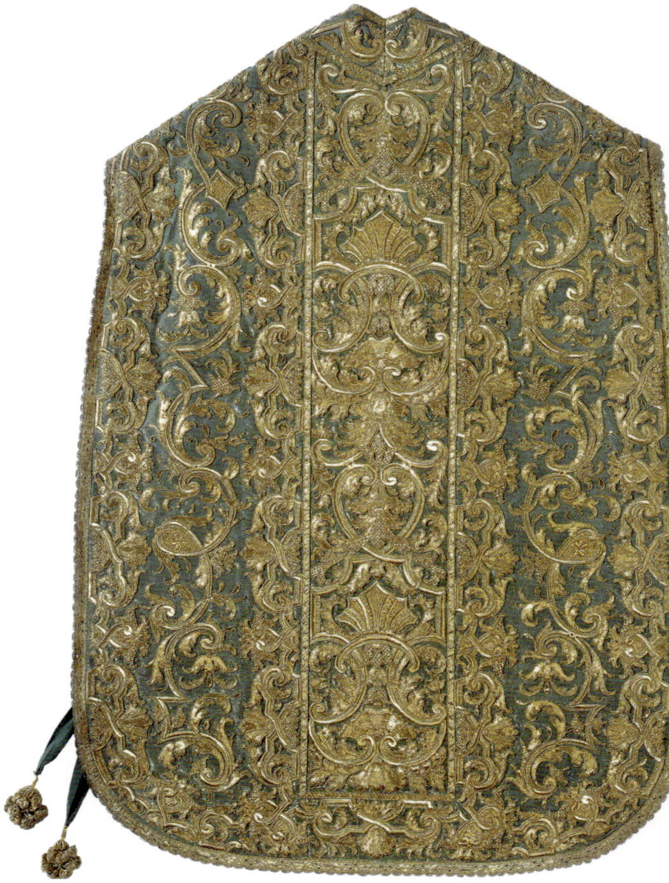

Figs 90 and 91
Chasuble (verso)
Green vestment
for holidays
Filippo Gabrielli
Rome, 1744–49
Silk and silver-gilt thread,
embroidered in gold
(inv. MT. 23)

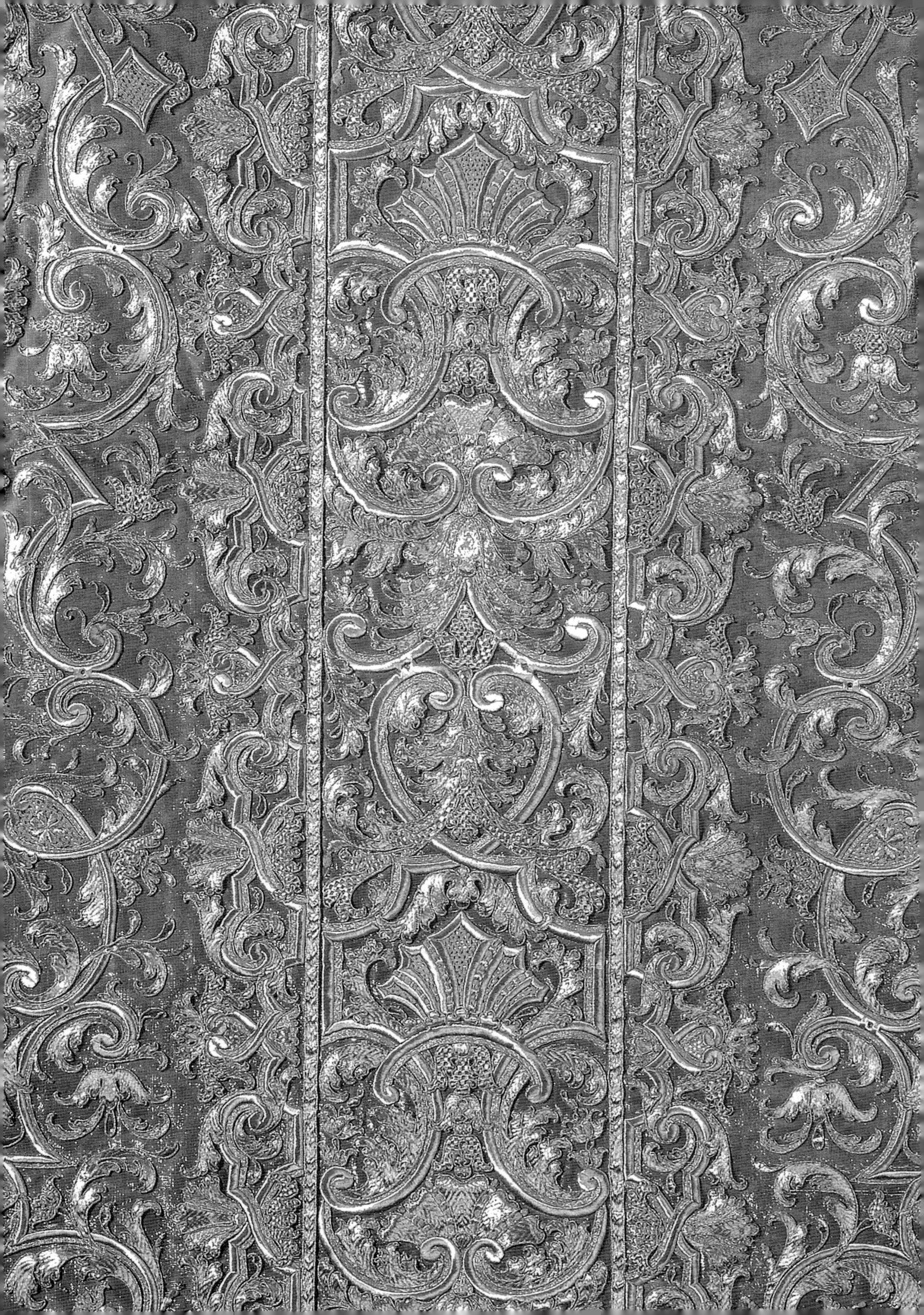

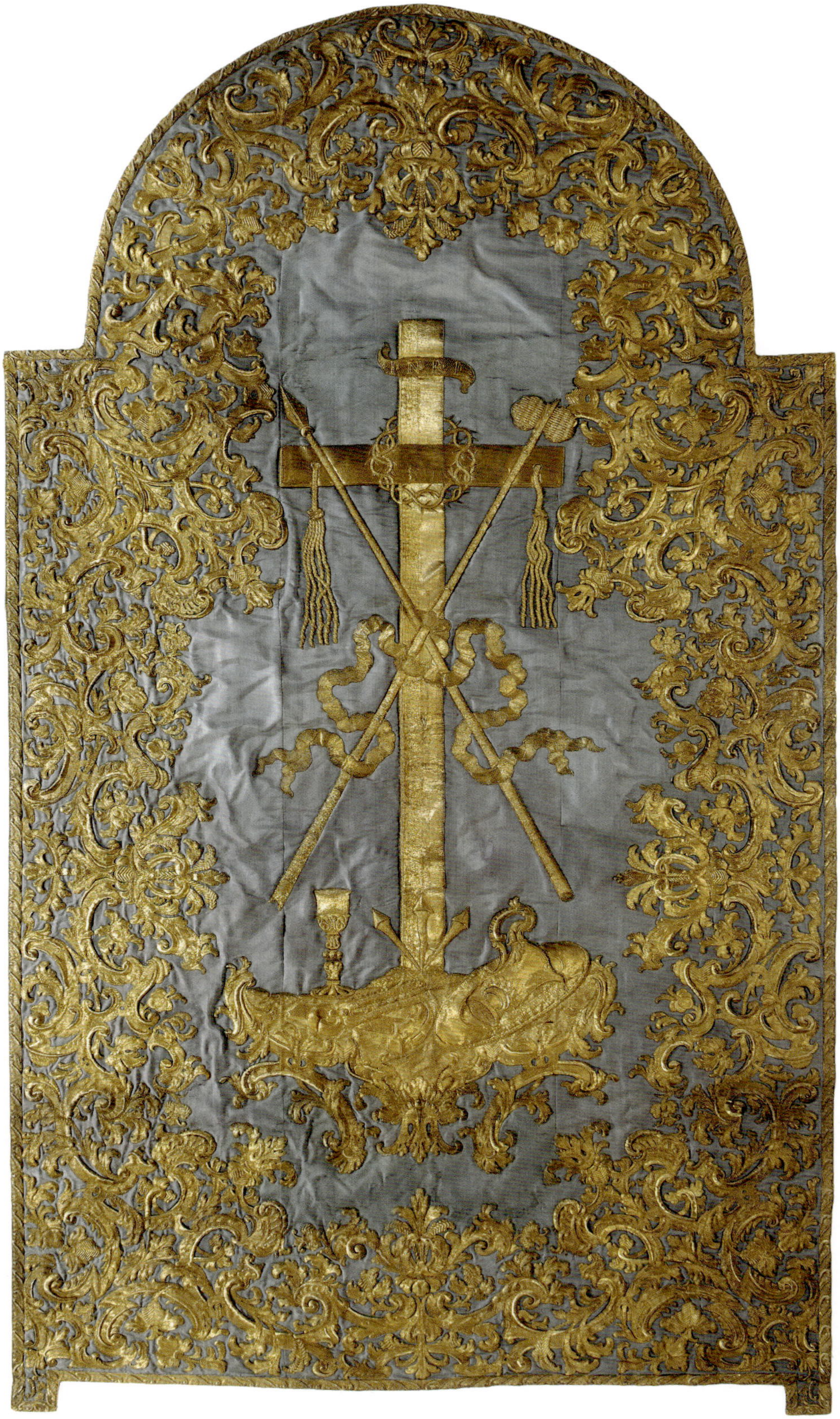

Fig. 92
Curtain of the Passion
(central)
Filippo Gabrielli, Cosimo Patrenostro
Rome, 1744–49
Silk and silver-gilt thread, embroidered in gold
(inv. MT. 155)

executed, decorated on both sides, elegant and of extremely refined appearance, thanks to the contrast obtained by the metallic effect of the gold embroidery against the dark purple velvet background.[23]

Although it was made by five different craftsmen, the set of vestments for everyday use – which has survived complete, including the altar frontals and the five pairs of door covers – constitutes a homogeneous whole in terms of its materials, and has a unified style perfectly matching the vestments for high days and holidays of which it purports to be a simplified version, by dint of using a less precious fabric. The fabric used here is robust and creates a great visual effect, however, as it is *gros de Tours moiré* (Tours grosgrain silk moiré – *Amuer* in the documents), which replaces the 'gilded' or lamé cloth, and yellow silk thread is used for the embroidery in place of gold thread. This is the joint work of a group, but no less original than the richest vestments; indeed, the artists followed a common compositional scheme and made use of the incredible variety of a shared decorative repertoire – lacy motifs, both stylised and naturalistic flowers, cartouches combining both straight and curved lines, and geometric forms, shells and volutes, all skilfully deployed in branching 'candelabrum-style' arrangements. These vestments for everyday use were commissioned on 4 March 1744, like the others, and by 28 May 1748 they were completed by the embroiderers Carlo Abbondio (white), Gio Batta Salandri (red), Benedetto Salandri (green), Filippo Gabrielli (purple) and Nicolò Bovi (fig. 93).[24]

The silk fabrics were supplied by Biagio Chelucci[25] and the trimmings – extremely refined and perfect in every way – were supplied by Giuliano Saturni.[26] The making-up of each piece was the responsibility of the tailor Francesco Giuliani.[27]

Fig. 93
Altar frontal
Black vestment
for everyday use
Nicolò Bovi
Rome, 1745–46
Grosgrain silk embroidered
in yellow silk (inv. MT. 154)

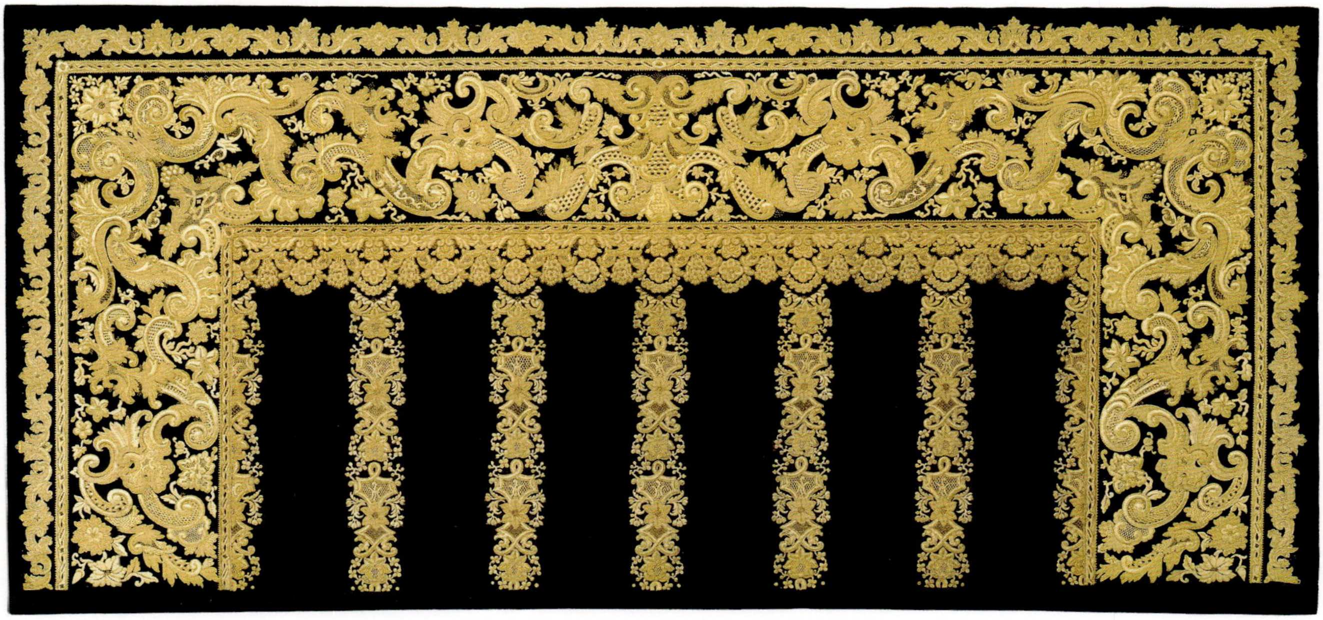

The carpet

Together with the textiles order for embroidered vestments and lace (9 March 1744), there is another for three carpets – for everyday use, for holidays and for high days, just as in the case of the liturgical vestments. Initially the work was entrusted to the carpet-maker Antonio Gargaglia, who established the prices on 29 May 1745. However, of the three carpets only one, the so-called *nobile* intended

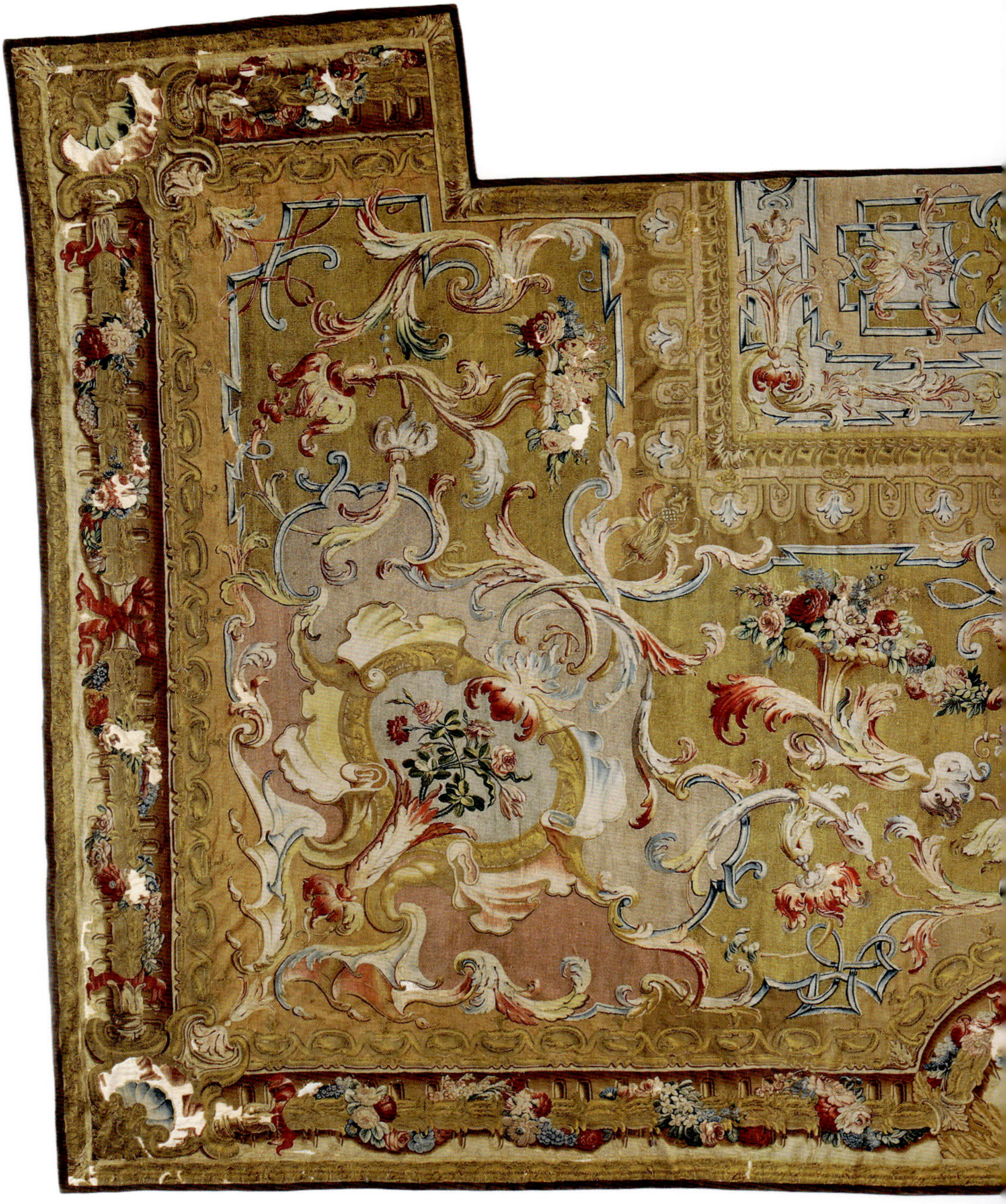

for high masses (5.60 x 3.52 m) is now included in the textile collections of the chapel (fig. 94).[28]

Antonio Gargaglia (who had been an assistant to the French craftsman Giovanni Simonet) and his partner Agostino Speranza, both of whom had trained in the San Michele workshop under the direction of Pietro Ferloni, had decided to set up their own workshop owing to disagreements with the latter. In the early

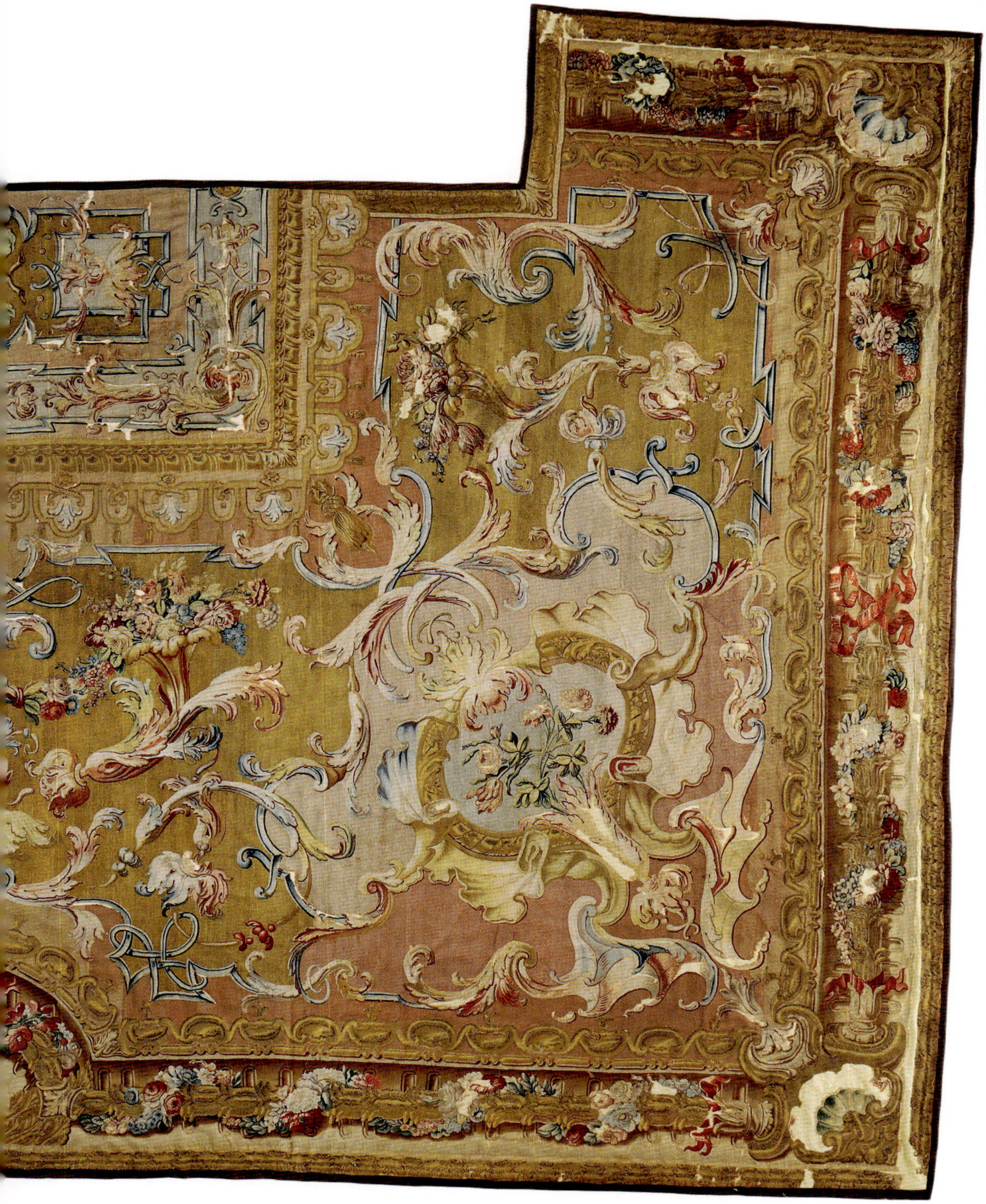

Fig. 94
Carpet
Agostino Speranza (carpet-weaver)
Biagio Chicci (painter)
Rome, *c.* 1747–50
Polychrome silk and silver thread (inv. MT. 165)

1740s, and under the protection of the Company of Jesus, they established a new workshop/factory located in Santa Maria Square in Trastevere, where they did indeed make extremely high-value carpets for the company.[29] The carpet in question was not executed in Antonio Gargaglia's Trastevere workshop, however, but in premises facing the palace of Cardinal Orsini,[30] that is to say, in the parish of Sant'Angelo, where the workshop of the master craftsman Pietro Durante[31] was also situated.

February 1748 brought the death of the decorator and painter Giuseppe Cucciolini, to whom execution of the cartoon had been entrusted on 20 December of the previous year. The commission for this drawing then passed to the younger artist Biagio Chicchi, a highly regarded flower painter and a friend of Cucciolini, and payment for this work was made on 8 July 1748.[32] Work began under the direction of Paolo Nicoli, who was commissioned for the purpose by the Jesuit Father Antonio Cabral (in charge of Portuguese affairs in Rome after the death of Ambassador Manuel Pereira Sampaio) and proceeded in two stages. During the first phase, according to an inspection carried out on 20 April 1750, Agostino Speranza, Mario Silvestri, Ferdinando Canziani, Michele Bastianelli, Filippo Fiorentini and Alessandro Zanetti had completed only 6 out of a planned length of 28 linear 'palms' or handspans, giving a total of 94 square palms.[33] This finding very probably incurred some kind of reprimand from Father António Cabral concerning the slow progress of the work, given that the documentation drawn up later reveals how Agostino Speranza – undoubtedly blaming the delay on some of the team members – took the task in hand himself in his role as master craftsman and contractually excluded the other workers (particularly Zanetti) from collaborating as partners, accepting them only as subordinate helpers.[34] The carpet took a whole year to complete, at the end of which Agostino Speranza signed it on the border of the lining: 'Agostinus Speranza F[ecit] Roma'.[35]

The technical and formal characteristics of the carpet derive from the fact that the professionals responsible for its creation had trained in the workshops of the Ospizio Apostolico or 'Apostolic Hospice' of San Michele. San Michele specialised particularly in the exclusive use of silk in their weaving, which makes the resulting work particularly valuable; they were also known for rendering effects of colour and volume inspired by painting, with the aim of imitating – albeit in moderation – the highly prized French productions of the day,[36] and for their linear flourishes whose flowing or geometric lines enclosed floral fantasies designed after the Chinese fashion in an exquisite synthesis of abstraction and naturalism. ■

NOTES

[1] cf. Angela DELAFORCE, 'Giovanni V di Braganza e le relazioni artistiche e politiche del Portogallo con Roma', in Sandra Vasco ROCCA and Gabriele BORGHINI (eds.), *Giovanni V di Portogallo (1707–1750) e la cultura romana del suo tempo*, Àrgos, Rome, 1995, p. 23. By the same author: *Art and Patronage in Eighteenth-Century Portugal*, Cambridge, Cambridge University Press, 2002.

[2] On the value and meaning of embroidery in the history of art: Marie SCHUETTE and Sigrid MULLER-CHRISTENSEN, *Il ricamo nella storia e nell'arte*, Rome, 1963, p. 13; Claude FOQUE, 'Broderie', in Régis DEBRAY and Patrice HUGUES (ed.), *Dictionnaire Culturel du Tissu*, Paris, Babylone/Fayard, 2005, pp. 42–45. On embroidery in gold: Isabella BIGAZZI, 'Ricami d'ogni sorte, d'oro, d'argento e seta', in Ricardo SPINELLI (ed.), *Arti fiorentine. La grande storia dell'Artigianato, Il Seicento e il Settecento*, vol. V, Florence, Giunti, 2002, pp. 207–29, p. 216.

[3] With regard to this important aspect see: Angela DELAFORCE in Sandra Vasco ROCCA and Gabriele BORGHINI, *op. cit.*, pp. 21–23.

[4] It should be remembered, for example, that just two years earlier the archbishop of Cologne, Clement Augustus of Bavaria, had marked the occasion of the imperial coronation of his brother Charles VII by having a set of vestments brought from Paris – an exceptionally rich set made in the best French workshops of the time: Dela von BOESELAGER, *Capella Clementina, Kurfürst Clemens August und die Krönung Kaiser Karsl VII*, Cologne, Kölner Dom, 2001.

[5] cf. Angela DELAFORCE, *op. cit.*, and see in the same volume Gabriele BORGHINI, 'Apparati Luso Romani tra chiesa e palazzo. II Il palazzo alla Pilotta del commendatore Sampaio', pp. 254–60, as also evidenced by the documents published by Teresa Leonor M. VALE, *Arte e Diplomacia. A Vivência Romana dos Embaixadores Joaninos. A figura e as colecções de arte de José Maria da Fonseca Évora (1690–1752)*, Lisbon, Scribe, 2015. Information obtained from books and prints such as that of Filippo BONANNI, *La gerarchia ecclesiastica considerata nelle vesti sagre, e civili, Roma 1720*, dedicated specifically to the *Sacra Magestade o Rei Portugal* (His Blessed Majesty the King of Portugal) available in the collections of the royal library of the Palace of Mafra.

[6] Biblioteca da Ajuda (Lisbon), Ms. 49-VIII-27, Doc. 9 (*Ordinazioni* ff. 53–60 v.); Francisco Marques de Sousa VITERBO and R. Vicente d'ALMEIDA, *A Capella de S. João Baptista Erecta na Egreja de S. Roque*, Lisbon, Livros Horizonte, 1997 (1902), pp. 52–55.

[7] B.A., Ms. 49-IX-22. *Contas de Manoel Pereira de Sampajo – annos de 1731 a 1750*, f. 190 et seq..

[8] It is interesting that the cost of the materials used is mentioned: 'Costo di lame d'oro e d'argento di varii colori, velluto, amuerre, fiocchi, frangie, galloni e cordoni di seta, barbanterie per contro fodere, Banderaro per fattura, ed altri minutami d'importo scudi 4.700:06' (Cost of gold and silver lamé of various colours, velvet, moiré, tassels, fringes, braids and cords of silk, *barbanterie* for linings, *banderaro* for making up, and other minutiae amounting to the sum of 4,700.06 scudi') (B.A., Ms. 49-VIII-25, ff. 25–27). It is not possible, however, to draw a precise comparison between the sum shown in the budget and the payment entries. In these, the artists appear with monthly regularity over several years – specifically between November 1744 and December 1749 – but without any clear link to the pieces that they were making at the time: B.A., Ms. 49-IX-22, *Contas de Manoel Pereira de Sampajo em Roma – annos de 1731 a 1750*.

[9] Without altar frontals in cloth, given that for pontifical masses the precious frontal of silver and lapis lazuli would be used.

[10] Francisco Marques de Sousa VITERBO and R. Vicente d'ALMEIDA, *op. cit.*, p. 54.

[11] Fausta FRANCHINI GUELFI, 'Theatrum sacrum: materiali e funzioni dell'apparato liturgico' in *Apparato liturgico e arredo ecclesiastico nella Riviera Spezzina*, Genoa, Sagep, 1986, pp. 9–19.

[12] For a more detailed analysis of this subject, see Magda TASSINARI, '*Et essendo la nostra arte sorella della pittura*: il ricamo a Roma tra Sei e Settecento e i corredi liturgici della Cappella di San Giovanni Battista nella chiesa di San Rocco a Lisbona', in *Romische Historische Mitteilungen*, no. 54, 2012, pp. 193–246.

[13] cf. Giulia FUSCONI, 'Disegni decorativi di Johan Paul Schor', in *Bollettino d'Arte*, no. 33–34 (1985), pp. 172–73; Giulia FUSCONI, *Disegni Decorativi del Barocco Romano* (exhibition catalogue), Rome, Edizioni Quasar, 1986, pp. 41–43, nos. 24–28. Around 1673, Johann Paul Schor's son Philipp, who was active in the papal court of Clement X (Altieri), as Giulia Fusconi records, also appears as a designer of embroidery. In addition to other

decorative work, Fusconi attributes to him authorship of the sketches for an embroidered livery (1682), cf. Giulia FUSCONI, 'Philipp Schor, gli Altieri e il Marchese del Carpio', in *Johan Paul Schor und die internationale Sprache des Barock* (Atti delle giornate di studio, Rome, 2003), Munich, Hirmer Verlag, 2008, pp. 175–91.

[14] Filippo PASSARINI, *Nuove inventioni d'ornamenti d'architettura e d'intagli diversi: utili ad argentieri, intagliatori, ricamatori et altri professori delle buone arti del disegno*, Rome, Domenico de Rossi, 1698.

[15] Francisco Marques de Sousa VITERBO and R. Vicente d'ALMEIDA, *op. cit.*, p. 55.

[16] Estimated at 8 *scudi* and 50 Roman *baiocchi* per square 'palm', the embroiderer was paid the total sum for this work of 416.30 *scudi* B.A., Ms. 49-VIII-16 (*Giustificazioni*, 1747), f. 135.

[17] B.A., Ms. 49-VIII-16 (*Giustificazioni*, 1747), ff. 234 and following; Ms. 49-VIII-19 (*Giustificazioni*, 1750), *Conto di Giuliano Saturni Ricamatore*, f. 162 (35) and following; in this list of accounts, the *porteiras* belonging to the purple and green holiday ensembles appear as having also been executed by Saturni.

[18] The cost submitted for the two sets of vestments was 3,589 *scudi* and 5 Roman *baiocchi*. Francisco Marques de Sousa VITERBO and R. Vicente d'ALMEIDA, *op. cit.*, p. 57. The pink holiday set of vestments by Filippo Salandri was recently exhibited in London – see Magda TASSINARI, in Michael SNODIN and Nigel LLEWELLYN (coord.), *Baroque. Style in the Age of Magnificence. 1620–1800*, London, V&A Publishing, 2009, nos. 110–14.

[19] Francisco Marques de Sousa VITERBO and R. Vicente d'ALMEIDA, *op. cit.*, p. 54.

[20] The embroiderer sets the corresponding price in a document dated 29 August 1745 in Rome, together with other works that had been commissioned from him: B.A., Ms. 49-VIII-25, f. 25.

[21] As can be seen from reading the payment notes recorded between 1748 and 1749 in the accounting books: B.A., *Contas de Manoel Pereira de Sampaio em Roma, 1731 a 1750*, Ms. 49-IX-22, cc. 805 et seq. The two curtains cost 1.323 and 710 Roman *scudi*: Francisco Marques de Sousa VITERBO and R. Vicente d'ALMEIDA, *op. cit.*, p. 58, no. 12, p. 59, no. 13, p. 169. B.A., Ms. 49-VIII-20, ff. 278 and 278v.

[22] B.A., Ms. 49-VIII-19 (*Giustificazioni*, 1750), *Conto di Giuliano Saturni Ricamatore*, f. 179.

[23] Commissioned in Rome on 9 March 1744, ('Tre Borze paonazze per le croci, cioè due ricche, et una meno ricca') (B.A., Ms. 49-VIII-25, f. 25); the three bags were budgeted for in Saturni's accounts at 99 Roman *scudi*, but only 88 were paid for them after the price was checked and adjusted, B.A., Ms. 49-VIII-19 (*Giustificazioni*, 1750), *Conto di Giuliano Saturni Ricamatore*, ff. 166, 167 v.

[24] B.A., Ms. 49-VIII-25, f. 26; Francisco Marques de Sousa VITERBO and R. Vicente d'ALMEIDA, *op. cit.*, pp. 55–58. Executed between Summer 1745 and Autumn 1746; 488 *scudi* and 25 Roman *baiocchi* were paid for each chasuble set: B.A., Ms. 49-VIII-14, ff. 592-594 ; B.A., Ms. 49-VIII-15, ff. 138–140; Ms. 49-VIII-16, ff. 234–236.

[25] The cost of which amounted, up to 1748, to 2.072 *scudi* and 72 *baiocchi*: B.A., Ms. 49-VIII-17, ff. 109–17.

[26] Estimated at 2.530 *scudi* and 36 *baiocchi*. A separate account has been identified for the curtain fringes, amounting to 978 *scudi* and 80 *baiocchi*: B.A., Ms. 49-VIII-19 (*Giustificazioni*, 1750), *Conto di Giuliano Saturni Ricamatore*, ff. 170–75.

[27] Giuliani submitted an account amounting to a total of 458.01 *scudi*, but in fact received the sum of 260 *scudi*: B.A., Ms. 49-VIII-16, ff. 301–22.

[28] Francisco Marques de Sousa VITERBO and R. Vicente d'ALMEIDA, *op. cit.*, pp. 67, 96, 168. In the commission this piece is referred to from the first as 'Un tappeto, o sia strato, per coprire ne'giorni più solenni la Pradella, e Scalini dell'Altare della Cappella del più Ricco, e miglior gusto possibile' (A carpet, that is to say a covering mantle, for use on the most solemn days to cover the predella, and altar steps of the chapel, of the richest and the best possible taste): B.A., Ms. 49-VIII-24, *Commissione delli tappeti di Arazzo per servizio della Cappella dello Spirito Santo e S. Gio Batta, con lettera delli 9 marzo 1744*; the design of the carpet, which exactly matches the work executed, is recorded in the drawings in the set known as the *Weale Album* (no. 82) accompanying the corresponding instructions with regard to materials and costs (f. 249), in accordance with what had been agreed with Antonio Gargaglia for its execution; cf. Teresa Leonor M. VALE (ed.), *De Roma para Lisboa. Um Álbum para o Rei Magnânimo*, Lisbon, Santa Casa da Misericórdia de Lisboa-Scribe, 2015, ff. 249–59, nos. 82, 83, 84.

[29] Luca Antonio CHRACAS, *Diario Ordinario*, Rome, no. 4218, 8 August 1744; Anna Maria DE STRÖEBEL, *Le Arazzerie Romane dal XVII al XIX Secolo*, Rome, Istituto Nazionale di Studi Romani, 1989, p. 62; Alvar GONZÁLEZ

PALACIOS, *Appunti per un lessico romano-lusitano ...*, p. 449; Pia TOSCANO, *Roma produttiva tra Settecento e Ottocento. Il San Michele a Ripa Grande*, Rome, Viella, 1996, p. 204.

[30] B.A., Ms. 49-VIII-19, f. 126 (VITERBO and ALMEIDA cite this document with the reference: Ms 49-VIII-12, f. 26, *op. cit.*, pp. 68, 95–96).

[31] Pietro Durante was 33 years old in 1750, and lived in the parish of Sant'Angelo in Pescheria together with his wife, four children and a servant; cf. Rita RANDOLFI, 'Parrocchia di Sant'Angelo Pescheria. Rione Sant'Angelo', in Elisa DEBENEDETTI (ed.), *Artisti e Artigiani a Roma I, Degli Stati delle Anime del 1700, 1725, 1750, 1775*, Rome, Bonsignore Editori, 2004, pp. 143–50.

[32] Alvar GONZÁLEZ PALACIOS, *Arte di corte del XVII e del XVIII secolo*, vol. I, Rome, Longanesi, 1993, p. 109; Alvar GONZÁLEZ PALACIOS, *Appunti per un lessico romano-lusitano, op. cit.*, p. 447, no. 45. B.A., Ms. 49-VIII-21, f. 78, this document shows the payment to Biagio Chicchi on 8 July 1748.

[33] The width of 147 palms was fixed, given that this corresponds to the side or width of the loom on which the carpet was made.

[34] B.A., Ms. 49-VIII-20, ff. 545–545 v.

[35] On 12 June 1751 Agostino Speranza was paid 1,969 Roman *scudi* and 40 *baiocchi* as the balance for the carpet-making work to complete the *nobile* carpet; cf. Francisco Marques de Sousa VITERBO and R. Vicente d'ALMEIDA, *op. cit.*, p. 68; Maria João Madeira RODRIGUES, *A Capela de S. João Baptista e as suas Colecções*, Lisbon, Inapa, 1989 (1988), p. 226. Appended to Speranza's contract there is a list of expenses (dated 29 August 1750) which totals six pages; this is a document of the greatest interest for a better understanding of the technical details of the work and also of the various individuals involved in its execution: B.A., Ms. 49-VIII-20, ff. 542–47 v. – *Conto del Tappeto Nobile, Ordinato dalla Reggia Corte di Portogallo*.

[36] Anna Maria DE STRÖEBEL, *L'Arazzeria di San Michele tra il Settecento e L'Ottocento attraverso le opere della collezione vaticana* in *Arte e artigianato nella Roma di Belli*, Rome, Edizioni Colombo, 1998, p. 119.

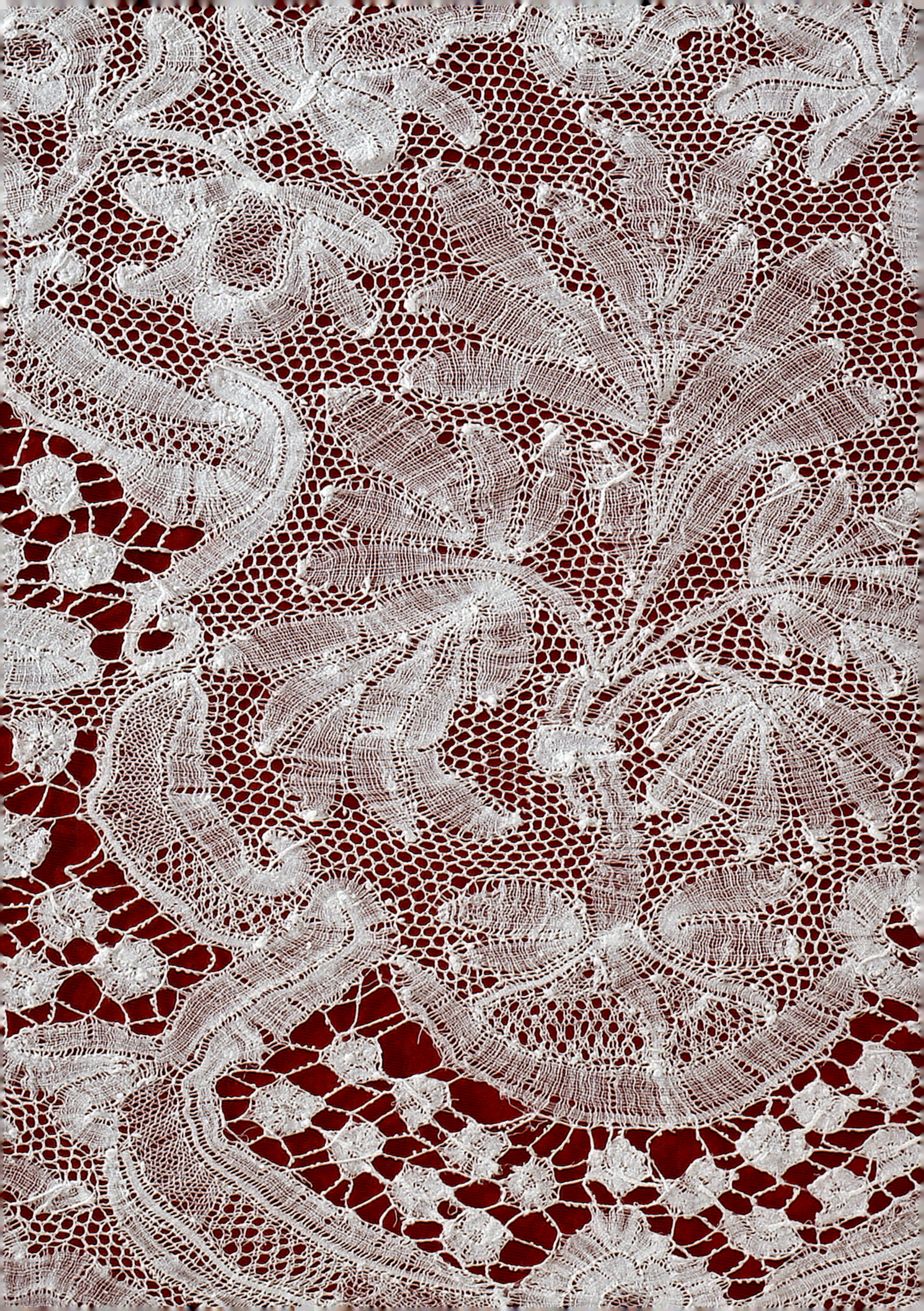

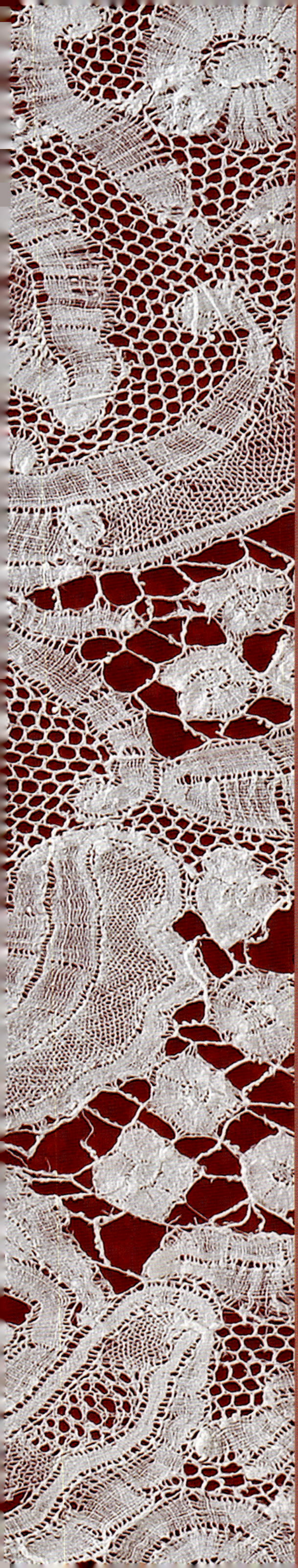

3. LACE

At the crossroads of Flanders, Rome and Lisbon: the lacework of the Chapel of St John the Baptist

Marialuisa Rizzini

The sumptuously rich endowment bestowed by John V on the Chapel of St John the Baptist included over 220 pieces of various linens and liturgical garments, trimmed with lace, of which 62 surviving pieces in a good state of preservation are now in the Museum of San Rocco in Lisbon.[1] Considering the very great extent to which such artefacts tended to be scattered and lost, this is a very significant number. The fact that it is possible to date the lace with certainty is also extremely rare, in a field of study which generally has to deal with specimens that have no documentary support at all.

This information, whose significance was first recognised in the archival research of Sousa Viterbo and Vicente d'Almeida (1900),[2] has in fact proved fundamental and has made it possible to reconstruct the stages of execution of the lacework. This would have taken place in Rome, as in the case of the other adornments and furnishings for the chapel. We know the identity of the person who coordinated the work, a noblewoman named Maria Anna Cenci Bolognetti, and we have the names of the Roman merchants (known as *trinaroli* because they sold *trine*, an Italian term equivalent to *merletti* or *pizzi* – lacework or lace) from whom the pieces were purchased as well as their probable workshops of origin. We even know the names of the women who sewed and made up the linens and who put in the gathers or 'ruffled' them, creating the dense pleats in the starched fabric that were in fashion at the time.

None of the lace itself came from a Roman studio, however, because the best workshops were in Flanders and France; nor were they made up to order, but purchased by the metre. Their designs do not therefore share the characteristic sumptuous Roman late baroque style of the chapel, but are instead more in line with the rococo style that was then in widespread use internationally in both religious and non-religious clothing. Nevertheless, their execution was probably set in motion thanks to the very close relations between John V and the papal court in Rome.

Maria Anna Cenci Bolognetti: a Roman noblewoman in the 'service of His Majesty the King of Portugal'

Among the elements supporting this hypothesis is the choice of Maria Anna Cenci Bolognetti (1705–94). She was a member of an old family, the Cenci, that had fallen into decline following the controversial trial for the murder of Francesco Cenci (1598); in fact it was Maria Anna Cenci Bolognetti's own marriage in December

pp. 138–139
Decorative hem of Alb (tunic) (detail)
Brussels, Brabant?
(See fig. 99)

1723 to Virginio Cenci (1700–55), a descendant of another branch of the family, that marked the birth of a new family line that would unite the two surnames, starting with their son Girolamo.[3] Maria Anna Cenci Bolognetti was the daughter of Count Ferdinand (born in Bologna but resident in Rome from the end of the seventeenth century) and the Roman Countess Flavia Theodoli. The family's social ascendency was enshrined by the appointment of her brother Mario (1690–1756) to the rank of cardinal, decreed on 9 September 1743 by Pope Benedict XIV (who was also from Bologna). Mario's successful ecclesiastical career, which flourished during the same period in the reign of John V, was characterised by his lively cultural interests and his taste as a collector, which made him a particularly noteworthy member of Pope Benedict XIV (Lambertini)'s political and cultural circle.

The family's prestige and particularly her brother's influence very probably determined the selection of Maria Anna Cenci Bolognetti to oversee the creation of the collection of liturgical linens for the chapel – although she boasted other personal qualities, being a charming and elegant woman, as can be seen from a portrait dated between 1736 and 1737 (fig. 95).[4] The painting shows her accompanied by her children, and depicts her as apparently fashion conscious but without extravagance, as her rank demanded. She is shown wearing a sumptuous *manteau* style gown, decorated with rococo motifs in gold embroidery and the finest, most delicate lace around the neckline and on the sleeves, as prescribed by the French fashion of the day. The skill and competence demonstrated in her choice of these exquisite trimmings showed how well suited she was for a task only slightly removed from the spheres of the feminine and fashionable.

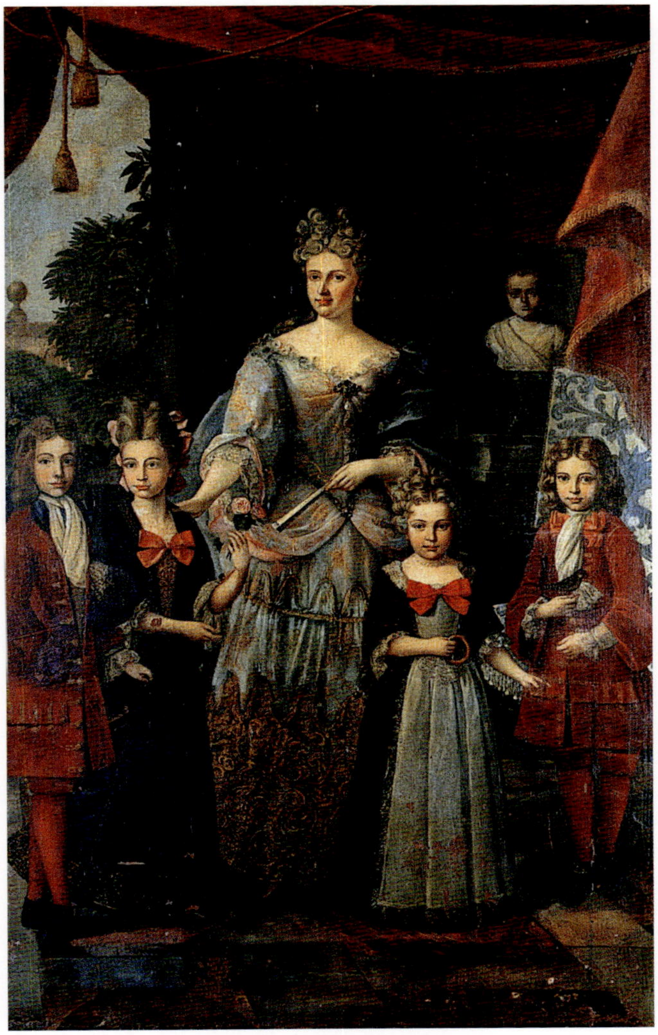

Fig. 95
Portrait of Maria Anna Cenci Bolognetti and her Family
Oil on canvas
Fondazione Principi di Vicovaro [Vicovaro Princes Foundation], Rome

In fact, the eighteenth century saw an extremely widespread use of lace, either in linen or metallic thread, as luxury decoration both for the formal garments of either sex and for religious use, and there was no distinction made in ornamental motifs between religious and secular use apart from for a few very rare and exceptionally prestigious commissions. The record showing that the merchant Giuseppe Girardi had delivered to 'her ladyship the Most Illustrious Madame Anna Maria Cenci ... two reels of *Ponto d'Inghiltera* [English point] lace a palm and a half wide, after the latest fashion',[5] highlights the novelty of the design. In fact, the decorations employed changed very rapidly during the eighteenth century precisely because they marked the latest innovations in fashion.

Making up the liturgical costumes

The *Commissione della Biancheria per servizio della cappella dello Spirito Santo, e S. Giovanni Battista ordinata con lettera delli 9 marzo 1744* (commissioning of the linens for the service of the Chapel of the Holy Spirit and St John the Baptist ordered by letter of 9 March 1744) by John V[6] contains a precise list of the items in the set of costumes, classified by type and intended purpose and accompanied by the different heights of the lace edging. Maria Anna Cenci Bolognetti oversaw every stage of execution, from the purchase of materials to making up.[7] Finally 'the chest no. 58 of linens' was lowered down the 'steps of the Palazzo Cenci' on 22 February 1746 to be taken on 'a cart' to the boat and transported to Lisbon.[8] Upon conclusion of her undertaking, Cenci received a gift 'per gradimento di sue fatiche e ingerenza nella sudetta biancaria ... una scatola d'oro' (in thanks for her labours and her intervention in the above-mentioned linens ... a gold box) of the value of 140 escudos.[9] The cost of executing the commission, including shipment and the gift of the box, amounted to a total of 4,200 Roman scudi.[10]

The making up of the pieces took place between September 1744 and August 1745. Lace, trimmings and fabrics were purchased from various merchants: Simone Gentili, Giuseppe Girardi, Piero Perucca, Sebastiano Porena, Giovanni Airoldi and Susanna Inghels. The last of these had a particularly conspicuous presence and may have come from Belgium – which would have been appropriate for the lace trade; having 'emissaries' present in all the most important marketplaces in Europe was in fact a method commonly adopted in the efficient Belgian trade system.[11]

Some of the *trinaroli* were suppliers to the Vatican Palace, as can be seen by comparison with the records of the papal accounts between 1740 and 1745.[12] These merchants, presumably among the most skilled in their fields, received a special 'select' (status) – conferred by official act – which ensured significant professional benefits. The fact that Maria Anna Cenci Bolognetti turned to merchants such as these, although not only to them, seems to confirm the influence of the papal court.

A 'Flemish' collection

In the invoices from the sellers, different types of lace are distinguished by price depending on their 'height' (i.e. their width) measured in Roman palms (a palm was about 22 cm). The most highly prized borders, between a palm and a palm-and-a-half wide, are referred to as being in 'English point' and described as 'noble', 'fine' or 'superfine with designs'; the less costly ones, which are narrower, are referred to as Flanders lace. The surviving examples show that these definitions correspond to the two main types of bobbin lace from Belgium and illustrate their different uses; those in English point were intended for costly undergarments, while the Flanders lace was for liturgical linens.

English point lace

The term 'English point' was used to circumvent the restrictions imposed by England on the importation of foreign lace, and in the eighteenth century it referred to lace from Brussels made in connected pieces;[13] that is to say, each decorative piece was made separately and then they were joined together. The division of labour among the lacemakers, each of whom specialised in different motifs, allowed the work to be done faster and the designs to be varied; it also made it possible to put together pieces of considerable size.

Brussels lace could be identified by various features. It uses very fine thread; the decorations are created in the form of a non-continuous ribbon, with a slightly raised border either along one edge or all round in order to gather up any threads not used in its execution; and there is a strong focus on chiaroscuro, even in the backgrounds such as the complex *fond de neige* or 'snow background', the extraordinarily fine and light *drochel* netting with its hexagonal mesh, and – until the mid-eighteenth century – the slender, dentillated irregular bars inspired by French needlepoint lace in *point de France* or French point that had become widespread since the late seventeenth century.[14]

Drochel netting and dentillated bars are present side-by-side in four borders of remarkable quality, tentatively included in the corpus of the Chapel of St John the Baptist (fig. 96).[15]

The other examples also have a background made using these tiny bars, but here they are supported on netting with a round mesh that was widespread from the second half of the seventeenth century. The motifs are less refined and sharp, and show the typical relief only in certain parts. Studies trace these features to a type

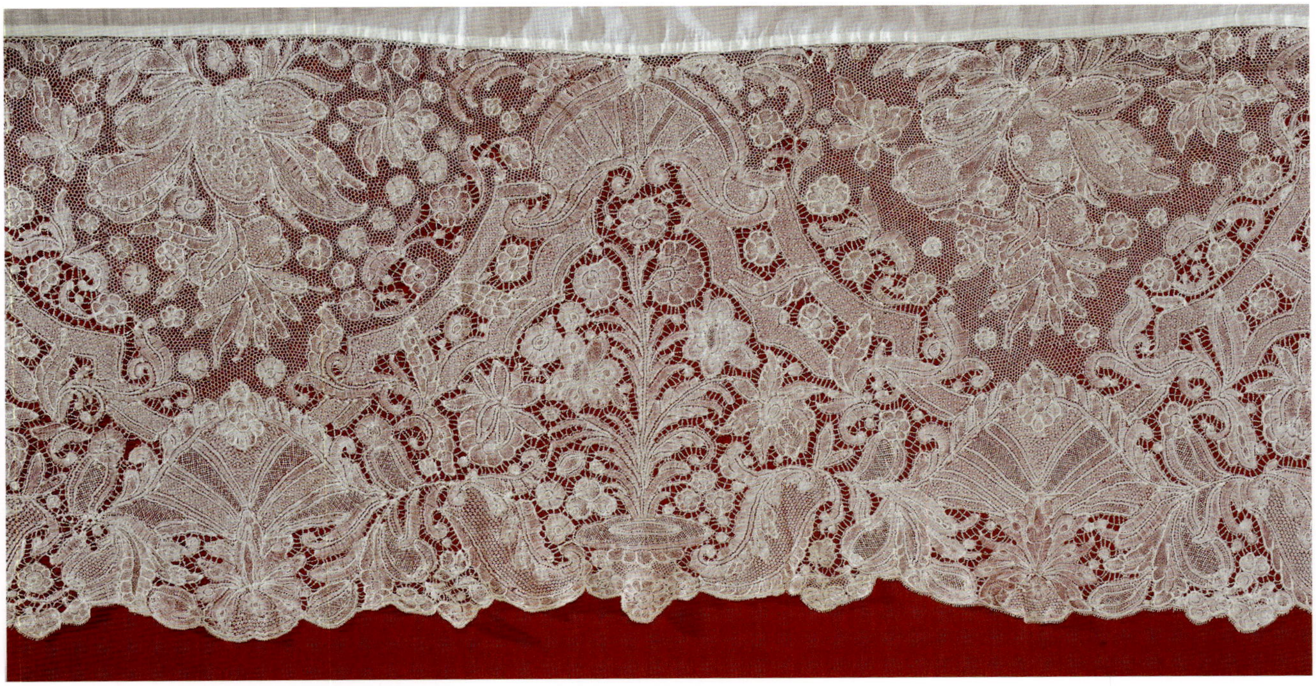

Fig. 96
Decorative hem of Alb (tunic)
Brussels, *c.* 1744–45
Linen
(inv. RT. 17/1)

generally referred to as Brabant lace, named for the region of Flanders where Brussels is situated. In fact, there are no reliable data permitting us to distinguish this specific type of lace, which is moreover similar to that of Brussels; furthermore, in the (very efficient) Flemish commercial communications the different types of lace are indicated by the names of the main centres of production even though they were executed throughout much larger areas. The different qualities of lace in terms of technique and style can thus be attributed not only to their execution in urban or outlying workshops but also to commercial differentiation by market sector.

The Portuguese lace considered here employs a wide range of compositional structures with closely linked modular sections in the Regency style, in harmony with the silk fabric decorations made between 1740 and 1745. There are noticeable differences between the repetitions of the same module due to the production system, in which the work was divided between many workers. This can clearly be seen, for example, by comparing one border in the Museum of the Palazzo Madama in Turin, which is identical to one of the Portuguese lace pieces (figs 97 and 98).[16] The decoration is elaborate but has a certain simplification, suggesting that it derives from a more refined prototype – which would support the argument that

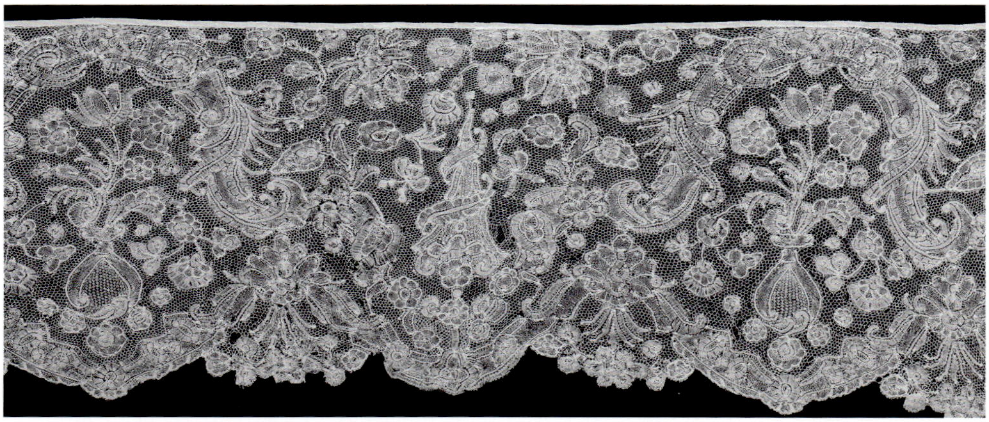

Fig. 97
Lace
Palazzo Madama – Museo Civico d'Arte Antica (Madama Palace – Civic Museum of Ancient Art), Turin (inv. 1889)

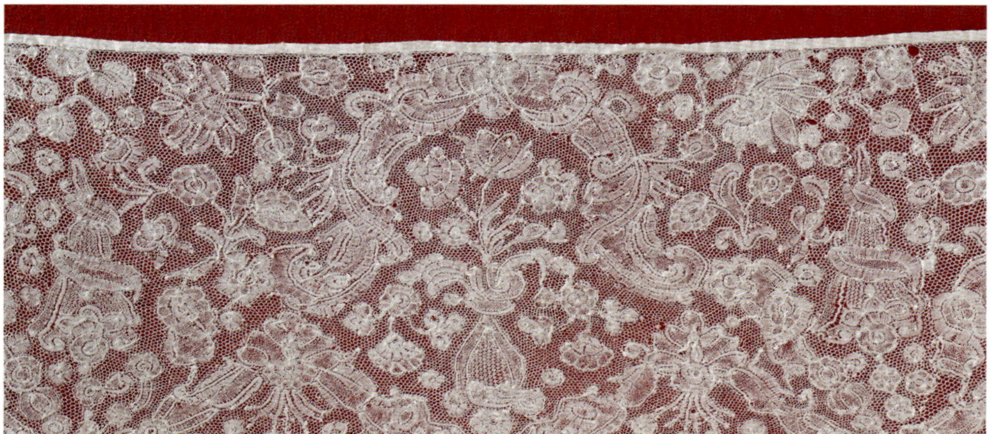

Fig. 98
Decorative hem of Alb (tunic)
Brussels, Brabant?, 1744–45
Linen
(inv. RT. 1/1)

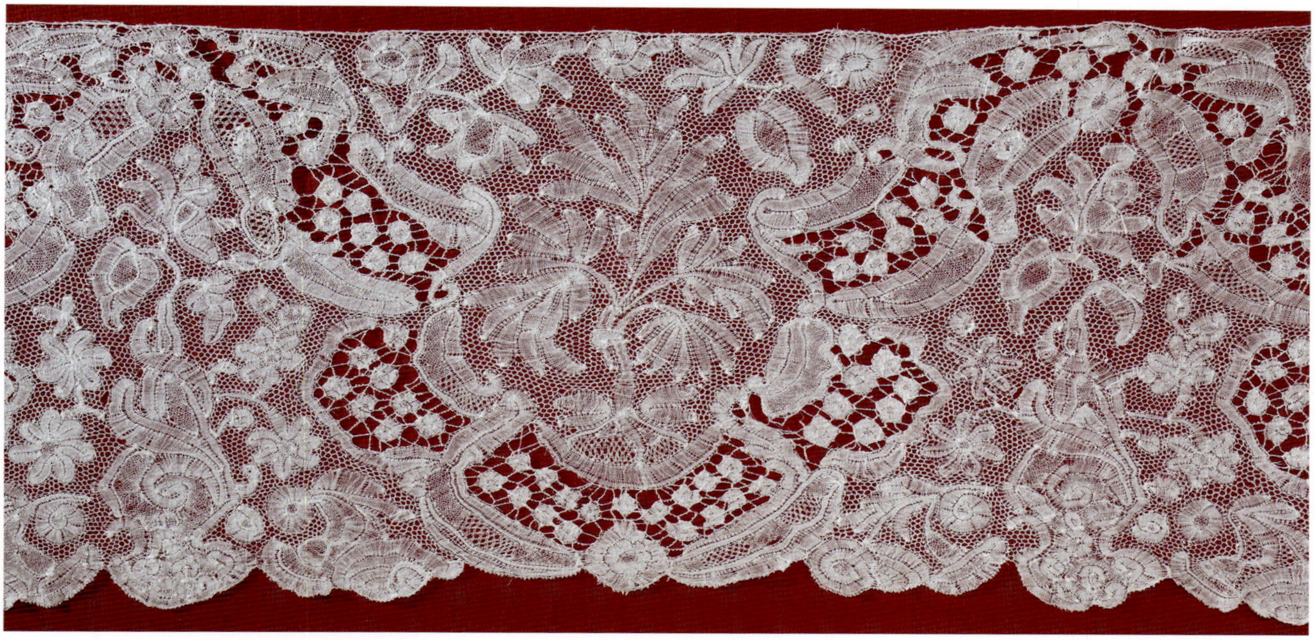

Fig. 99
Decorative hem of Alb (tunic)
Brussels, Brabant?, 1744–45
Linen
(inv. RT. 6/1)
The cornucopia motif is similar to that on the hem in the previous figure, but the decoration is less elaborate

it comes from a provincial workshop. There are obvious possibilities for variation, whether in the background or in the arrangement of the motifs, but also in the fact that the same motif is reprised in examples that differ in stylistic quality (inv. 0001 and 0006) (fig. 99), which may support the hypothesis of different grades of product being made in the same workshops.

Fine Flanders lace

The term 'Flanders' indicated a bobbin lace made with continuous threads – that is to say, with the motifs and the background executed together. This can be seen from examination of an original sample book in the Vatican Secret Archive containing 11 pieces of Flanders lace that are very close to the Lisbon borders in both technique and style (fig. 100).[17]

Fig. 100
Lace
Archivio Segreto Vaticano [Vatican Secret Archive]
(inv. 160r, 9)

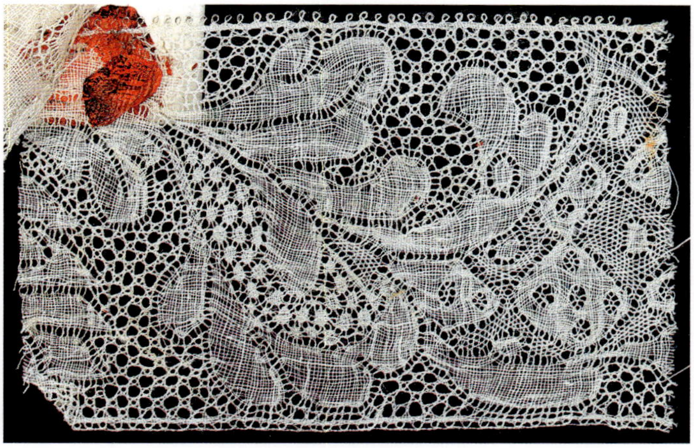

The best known workshops were in Mechelen, Antwerp and Binche, to which examples have been traced that differ in technique but share the common feature that they were made by working with continuous threads. This allowed only limited widths of lace to be made, and demanded a very great deal of time for the most refined examples; bearing in mind that each lacemaker had her own 'signature' handiwork – that is to say, each individual tensioned the thread differently – this meant that a given piece could not be handed over to other workers.

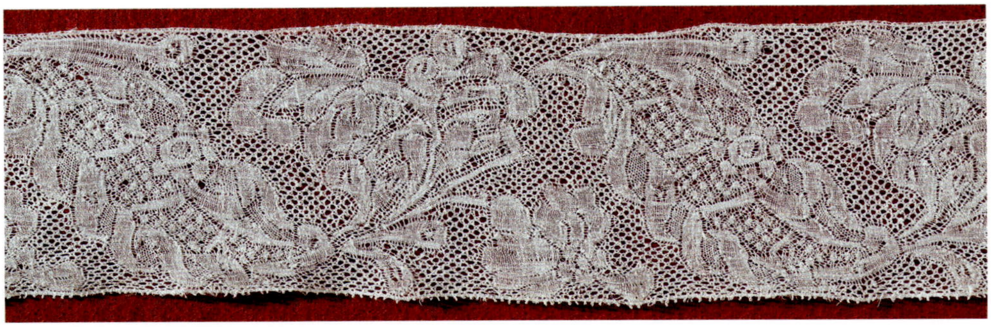

Fig. 101
Decorative hem of Alb (tunic)
Flanders, Valenciennes type, 1744–45
Linen
(inv. RT. 14/1)

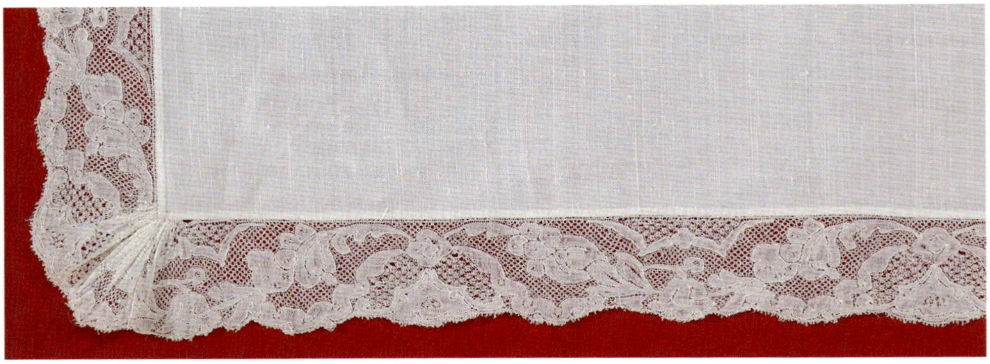

Fig. 102
Border of corporal altar cloth
Flanders, Malines (Mechelen) type, 1744–45
Linen
(inv. RT. 43/1)

Despite the small size of the pieces executed, the Lisbon lace shows remarkable inventiveness in the variety of its motifs and decorations, which although simplified are always in the Regency style. The likely origins cover the range of the main Flemish centres: Binche and Mechelen, and also Valenciennes (which despite having been ceded to France in 1678 was technically still linked to lace production in Belgium). Some of the specimens, however, cannot be attributed to a precise type – which shows that in reality production was structured in much finer divisions than the classifications commonly used in studies, and that it was probably differentiated with reference to the markets for which it was intended.[18] In general, these borders share the common features of extremely fine thread, highly accurate execution and a background mesh known as rose or 'five-hole' ground punctuated with various 'filler' details, confirming that this background – already in widespread use in the second half of the seventeenth century – continued to be used in Flanders until the mid-eighteenth century. As lacemakers had already had extensive experience with this ground, it was easier to work with than other new, and therefore more expensive ones; it also it gave the lace a 'dense' appearance well suited to the tightly filled designs then in vogue (figs 101 and 102). It offers further proof not only of the technical quality of Flemish lacemaking, but also of the efficiency of Flemish commerce, of which the lace of the Chapel of St John offers a very significant example. ■

NOTES

[1] See the following essay for further information and greater detail on the topics covered: Marialuisa RIZZINI, 'Entre a Flandres, Roma e Lisboa: as rendas para a Capela de de S. João Baptista', in Teresa Leonor M. VALE (coord.), *A Capela de S. João Batista da Igreja de São Roque. A encomendas, a obra, as coleções*, Santa Casa da Misericórdia de Lisboa- Imprensa Nacional-Casa da Moeda, 2015, pp. 321–51; on the collection, see also Maria Filomena BRITO, *Rendas Barrocas em Portugal Colecção da Capela de S. João Batista*, Lisbon, Santa Casa da Misericórdia de Lisboa e Livros Horizonte, 1997.

[2] Francisco Marques de Sousa VITERBO and Rodrigo Vicente d'ALMEIDA, *A Capella de S. João Baptista erecta na egreja de S. Roque*, Lisbon, Livros Horizonte, 1997, pp. 61–65 (1st edition 1900).

[3] Michele DI SIVO (ed.), *I Cenci nobiltà di sangue*, Fondazione Marco Bresso, Rome, Editore Colombo, 2002. Unpublished and important documentation regarding Maria Anna [Cenci Bolognetti] and her family has been found in the Archivio di Stato di Roma, *Famiglia Cenci-Bolognetti, B2, Patrimoniali, mazzi* [bundles] 30, 32, 33, 34, 35, 36. Thanks to Michele di Sivo for this invaluable advice.

[4] The portrait is located in the Fondazione Principi di Vicovaro. There is also a sonnet dedicated to Cenci's beauty that can be dated to approximately 1726, by Niccolò FORTEGUERRI (*Il Ricciardetto*, Milan, Societa Tipografica de' Classici italiani, 1813, vol. II, pp. 290–91).

[5] Biblioteca da Ajuda (Lisbon), Ms. 49-VIII-14, f. 18 September 1744.

[6] B.A., 49 VIII 24, s.n.p and 49-VIII-25, ff. 28–29. The document was published by F.M.S. VITERBO and R.V. d'ALMEIDA, *op. cit*.

[7] B.A., Ms. 49-VIII-14: ff. 195r, 310r, 518r.

[8] B.A., Ms. 49-VIII-15, ff. 415v–17r.

[9] F.M.S. VITERBO and R.V. d'ALMEIDA, *op. cit*., pp. 61, 98 without the source. The document is in B.A., 49-IX-22, *Livro de pagamentos de Manuel Pereira Sampaio em Roma*, f. 289, 3 January 1746. Thanks to Magda Tassinari for this information.

[10] F.M.S. VITERBO and R.V. d'ALMEIDA, *op. cit*., p. 61, and B.A., 49 VIII 24 (in identical copy in *ibid*., 49 VIII 25, ff. 28–29).

[11] The accounts, cited in part in F.M.S. VITERBO and R.V. d'ALMEIDA, *op. cit*., pp. 61–63, without archival placement reference, are in B.A., Ms. 49-VIII-14: ff. 2, 18, 194, 194b, 311, 312, 313, 504, 505.

[12] The following volumes have been consulted at the Vatican Secret Archives in the Papal Palace: *Palazzo Apostolico, Computisteria* 218, 225, 226, 229, 230, 234, 236, 239. The lace suppliers included Sebastiano Porena, Pietro Fedele, Susanna Inghels and Francesco Inghels in association with Fabio Devoti. There is a very important study by Antonella PAMPALONE, 'Merletti tra le carte', in Angela NEGRO, Angela (ed.), *Storie di abiti e merletti. Incontri al museo sull'arte e il restauro del pizzo*, Rome, Gangemi, 2014, pp. 53–71, with many previously unpublished lace samples (preserved in the Archivio di Stato di Roma, Giustificazioni di Tesoreria) which were sold between 1700 and 1730 to the Curia by a Roman merchant, Alberto Devoti, who may have been a relative of Fabio Devoti.

[13] Marie RISSELIN-STEENBRUGEN, *Trois siècles de dentelles aux Musées Royaux d'Art et d'Histoire*, Brussels, Musées Royaux d'Art et d'Histoire, 1987 (12th edition), pp. 337–38. The term was already interpreted in this sense by Maria Filomena BRITO, *op. cit*., p. 30.

[14] Marie RISSELIN-STEENBRUGEN, *op. cit*., pp. 383–85.

[15] Maria Filomena BRITO, *op. cit*., nos. 16, 17, 18 and 19, pp. 47–49.

[16] Example no. inv. 1889/T is identical in width to the Lisbon RT/0001 border cf. Marialuisa RIZZINI, card no. 44 in Marina CARMIGNANI, Marialuisa RIZZINI and Maria Paola RUFFINO (eds.), *Merletti dalle collezioni di Palazzo Madama*, Cinisello Balsamo, Silvana Editoriale, 2013, pp. 96–97.

[17] The sample book, with lace samples of widths varying between 4.5 and 7.5 cm, is attached to a letter dated 12 February 1740 (ASV, *Palazzo Apostolico, Computisteria*, vol. 218, ff. 159–61).

[18] This issue has already been raised with regard to the reserve of extremely rare Flemish samples; cf. Marie RISSELIN-STEENBRUGEN, 'Un livre de patrons de dentelles du XVIII sìecle', in *Bullettin des Musées royaux d'Art et d'Histoire*, Brussels, vols 43–44, 1971–72, pp. 131–41; Marguerite COPPENS, 'Un cahier de dessins de dentelles, daté de 1750, et son contexte commercial. d'après les archives d'une famille de fabricants anversois. Les Reyns', *op. cit*., pp. 49–72.

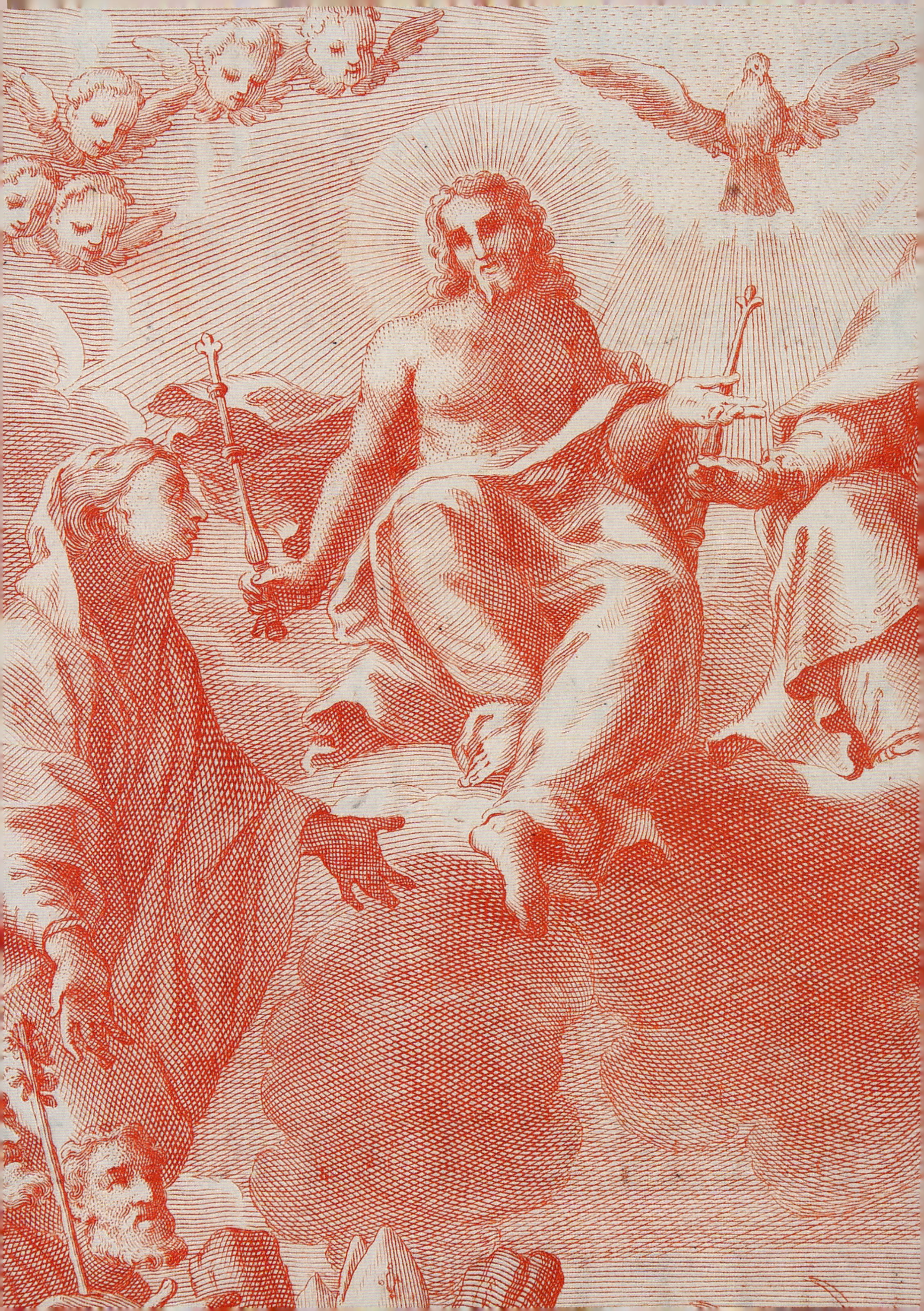

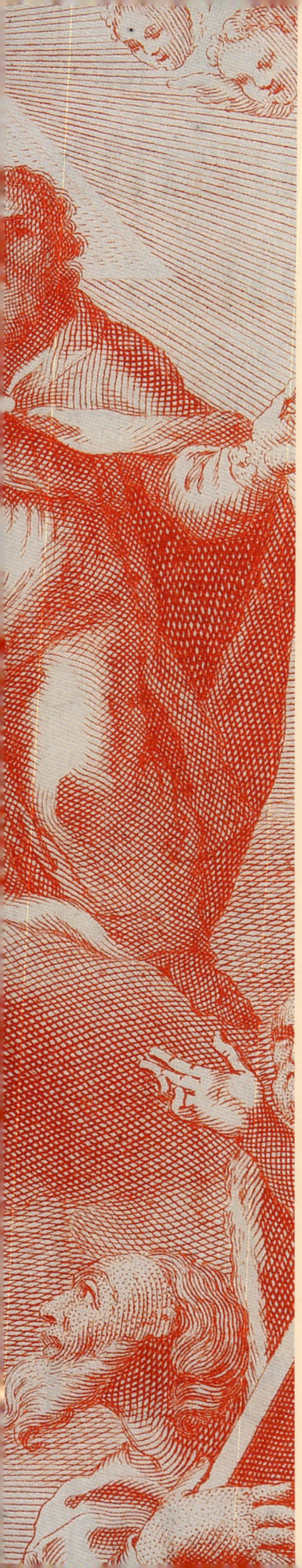

4. BOOKS

Reading the divine word in secular writings

Cristina Pinto Basto and Maria de Fátima Rezende Gomes

Quem com animo tão generoso se empenhou em mandar executar expressamente as alfaias da capella … não se esqueceria dos livros de canto e reza para os dias de festa e uso quotidiano.
(Anyone who showed such generosity of spirit and took such pains to give specific orders in having the accoutrements for the chapel executed … could not forget the song and prayer books for holidays and for everyday use.)
Francisco Marques de Sousa Viterbo and R. Vicente d' Almeida,
A Capella de S. João Baptista Erecta na Egreja de S. Roque (…), 1900

pp. 148–149
The Holy Trinity surrounded by the Virgin and Saints (detail)
Engraving by Aureliano Melani (designer) and Gio Batta (sculptor)
Red chalk imprint
Epistolary
Rome: Salvioni, 1746
(Inv. LA.Mp.XVIII.985)

– Two missals – *Missale Romanum* – Rome: Salvioni, 1735 (fig. 103)
– An 'Epistolary' or book of Epistles – *Epistolae Totius Anni* – Rome: Salvioni, 1746 (fig. 104)

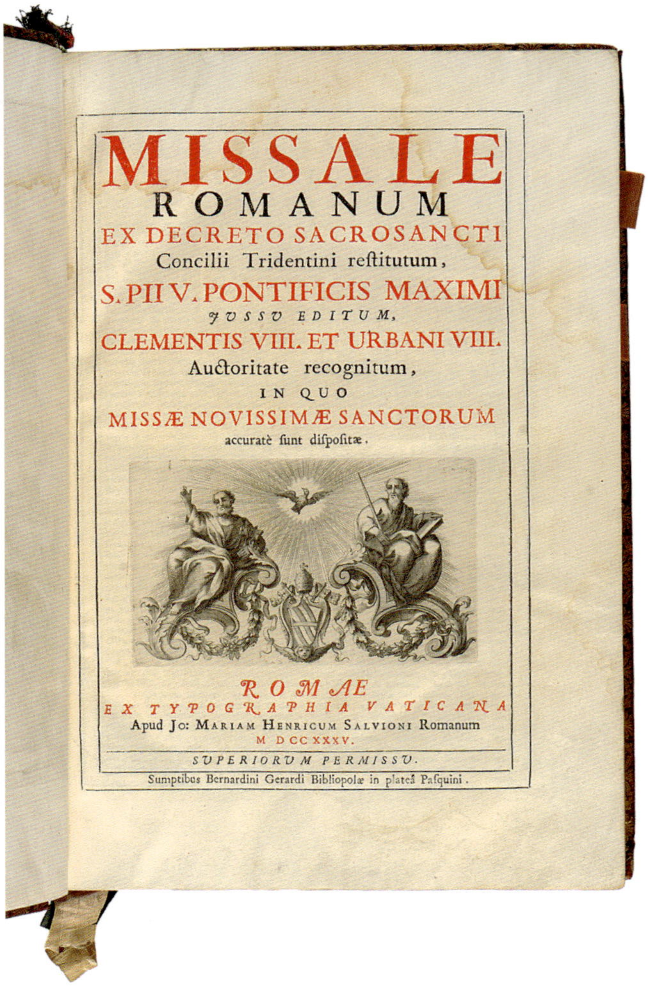
MISSALE
ROMANUM
EX DECRETO SACROSANCTI
Concilii Tridentini reſtitutum,
S. PII V. PONTIFICIS MAXIMI
JUSSU EDITUM,
CLEMENTIS VIII. ET URBANI VIII.
Auctoritate recognitum,
IN QUO
MISSÆ NOVISSIMÆ SANCTORUM
accuratè ſunt diſpoſitæ.
ROMAE
EX TYPOGRAPHIA VATICANA
Apud Jo: Mariam Henricum Salvioni Romanum
M DCC XXXV.
SUPERIORUM PERMISSU.
Sumptibus Bernardini Gerardi Bibliopolæ in plateâ Paſquini.

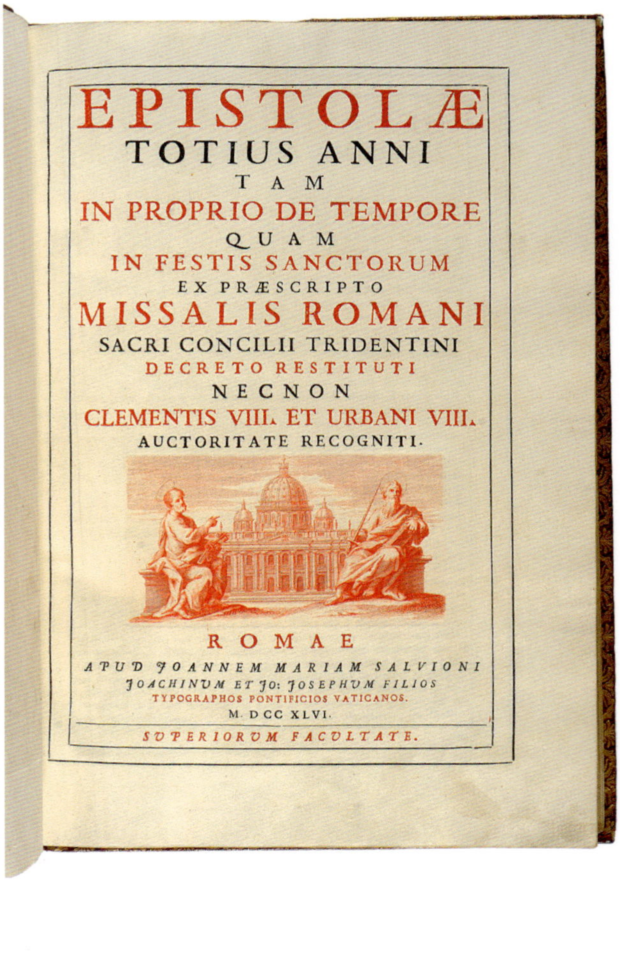
EPISTOLÆ
TOTIUS ANNI
TAM
IN PROPRIO DE TEMPORE
QUAM
IN FESTIS SANCTORUM
EX PRÆSCRIPTO
MISSALIS ROMANI
SACRI CONCILII TRIDENTINI
DECRETO RESTITUTI
NECNON
CLEMENTIS VIII. ET URBANI VIII.
AUCTORITATE RECOGNITI.
ROMAE
APUD JOANNEM MARIAM SALVIONI
JOACHINUM ET JO: JOSEPHUM FILIOS
TYPOGRAPHOS PONTIFICIOS VATICANOS.
M. DCC XLVI.
SUPERIORUM FACULTATE.

Fig. 103
Roman Missal (front)
Rome: Salvioni, 1735
(Inv. LA.Mp.XVIII.115)

Fig. 104
Epistolary (front)
Rome: Salvioni, 1746
(Inv. LA.Mp.XVIII.985)

Fig. 105
Evangelion or Gospel Book (front)
Rome: Salvioni, 1746
(Inv. LA.Mp.XVIII.112)

Fig. 106
Canon Mass (front)
Rome: Salvioni, 1745
(Inv. LA.Mp.XVIII.113)

– An 'Evangelary' or Gospel Lectionary (book of Gospels) – *Evangelia Totius Anni* Rome: Salvioni, 1746 (fig. 105)
– A canon mass book – *Canon Missae* – Rome: Salvioni, 1745 (fig. 106)

This group of books is generally thought to be the complete set of liturgical works allocated to the chapel, based on a tradition that began with the *Inventario da Fabrica da Real Capella de S. João Baptista, em 1784* (Inventory of the fabric of the Royal Chapel of St John the Baptist, in 1784) that was drawn up by Luiz Francisco Xavier Telles de Mello as the administrator of the Royal Chapel of St John the Baptist.[1] It has therefore been decided to include them within the sphere of the commissions by John V, an ensemble comprising a vast trove of manuscripts made up of correspondence, inventories, reports and accounts of the various ambassadors and agents who were in charge of the royal commissions in Italy from 1707.

Knowing that the commissions executed in Rome for the Chapel of St John the Baptist lie between 1742 and 1752 (the dates of the initial 'orders' and of the *assentamento* [founding or establishment] of the chapel in São Roque), priority has

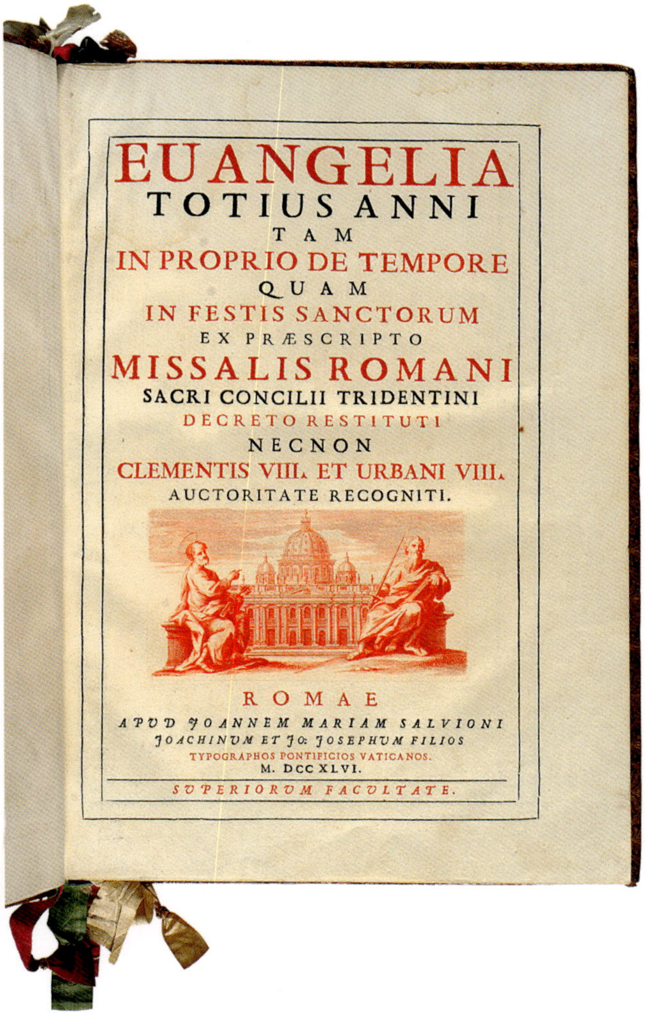

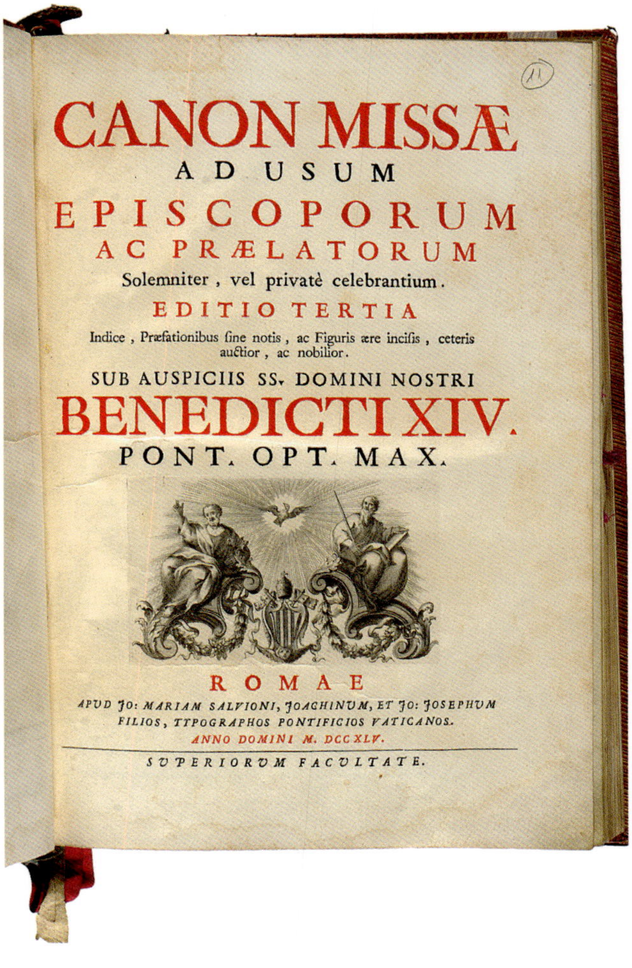

been given to the primary sources that referred explicitly to the commissioning of books and their appurtenances, namely the following:

- Correspondence sent from Lisbon to Rome and vice versa, between Giovanni Battista Carbone S.J. and Comendador Manuel Pereira de Sampaio;
- Books of accounts for the orders placed: orders, budgets, receipts, the *ristretos* or summaries of sums received, and bills of lading;
- Handwritten catalogues of the *Livraria das Necessidades* (Library of the Convent of Necessidades – 'Necessities') or set of books required.

Commissions for books

The first commission relating to the Chapel of St John the Baptist is dated 26 October 1742,[2] and it establishes the methodology for the architectural plans. On 29 May 1744[3] the first order that specifies the desired books was issued, emphasising that the books and their bindings were to be of the highest quality. This idea is further reinforced by the richness of the accessories made for them – namely the bookmarks, cushions and cloths – as can be seen from the receipts, of which those for Bernardino Gerardi's silk bookmarks offer an example.[4]

The commissions for **Epistolaries** and **Evangelaries** were documented by purchase instructions in 1743, with further documentation in 1744, and they were received in accordance with instructions in 1745: 'agradou a letra do Epistolario, e do Livro de Evangelhos os quaes devem vir absolutamente separados, e encadernado cada hum sobre si; e se estimou, q[ue] se pozesse[m] accentos nas palavras, p.ª distinção das penultimas breves, ou longas'[5] (pleased with the writing of the Epistolary, and of the book of Gospels, which must come absolutely separate, and bound each one in itself alone; and it was considered that accents should be placed upon the words, in order to distinguish the short or the long penultimate syllables). It is probably to these copies with accents that receipt no. 675 refers (fig. 107); issued by Giovanni Maria Salvioni[6] and dating from February 1745, they record the separate printing of 15 volumes of the Epistles and the Gospels.[7] In fact, between 1742 and 1748 there are multiple orders for various quantities of these two books,[8] which indicates that they were initially for distribution to various churches and for different altars.

Making the bindings for these works is generally attributed to Bernardino Gerardi, although a separate account and receipt have been found for the craftsman responsible for the *legatura* or binding, namely Muzio Bona (1641–1747). Both were booksellers established in Rome in the Piazza Pasquino, and both had professional links to the papal printing house (Salvioni). There is also, for example, a receipt (no. 1522) naming Muzio Bonn, dated 22 March 1747, referring to the 'legatura di un corpo di Libro divito in due Tomi, e sono uno di l'Epistole e l'altro li Evangeli di tutto canno in foglio magno stampa del Salvioni in cremis di Levante ornato d'oro' (binding of the body of a book divided into two tomes, and they are one of the

Epistles and the other the Gospels of the whole canon, printed in folio *magno* by Salvioni in crimson Levant [leather] adorned with gold).[9]

With regard to the **missals**, the order of 1744 indicates the 'compra de livros p.ª as Missas. Trez Missaes com differentes encadernações p.ª a differença dos dias em q[ue] servirê, todos porem dos melhores, e excelentem.te encadernados' (the purchase of books for masses. Three missals, with different bindings for the various days on which they shall serve, but all of the finest, and excellently bound).[10] The corresponding receipt (no. 747, of 9 July 1745) confirms these details: 'legatura de tre Messale della Stampa del Salvioni in foglio, con les giunte de S. di Spagna ligatti in Cremesino di Levante com Carte dorate e miniate, e coperte piene d'oro com disegno' (binding of three missals from Salvioni's press, in folio, with the clasps of Spanish silk [and] bound in Levant cramoisy, with papers that are gilded and illuminated, and covers full of gold designs).[11]

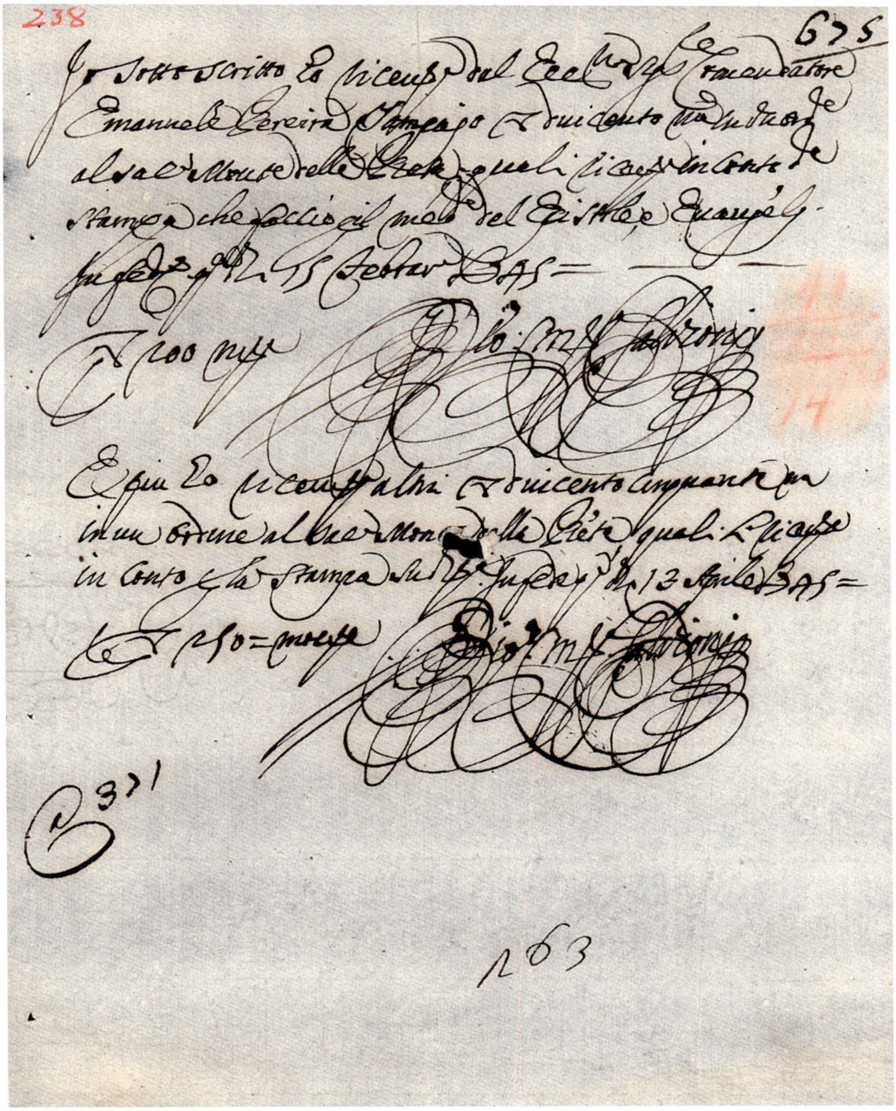

Fig. 107
Justificatory documents for payments in Rome on the account of the court of Lisbon
B.A. Ms. 49-VIII-14, f. 263
Salvioni, receipt no. 675, Feb./April 1745

It is on the basis of this description that a connection has been established between this purchase and the bindings of the missals for the Chapel of St John the Baptist, since one of them is decorated with the design of the royal arms of Portugal and another with a miniature of the baptism of Jesus – the subject depicted in the central mosaic in the Chapel of St John the Baptist and directly associated with the name of the monarch and patron. It is also the miniatures on the bindings that establish that these books belonged to the estate of the Chapel of St John the Baptist. Recognition of the same fact may also be extended to the bindings of the books of Epistles and Gospels, a hypothesis corroborated by a receipt from Gerardi that refers to bindings for these two books: 'Per Aver Ligato in Marochino di Levante Cremesi tutti dorati dui Tomi in foglio reale uno del. Epistole e laltro del. Evangeli' (For having bound in crimson moroccan leather, all gilded, two tomes in royal folio, one of the Epistles and the other of the Gospels) (7 May 1747).[12]

The order for the purchase of the **Canon Mass** book does not appear in any specific document or explicit reference apart from the correspondence analysed, and can only be linked to an order placed in 1742 (previous to the orders for the books for the chapel) which refers to 'dois Rituais romanos ordinários' (two ordinary Roman rituals or mass books) recently printed and which accompany the purchase order for 'meia duzia de Ritos Pontificios' (half a dozen pontifical missals).[13] The most concrete reference is to be found in the books of accounts, which include a receipt from Bernardino Gerardi (no. 961, Dec. 1745) referring, among other works, to the binding of 'otto canoni in Cremesi dorato dentro e fuora' (eight canons in cramoisy gilded within and without) and including an amount detailed separately, paid to Salvioni, for the printing of 'Canone Pontificio della nuova stampa del Salvioni' (a pontifical canon from Salvioni's new press).[14]

Considering the internal organisation of this book, which corresponds to the fixed part of the missal, and which in this particular case is preceded by an extended introduction, its purpose might have been for use in the liturgical celebration instead of as a missal. With regard to the bindings of the two missals, the fact that one has the engraving of the royal arms and one has a miniature of the baptism of Jesus links them directly to the treasury of the Chapel of St John the Baptist, and suggests that this may well be a book that replaced a third missal – one that was ordered, bought and bound but was already no longer to be found in the inventory of books drawn up by Father Luiz Francisco Telles de Mello.

Engravings and bindings

The large-format **engravings** that are included in all these copies, varying in number from 4 (those of the Epistles and Gospels) to 16 (those of the canon) all show a date of 1735 – the same date as the two missals that would have been the only ones already printed by the time the order was placed for the books for the chapel. The same images are repeated throughout the various books, arranged according to

Fig. 108
Annunciation
Engraving by Carolus Lovaniensis (designer) and B. Thiboust (sculptor)
Red chalk imprint
Epistolary
Rome: Salvioni, 1746
(Inv. LA.Mp.XVIII.985)

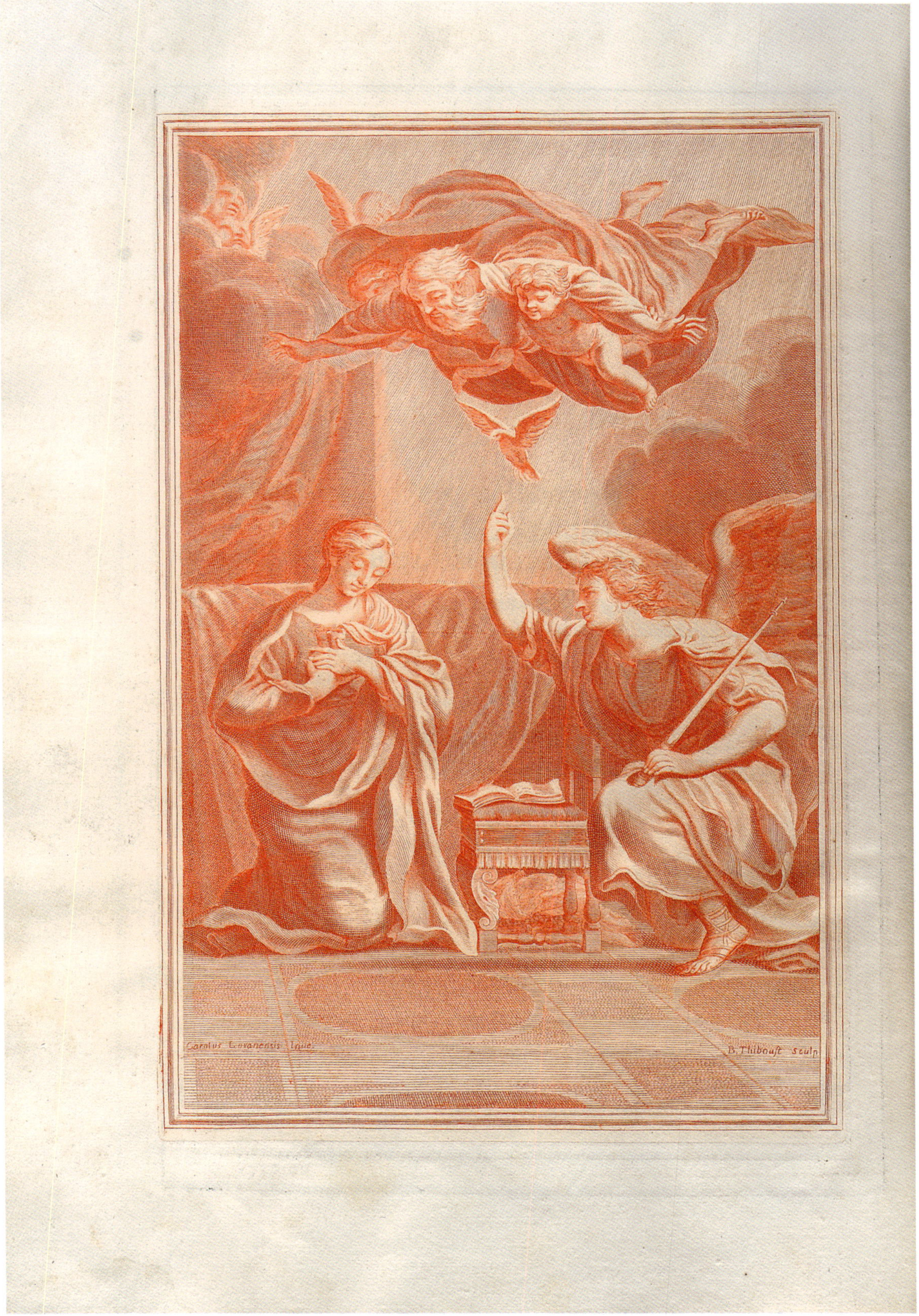
B. Thibouſt sculp

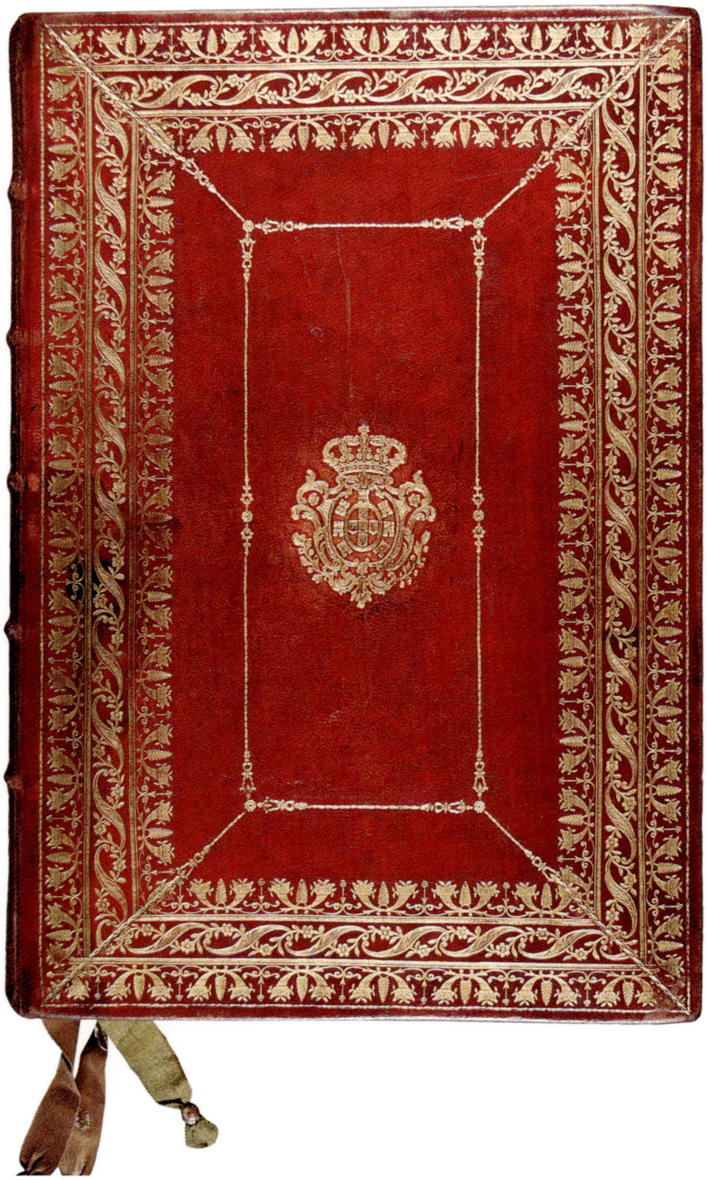

Fig. 109
Roman Missal (binding)
Rome: Salvioni, 1735
Red moroccan (leather) with fillets and royal escutcheon embossed in gold
(Inv. LA.Mp.XVIII.114)

subject. The authors of the engravings are all important names in the Italian visual arts, directly or indirectly linked to the Accademia San Luca (St Luke's Academy) and – perhaps for this very reason – there are no comments of any kind on these pieces to be found in the correspondence, or even receipts for payment issued to their authors. This appears to confirm that the quality of the engravings in the books sent as an example met with immediate satisfaction.

The **bindings** of these five books are the first indication that the Chapel of St John the Baptist and its appurtenances were considered as 'treasure' (fig. 109). They are richly and profusely decorated in gold, and the symbols chosen for their central motifs refer to a royal chapel. A depiction of the baptism of Jesus is an obvious choice in the context of the chapel and its dominant themes (fig. 110),

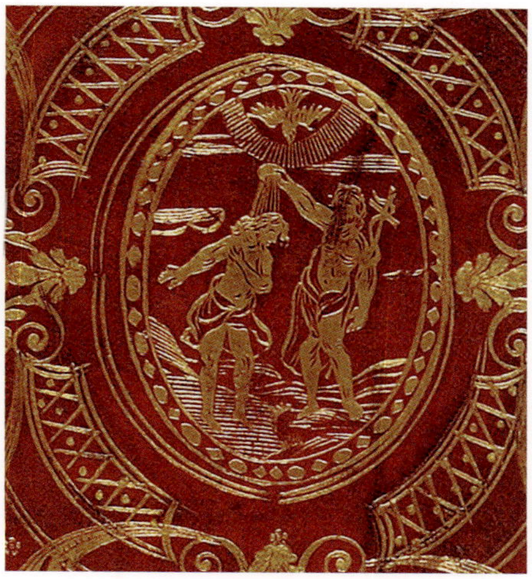

Fig. 110
Roman Missal (detail of miniature with scene of the baptism of Christ)
Rome: Salvioni, 1735
Red moroccan (leather) with fillets and various designs embossed in gold
(Inv. LA.Mp.XVIII.115)

but that of the royal arms could not be considered in the same light. Decoration with the royal coat of arms is, however, known to reflect the high value placed on a book's content and/or ownership of it, and is associated with works of great importance, scope or prestige aimed at consolidating John V's political and cultural position vis-à-vis other European monarchs while also pleasing the pope. Similarly, the paper used for the back and front endpapers is identical in all the books; it is of Italian origin, and distinguished by its excellent quality and the decorative motifs and colours used.

From the moment that the idea of the Chapel of St John the Baptist was first conceived, it was seen by the various individuals involved in its creation as a work of art in whose design and execution no detail was overlooked. Confirmation of this can clearly be seen in the surviving contemporary sources, and in the liturgical books – with the exception of the canon, which is a particular case. It is expressed in their external appearance (the bindings) as well as in details that add value to their interior (engravings in red shades known as *sanguine*). It was precisely in the ritual practices performed 'on the different days', with all their associated accessories, vestments and adornments, that the sumptuousness of these books would be clearly visible, in harmony with the surrounding context. ■

NOTES

[1] Transcription of this document in Francisco Marques de Sousa VITERBO and R. Vicente d' ALMEIDA, *A Capella de S. João Baptista Erecta na Egreja de S. Roque*, Lisbon, Livros Horizonte, 1997, p. 71. (1st edition 1900)

[2] Date established on the basis of the letter that accompanies this order: cf. Biblioteca da Ajuda (Lisbon), Ms. 51-X-32, f. 85.

[3] B.A., Mss. 49-VIII-27, p. 55 and 49-VIII-41, f. 20v.

[4] B.A., Ms. 49-VIII-16, ff. 163, 172.

[5] cf. B.A., Ms. 49-VIII-41, f. 147v.

[6] Salvioni, a native of Rome, established himself first as a bookseller. From 1707 to 1714 he ran his own press in the Campo de Fiori. From 1715 he was commissioned by Pope Clement XI to direct the Stamperia Vaticana, the Vatican press, in the Palazzo della Sapienza.

[7] cf. B.A., Mss. 49-VIII-14, f. 263, 49-IX-22, f. 232 and 49-IX-23, f. 371.

[8] With regard to the question of receipts cf. BA, Mss. 49-VIII-14 (no. 1745), ff. 306, 436, 499; 49-VIII-15 (no. 1746), ff. 30, 229.

[9] cf. B.A., Ms. 49-VIII-16, f. 33.

[10] cf. B.A., Ms. 49-VIII-27, f. 55.

[11] cf. B.A., Mss. 49-VIII-14, f. 332, 49-IX-23, f. 390 and 51-XIII-49, f. 316.

[12] cf. B.A., Ms. 49-VIII-16, f. 88.

[13] cf. B.A., Ms. 49-VIII-40, f. 117v.

[14] cf. B.A., Mss. 49-VIII-14, f. 636 and following, and 49-IX-23, f. 450.

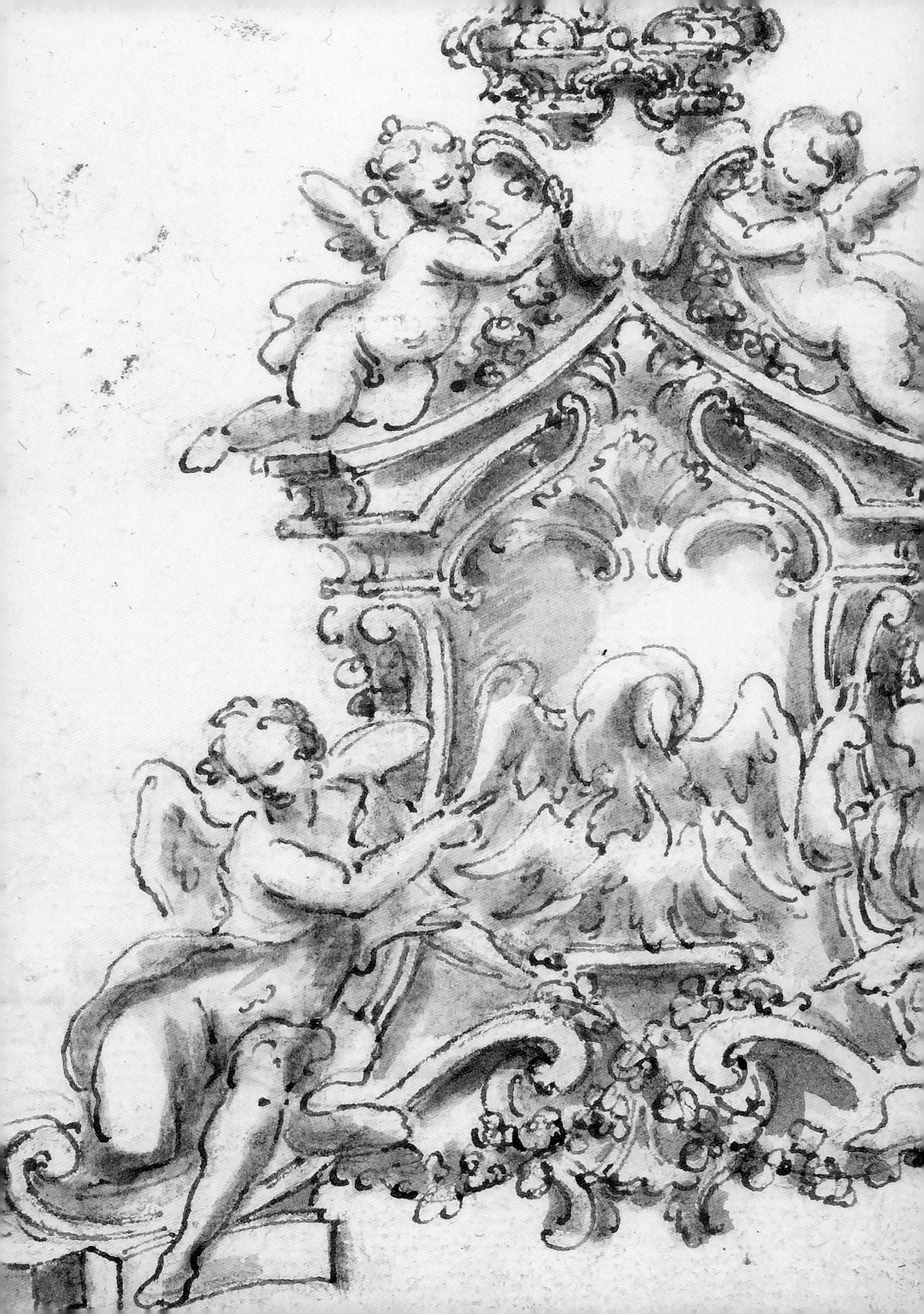

5. OTHER PIECES

Peripheral items and aspects of the commission of the Chapel of St John the Baptist

Teresa Leonor M. Vale

The Chapel of St John the Baptist was commissioned as a coherent ensemble, as can clearly be seen from the various texts presented in this book. In addition to its artistic constituent elements, understood in the strict sense of the word, this commission therefore also included other aspects and items related to the functioning and daily life of the chapel. These aspects, which might be considered peripheral or minor in relation to the scope of the commission, are briefly addressed in this chapter.

In fact, in addition to all the implements related to making hosts, the containers for water and wine, and the utensils for the cleaning and maintenance of the chapel which were ordered in the letter of 9 March 1744, it was anticipated from the first that there would be a need for – and inevitably orders to make – cupboards or cabinets intended to house the pieces in gold and silver (and also the candles, as specifically mentioned).

Among the vast volumes of documentation to have come out of the Portuguese embassy in Rome during the reign of John V, which are preserved in the Ajuda Library, it has proved possible to locate a set of documents consisting of five lists detailing the packing cases – and their respective contents – which were dispatched from Rome to Lisbon in the years 1741, 1744, 1745, 1748–49 and 1750. There is also a sixth list corresponding to 44 packing cases which would have been sent to Lisbon between 1751 and 1752.[1]

The first five lists reveal the contents of a total of 280 crates that were sent from Rome to the Portuguese capital between 1741 and 1750, the last year of the reign of John V. The 44 boxes sent between 1751 and 1752, which are shown in the sixth list, must also be added to this number.

The last set to be sent during John V's lifetime, consisting of 97 boxes and corresponding to the fifth list,[2] was sent from Rome in February 1750. It is among the contents of this last set of nearly 100 boxes that four cabinets can be identified as those intended to house the precious implements for the royal chapel in the Church of São Roque. These were to be placed in the area that was going to be the sacristy of the Chapel of St John the Baptist, which has recently been identified within the context of the architectural complex of Santa Casa da Misericórdia as a room referred to in early twentieth-century documentation as the 'Sacristy of St John', located underneath the treasury.[3]

pp. 158–159
Lost Pieces: monstrance
in gold (detail)
(See fig. 82)

Fig. 111
Confessional
Giovanni Palmini
Rome, c. 1750
Walnut and gilded bronze
(inv. Mb 349)

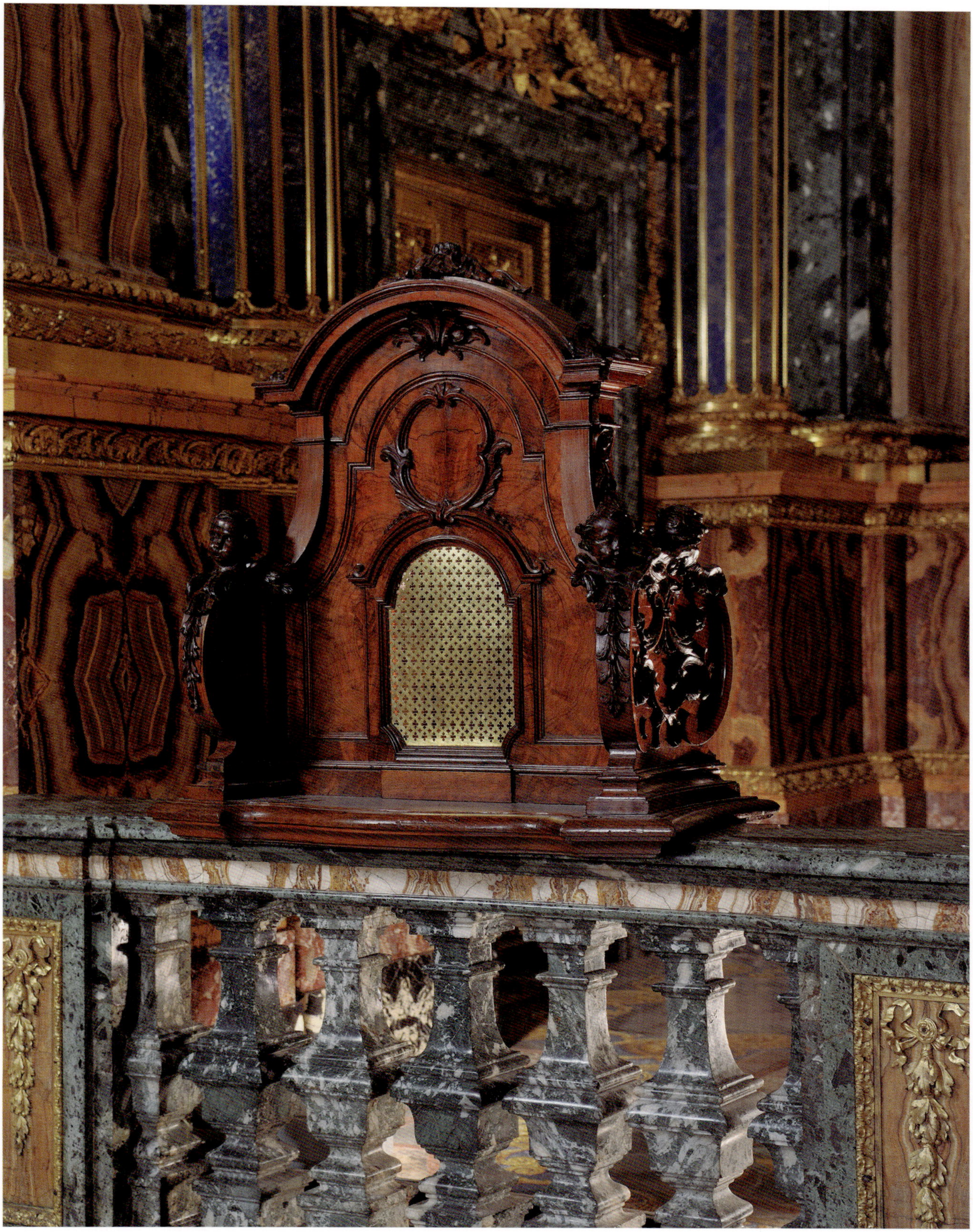

It is specifically mentioned that the contents of the first of the crates corresponding to the various parts of these cabinets (which are referred to as *credenzoni,* cabinets or dressers of considerable size) were intended for the sacristy and that their purpose was to house the chapel vestments and silver accoutrements.

Payments made between May 1749 and January 1750 to the carpenter Lucino Cittadini for making these cabinets can also be identified among the documentation referring to work on the Chapel of St John the Baptist which is held in the Ajuda Library.[4]

Entries recording payments made to the silversmith and metalworker Lorenzo De Caporali (*c.* 1712–77) for fashioning gilded metal ornaments for these same cabinets can also be identified among the books of accounts of the Portuguese embassy in Rome. Between 1749 and 1750, for example, a number of payments were recorded 'a conto delli Ouali di Metallo dorati che stò facendo per li quatro Arnmarij della Corona di Portogallo' (on account of the ovals of gilded metal that I am making for the four armoires of the Crown of Portugal),[5] while the total for these tasks appears in the account submitted by De Caporali in 1750. It is inferred from this fact that the Roman silversmith and metalworker made designs and models in addition to executing the pieces in metal, which would explain the high cost of 5,728.50 Roman scudi – a sum that was later revised by Antonio Arrighi (as was the practice at the time) and finally set at 5,100 Roman scudi.[6]

It appears that the silversmith Matteo Piroli (1701–77) was also involved in creating these ornamental components in metal for the cabinets intended to house the vestments and accoutrements of the royal chapel in São Roque, as there is a reference to metal elements and metal trimmings for two of the four cabinets in the chapel sacristy[7] to be seen among the multiple items of the account he submitted on 27 June 1750. It should be noted that Lorenzo De Caporali also made a gold chalice and matching paten, which have since been lost, as part of the work commissioned for the chapel's gold and silver collection.[8]

A pair of confessionals in walnut wood was also made for the Chapel of St John the Baptist, by the cabinet-maker Giovanni Palmini (fig. 111). It is once again thanks to the set of lists of the crates sent to Lisbon referred to above that these two confessionals can be identified; they were sent to the capital in February 1750[9] or possibly in 1751 or 1752, after the reign of John V had come to an end, since two confessionals in walnut[10] also appear in the contents of case 34 (List 6).

These confessionals, which can now be seen in the Museum of São Roque,[12] are small pieces designed to be placed on the balustrade that separates the royal chapel from the nave of the Jesuit church 'da levarsi, e mettersi, che va posto sù la balaustrata della cappella, ornato di metalli dorati' (that can be taken up, and set down; which should be placed upon the balustrade of the chapel, adorned with gilded metal) (fig. 112).[11]

One final detail worthy of mention is another item of great interest that was included among the contents of the cases sent from Rome to Lisbon during the last

Fig. 112
General view of the Chapel of St John the Baptist
with the pair of confessionals located within the balustrade

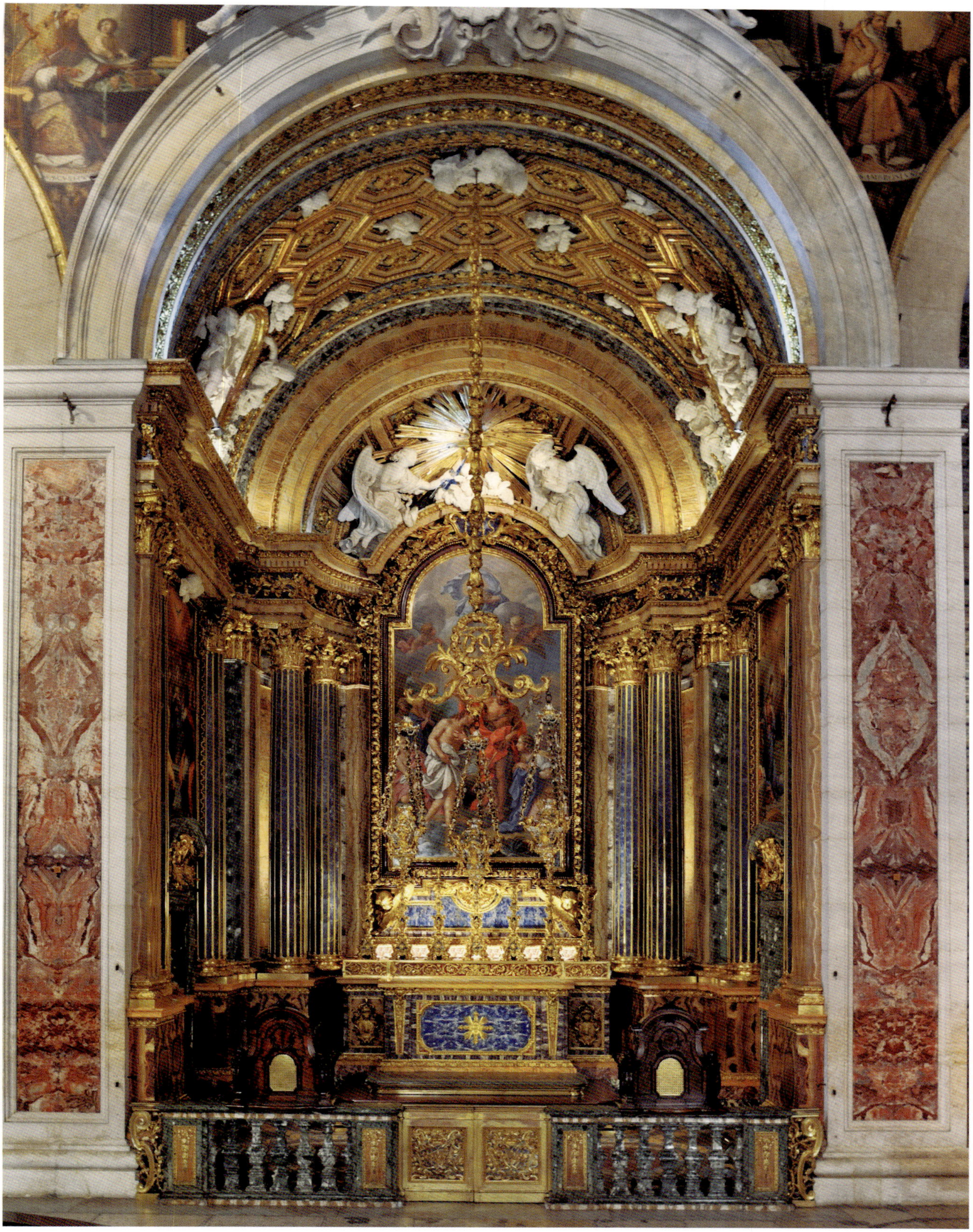

decade of the reign of John V: namely, extra pieces of the various types of stone used for the Chapel of St John the Baptist which were intended for use as replacements in the event of damage. A reading of List 5, in fact, reveals that the contents of Box 85 are given as follows: 'Varie Pietre mischie, dure, e tenere di tutte le qualità, che sono andate in opera della Cappella, e che si mandano per provedimento, e supplemento, in caso che potessero bisognare' (Various stones, mixed, hard and soft of every quality that went into the work of the chapel, and which are sent in provision, and supplement, in case they should be needed).[13] In the inventory drawn up on 3 October 1892 by the visitor Ernesto Manuel Quintans, the appurtenances of the chapel are still referred to as including 'Dois embrulhos com bocados de lápis lazúli e a declaração escrita da sua proveniência' (Two parcels, with bits of lapis lazuli, and the written declaration of their provenance),[14] from which it can be deduced that some of these stones still existed at that time. ■

NOTES

[1] cf. Biblioteca da Ajuda (Lisbon), Ms. 49-VIII-22, f. 433-433v.

[2] B.A., Ms. 49-VIII-26, ff. 1-40.

[3] Information resulting from the research of Dr João Simões, who has generously shared it with us.

[4] B.A., Ms. 49-VIII-18, f. 63 (5 May 1749: 300 Roman scudi), f. 75 (12 July 1749: 320 scudi), f. 103 (5 August 1749: 300 scudi), f. 157 (3 October 1749: 100 scudi), f. 264 (8 December 1749: 300 scudi) and f. 292 (5 January 1750: 40 scudi).

[5] B.A., Ms. 49-VIII-18, f. 89.

[6] B.A., Ms. 49-VIII-19, f. 301.

[7] B.A., Ms. 49-VIII-20, f. 234.

[8] The last record that it is thought may refer to these cabinets (now lost) dates from 1892, specifically 3 October. This is the date of an inventory drawn up by the visitor Ernesto Manuel Quintans in the presence of Jorge Camelier, adjunct to the administration of the Santa Casa da Misericórdia de Lisboa, and Father José António da Conceição Vieira, the church treasurer. In this document the cabinets are referred to as being six in number, and their very brief description suggests that they had probably been altered or replaced – cf. Arquivo Histórico da Santa Casa da Misericórdia de Lisboa, *Inventário de Bens. Tesouro da Real Capela de S. João Baptista*, ch. 1, f. 7v.

[9] cf. B.A., Ms. 49-VIII-35, pp. 43–196.

[10] cf. B.A., Ms. 49-VIII-22, f. 433–33v.

[11] B.A., Ms. 49-VIII-35, p. 187.

[12] Inv. MB. 0349.

[13] B.A., Ms. 49-VIII-35, pp. 174–75.

[14] A.H.S.C.M.L., *Inventário de Bens. Tesouro da Real Capela de S. João Baptista*, ch. 1, f. 7v.

Lost Pieces: pyx in gold (detail)
(See fig. 84)

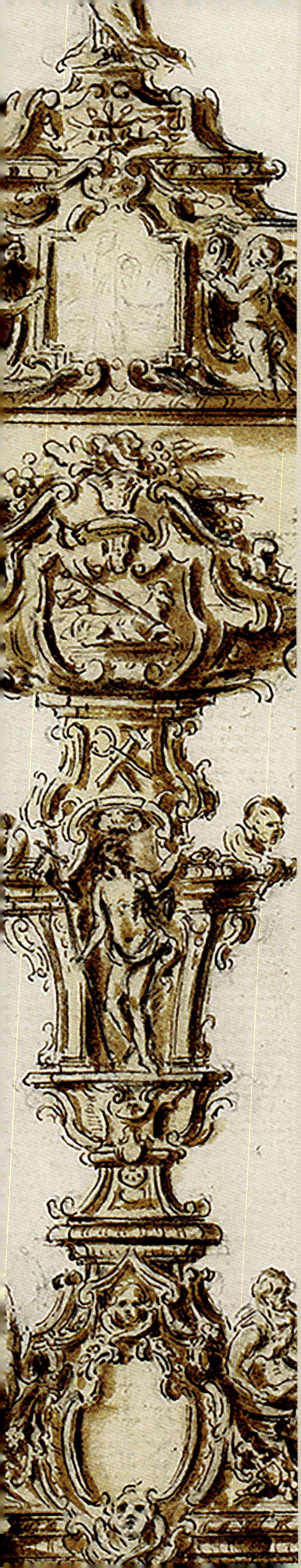

SELECTED BIBLIOGRAPHY

Archivio Reverenda Fabbrica di San Pietro (Fabric of St Peter's archive) (Vatican)

ARM. 12 G 14 B, c. 496. c. 497

ARM. 43, E, N. 90 c.479

Arm. 43, E., n. 92, Arm. 43, E., n. 91

Arquivo Histórico da Santa Casa da Misericórdia de Lisboa (Historical Archive of the Santa Casa da Misericórdia de Lisboa, Lisbon)

SCML/IG/SJB/01/Lv. 001

Ch. 01. *Inventários de Bens. Tesouro da Real Capela de S. João Baptista*, 1892

Ch. 02. *Inventários de Bens. Tesouro da Real Capela de S. João Baptista – relatório do adjunto Camelier* [Report by Adjunct Camelier], 1892

Ch. 08. Doc. 3, *Certidão da prata fundida na Casa da Moeda* (29 October 1808)

Codice Ottoboniano Latino, N° 3118

Biblioteca da Ajuda (Ajuda Library, Lisbon)

Ms. 46-XIII-9, Ms. 46-XIII-10

Ms. 49-VI-15, Ms. 49-VI-16, Ms. 49-VI-23, Ms. 49-VI-28

Ms. 49-VII-11, Ms. 49-VII-13, Ms. 49-VII-13a (cota provisória), Ms. 49-VII-16, Ms. 49-VII-32, Ms. 49-VII-33, Ms. 49-VII-34, Ms. 49-VII-35, Ms. 49-VII-36, Ms. 49-VII-37, Ms. 49-VII-38, Ms. 49-VII-43

Ms. 49-VIII-12, Ms. 49-VIII-13, Ms. 49-VIII-14, Ms. 49-VIII-15, Ms. 49-VIII-16, Ms. 49-VIII-17, Ms. 49-VIII-18, Ms. 49-VIII-19, Ms. 49-VIII-20, Ms. 49-VIII-21, Ms. 49-VIII-22, Ms. 49-VIII-23, Ms. 49-VIII-24, Ms. 49-VIII-25, Ms. 49-VIII-26, Ms. 49-VIII-27, Ms. 49-VIII-28, Ms. 49-VIII-29, Ms. 49-VIII-31, Ms. 49-VIII-32, Ms. 49-VIII-33, Ms. 49-VIII-35, Ms. 49-VIII-40, Ms. 49-VIII-41

Ms. 49-IX-1, Ms. 49-IX-9, Ms. 49-IX-10, Ms. 49-IX-11, Ms. 49-IX-12, Ms. 49-IX-22, Ms. 49-IX-23, Ms. 49-IX-31, Ms. 49-IX-3, Ms. 49-XI-12, Ms. 49-XI-19

Ms. 51-X-1, Ms. 51-X-31, Ms. 51-X-32

Ms. 51-XIII-16, Ms. 51-XIII-17, Ms. 51-XIII-18, Ms. 51-XIII-49

Ms. 54-IX-9, N° 76, Ms. 54-XI-25, N° 51 a N° 54

Printed sources

ALBERTI, Leon Battista, *L'architettura* (ed. Giovanni Orlandi, introduction and notes by Paolo Portoghesi), Milan, Ed. Il Polifilo, 1966

CHRACAS, Luca Antonio, *Diario Ordinario*, Rome [various dates]

DEBENEDETTI, Elisa (ed.), *Artisti e Artigiani a Roma I e II, Degli Stati delle Anime del 1700, 1725, 1750, 1775* (col. *Studi sul Settecento Romano*, vols 20–21), Rome, Bonsignori Editore, 2004–5

FORTEGUERRI, Niccolò, *Il Ricciardetto*, vol. II, Milan, Societa Tipografica de' Classici Italiani, 1813

MARIETTE, Pierre-Jean, *Catalogues de la Collection d'Estampes de Jean V, Roi de Portugal* (ed. Marie-Thérèse Mandroux-França and Maxime Préaud), Lisbon–Paris, Fundação Calouste Gulbenkian-Fundação da Casa de Bragança-Centre Culturel Calouste Gulbenkian-Bibliothèque Nationale de France, 1996–2003

PASSARINI, Filippo, *Nuove inventioni d'ornamenti d'architettura e d'intagli diversi: utili ad argentieri, intagliatori, ricamatori et altri professori delle buone arti del disegno*, Rome, Domenico de Rossi, 1698

GUERRA, Luís Bívar, *Colégios de Santo Antão, S. Roque, S. Francisco Xavier e Noviciado de Arroios (Companhia de Jesus): Arquivo do Tribunal de Contas* (col. 'Documentos para a História da Arte em Portugal', vol. 5), Lisbon, Fundação Calouste Gulbenkian, 1969

MANOEL, Francisco d'Orey (ed.), *Fundo Musical. Século XVI ao Século XIX*, 2 vols, Lisbon, Santa Casa da Misericórdia de Lisboa, 1994

VELOSO, Júlio Caio, *Catálogo das obras impressas no século XVIII. A colecção da Santa Casa da Misericórdia de Lisboa*, 2 vols, Lisbon, Santa Casa da Misericórdia de Lisboa, 1999

General Works and Studies

Aa.Vv. *Antichi telai. I Tessuti d'Arte del Patrimonio del Fondo Edifici di Culto del Ministero dell'Interno*, Rome, Elio De Rosa Editore, 2009

Aa.Vv., *Le Botteghe degli Argentieri Lucchesi del XVIII Secolo* (exhibition catalogue), Florence, Study for Edizione Scelte, 1981

AAVV, *Luigi Vanvitelli*, Naples, Edizione Scientifiche Italiane, 1973

ALMEIDA, Luís Ferrand de, 'D. João V e a Biblioteca Real', in *Revista da Universidade de Coimbra*, vol. 36, 1991

AVERY, Charles, *Fingerprints of the Artist. European Terracotta Sculpture from the Arthur M. Sackler Collections*, Washington, The Arthur M. Sackler Foundation – The Fogg Art Museum, 1981

BARUCCA, Gabriele, and Jennifer MONTAGU (ed.), *Ori e Argenti. Capolavori del '700 da Arrighi a Valadier*, Milan, Skira Editore, 2007

BÉNÉZIT, Edouard, *Dictionnaire Critique et Documentaire des Peintres, Sculpteurs, Dessinateurs et Graveurs* [Paris], Librairie Gründ, 1966

BERINGER, Joseph August, *Peter A. von Verschaffetlt*, Strasbourg, 1902

BEVILACQUA, Mario, and Elisabetta MORI (ed.), *Beatrice Cenci: la storia, il mito*, Rome, Fondazione Marco Bresso, 1999

BEVILACQUA, Mario, *Il monte dei Cenci: una famiglia romana e il suo insediamento urbano tra Medioevo e età baroca*, Rome, Gangemi, 1988

BIGAZZI, Isabella, 'Ricami d'ogni sorte, d'oro, d'argento e seta', in Riccardo SPINELLI (ed.), *Arti fiorentine: la grande storia dell'Artigianato, Il Seicento e il Settecento*, vol. V, Florence, Giunti, 2002

BONANNI, Filippo, *La gerarchia ecclesiastica considerata nelle vesti sagre, e civili usate da quelli, li quali le compongono, Espresse, e spiegate con le immagini di ciascun grado della medesima. Offerta alla Maestà di GIOVANNI QUINTO RE' DI PORTOGALLO e DELL'ALGARVE*, Rome, Stamperia Giorgio Placho, 1720

BOWRON, Edgar Peters, and Joseph J. RISHEL (ed.), *Art in Rome in the Eighteenth Century*, Philadelphia, Merrell – Philadelphia Museum of Art, 2000

BRAZÃO, Eduardo, 'A Cultura Portuguesa no Reinado de D. João V', in *Estudos Italianos em Portugal*, no. 2, Lisbon, 1940

BRAZÃO, Eduardo, *D. João V e a Santa Sé*, Coimbra, Coimbra Editora, 1937

BRIGGS, Martin S., 'St John's Chapel in the Church of St Roch, Lisbon', in *Burlington Magazine*, no. XXVIII (1915)

BRITO, Maria Filomena, *Rendas Barrocas em Portugal Colecção da Capela de S. João Baptista*, Lisbon, Santa Casa da Misericórdia de Lisboa e Livros Horizonte, 1997

BULGARI, Costantino, *Argentieri, Gemmari e Orafi d'Italia*, 2 vols, Rome, Lorenzo del Turco, 1958–59

CAHEN, Antoine, 'Les Prix de Quartier à l'Académie Royale de Peinture et de Sculpture', in *Bulletin de la Societé de l'Histoire de l'Art Français*, 1993 (1994)

CALISSONI, Anna Bulgari, *Argentieri, Gemmari e Orafi di Roma*, Rome, Fratelli Palombi Editori, 1987

CANDIAGO, Anna, 'Un Tesoro di Oreficeria Romana del Secolo XVIII a Lisbona: Gli Argenti di S. Rocco', in *Estudos Italianos em Portugal*, no. 24 (1965)

CARMIGNANI, Marina, *Tessuti Ricami e Merletti in Italia*, Milan, Electa, 2005

CARMIGNANI, Marina, Marialuisa RIZZINI and Maria Paola RUFFINO (ed.), *Merletti dalle collezioni di Palazzo Madama*, Cinisello Balsamo, Silvana Editoriale, 2013

CARVALHO, A. Ayres de, *D. João V e a Arte do Seu Tempo*, vol. 2, Lisbon, Edição do Autor, 1962

CATALDI GALLO, Marzia, *Le vesti dei Papi: i parati della Sacrestia pontificia. Seicento e Settecento*, Genoa, De Ferrari, 2011

CELLINI, Antonia Nava, *La Scultura del Settecento*, 2nd edition, Milan, Garzanti, 1992 (1st edition 1982)

COGO, Bruno, *Antonio Corradini Scultore Veneziano*, Este, Libreria Gregoriana Estense, 1996

COLLE, Enrico, Angela GRISERI and Roberto VALERIANI, *Bronzi Decorativi in Italia. Bronzisti e Fonditori Italiani dal Seicento all'Ottocento*, Milan, Electa, 2001

CONCEIÇÃO, Frei Cláudio da, *Gabinete Histórico*, Lisbon, Imprensa Nacional, 1823–29

CONTARDI, Bruno, 'L'altare di San Luigi Gonzaga in Sant'Ignazio', in Alberta BATTISTI (ed.), *Andrea Pozzo*, Milan–Trento, Luni Editore, 1996

COPPENS, Marguerite, 'Un cahier de dessins de dentelles, daté de 1750, et son contexte commercial. D'après les archives d'une famille de fabricants anversois. Les Reyns', in *Bullettin des Musée Royaux d'Art et d'Histoire*, vol. 53, fasc. 1, 1982

D'AMELIO, Maria Grazia, and Carlo Stefano SALERNO, 'Virtù e difetti degli smalti settecenteschi di Alessio Mattioli: la qualità delle tinte e la loro alterazione dalle prime critiche del chimico Alessandro Martelli alle indagini sui mosaici della Basilica Vaticana nel periodo dell'occupazione francese', in C. FIORI and M. VANDINI (ed.), *Ravenna Musiva. Conservazione del Mosaico Antico e Contemporaneo. Atti del Convegno*, Bologna, Ante Quem, 2010

DEBENEDETTI, Elisa, 'Gli Altari in Duomo e altri altari urbinati' in Giuseppe CUCCO (ed.), *Papa Albani e le arti a Urbino e a Roma 1700–1721*, Rome, Marseilles, 2001

DEBENDETTI, Elisa (ed.), *Carlo Marchionni. Architettura, decorazione e scenografia Contemporanea* (col. Studi sul Settecento Romano, 4), Rome, Bonsignori Editore, 1988

DEBENEDETTI, Elisa (ed.), *Sculture romane del Settecento. La Professione dello Scultore* (col. *Studi sul Settecento Romano*, 17, 18 and 19), 3 vols, Rome, Bonsignori Editore, 2001–3

DEBENEDETTI, Elisa (ed.), *Palazzi, chiese, arredi e scultura*, vol. I (col. *Studi sul Settecento Romano*, 27), Rome, Bonsignori Editore, 2011

DE FEO, Vittorio, 'Le cappelle e gli altari', in Vittorio DE FEO and Valentino MARTINELLI (ed.), *Andrea Pozzo*, Milan, Electa, 1996

DELAFORCE, Angela, *Art and Patronage in Eighteenth-century Portugal*, Cambridge, Cambridge University Press, 2002

DEL RICCIO, Agostino, *Istoria delle Pietre*, 1597 (ed. P. Barocchi), Florence, Study for Edizioni Scelte, 1979

DI SIVO, Michele (ed.), *I Cenci nobiltà di sangue*, Rome, Fondazione Marco Bresso – Edizioni Colombo, 2002

DESMAS, Anne-Lise, *Le Ciseau et la Tiare. Les sculpteurs dans la Rome des Papes 1724–1758* (col. De l'École Française de Rome, 463), Rome, École Française de Rome, 2012

DESMAS, Anne-Lise, 'Pierre de L'Estache (*c.* 1688–1774): un Sculpteur Français à Rome entre Institutions Nationales et Grands Chantiers Pontificaux', in *Studiolo: Revue d'Histoire de l'Art de l'Académie de France à Rome*, no. 1 (2002)

DESMAS, Anne-Lise, 'Portraits de Français Sculptés à Rome par un Français, Pierre de L'Estache, entre 1720 et 1750', in *Gazette des Beaux-Arts*, 144, ser. 6, vol. CXL, no. 1607 (2002)

DE STROEBEL, Anna Maria, *L'Arazzeria di San Michele tra il Settecento e L'Ottocento attraverso le opere della collezione vaticana* in *Arte e artigianato nella Roma di Belli*, Rome, Edizioni Colombo, 1998

DE STROEBEL, Anna Maria, *Le Arazzerie Romane dal XVII al XIX secolo*, Rome, Istituto Nazionale di Studi Romani, 1989

DE VICENTI, Monica, '*Piacere ai Dotti e ai Migliori. Scultori Classicisti del Primo '700*', in Giuseppe PAVANELLO (ed.), *La Scultura Veneta del Seicento e del Settecento. Nuovi Studi*, Venice, Istituto Veneto di Scienze, Lettere ed Arti, 2002

ELIAS, Norbert, *A Sociedade de Corte*, Lisbon, Editorial Estampa, 1987

ENGGASS, Robert, 'Bernardino Ludovisi III: his work in Portugal', in *Burlington Magazine*, vol. CX, no. 788 (Nov. 1968)

ENGGASS, Robert, *Early Eighteenth-century Sculpture in Rome. An Illustrated Catalogue*, University Park and London – The Pennsylvania State University Press, 1976

FARANDA, Franco, *Argentieri e Argenteria Sacra in Romagna dal Medioevo al XVIII Secolo*, Rimini, Luisè Editore, 1990

FERREIRA, Carlos Alberto, 'As livrarias reais de D. João IV a D. João VI', in *Memórias e comunicações apresentadas ao Congresso de História da Monarquia Dualista e Restauração, Tomo II. Congresso do Mundo Português (IV), II Secção: Restauração e Guerra da Independência*, Lisbon, Comissão Executiva dos Centenários and Bertrand Editora, 1940

FOQUE, Claude, 'Broderie', in Régis DEBRAY and Patrice HUGUES (ed.), *Dictionnaire Culturel du Tissu*, Paris, Babylone/Fayard, 2005

FRANÇA, José-Augusto, *Lisboa Pombalina e o Iluminismo*, Lisbon, Bertrand, 1987 (1st edition 1983)

FRANCHINI GUELFI, Fausta, 'Theatrum sacrum: materiali e funzioni dell'apparato liturgico', in *Apparato liturgico e arredo ecclesiastico nella Riviera Spezzina*, Genoa, Sagep, 1986

FUSCONI, Giulia, *Disegni Decorativi del Barocco Romano* (exhibition catalogue), Rome, Edizioni Quasar, 1986

FUSCONI, Giulia, 'Disegni decorativi di Johan Paul Schor', in *Bollettino d'Arte*, 33–34 (1985)

FUSCONI, Giulia, 'Philipp Schor, gli Altieri e il Marchese del Carpio', in *Johan Paul Schor und die internationale Sprache des Barock* (Atti delle giornate di studio, Rome, 2003), Munich, Hirmer Verlag München, 2008

GARMS, Jörg, 'Altari e tabernacoli di Luigi Vanvitelli', in *Luigi Vanvitelli e il '700 Europeo* I (Atti del Convegno Internazionale di Studi, Naples–Caserta. 1973), Naples, Istituto di Storia dell'Architettura dell' Università di Napoli, 1979

GOMES, Paulo Varela, *A Confissão de Cyrillo. Estudos de História da Arte e da Arquitectura*, Lisbon, Hiena, 1992

GOMES, Paulo Varela, *A Cultura Arquitectónica e Artística em Portugal no Século XVIII*, Lisbon, Editorial Caminho, 1988

GONZÁLEZ-PALACIOS, Alvar, *Arredi e Ornamenti alla Corte di Roma 1560–1795*, Milan, Mondadori Electa, 2004

GONZÁLEZ-PALACIOS, Alvar, 'Giovan Battista Calandra, un mosaicista alla corte dei Barberini', in *Ricerche di Storia dell'Arte*, nos. 1–2, Rome (Dec. 1976)

GONZÁLEZ-PALACIOS, Alvar, *Il Gusto dei Principi. Arte di Corte del XVII e del XVIII Secolo*, vol. I, Milan, Longanesi, 1993

GONZÁLEZ-PALACIOS, Alvar (ed.), *L'Oro di Valadier: Un Genio nella Roma del Settecento*, Rome, Fratelli Palombi Editori, 1997

GONZÁLEZ-PALACIOS, Alvar, 'Provenzale e Moretti: indagini su due mosaici', in *Antichità viva*, Year XV, no. 4 (Dec. 1976)

HARRIS, Ann Sutherland, *Andrea Sacchi*, Oxford, Phaidon, 1977

HAUTECOEUR, Louis, 'I musaicisti sampietrini del Settecento', in *L'Arte*, Year XIII (1910)

HONOUR, Hugh, *Goldsmiths and Silversmiths*, London, Weidenfeld & Nicholson, 1971

LAVAGNINO, Emilio, *Il Genio Italiano all'Estero: Gli Artisti in Portogallo*, Rome, La Libreria dello Stato, 1940

LEVENSON, Jay A. (ed.), *The Age of Baroque in Portugal*, London – New Haven, Yale University Press, 1993

LEVRON, Jacques, *La vie quotidienne à la cour de Versailles aux XVIIe–XVIIIe siècles*, 3rd edition, Poitiers–Ligugé, Hachette, 1986

LIPINSKY, Angelo, 'Il Tesoro di San Giovanni in Lisbona', in *Fede e Arte*, IX, no. 1 (Jan.–Mar. 1961)

LO BIANCO, Anna, and Angela NEGRO (ed.), *Il Settecento a Roma* (exhibition catalogue), Rome, Silvana Editoriale, 2005

MACHADO, Cirilo Wolkmar, *Colecção de Memórias Relativas às Vidas dos Pintores e Escultores, Arquitectos e Gravadores Portuguezes e dos Estrangeiros que Estiverão em Portugal* (ed. J.M. Teixeira de Carvalho and Vergílio Correia), Coimbra, Imprensa da Universidade, 1922 (1st edition 1823)

MANDROUX-FRANÇA, Marie-Thérèse, 'La Patriarcale du Roi Jean V de Portugal', in *Colóquio.Artes*, 2nd Série [2nd series], 31st year, no. 83 (Dec. 1989)

MANDROUX-FRANÇA, Marie-Thérèse, 'Rome, Lisbonne, Rio de Janeiro, Londres et Paris: Le Long Voyage du Recueil Weale, 1745–1995', in *Colóquio-Artes*, 2nd Série [2nd series], 38th year, no. 109 (Apr.–Jun. 1996)

MARCONI, Nicoletta, 'La prestigiosa collazione delle macchine del Zabaglia e la "scuola" di meccanica pratica della Fabbrica di San Pietro', in Angela MARINO (ed.), *Sapere e saper fare nella Fabbrica di San Pietro: 'Castelli e ponti' di maestro Nicola Zabaglia 1743* (ed. Paolo Portoghesi), Rome, Gangemi, 2008

MARCONI, Nicoletta, 'Glossario dei termini tecnici', in Angela MARINO (ed.), *Sapere e saper fare nella Fabbrica di San Pietro: 'Castelli e ponti' di maestro Nicola Zabaglia 1743* (ed. Paolo Portoghesi), Rome, Gangemi, 2008

MINOR, Vernon Hyde, 'A portrait of Benedict XIV by Bernardino Ludovisi', in *Antologia di Belle Arti. Studi sul Settecento II*, Nova Série [new series], nos. 59–62 (2000)

MOITA, Irisalva, 'O Aqueduto das Águas Livres e o abastecimento de água a Lisboa', *D. João V e o abastecimento de água a Lisboa*, vol. I (exhibition catalogue), Lisbon, Câmara Municipal de Lisboa, 1990

MONTAGU, Jennifer, *Antonio Arrighi: A Silversmith and Bronze Founder in Baroque Rome*, Todi, Tau Editrice, 2009

MONTAGU, Jennifer, 'Gagliardi versus Sampajo, the case for the defence', in *Antologia di Belle Arti. Studi Romani. I*, Nova Série [new series], nos. 67–70 (2004)

MONTAGU, Jennifer, 'Giovanni Battista Maini's role in two sculptural projects: the evidence of the drawings', in *Master Drawings. Essays in Memory of Jacob Bean (1923–1992)*, vol. 31, no. 4 (1993)

MONTAGU, Jennifer, *Gold, Silver and Bronze. Metal Sculpture of the Roman Baroque*, New Haven – London, Yale University Press, 1996

MONTAGU, Jennifer, 'The practice of Roman baroque silver sculpture', in *The Silver Society Journal*, no. 12 (Autumn 2000)

MORETTI, Cesare, and Carlo Stefano SALERNO, 'Contributi allo studio dei materiali e delle composizioni degli smalti per i mosaici della Basilica di San Pietro tra il XVI e il XVIII secolo', in *Quaderni Friulani di Archeologia*, XVI, no. 1 (Dec. 2006)

MORETTI, Cesare, Teresa MORNA, Teresa MEDICI, Carlo Stefano SALERNO and Marco VERITÀ, 'Glass weathering in eighteenth century mosaics: the St John's Chapel in the St Roch Church in Lisbon and the St Peter's Basilica in Rome', *II International Conference on Glass Science in Art and Conservation. Supplement*, Valencia, no. 9 (Dec. 2008)

MORNA, Teresa Freitas (ed.), *100 Anos do Museu de S. Roque*, Lisbon, Santa Casa de Misericórdia de Lisboa, 2005

MORONI, Gaetano, *Dizionario di erudizione storico-ecclesiastica da S. Pietro sino ai nostri giorni*, Venice, Tipografia Emiliana, 1840–61

OLIVEIRA, Helena, and Teresa Freitas MORNA (ed.), *Museu de São Roque*, Lisbon, Santa Casa da Misericórdia de Lisboa, 2008

OROZCO DÍAZ, Emilio, *El teatro y la teatralidad del Barroco*, Barcelona, Planeta, 1969

PAMPALONE, Antonella, "Merletti tra le carte", in NEGRO, Angela (ed.), *Storie di abiti e merletti: incontri al museo sull'arte e il restauro del pizzo*, Rome, Gangemi, 2014

PECCHIAI, Pio, *Il Gesù di Roma*, Rome, Società Grafica Romana, 1952

PEREIRA, Paulo, 'A simbólica manuelina. Razão, celebração, segredo', in *História da Arte Portuguesa*, vol. II, Lisbon, Círculo de Leitores, 1995

PEREIRA, Paulo, *A Obra Silvestre e a Esfera do Rei, iconologia da arquitectura manuelina na Grande Extremadura*, Coimbra, 1990

PEREIRA, Sheila Sousa, *O Arquitecto João Frederico Ludovice e a Quinta da Alfarrobeira*, (Master's dissertation in theory of art, the Faculty of Fine Arts of the University of Lisbon), Lisbon, 2003

PETRUCCI, Francesco, 'Contributti su Carlo Marchioni Scultore', in Elisa DEBENEDETTI (ed.), *Sculture Romane del Settecento. La Professione dello Scultore*, vol. I, Rome, Bonsignori Editore, 2001

PIMENTEL, António Filipe, 'Antonio Canevari e a Arcádia Romana: subsídios para o estudo das relações artísticas Lisboa/Roma no reinado de D. João V', in Teresa Leonor M. VALE (ed.), *Lisboa Barroca e o Barroco de Lisboa*, Lisbon, Livros Horizonte, 2007

PIMENTEL, António Filipe, 'Antonio Cannevari e a Torre da Universidade de Coimbra', in *Artistas e artífices e a sua mobilidade no mundo de expressão portuguesa*, Actas [Minutes], VII Colóquio Luso-Brasileiro de História da Arte [Portuguese-Brazilian Colloquium on the History of Art], Oporto, Faculdade de Letras da Universidade do Porto [Faculty of Letters of the University of Oporto], 2005

PIMENTEL, António Filipe, *Arquitectura e Poder. O Real Edifício de Mafra*, Lisbon, Livros Horizonte, 2002

PIMENTEL, António Filipe (ed.), *A Encomenda Prodigiosa. Da Patriarcal à Capela Real de S. João Baptista* (exhibition guide), Lisbon, Museu Nacional de Arte Antiga – Museu de São Roque – Imprensa Nacional-Casa da Moeda, 2013

PIMENTEL, António Filipe, 'D. Tomás de Almeida (1716-1754)', in D. Carlos A. Moreira AZEVEDO (ed.), *Os Patriarcas de Lisboa*, Lisbon, Centro Cultural do Patriarcado – Aletheia Editores, 2009

PIMENTEL, António Filipe, 'Nobre, séria e rica: a encomenda da capela lisboeta de S. João Baptista em S. Roque e a controvérsia barroco versus classicismo', *Anais* do *VI Colóquio Luso-Brasileiro de História da Arte* [Annals of the VI Portuguese–Brazilian Colloquium on the History of Art], Rio de Janeiro, Fundação Universitária José Bonifácio, 2004

PIMENTEL, António Filipe, 'Real Basílica de Mafra: salão de trono e panteão de reis', in *Boletim Cultural*, 93 (Feb. 1994)

PIMENTEL, António Filipe, 'Uma jóia em forma de templo: a Capela de São João Baptista', in *Oceanos*, no. 43 (Jul./Sept. 2000)

PORTOGHESI, Paolo, *Roma Barocca*, 4th edition, Rome–Bari, Laterza, 1988 (1st edition 1966)

QUIETO, Pier Paolo, *D. João V de Portugal e a Sua Influência na Arte Italiana do Século XVIII*, Lisbon–Mafra, Elo, 1990

RACZYNSKI, Athanasy, *Dictionnaire Historico-Artistique du Portugal*, Paris, Jules Renouard & Cie, 1847

RIBEIRO, José Silvestre, *História dos estabelecimentos scientificos litterarios e artísticos de Portugal nos successivos reinados da monarchia*, vol. I, Lisbon, Typographia da Academia Real das Sciencias, 1871

RISSELIN-STEENEBRUGEN, Marie, *Trois siècles de dentelles aux Musées Royaux d'Art et d'Histoire*, 12th edition, Brussels, Musées Royaux d'Art et d'Histoire, 1987

RISSELIN-STEENEBRUGEN, Marie, 'Un livre de patrons de dentelles du XVIII siècle', in *Bulletin des Musées Royaux d'Art e d'Histoire*, Brussels, 6th series, nos. 43–44 (1971–72)

RIZZINI, Maria Luisa, '"*Essendo che sono cose che resteranno a perpetua memoria*". Due ricami milanesi del primo Seicento', in Flavia FIORI and Margherita ZANETTA ACCORNERO (ed.), *Il ricamo in Italia dal XVI al XVIII secolo* (Atti delle giornate di studio [Minutes of Study Sessions], Novara 21–22 Nov. 1998), Novara, Interlinea Edizioni, 2001

ROCCA, Sandra Vasco, and Gabriele BORGHINI (ed.), *Giovanni V di Portogallo e la Cultura Romana del suo Tempo (1706–1750)*, Rome, Àrgos Edizioni, 1995

ROCCA, Sandra Vasco, Gabriele BORGHINI and Paola FERRARIS (ed.), *Roma Lusitana, Lisbona Romana* (exhibition catalogue), Rome, Àrgos Edizioni, 1990

ROCCA, Sandra Vasco, and Gabriele BORGHINI (ed.), *S. Antonio dei Portoghesi*, Rome, Istituto per il Catalogo e la Documentazione – Edizioni Argos, 1992

ROCCA, Sandra Vasco, and Natália Correia GUEDES (ed.), *Thesaurus. Vocabulário de Objectos do Culto Católico*, Vila Viçosa, Fundação da Casa de Bragança, 2004

RODRIGUES, Maria João Madeira, *A Capela de S. João Baptista e as suas Colecções*, Lisbon, Inapa, 1989

RODRIGUES, Maria João Madeira, *Museu de São Roque*. Metais, 2nd edition, Lisbon, Museu de São Roque, 1988

ROTILI, Mario, *La vita di Luigi Vanvitelli*, Naples, Società Editrice Napoletana, 1975

SALDANHA, Nuno (ed.), *Joanni V Magnifico*, Lisbon, Instituto Português do Património Arquitectónico, 1994

SALDANHA, Sandra Costa, 'Os apóstolos em prata para a Patriarcal de Lisboa: modelos de ourivesaria dos escultores José de Almeida (1708–1770) e Joaquim Machado de Castro (1729–1822), in *Revista de Artes Decorativas*, Oporto, Universidade Católica Portuguesa, no. 2 (2008)

SALERNO, Carlo Stefano, 'L'interesse di Ghezzi per le pietre e le paste vitree', in Paolo COEN and G.B. FIDANZA (ed.), *Le pietre rievelate. Lo Studio di molte pietre di Pier Leone Ghezzi. Manoscritto 322 della Biblioteca Universitaria Alessandrina*, Rome, Istituto Poligrafico e Zecca dello Stato, Libreria dello Stato, Rome, 2011

SANTANGELO, Antonino, *Tessuti d'Arte Italiani dal XII al XVIII secolo*, Milan, Electa [1959]

SCHIAVO, Armando, *La Fontana di Trevi e le altre opere di Nicola Salvi*, Rome, Istituto Poligrafico dello Stato, 1956

SCHUETTE, M., and M. MULLER-CHRISTENSEN, *Il ricamo nella storia e nell'arte*, Rome, Edizioni Mediterranee, 1963

SILVA, Francisco Xavier da, *Elogio fúnebre e histórico do muito alto ... Rei de Portugal, o Senhor D. João V*, Lisbon, Regia Officina Sylviana, e da Academia Real, 1750

SMITH, Robert. C., 'João Frederico Ludovice, an eighteenth century architect in Portugal', in *Art Bulletin*, vol. XVIII, 3, Chicago, 1936

SNODIN, Michael, Nigel LLEWELLYN (ed.), *Baroque 1620–1800: Style in the Age of Magnificence* (exhibition catalogue), London, V&A Publishing, 2009

SOUCHAL, François, 'Quelques Sculptures Retrouvées du XVIIIe Siècle', in *Bulletin de la Societé de l'Histoire de l'Art Français*, Paris, 1996 (1997)

SPAGNIESI, Gianfranco, 'Rome et sa culture à l'époque du voyage de Soufflot', in *Soufflot et l'Architecture des Lumières*, Actes [Minutes], École Nacional Supérieure de Beaux Arts, Paris, 2001

SPESSO, Marco, *La cultura architettonica a Roma nel XVIII secolo: Gerolamo Theodoli (1677–1766)*, Rome, Bulzoni, 1991

TASSINARI, Magda, '"Et essendo la nostra arte sorella della pittura": il ricamo a Roma tra Sei e Settecento e i corredi liturgici della Cappella di San Giovanni Battista nella chiesa di San Rocco a Lisbona', in *Römische Historische Mitteilungen*, no. 54 (2012)

TEMPESTA, Claudia, 'Le storie del Battista in San Giovanni in Fonte', in R. BARBIELLINI AMIDEI, L. CARLONI and C. TEMPESTA (ed.), *Andrea Sacchi 1599–1661* (exhibition catalogue), Rome, Ed. De Luca, 1999

TITI, Filippo, *Descrizione delle Pitture, Sculture e Architetture Esposte al Pubblico in Roma com l'Aggiunta di Quanto è Stato Fatto di Nuovo fino all'Anno Presente*, Rome, Stamperia di Marco Pagliari, 1763

TORGAL, Luís Reis, *Ideologia política e teoria do Estado na Restauração*, vol. I, Coimbra, Biblioteca Geral da Universidade, 1981

TOSCANO, Pia, *Roma produttiva tra Settecento e Ottocento. Il San Michele a Ripa Grande*, Rome, Viella, 1996

VALE, Teresa Leonor M., *Arte e Diplomacia. A Vivência Romana dos Embaixadores Joaninos. A figura e as colecções de arte de José Maria da Fonseca Évora (1690–1752)*, Lisbon, Scribe, 2015

VALE, Teresa Leonor M., 'Eighteenth-century Roman silver for the Chapel of St John the Baptist of the Church of S. Roque, Lisbon', in *Burlington Magazine*, vol. CLII, no. 1.289 (Aug. 2010)

VALE, Teresa Leonor M., *Escultura Barroca Italiana em Portugal. Obras dos Séculos XVII e XVIII em Colecções Públicas e Particulares*, Lisbon, Livros Horizonte, 2005

VALE, Teresa Leonor M., *A Escultura Italiana de Mafra*, Lisbon, Livros Horizonte, 2002

VALE, Teresa Leonor M., 'A Estátua de Nossa Senhora da Conceição da Patriarcal de Lisboa e a eleição de modelos pictóricos para obras de escultura, num texto de João Frederico Ludovice', in *Artis – Revista do Instituto de História da Arte da Faculdade de Letras de Lisboa*, nos. 7–8 (2009)

VALE, Teresa Leonor M., 'Di bronzo e d'argento: sculture del Settecento italiano nella magnifica Patriarcale di Lisbona', in *Arte Cristiana. Rivista Internazionale di Storia dell'Arte e di Arti Liturgiche*, 100, no. 868 (Jan.–Feb. 2012)

VALE, Teresa Leonor M., 'Mettere in scena il lusso le mostre di opere d'arte commissionate da Giovanni V di Portogallo in due palazzi romani (1747 e 1749)', in Elisa DEBENEDETTI (ed.), *Studi sul Settecento Romano. Palazzi, chiese, arredi e scultura*, vol. II (col. *Studi sul Settecento Romano*, 28), Rome, Bonsignori Editore, 2012

VALE, Teresa Leonor M., 'Roma em Lisboa: as artes decorativas no contexto das obras de arte enviadas da cidade pontifícia para a capital portuguesa no reinado de D. João V', *Revista de Artes Decorativas*, no. 5 (2011)

VALE, Teresa Leonor M., 'Roman baroque silver for the patriarchate of Lisbon', in *Burlington Magazine*, vol. CLV, no. 1.323 (Jun. 2013)

VALE, Teresa Leonor M., *Scultura barocca italiana in Portogallo: Oper, artisti, committenti*, Rome, Gangemi Editore, 2010

VALE, Teresa Leonor M., '"Só para ostentação da magestade, e grandeza". Aproximação à encomenda de ourivesaria barroca italiana para a basílica de Nossa Senhora e Santo António de Mafra', in *Revista de Artes Decorativas*, no. 2 (2008)

VALE, Teresa Leonor M. (ed.), *A Capela de S. João Batista da Igreja de S. Roque, A encomenda, a obra, as coleções*, Lisbon, Imprensa Nacional Casa da Moeda – Santa Casa da Misericórdia de Lisboa, 2015

VALE, Teresa Leonor M. (ed.), *From Rome to Lisbon. An Album for the Magnanimous King*, Lisbon, Santa Casa da Misericórdia de Lisboa – Scribe, 2015

VARIGNANA, Franca (ed.), *Il Tesoro di San Pietro in Bologna e Papa Lambertini*, Bologna, Minerva Edizioni, 1997

VERITÀ, Marco, 'La tecnologia vetraria veneziana e i contenuti dell'opera', in Luigi ZECCHIN (ed.), *Il ricettario Darduin: un codice vetrario del Seicento trascritto e commentato*, Venice, Arsenale, 1986

VITERBO, Francisco Marques de Sousa, and R. Vicente d'ALMEIDA, *A Capella de S. João Baptista Erecta na Egreja de S. Roque. Fundação da Companhia de Jesus e Hoje Pertencente à Santa Casa da Misericordia. Noticia Historica e Descriptiva*, Lisbon, Livros Horizonte, 1997 (1st edition 1900)

(overleaf)
Lost Pieces: monstrance in gold (detail)
(See fig. 82)

p. 176
Pentecost (detail)
Mosaic panel on the wall on the Gospel (left-hand) side
(See fig. 22)

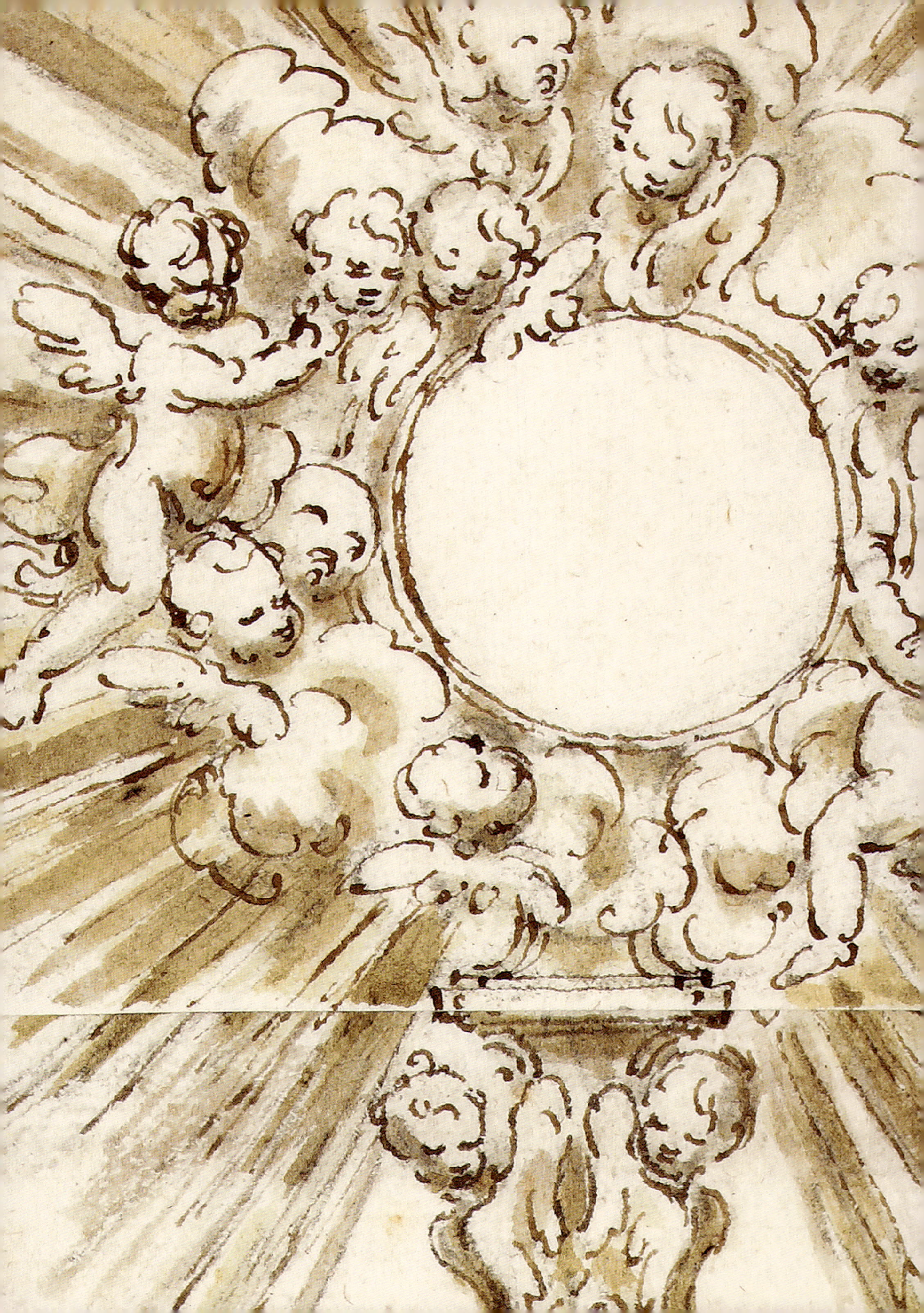

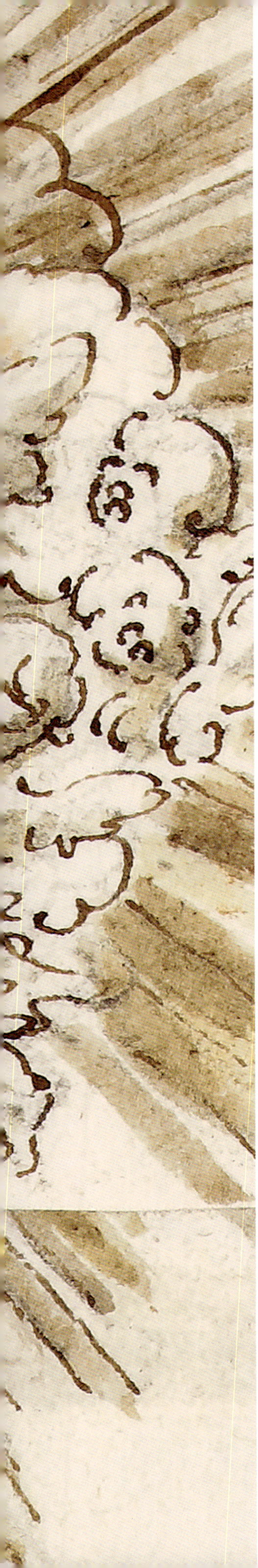

NOTES ON CONTRIBUTORS

António Filipe Pimentel
BA (1985), MA (1991) and PhD (2003) in History of Art. Professor in the Faculty of Letters of the University of Coimbra and researcher at the Centre for Archaeological Studies of the Universities of Coimbra and Porto – CEAUCP (Multidisciplinary Studies in Art). Director of the Museu Nacional de Arte Antiga (National Museum of Ancient Art) since 2010.

Author of various books and articles in the field of art history and especially on baroque art and culture, published in Portugal, Spain, France, Italy, England, Belgium, Germany, Poland, Slovakia, Slovenia and Brazil.

Carlo Stefano Salerno
BA in History of Art from the Università la Sapienza in Rome (1989). Senior technical specialist in restoration at the Istituto Centrale del Restauro in Rome (1987). Lecturer in the theory and history of restoration at the University of Calabria (Unical) since 2005.

In charge of various conservation and restoration projects in the field of mural painting, sculpture and mosaics, and author of books and articles on artistic techniques, conservation and art history.

Cristina Pinto Basto
BA (1989) in History from the Universidade Autónoma de Lisboa; postgraduate qualification in archiving (1993) from the same university. Director of the Biblioteca da Ajuda ('Assistance' Library) (2005–12). Senior technical specialist at the Biblioteca da Ajuda.

Magda Tassinari
BA in Literature (University of Genoa, 1975), Professional Vocational Course in Cataloguing Cultural Heritage Items (Regione Liguria, 1978–81), Specialisation in History of Art (University of Genoa, 1983), teaching qualification in Art History (1989).

Worked in the region of Liguria Ufficio Musei (Museums Department) (1981–92) and lectured in History of Art at the G. Chiabrera de Savona School (1992–2011). Author of various articles and books on the history of art in Liguria, and on the history of embroidery and textiles, published in Italy and Portugal.

Maria de Fátima Rezende Gomes
BA (1984) in Philosophy from the Universidade Católica; Postgraduate qualification in Chinese Studies (2000) from the University of Aveiro. Senior technical specialist at the Biblioteca da Ajuda.

Marialuisa Rizzini
BA from the Università Statale of Milan (1988). Lecturer in history of art, secondary school with arts speciality (since 1993), associate contributor to the IULM University of Milan (since 2001, in relation to courses and seminars on the history of fashion and contemporary fashion). Lecturer in the history of costume and fashion at the Istituto Marangoni in Milan since 2006. Author of various books and articles on the history of lace and embroidery, and cataloguer of numerous collections of lace and embroidery in various museums in Italy. A consultant since 1994 for the Biennale Internazionale del Merletto (International Lace Biennale) in Cantù (Como).

Teresa Leonor M. Vale
BA (1989), MA (1994) and PhD (1999) in History of Art. Professor in the School of Arts and Humanities of the University of Lisbon and researcher attached to ARTIS – Institute of the History of Art of the same university.

Author of various books and articles in the field of art history and especially on baroque art and culture, published in Portugal, Spain, France, Italy and the United Kingdom.

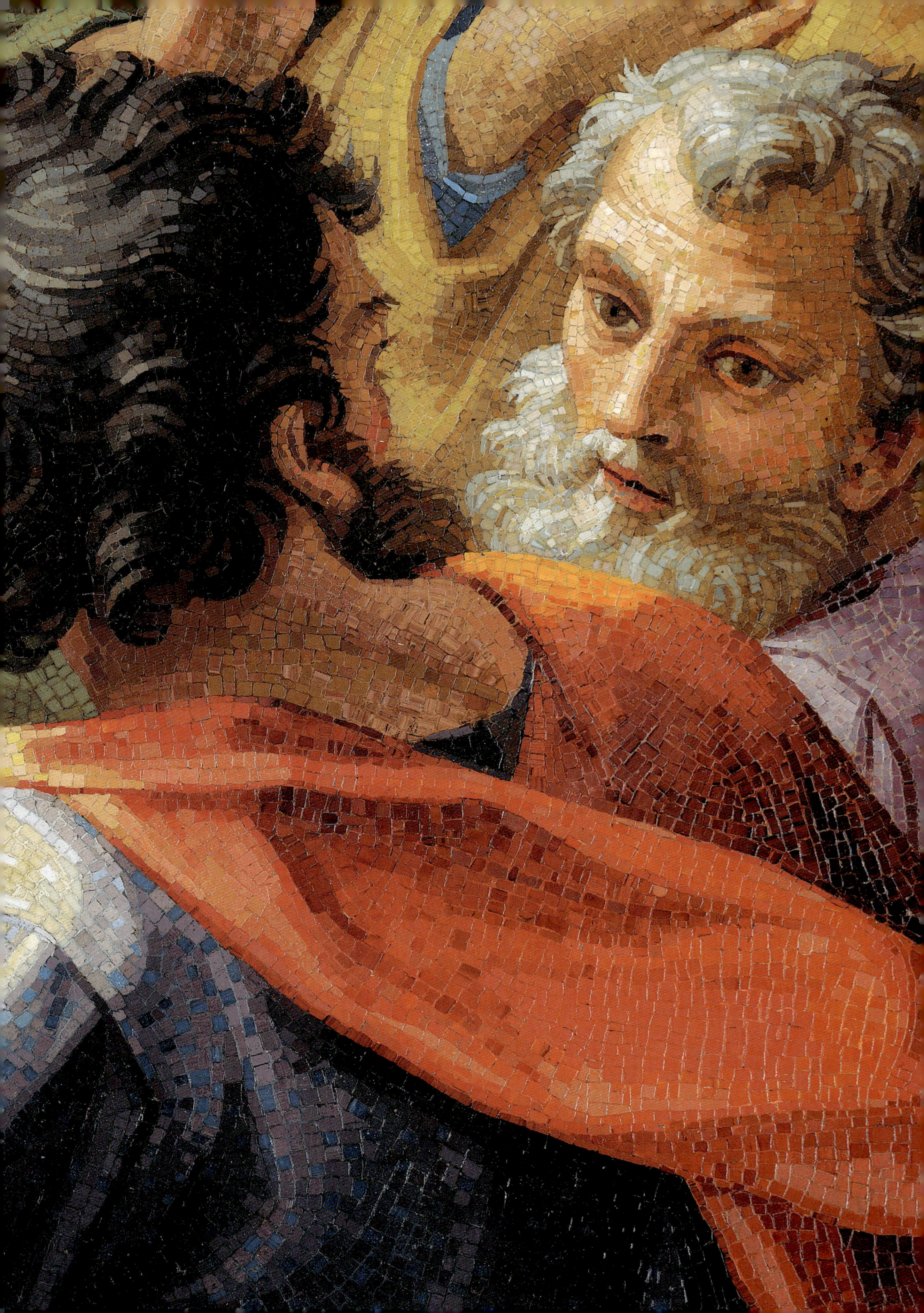